THE COMPLETE POEMS OF JOHN KEATS

Introduction by ROBERT BRIDGES

The Complete Poems of John Keats
By John Keats
Introduction by Robert Bridges

Print ISBN 13: 978-1-4209-5184-4
eBook ISBN 13: 978-1-4209-5185-1

Cover Image: A detail of a portrait of John Keats of unknown date by William Hilton the Younger (1786-1839).

Please visit *www.digireads.com*

CONTENTS

THE POEMS

Introduction

I.

If one English poet might be recalled today from the dead to continue the work which he left unfinished on earth, it is probable that the crown of his country's desire would be set on the head of John Keats; and this general feeling is based on a judgment of his work which we may unhesitatingly accept, namely, that the best of it is of the highest excellence, but the mass of it disappointing.

Nor is there any likelihood of this verdict being overset, although some may always unreservedly admire him on account of his excellences,—and this because his fault is often the excess of a good and rare quality,—and others again as unreservedly depreciate him on account of that very want of restraint, which in his early work, besides its other immaturities, is often of such a nature as to be offensive to good taste, and very provocative of impatient condemnation.

Among Keats' poems, too, a quantity of indifferent and bad verse is now printed, not only from a reverence for his first volume, which he never revised, and which is very properly reprinted as he issued it, but also from a feeling which editors have had, that since anything might be of value, everything was; so that any scrap of his which could be recovered has gone into the collections. Concerning which poor stuff we may be consoled to know that Keats himself would have had no care; for, not to speak of what was plainly never intended for poetry at all, he seems to have regarded at least his earlier work as a mere product of himself and the circumstances, now good now bad, its quality depending on influences beyond his control and often adverse, under which he always did his best. On one point only was he sensitive, and that was his belief that he sometimes did well, and would do better. The failures he left as they were, having too much pride to be ashamed of them, and too strong a conviction of an ever-flowing, and, as he felt, an increasing and bettering inspiration to think it worthwhile to spend fresh time in revising what a younger moment had cast off.

The purpose of this essay is to examine Keats' more important poems by the highest standard of excellence as works of art, in such a manner as may be both useful and interesting; to investigate their construction, and by naming the faults to distinguish their beauties, and set them in an approximate order of merit; also, by exhibiting his method, to vindicate both the form and meaning of some poems from the assumption of even his reasonable admirers that they have neither one nor other. Within the limits of an introductory chapter this cannot be done, even imperfectly, without the omission of much which the reader may look for in an account of Keats' poetry, but such omissions can be easily supplied: a knowledge, too, of the circumstances of Keats' life will be assumed,[1] and some acquaintance with his letters to his friends; and since these make of themselves a most charming book,[2] and one that can never be superseded as a commentary on his work in its personal aspect, this view of the subject will here be disregarded except when required to aid the criticism or interpretation of a poem.

I shall take the poems in what seems the most convenient order for my purpose, and shall not trouble the reader with any other artificial connection, reserving general remarks till the end. The worser pieces I shall not notice at all.

II. ENDYMION.

Endymion is Keats' longest poem. It is the story of how Cynthia, the moon-goddess, who is also herself the moon, fell in love with the mortal Endymion. "A great trial of invention," wrote Keats, for he had "to fill 4000 lines with one bare circumstance." When he composed the poem, he was in a state of mental excitement varied by fits of depression; he grew tired of it, had a poor opinion of it, and in his preface described it as a feverish attempt.

To one who expects to be carried on by the interest of a story, this poem is more tedious and unreadable than can be imagined; and parts of it merit at least some of the condemnation which fell on the whole. Keats thought to "surprise by a fine excess;" his excess rather confuses and blurs, and it is a severe task to keep the attention fixed. A want of definition in the actual narration,—so that important matters do not stand out,—a sameness in the variety, and the reiteration of languid epithets, are the chief cause of this; and in the second book, where Endymion is wandering in strange places, the uncertainty as to where he is, in the absence of explanatory statement as to what is intended, reduces the reader to despair. And yet it is nothing less than a marvel how even these faults can have obscured so completely the poetic excellences from a more general recognition.[3] I shall give a short analysis of the outward events of the poem, such as the reader may find useful both as a guide and for reference or index, and will add some explanation of the allegory. But first with respect to the allegory I would say this, that the minor characters and incidents are so numerous and so yielding to various interpretation, that for the sake of brevity and simplicity I must confine myself to the main points, without which

---

[1] Mr. Sidney Colvin's *Life of Keats*, in the *English Men of Letters* series, supplies all these desiderata most satisfactorily.

[2] And a beautiful book if some of the letters were emitted. *Letters of John Keats to his Family and Friends*. Edited by Sidney Colvin. Macmillan & Co., 1891.

[3] As an example of what is meant, see the poverty of the selections from *Endymion* in Ward's *English Poets*.

there is no sense in the whole; and since, even with these, the mere putting their explanation into definite statement cannot be done without throwing the whole temporarily out of focus, I am the more content to neglect those lesser matters, in which the poet should be regarded as having, in his own words, "let himself go from some fine starting-point towards his own originality;" nor would I wish to represent the poem other than he meant it, "a little region in which lovers of poetry may wander" at their will.

ANALYSIS OF ENDYMION.

BOOK I.—ON THE EARTH.

1. *Author's prologue, 1-62.
2. Festival of Pan on Latmos, 63-406.
    [Endymion enters, 168 ; *Ode to Pan, 232-306.]
3. Peona takes E. to her bower, 407-515.
    [Address to Sleep, 453-463.]
    E. tells of his vision of an unknown goddess among the poppies—he dreamt he was asleep, 516-710.
    Peona rallies him on his love, 710-768.
    E. replies with his *argument on the meaning of Love, 769-857, and gives an account of a second, 893, and third, 963, meeting with the same vision, to end of book.

BOOK II.—WANDERINGS UNDER THE EARTH.

1. *Prologue on supremacy of love above heroism, &c, 1-43.
2. E., while enjoying the pleasures of nature, reads a message on a butterfly's wings, 43-63.
    The butterfly leads him to a nymph, who foretells his wanderings and ultimate success, 64-130.
    E. meditates on the disappointment of desire, and prays to Cynthia as his especial goddess, but not recognised as his visitant; and receives answer bidding him descend into the silent mysteries of earth, 131-214.
    He obeys, -218.
    Description of an underworld of gems, 219-280.
    E. feels horror of solitude, and wishes to return to the earth. He comes to a temple of Diana, his goddess, and prays Diana to deliver him from the underworld, 281-332.
    Flowers spring out of the marble, 333-350.
    He goes on to soft music, 351-363.
    Is tortured by the music, 364-375.
    Comes to a lightsome wood of myrtles, 376-386.

3. Description of Adonis, 387-427.
    The waking of Adonis, 428-533.
    Venus encourages E., and enjoins secrecy, 534-587.
4. E. follows a diamond balustrade through waterworks to a gloom where he sees Cybele, 588-649.
    Balustrade breaks off, and he goes on an eagle to a jasmine bower, where he soliloquizes, 649-706.
    Cynthia comes unknown to him in bower, 707-827,
    And leaves him asleep, 853.
    [*The poet speaks of the mystery of his legend, 827-853.]
5. E. wakes to melancholy thought, and strays to a grotto where he sees Alpheus and Arethusa—he prays for them, 854-1017.
    He goes altogether under the sea, -1023.

BOOK III.—UNDER THE SEA.

1. *Prologue on regalities and supremacy of the Moon, 1-71.
2. A moonbeam reaches E. under sea, 72-102, and shines on him till morning, 102-119.
    [Description of sea-floor, 119-141.]
    [*Address to the Moon, 142-187.]
3. He meets with Glaucus and Scylla, 187-1027.
    Neptune's hall, 866-887.
    Venus cheers E., 887-923.
    Neptune's feast, 924-937.
    Hymn to Neptune, 943-990.
    Nereids carry off E., 1005-1018.
    E. hears a heavenly voice promising to take him up, 1019-1027.
4. E. finds himself back on the earth, 1028-1032.

BOOK IV.—IN THE AIR.

1. Prologue to English Muse, 1-29.
2. E. finds a beautiful Indian maid bewailing her loneliness. He falls in love with her, 30-330,
    [*Her song, 146-290.]
    And accompanies her in the air on flying horses, 330.
    *Vision of Sleep journeying, 367-397.
    E. and Indian sleep on the sleeping horses, 398.
    Cynthia appears to E. as the moon, 430.
    The Indian disappears, -512.
    *Cave of quietude described, 512-562.
    Diana's feast and hymn to D., 563-611.

3. In midst of hymn E. is borne to Latmos again, and finds there and addresses the Indian lady, 611-797.
   [The poet speaks, 770-780.]
4. Peona reappears, and by the identification of the Moon, Cynthia, and the Indian lady as one, the tale concludes, -1003.

In so far as the poem has an inner meaning, Endymion must be identified with the poet as Man. The Moon represents "Poetry" or the Ideality of desired objects, *The principle of Beauty in all things*: it is the super-sensuous quality which makes all desired objects ideal; and Cynthia, as moon-goddess, crowns and personifies this, representing the ideal beauty or love of woman: and in so far as she is also actually the Moon as well as the Indian lady,—who clearly represents real or sensuous passion,—it follows that the love of woman is in its essence the same with all love of beauty; and this proposition and its converse will explain much that is otherwise strange and difficult.

Man in Keats' poem begins with a desire for excellence, renown, and fame, and connects the Moon with his passion, iii. 142 *seq.*, that is, he sees beauty or "poetry" or ideality in his desire. This Ideality, assuming the form of the goddess, that is, of woman, *which it is*,[4] makes him renounce ambition and pursue poetic love. Next he has to humanize the ideality of his passion; and this comes about by his contact with the mystery of life, and by sympathy with dead lovers' tragedies; and this sympathy leaves him a prey to real sensuous passion. In this he falls, as he thinks, from his faith; and his sensuous passion, coming into sudden contact with his old ideals, vanishes at one moment quite away, and leaves him a prey to utter despair, iv. 507 *seq.*; and he is at discord with himself, until he unexpectedly discovers that his real and ideal loves are one and the same.

The circumstance that ideal beauty, if it is the Moon, is represented as falling in love with man, merely implies selection or election, and narrows down the application of the allegory to those men who feel supernatural visitations (*End.* i. 795), such as are the *Visionaries* of the *Revision of Hyperion.* Also, to follow Keats' meaning, it must not be lost sight of that when Endymion is visited by Cynthia, he never recognises her to be the Moon,[5] although her advent was heralded by "the loveliest moon," &c, i. 591. The identity is not revealed to him till Book IV. 430, &c.; and so, when he finds himself loving both Cynthia and the Indian lady at the same time, he remembers his first love, the Moon, as distinct from them, and says, that he has a *triple* soul. There is no doubt about this, and it seems to me one of the two keys to the

---

[4] The absolute identification must be intended in iv. 430, &c.

[5] See i. 606, 894, 943-959; ii. 128, esp. 168-195, and 302-332, 576, esp. 686 *seq.*, and 739, 753; iii. 175. &c., 913-914.

allegory. That it has escaped the attention of diligent readers is a proof that it is not insisted on with sufficient clearness in the poem, and it is a good example of the lack of definition in the presentation of Keats' main designs.

Keats was not making an allegory, but using a legend, and he never, so far as I know, stated that he intended his poem for an allegory (unless this is implied in ii. 838-9), so that it may naturally shock the reader to find the Moon identified with such an abstraction as the principle of beauty in all things. But as a matter of fact, the symbolism may be arrived at in the simplest way: the poet was very sensible to the mysterious effects of moonlight,[6] and felt the poetry of nature more deeply under that influence; and, that mood being given, one step further only is necessary, which is that other ecstatic and poetic moods should be likened to it, and the conditioning cause of the first, which is known, be taken for a symbol of the other unknown causes, or of that which is common to all. This is, I think, the other chief key to the sense, and it makes the difficult passage in *End.* iii. 142-187 (and see especially lines 163-169) intelligible and plain; and the poem becomes, with these explanations, readable as a whole, suggestive of meaning, and full of shadowy outlines of mysterious truth.

The general scheme of the poem is broad and simple. The four books (see the Analysis) correspond with the four elements—I. Earth; II. Fire—for it is more probable that this element has been somewhat lost sight of in its necessary modifications than that it was not intended in its proper home beneath the earth's crust; III. Under sea = Water; IV. Air; and these typify respectively—I. Natural beauty; II. The mysteries of earth; III. The secrets of death; IV. Spiritual freedom and satisfaction. The first idea needs little comment: the last three books are concerned with states of mind which, on his own confession, lay beyond the poet's experience; and here he must be regarded as a searcher for truth rather than as full prophet. What the mysteries of earth are will appear in the explanation of *Sleep and Poetry*. Their region "beneath in the earth" is moonless, *i.e.*, unlovely, and oppresses Endymion with the horror of solitude; but even here he finds a cold shrine to Diana and immortal bowers of beauty; and at last the

---

[6] And see Wordsworth's two *Odes to the Moon*:—

> "O still beloved! for thine, meek Power, are charms
> That fascinate the very babe in arms."

And better Guy de Maupassant:—

> "Pourquoi ces frissons de coeur, cette émotion de l'âme? . . . A qui étaient destinés ce spectacle sublime, cette abondance de poésie jetée du ciel sur la terre? . . . Dieu peut-être a fait ces nuits-là pour voiler d'idéal les amours des hommes."

mysteries flush into love, and he holds unexpected communion with Cynthia herself. After this "the blank amazements amaze no more," and he meets with Alpheus and Arethusa. The reason for the choice of this legend is very clear; they are two lovers, who, like Endymion himself, have left the earth, and are pursuing their passion underground, whence they are destined, as he too is, to arrive again at the upper air through the sea. So in the third book the story of Glaucus and Scylla has a similar fitness. Glaucus is a mortal, who, of his own curiosity and instinctive desire, has plunged straight into the "secrets of Death" from the world of natural beauty, where he was living on the brink of them. Scylla may have done the same; but the general meaning of this third book I am not at all able to interpret. The region is one where the moonbeams can reach, and the phenomena of earth's day and night are dimly seen. The secrets of Death are in some way connected with magic, of which there are two kinds—the first, the earthly magic or witchcraft of Circe, who is "arbitrary queen of sense," and can gratify the sense but not resolve the secrets of Death, whose evil power she seems rather to aid; and the second, a serious magic, which Glaucus has to learn before he can win redemption from Circe's curse. The meaning of the secrets of Death is probably the same as the imagination in *Rev. of Hyperion* (q.v.), but whether Glaucus is a visionary who lives entirely in the past (see *End.* iii. 327-337, 122, &c.), or whether Death has a more realistic meaning, or whether, as is not impossible, the two ideas are combined, I cannot guess. It seems intended that the sorrow of the secrets of Death can only be surmounted and their magic resolved by a soul who has been in perfect communion with ideal beauty, and has traced her presence through the whole of creation.

The episode of Glaucus and Scylla, bk. iii. from line 188 onwards, may be omitted at first reading, and it must always, though most consecutive in narration, please the least, even though a key should be found for it. Of the four books, of almost equal length, the fourth reads by far the shortest. As for the beauties of the poem, they are innumerable, and the reader will find them for himself, if he will be patient with the defects that so curiously hide them. Of these I would say no more here, if they did not very many of them depend on a lamentable deficiency Keats' art, which, while it affects much of his work, is brought into unusual prominence by the subject of *Endymion*; and that is his very superficial and unworthy treatment of his ideal female characters. It may be partly accounted for thus: Keats' art is primarily objective and pictorial, and whatever other qualities it has are as it were added on to things as perceived; and this requires a satisfactory pictorial basis, which, in the case of ideal woman, did not exist in Keats' time. Neither the Greek nor the Renaissance ideals were understood, and the thin convention of classicism, which we may see in the works of West and Canova, was played out; so that the rising artists, and Keats with them, finding "nothing to be intense upon," turned to nature, and produced from English models the domestic-belle type, which ruled throughout the second quarter of the century, degrading our poets as well as painters. It was *banal*, and the more ideal and abstract it sought to be, the more empty it became; so that it was the portrait-painters only, like Lawrence, who, having to do with individual expression of subjective qualities, escaped from the meanness, and represented women whom we can still admire. Now Keats was clearly in a predicament from which neither circumstances nor disposition provided him an escape. The social condition of his parents probably excluded him from contact with the best types, and he seems to have had some idiosyncrasy. He deplores in one of his letters that he was not at ease in women's society; and when he attributes this to their not answering to his preconception of them, it looks as if he were seeking his ideal among them. Certainly what appears to be the delineation of his conception often offends taste without raising the imagination, and it reveals a plainly impossible foundation for dignified passion, in the representation of which Keats failed, as we shall see later. I conclude that he supposed that common expressions became spiritualised by being applied to an idea. Whatever praise is given to Keats' work must always be with this reservation; and he generally does his best where there is no opportunity for this kind of fault. There are exceptions, and these are, as one would expect, among the more personally inspired poems; for such sonnets as *Time's Sea*, *I cry your Mercy*, *Bright Star*, though perhaps not quite untainted by this weakness if interpreted by the rest of his work, are yet, if considered alone, above reproach.

This ideal carries much better his other more homely type of woman, represented to him by his sister-in-law, who was no doubt the model of Peona, a lady who has no aspirations after the moon, a simple nature which he grew to value even more, of which in the revised *Hyperion* he says—

> "They seek no wonder but the human face,
> No music but a happy-noted voice."

And it must be remembered that his behaviour towards his own younger sister was a pattern of brotherliness and natural affection, full of sympathy, chivalry, devotion, and commonsense.

III. THE SHORT "ENDYMION" AND "SLEEP AND POETRY."

The first poem in Keats' first volume, "I stood tiptoe upon a little hill," must be considered in relation to *Endymion*, for "Endymion" was its original title, and it may be regarded as a prelude to the longer poem. It was written in December 1816, and was more worked at[7] than one might suppose from what Keats tells us of his habits at that time. The argument of the poem, though much disguised by its objective manner, is carefully elaborated. It begins with a description of Nature as seen in a walk in the then suburbs of London—already romantically remote from us—and from this passes insensibly to other descriptions of Nature, with incidental reference to the new school of poetry, which promises to celebrate Nature (51, &c.). Then (l. 94 *seq.*), in an unfortunate passage, maiden beauty intrudes, and then (113) the moon

> "Coming into the blue with all her light."

And this moon is the same symbol as in the long poem—

> "O Maker of sweet poets! dear delight
> Of this fair world . . .
> Lover of loneliness and wandering,
> Of upcast eye."

And then (125) follows a poetic statement of the inspiration of poetry by Nature, which is unique in its bold and fanciful identification of versification with natural forms, *e.g.* l. 127—

> "In the calm grandeur of a sober line
> We see the waving of the mountain pine," &c.

He then suggests that this ecstasy in Nature may have given origin not only to the music of verse, but to the poetic ideas of such myths as Psyche, Syrinx, and Narcissus, and lastly (181) of Endymion, asserting his preference for that tale, and his wish to write it; and the poem ends (210-242) with a passage of human sympathy, as the direct effect of the marriage of Endymion and Cynthia.

This will give some notion of Keats' poetic method, but I will take one other poem to illustrate it, the last in the first volume, called *Sleep and Poetry*; and it is conveniently grouped here, because, like the one just noticed, it is in the same meter as *Endymion*, and both are good

---

[7] Letters iv.

examples of Keats' early style.[8] They often fall into the feeble manner which he caught from Leigh Hunt,[9] and they never rise to Keats' full height, but here and there, especially in single lines, they do touch on it, and, quite apart from their inner meaning, have a beauty worthy of their author, and are very pleasant reading.

Sleep and Poetry is crowded with meaning. The short analysis of it is thus. Sleep, which figures the unawakened state of mind,[10] is for its gentle soothing and inspiring qualities (1-18, and *cf. End.* i. 453 *seq.*) subordinated to Poetry, which reveals more (19-34). Poetry, which represents the mind awakened to mystery, inspires with ambition and confidence (-40).

Keats then states his own devotion to Poetry (47-55), and prays to her for inspiration to penetrate the mysteries of Nature and human life (-84). He doubts whether fate will grant him length of life, and figures images of life which bring him back to a picture of the state of mind described in the opening lines of the poem (85-95).

Then in an important passage (101-162), to which I will recur, he states the spheres of emotion through which this poetic love of Nature will carry him. Then (162-235) follow the well-known invective against the Augustan school, and his prophecy of the coming revival; and at 235 a definition of the true object of poetry, to comfort mankind; implying sympathy with human misery. The rest of the poem, 270 to end, is his peroration to his first publication, an apology for presumption, a determination to write, a tribute to the sympathetic support of his friends, a description of his refuge in Leigh Hunt's study, and he ends his book saying of his verses—

"Howsoever they be done,
I leave them as a father does his son."

This argument seems consecutive enough, but the passage 101-162 requires explanation. The meaning of it is exactly the same with that of Wordsworth's *Tintern Abbey*. In that poem Wordsworth distinguishes three states of mind following by development one on another; 1st. boyhood—mere animal pleasure; 2nd. simple unreflective ecstasy in Nature; 3rd. reflective pleasure in nature, *i.e.* pleasure accompanied by or inwoven with that sense of mystery which it is the object of his

---

[8] Concerning the versification of *Endymion* there is no reason to repeat objections which were evident from the first to their Serene Caecities the *Edinburgh* and *Blackwood*, but some remarks will be found under *Lamia*, and on p. lxxxv. *seq.*

[9] I have not read Hunt's poems, but this assertion of critics is unmistakably confirmed in Keats' Letters.

[10] As pointed out by Mrs. F. M. Owen in "Keats, a Study," Kegan Paul, 1880—an important book in the history of the criticism of Keats' genius.

poem to exhibit. Now Keats, in a letter to Reynolds, May 1818,[11] refers to these lines on *Tintern Abbey*, and sets out his own ideas in the following language:—

"I compare human life to a large Mansion of many apartments, two of which I can only describe, the doors of the rest being as yet shut upon me. The first we step into we call the infant or thoughtless Chamber, in which we remain as long as we do not think. We remain there a long while, and notwithstanding the doors of the second Chamber remain wide open, showing a bright appearance, we care not to hasten to it; but are at length imperceptibly impelled by the awakening of the thinking principle within us. We no sooner get into the second Chamber, which I shall call the Chamber of Maiden-Thought, than we become intoxicated with the light and the atmosphere, we see nothing but pleasant wonders, and think of delaying there forever in delight. However, among the effects this breathing is father of, is that tremendous one of sharpening one's vision into the heart and nature of Man—of convincing one's nerves that the world is full of Misery and Heartbreak, Pain, Sickness, and Oppression—whereby this Chamber of Maiden-Thought becomes gradually darkened, and at the same time, on all sides of it, many doors are set open—but all dark—all leading to dark passages—We see not the balance of good and evil—we are in a mist—*we* are now in that state—We feel the 'burden of the Mystery.'

"To this point was Wordsworth come, as far as I can conceive, when he wrote 'Tintern Abbey,' and it seems to me that his Genius is explorative of those dark Passages."

I do not think that anyone who knows Keats' letters would suppose that he was merely borrowing from Wordsworth, but there is no objection to supposing that he may have learnt some of his obstinate questionings from that master, though he thought them out for himself. The sense in the two poems is, however, identical, and it will repay us to examine the extreme difference between Keats' objective treatment and Wordsworth's philosophizing. For instance, here is Wordsworth's description of what Keats calls the infant or thoughtless chamber—

"The coarser pleasures of my boyish days
And their glad animal movements."

Keats speaks directly of this first state in the opening lines, and incidentally, though not without full contrastive purpose, he describes it last among his images of human life, where "knowledge is sorrow,

---

[11] Letters lii.

sorrow is wisdom, and wisdom is folly." These images are of life considered first as a mere atomic movement in a general flux, then as a dream on the brink of destruction, then as a budding hope, then as an intellectual distraction, then as an ecstatic glimpse of beauty, and lastly as an instinctive pleasure; and this corresponds exactly with what Wordsworth describes above. But how does Keats put it?—

"A pigeon tumbling in clear summer air;
A laughing school-boy, without grief or care,
Riding the springy branches of an elm."

Of the Second Chamber Wordsworth's lines may serve the general purpose of this essay, as giving an excellent plain description of Keats' mental condition when he wrote most of his earlier poetry—

"The sounding cataract
Haunted me like a passion: the tall rock,
The mountain, and the deep and gloomy wood,
Their colours and their forms, were then to me
An appetite; a feeling and a love,
That had no need of a remoter charm,
By thought supplied," &c. (Cp. *End.* iii. 142, &c.)

And when they both describe the Third Chamber here are the parallel passages: Wordsworth has—

"And I have felt
A presence that disturbs me with the joy
Of elevated thoughts; a sense sublime
Of something far more deeply interfused,
Whose dwelling is the light of setting suns,
And the round ocean and the living air,
And the blue sky, and in the mind of man:
A motion and a spirit, that impels
All thinking things, all objects of all thought,
And rolls through all things."

And Keats has—

'Lo, I see afar,
O'er-sailing the blue cragginess, a car
And steeds with streamy manes—the charioteer
Looks out upon the winds with furious fear:
And now the numerous tramplings quiver lightly
Along a huge cloud's ridge; and now with sprightly

Wheel downward come they into fresher skies.

And now I see them on a green-hill's side
In breezy rest among the nodding stalks.
The charioteer with wondrous gesture talks
To the trees and mountains; and there soon appear
Shapes of delight, of mystery. . . .
. . . . Most awfully intent
The driver of those steeds is forward bent
And seems to listen."

It is impossible to read Wordsworth's statement without seeing his meaning. Keats' poetry is as obscure as the "dark passages" themselves; but it must be acknowledged that it is a definitely aimed attempt to express a definitely conceived thought in poetical terms. If the imagery fails to define the poet's thought, it must be remembered that definition is hardly to be reached in this field; and if there does lie behind Keats' poetry a meaning which it is impossible to make absolutely distinct in his objective manner, then it is not strange that his poetry should attract many who have to confess that they do not entirely understand it.

There must be thousands and thousands of persons alive at this moment in England, who, if they could only give poetic expression to those mysterious feelings with which they are moved in the presence of natural beauty, would be one and all of them greater poets than have ever yet been; but this objective presentation of ecstatic moods is only given in rare touches, and seems to be the reward of consummate art. The old simile, which in the *Iliad* is seldom more than an ornament used to enliven the description in an almost barbaric taste, may be used for a device to secure something of this evasive wonder. The poet having put his reader into the fit mood, then thrusts a natural picture before him, which is seen by him from the human or mysterious point of view; for instance, in *Hyperion*, the exquisite passage—

"Like a dismal cirque
Of Druid stones upon a forlorn moor,
When the chill rain begins at shut of eve
In dull November, and their chancel vault,
The heaven itself, is blinded throughout night,"

is not so much a heightening of the picture of those old monstrous gods, lying out "at random, carelessly diffused,"—which is its excuse and opportunity,—so much as it is a glorifying of the mystery of Stonehenge and the forlorn moor, the poetry of which is seized at once by the reader, whose mood has been created for him by the story.

Nothing can exceed the force of such a reserved method as this. The intention is artistically concealed by the very means which are taken to prepare the effect, and the picture bursts unexpectedly on the reader with all the force of a landscape seen suddenly upon reaching the brow of a hill. But it is of course much more difficult to picture ideas than moods. The purely objective picturing of an idea in poetry is very like a musical presentation; and as instrumental music can give a mood, but cannot be trusted to suggest the simplest idea without the interpretation of words or action either accompanying or preparing it, so the poetic picture requires a statement of its intention; and even then it seems as vague in itself as music, because it would equally well picture some other intentions. Keats gives a statement of the intention of his charioteer in 123-125 and 157, and also by a few words in the picture; yet it must be confessed that he is not quite successful; and if it may be said that in Wordsworth the statement is overdone, and that what poetry there is, is swamped in a self-conscious disquisition, Keats reads like an Apocalypse.

IV. HYPERION.

Keats was twenty-two years old when he finished *Endymion* in November 1817. It represents his youthful effort towards a reconstruction of English poetry on Elizabethan lines, in sympathy with the romantic and natural schools of his time, and in reaction against the poetry of the last century. A year passed before he began *Hyperion*, his other long poem, and in that time he fell under the influence of Milton, recognizing in *Paradise Lost* the model of that workmanship, the neglect of which had spoiled his first attempt. *Hyperion* was to be an epic in Milton's manner, narrating the overthrow of the old elemental Greek gods by the new Olympian hierarchy. The difficulty that the events are supra-mundane is met by reliance on ancient sculpture for the types of the gods, with some hints from Milton's Pandemonium, and by placing the scene on earth, where his romantic love of Nature could have full play. Hyperion has a palace in the sky, which is luxuriantly described, and he is pictured as resting awhile on the clouds, where he is addressed by Coelus from space; but he is quickly brought down to earth, where also the other gods are wandering.

The opening promises well; we are conscious at once of a new musical blank verse, a music both sweet and strong, alive with imagination and tenderness. There and throughout the poem are passages in which Keats, without losing his own individuality, is as good as Milton, where Milton is as good as Virgil; and such passages rank with the best things that Keats ever did; but in other places he seems a little overshadowed by Milton, while definite passages of the *Paradise Lost* are recalled, and in some places the imitation seems frigid. Milton's grammar and prosody are apparently aimed at, but they are not strictly kept, nor is the poem maintained at the Miltonic elevation. Here and there, too, a fanciful or weak expression betrays the author of *Endymion*. When, in April 1819, Keats had written little more than the first two books, he broke it off; and though it was not finally discarded till five months afterwards, he never continued it. In his letters he attributes his dissatisfaction to the style; but one cannot read to the end without a conviction that the real hindrance lay deeper; for although we may say that this torso of Keats' is the only poem since Milton which has seriously challenged the epic place, it is to the style mainly that this is due; the subject lacks the solid basis of outward event, by which epic maintains its interest: like *Endymion*, it is all imagination; or, if we should accept Keats' personifications as sufficiently real for his purpose, even then the poem fails in conduct. The first two books describe the conditions of the older gods, and are impassioned with defeat, dismay, and collapse; the third introduces the new hierarchy, and we expect to find them radiant, confident, and irresistible; but there is no change in the colour of the poem; of the two deities introduced, Apollo is weeping and raving, and Mnemosyne, who has deserted the old dynasty for her hope in the new, "wails morn and eventide." It is plain that the story was strangling itself.

This failure is really the same in kind as the fault of *Endymion*: there is little but imagination, and a one-sidedness or incompleteness of that; a languor which, though it has now generally left the language, lingers in the main design. That Keats was conscious, too, that some of his earlier weaknesses were still visible will appear when we come to consider the *Revision of Hyperion*; but his own criticism of the poem was that it was Miltonic and artificial, and he confesses in a letter of September 1819[12] to a revulsion of taste. *Paradise Lost*, which not a month before had been "every day a greater wonder" to him, is now "a corruption of our language, accommodating itself to Greek and Latin inversions and intonations. I have but lately (he writes) stood on my guard against Milton. Life to him would be death to me." These last words mean a great deal, and remind one of Milton's ambitious avoidance of Shakespeare in his own later work. But Keats' condemnation of grammatical inversion seems a going back from the great advance in style which he had made, and it is worthwhile to inquire what he meant. It might seem at first that he attributed to inversions the appearance of Miltonism in his poem, and that he could not afford to be imitative. But he had not abused inversion in *Hyperion*, nor is it absent from his revision, nor wholly from his other poems; and the truth is that it is of the essence of good style. In ordinary speech the words follow a common order prescribed by use, and if that does not

[12] Letters cxvi.

suit the sense, correction is made by vocal intonation: but the first thing that a writer must do is to get his words in the order of his ideas, as he wishes them to enter the reader's mind; and when such an arrangement happens not to be the order of common speech, it may be called a grammatical inversion. To take the simplest case, the position of the adjective with regard to its substantive: in French it generally follows the substantive, and this is in most cases its proper place,[13] and for this reason alone descriptions of scenery are generally more pictorial in French prose than in English, the necessarily frequent predicates being in their natural position: in English the common use sets the epithet before the object, and when this is a malposition of ideas, a poet must invert either his grammar or his ideas; and what is true of adjectives is true also of every word in the sentence. The best simple writers have the art of making the common grammatical forms obey their ideas, and Keats has usually a right order of ideas in a simple grammatical form, and a preference for this style over more elaborate constructions is no doubt what he intended to advocate, and this is well enough: but it must be remembered that he often gets good effect from the proper use of inversion, which is present where least suspected; and also that he does not refuse to invert the grammatical order for the sake of rhyme or meter, which, though it may occasionally be a beauty, is generally a license or abuse, a resource of bad writers, and almost as much to be condemned as those needless or false inversions which are sometimes used in the mechanical avoidance of the appearance of prose.

If now, for the convenience of pursuing our subject, we consider the *Revision of Hyperion*, we must remember that we are passing over Keats' most important work,—for it was between his beginning the *Hyperion* in September 1818 to September 1819, when he discarded it, that is, when he was under the Miltonic influence, that almost all his best work was done,—and we shall now be dealing with what was really a transitional period, though its development was arrested, as under the torture of passion, disappointment, and mortal disease his bright hopes of poetic attainment faded from him, and his voice was silenced forever.

He had been disappointed, too, in a resolution which he had made to support himself and those whom his generosity invited to look to his talents for assistance, by doing some hackwork independent of his poetry; and he had returned dispirited to Hampstead (October 1819), the home of his unfortunate passion, and there, hiding from his friends his restlessness and gloom, had betaken himself again to composition. By some paradoxical devilry, moreover, he devoted the best hours of

[13] Diderot asserts the contrary; but he seems to me to have confused himself with a metaphysical argument. His disquisition on this subject raises the general questions with his usual perspicacity. *Lettre sur les Sourds et Muets*.

the day to supplying the market with a comic poem in the Byronic vein, *The Cap and Bells*, and worked in the evenings only, when fatigued and distracted, at the *Revision of Hyperion*, which might be in itself enough to account for any inferiority in the execution. This fragment is very interesting; first, it shows a new departure in style; secondly, a deliberate resumption of his old allegorizing vein, which we found in *Endymion* and the early poems; thirdly, the most mature attempt that he ever made to express some of his own convictions concerning human life. It is in this third aspect that the chief interest lies, and it is strange that its matter should not have prevented the *Revision* from passing for a first draught, with such critics as might overlook the evidence of the form. The style, being evidently less mastered than in the longer poem, might at first sight deceive; but it should not have deceived, for, in spite of the inefficient execution, it is in some respects an advance; it aims at a greater severity and has a more thoughtful power than any of Keats' other work. But the evidence of the alterations of the passages common to the two versions is glaring. For instance, an old trick of Keats' is the abuse of invocation, as almost any page of *Endymion* will show: now in the *Revision of Hyperion* there is not a single vocative O admitted; and if we examine a passage which contained them in the original, and which is kept in the *Revision*, we shall see how their exclusion accounts for the alterations: for example, *Hyp.* i. 50.—

> "Would come in these like accents; O how frail
> To that large utterance of the early gods!
> Saturn, look up! though wherefore, poor old king?
> I have no comfort for thee, no not one:
> I cannot say 'O wherefore sleepest thou?'
> For heaven is parted from thee, and the earth
> Knows thee not, thus afflicted, for a god."

The O's being proscribed, the first line is altered in *Revision*, 328, to

> "Would come in this like accenting: how frail!"

and the fifth line to

> "Wherefore thus sleepest thou?"

And this new *thus* drives out the original *thus* from line 7, which now becomes so *afflicted*. He then sees the two *wherefores* and alters the third line to *and for what, poor lost king*; the change of *lost* for *old* being made to avoid the hackneyed *poor old*.

And besides this conscious correction of old faults, it is now for the first time that the influence of Dante appears, and that not merely in the gravity of the vision in this poem, which is unlike any other of his embodiments, and in the sort of connection conceived between his vision of doom and his own experience and poetic meaning, all which he might have come at through a translation, but in echoes of the Italian balance in passages where the sense is like Dante's, as in this—

> "High prophetess, said I, purge off,
> Benign, if so it please thee, my mind's film."

And also where there is only the indefinable and individual touch to point to, as in—

> "When in mid-day the sickening east-wind
> Shifts sudden to the south, the small warm rain
> Melts out the frozen incense from all flowers,"

where the last line shows that Keats has now added to his style a mastery of Dante's especial grace: and such passages as this, or again when he calls written words

> "The shadows of melodious utterance,"

which is also Dantesque in thought, should, I think, have forbidden the later critics, who knew from external evidence when the *Revision* was written, from judging that the new style came from decay of poetic power. In these quotations there is certainly no falling off in the magic of his pen, while faults so foreign to him as the wrongness, lowness, and awkwardness in the diction of these lines—

> "Therefore, that happiness be somewhat *shared*,
> Such *things* as thou *art* are admitted oft
> Into *like gardens thou didst pass* erewhile,"

show want of mastery in his new, not failure in his old manner, and are like fatigue.

To conclude this question of style, it may be added, that though the effect of an imitation of Milton is fairly got rid of from the *Revision*, and whole passages are excluded because they were too Miltonic, yet inversions and classicisms are used, and in the line—

> "Saturn, sleep on; O thoughtless, why did I,"

a Latinism is actually introduced to supplant a mannerism of his own; for *O thoughtless* is changed to *me thoughtless*.

To pass now to the meaning of the poem, we will begin with what is certain, and so lead up to the more doubtful matters. First, it is certain that the poem was intended as an allegory; it is named *A Vision*, but of Knowledge now, not of Love, and it begins in a figurative garden, as the *Divina Commedia* in a wood, and there is a supernatural guide, who is to explain things unseen by what is seen. It is also clear that the first version of *Hyperion* was to be used to supply the vision, and from this it follows that the old *Hyperion* had also an inner meaning, for it is impossible that Keats would have forced into an allegory a poem which he had conceived and written without such intention. But the original poem being unfinished, this did not clearly appear; there are, however, indications of it, and one passage, the speech of Oceanus in Bk. ii., fairly supplies the argument, which is that there is a self-destructive progress in Nature towards good, and that beauty, and not force, is the law of this flux or change. It seems also probable that Keats intended to make Hyperion and Mnemosyne instruct Apollo, and thus to show Light and Song passing into union and perfection out of elemental chaos and crudeness. However this may be, Oceanus bids Saturn take comfort in his dethronement, "for," he says,

> "To bear all naked truths,
> And to envisage circumstance, all calm
> That is the top of sovereignty."

And it is further clear in the *Revision* that this *top of sovereignty* is the reward of the poet for conduct in certain circumstances of real life, and that the whole of the introduction (lines 19-266) is an objective picture of those circumstances. Here the allegory is complete, and it is here that it should be intelligible.

And this will serve to guide us at once to separate the *Revision* into two parts, the first down to line 266, which is the new allegory, and the second from line 267 onward, which is an adaptation of the original poem. This latter part we may neglect; it is only a maiming of his earlier fine work; but the first part is original, and though it opens badly, and has some poor places, it is from line 19 onwards, generally worthy to be reckoned with Keats' best work.

Although one cannot be wrong in assuming that this allegory is a description of Keats' own life, and of his latest convictions, and one would think that his letters and poems should supply the key with some certainty, yet I would not take on myself the responsibility of venturing very far, and would leave what I say as suggestion only.

As I read it, the visionaries are those who neglect conduct for the pursuit of any ideal. The garden and feast represent the beauties of Nature, and the drink is poetry, which is made from the fruits of the feast. The intoxication which followed the draught represents that complete and excited absorption by poetry which Keats describes himself as suffering when he was writing *Endymion*, and the swoon would be that state of selfish isolation into which he fell in his Miltonic period. His awaking in the temple is his recovery from this to a sympathy with the miseries of the world; and the temple itself is the temple of Knowledge, which it is death for a visionary to enter if he have not that sympathy. The steps to the altar are the struggle of such a mind to reach truth: and truth itself is revealed by knowledge. The leaves burning on the altar are years of the poet's life, or his youthful faculties.

Whether or no any or all of these points are rightly interpreted, it is sure that the general meaning is, that though Keats conceived of the true poet as a prophet and seer, yet he now valued the life of action and conduct above that of meditation and poetry, and condemns as selfish the merely artistic life which he had been leading; and he is now preaching that actual contact and sympathy with human misery and sorrow are the only school for real insight, which is the reward of true human conduct, and not to be arrived at by any other path. In this way only can the poet hope to create anything of value and become himself immortal.

Moneta, the new name for Mnemosyne, must be connected with *moneo*, and Memory is the same as Knowledge, and she can *admonish* or teach a knowledge of the mysteries of earth." And this knowledge is what is required to make a poet of a visionary. She is thus foster-mother of Apollo as well as mother of the Muses. She has a harp; and when Apollo says, "For me dark, dark, and painful vile *oblivion* seals my eyes," this oblivion must be ignorance regarded as the opposite of that knowledge which is memory. Compare *Hyperion*, iii., where Apollo "becomes immortal" by reading in Mnemosyne's eyes, just as the poet is to do in the *Revision*. Thus the temple must be the temple of Knowledge = Memory;[14] and it is fit that Mnemosyne, the Memory of all things, should be primeval, and sister to the oldest god.

The conception of her temple, all that is spared from the thunder of the war, is extremely fine in its allegorical manner, with its doors barred to the sunrise, and the western past closed by a mighty mythical image of a dead god, and an altar, beside which the goddess of the memory of all change stands veiled in the smoke of the sacrifice of the poet's life. The marble palace in *End.* ii. 256-270, corresponds somewhat closely with this temple, though the meaning is now changed, and it should be compared; but in taking this allegory to interpret Keats' mind, it must be remembered first, that all the different states through which he may represent himself as having passed, were only consecutive in the sense that he may have been at one time more dominated by one view of things, at another time by another; and

[14] *Cf.* Letter xxxvii., "Memory should not be called Knowledge." February 1818.

though in the changing strength of his convictions there may have been a real growth, yet the different feelings were most of them known to him almost from the first, as his letters show: and secondly, that what he condemned as his selfish period was the period in which he most benefited mankind; and he saw at the time the truth of the paradox, and was tortured by the "solitariness," which proved his sympathy to be alive; and that very torture may have been his misery at the foot of the altar-stairs, on which, when he once stepped, they filled his freezing body with natural heat. There is a great nobility in all this, and considering what vile treatment he had met with, it is very beautiful that there is not only no word of resentment, but no place for complaint: he takes all the blame on his own unworthiness. But it is also very sad: how changed now is his faith in the meaning of natural beauty to men: his old ideal mistress, Cynthia, the "lover of the upcast eye," is likened with the eyes of the goddess of memory, of which he says—

"They saw me not,
But in blank splendour beam'd, like the mild moon,
Who comforts those she sees not, who knows not
What eyes are upward cast."

V. THE TALES.

There are three finished tales or short narrative poems by Keats, *Isabella*, *The Eve of St. Agnes*, and *Lamia*. They are all famous for their beauty, and the first two, which are in stanza, may be said to have become almost popular. *Isabella* has, in fact, caused the story of the pot of basil to be widely known in England, as much perhaps from the pictures of artists who took their subject from Keats as from the poem itself. The story is unpleasant, and is the worst executed of the three; but the poet has overcome the gruesomeness with skill—he parenthetically interrupts his narration to confess the difficulty,—yet he seldom stays for many lines together above his weaker vein: the appearance of Lorenzo's ghost to Isabella, from stanza xxxi. onwards, being the best sustained passage. The poem has many examples of Keats' originality of imagination and felicity of phrase, but is tainted throughout by a characteristic egritude of passion, which makes the best occasion to speak of the curiously close similarity which exists between him and the school of painting which had Rossetti for its head. The lovers who "could not in the self-same mansion dwell without *some malady*," the "sick longing" of Isabella, the "passion both meek and wild," the "little sweet among much bitterness," and the consciousness of something too horrible to speak of behind the scene; with all the passionate faintness of the personages of the romance, in whom, as in a faded tapestry, the brilliance of the dresses has outlasted the flesh-colour, have a likeness to the creations of this school so remarkable, that Keats may be safely credited with a chief share of the parentage. *Isabella* was written in February-April 1818, when *Endymion* was in the press.

The Eve of St. Agnes, written in January 1819, and revised in September, that is, in the *Hyperion* period, is much more powerful. It is well done throughout, and except for some expressions, criticism could only quarrel with the machinery of the story. This opens with four stanzas about an "ancient bedesman," who has personally nothing whatever to do with the tale; he provides contrast to the revelry, which he introduces by hearing it, and he also makes opportunity for describing his haunt in the chapel of the heroine's castle: but the chapel is never used again. The feast, too, which Porphyro sets out in Madeline's chamber is robbed of its motive and serves no purpose but to enrich the description. Both these strands should have been woven in; but they are selected in sympathy with the story, and make some of the most successful colouring. *The Eve of St. Agnes* is not only a passionate tale, but it is very rich in the kind of beauty characteristic of Keats, and contains high poetry both of diction and feeling: the majority of readers would not wish it different from what it is.

Lamia, which was written between July and September 1819, that is, in the interval between the discontinuing and the rejection of *Hyperion*, is in rhymed couplets. These differ from those of *Endymion* in showing an approach to Dryden's versification,[15] and in so far a return from the extreme reaction against Pope with which Keats began. There will always be difference of opinion as to what the excellence of this meter is, but the source of the uncertainty in which Keats found himself is easy to explain. The meter in Chaucer's hands came to be perfectly successful, and chiefly because it was light; and the lightness was due to the presence in his language of terminal vowels and inflexions which have since become mute or entirely disappeared. For instance, Chaucer wrote—

> "As thick as motës in the sonnë beam."

Milton's ten syllables are

> "As the gay motes that people the sunbeams."

All the buoyancy is gone; and this exemplifies the change which necessarily came over the rhymed heroic verse. It became heavier and

---

[15] So the critics say; and Charles Brown told Lord Houghton that Keats purposely studied Dryden's verse: I have not myself any intimate acquaintance with it.

less adapted for narration, and at last was cast mechanically in polished couplets, which passed in a dull generation for a triumph of classic grace, and were prescribed by the Universities as the only form in which they would recognise English poetry. Later poets have used different devices for lightening the meter, so as to make it again do Chaucer's work, but the general result is that their lightly constructed verse is slovenly. *Endymion* was very successful in the quality of lightness, but it met with no favour, and the lightness was gained at the cost of other qualities which Keats could now regard without prejudice. In *Endymion* the couplet and line units are reduced to a minimum of value, and with these the rhyme value sinks, so that the unrhymed lines in the poem are scarcely noticed: on the other hand, the verses are frequently tagged by evidently foisted rhymes. But in reading the first dozen lines of *Lamia*, the problem seems solved; all is both light and sure, and there are neither tags nor self-conscious couplets: nothing could be better, and a great deal of the poem is as good as this. The device of separating the couplets by a pause in the sense after the first rhyme is retained from *Endymion*, and rhyme-triplets and twelve-syllable lines are introduced. But the poem is not all equally well written, the whole passage, i. 300-350, where the subject does not suit him, is plainly below the mark, and here the tags reappear, and they are much more self-evident and offensive in this kind of verse than in *Endymion*, where they were an avowed means of construction, and where their frequency became familiar and had the advantage of giving great force to any unbroken couplets that were introduced. As for the triplets and twelve-syllable lines, these are no doubt used sometimes with skill, but among regular 'heroics' they are a device of the most transparent artificiality, and by their carefully irregular intrusion they openly expose the monotony which they would awkwardly obviate. From which it would seem that they would find a better home in the less regular verse.

The problem how to match Chaucer's narrative in modern English is much more nearly solved in the unfinished Tale, *The Eve of St. Mark*, written in eight-syllable couplets with the same sort of latitude which Coleridge advocated in *Christabel*. This meter carries the description of the cathedral town on a showery Sunday evening in spring with an easy geniality combining beauty and homeliness, and suits just as well the indoors picture, which is a light combination of mystery and real life; and his mastery of all this, quite as much as his playful and charming imitation of the dainties and delicacies of middle English, assure one that Keats had Chaucer in his mind when he wrote it, and might have succeeded perfectly in this manner.

As for the poetry of *Lamia*, it does not all go on as well as it begins, and sometimes fails too in its most highly-wrought passages. The description of the serpent is overdone to vagueness, and her transformation has the same fault. Words like *rosy* and *phosphor* assert themselves; others are dressed at the call of the rhyme; while very common expressions occasionally produce a bathos, i. 201, 330, 335; ii. 12, 15, 89, 128. Yet Keats was trying to correct his old faults; for instance, in revising he appears to have written silently in ii. 134 for *silverly*; and *Lamia* is constructively the most perfect of his three narratives. I remark that "the taller grasses and full flowering weed" of i. 44 do not agree with the daffodils of line 184: and I consider it a blot that Lycius should die at the end; because he is killed by Apollonius, who, if he could not rescue him, should have let him alone. Philosophy or Reason is made unamiable: but I am afraid that Keats may have intended this; and he makes Apollonius laugh, which is almost diabolic. The general meaning is, no doubt, the antagonism of reason and pleasure, or of science and imagination (ii. 229 *seq.*), or both; and that reason should take delight in destroying pleasure is only one of the ugly doctrines that lurk beneath the text if it be read as a parable. But it is very uncertain how much Keats intended. He may have had in his mind the selfishness of the artist absorbed in his ideals, and his catastrophe in the justifiable indifference of the world to the creations of mere art. On August 23, 1819, he wrote thus: "A solitary life engenders pride and egotism, but this pride and egotism will enable me to write finer things than anything else could,—so I will indulge it." And in less than a month he had wholly banished from himself as unworthy this strong conviction of his duty.

VI. THE ODES.

Had Keats left us only his Odes, his rank among the poets would not be lower than it is, for they have stood apart in literature, at least the six most famous of them; and these were all written in his best period, when he was under the Miltonic influence—that is, between the early spring of 1819, while he was still engaged on *Hyperion*, and the autumn, when he discarded it. These are the six: 1. *Psyche*; 2. *Melancholy*; 3. *Nightingale*; 4. *Greek Urn*; 5. *Indolence*; 6. *Autumn*.

To these should be added 7. the fragment of the *May Ode*, May 1st, 1818, and 8. the *Ode to Pan*, from *Endymion*, bk. i., and 9. the *Bacchic Ode to Sorrow* in *Endymion*, bk. iv. But the two hymns to *Neptune* and *Diana* in *Endymion* are only worth enumeration, and the two early odes to *Apollo* and the *Ode to a Lock of Milton's Hair* are, as are the two later *Odes to Fanny*, chiefly or entirely of personal interest.

Of the seven odes first enumerated, the first place must be given for its perfection to that last composed—that is, the *Ode to Autumn*. This is always reckoned among the faultless masterpieces of English poetry; and unless it be objected as a slight blemish that the words "Think not of them" in the 2nd line of the 3rd stanza are somewhat awkwardly addressed to a personification of Autumn, I do not know that any sort of fault can be found in it. But though this is the best as a whole, it is yet left far behind by the splendour of the *Nightingale*, in which the mood is more intense, and the poetry vies in richness and variety with its subject.

The song of the nightingale is, to the hearer, full of assertion, promise, and cheerful expectancy, and of pleading and tender passionate overflowing in long drawn-out notes, interspersed with plenty of playfulness and conscious exhibitions of musical skill. Whatever pain or sorrow may be expressed by it, it is idealized—that is, it is not the sorrow of a sufferer, but the perfect expression of sorrow by an artist, who must have felt, but is not feeling; and the ecstasy of the nightingale is stronger than its sorrow, although different hearers may be differently affected according to their mood. Keats in a sad mood seized on the happy interpretation and promise of it, and gives it in this line—

> "Singest of *summer* in full-throated case."

But the intense feeling in his description of human sorrow (stanza 3) is weakened by the direct platitude that the bird has never known it; and in the penultimate stanza the thought is fanciful or superficial,—man being as immortal as the bird in every sense but that of sameness, which is assumed and does not satisfy. The introduction, too, of the last stanza is artificial, while his choosing *elf* to rhyme to *self*[16] turns out disastrously; and he loses hold of his main idea in the words "plaintive anthem," which, in expressing the dying away of the sound, changes its character. No praise, however, could be too high for those last six lines; and if grammar and sense are a little obscure in the first ten, I could not name any English poem of the same length which contains so much beauty as this ode.

Next to this I should rank *Melancholy*. The perception in this ode is profound, and no doubt experienced. The paradox that melancholy is most deeply felt by the organization most capable of joy is clinched at the end by the observation of the reaction which satiety provokes in such temperaments, so that it is also in the moment of extremest joy that it suddenly fades—

---

[16] The elf belongs to W. Brown of Tavistock, whom I suspect to have been the remote cause of the hitch in the first stanza—

> "Philomel, I do not envy thy sweet carolling."
>
> *Brit. Past.*, i. 3, 164.

"Turning to poison while the bee-mouth sips:
Ay, in the very temple of Delight
Veil'd Melancholy has her sovran shrine."

In spite of the great beauty of this ode, especially of the last stanza, it does not hit so hard as one would expect. I do not know whether this is due to a false note[17] towards the end of the second stanza, or to a disagreement between the second and third stanzas. In the second stanza the melancholy is, as Lord Houghton said, a "luxurious tenderness," while in the third it is strong, painful, and incurable.

The line—

"That fosters the droop-headed flowers all,"

means all the flowers only that are sacred sorrow. See *End.* iv. 170.

Next in order might come *Pysche*, for the sake of the last section (l. 50 to end), though this is open to the objection that the imagery is worked up to outface the idea—which is characteristic of Keats' manner. Yet the extreme beauty quenches every dissatisfaction. The beginning of this ode is not so good, and the middle part is mid-way in excellence.

Next, and disputing place with the last, comes the *Grecian Urn.* The thought as enounced in the first stanza is the supremacy of ideal art over Nature, because of its unchanging expression of perfection; and this is true and beautiful; but its amplification in the poem is unprogressive, monotonous, and scattered, the attention being called to fresh details without result (see espec. ll. 21-24, anticipated in 15, 16), which gives an effect of poverty in spite of the beauty. The last stanza enters stumbling on a pun, but its concluding lines are very fine, and make a sort of recovery with their forcible directness.

The last of the six. *Indolence*, is the objective picturing of a transient mood, and may be the description of an actual half-waking vision. If the details, such as the appearing of the figures four times, have no definite meaning, and I cannot fix any, they are too arbitrary. Parts of stanzas 2 and 3 and all the 5th are of the best work; but the whole ode scarcely earns its title; and its main interest, that is its fervour and feeling, betrays the poet into an undignified utterance in line 4 of the last verse.

The fragment of the *May Ode* is immortal on account of the famous passage of inimitable beauty descriptive of the Greek poets—

"Leaving great verse unto a little clan," &c.

---

[17] For its explanation, see p. xcvi.

With these seven the two chief odes in *Endymion* are worthy to rank. The ode to Pan in Book I. is good enough in design. Pan is first invoked as ruler in dark and moist woods; secondly, as the god to whom all natural products are sacred, with contrast of sunny places; thirdly, as king of fauns and satyrs; fourthly, for six lines as farm-god. But this last idea has been anticipated by interpolation in the previous section. Then the last part of the ode connects Pan with the secrets and power of Nature. The expression *But no more*, however interpreted, is unfortunate at the end of the ode. The diction throughout is rich and the imagery chosen well for the work that it has to do in the various aspects of the god's energy, the different objects being seized and shown in happy phrases full of knowledge and feeling; and though it might perhaps have been better if the second section had immediately preceded the last, rather than that the mysteries should follow close on the farm, there is no great fault to find. But yet the ode does not at first reading make an impression corresponding to these merits, nor has it won, like the others, a high reputation; and this may be due partly to the vagueness of the personification, caused by the variety of attributes and objects, and partly to the versification, which, though generally easy and fluent, pauses, especially in the second division, too frequently in the mid-line, in the manner of tagging, and produces there something of the effect of a catalogue, very foreign to the repose and finish which we look for in a set ode.

Lastly, as to the *Ode to Sorrow* in the 4th book of *Endymion*, I regard this as one of the greatest of Keats' achievements, and agree with all that Mr. Sidney Colvin has said in its praise in his Life of Keats. It unfortunately halts in the opening, and the 1st and 4th stanzas especially are unequal to the rest, as is again the 3rd from the end, "Young stranger," which for its matter would with more propriety have been cast into the previous section; and these impoverish the effect, and contain expressions which might put some readers off. If they would begin at the 5th stanza and omit the 3rd from the end, they would find little that is not admirable. And, as it stands, the ode is, I think, the better for these omissions. The pictorial description of the Bacchic procession is unmatched for life, wide motion, and romantic dreamy Orientalism, while the concluding stanzas, returning to the first movement, are as lovely as any Elizabethan lyric, and in the same manner. The bold contrast and passion of the ode, in spite of its weaker opening and the few expressions which remind one that it is an early work, give it a unique place among the richest creations of the English Muse.

VII. SONNETS.

There are nearly sixty sonnets in the latest editions of Keats' poems, but the most of them are sonnets only in external form. The metrical laws and liberties of sonnet-writing have been much inflicted on readers, and sonnets are usually classified by their differences in these minor particulars. But a more useful classification would be by their contents and form of thought. The typical sonnet is a reflective poem on love, or at least in some mood of love or desire, or absorbing passion or emotion; and such a definition includes almost everything which cannot be readily referred to some quite different species of poetry, as a few considerations may illustrate.

The Greek epigram, for instance, was originally, as the name implies, an inscription: its business was to record some event or mark some place, and its excellence to raise an emotion in the reader's mind. Its qualities, terseness with pathos, soon established a form which poets used for other purposes, until in the hands of city wits the name wholly changed its signification, and often now the record is a piece of scandal, and the emotion such as may be expressed by a well-bred jeer; a sad fall from Simonides. The sonnet form has been as loosely and variously used as the epigram, and the many varieties of the two have more than one point of contact; but it is plain that an epigram proper cannot become a sonnet by mere expansion to fourteen lines;—this happens to exceed epigrammatic length, but is possible in dedications and temple inscriptions,—and such a hybrid may at least be separated off as an epigrammatic sonnet.

Again, Horace elaborated a form of ode which it is easier to recognize than in few words describe; and a number of Milton's sonnets may be referred to this ode form. If we compare, for example, his *Cyriack, whose grandsire*, with *Martiis coelebs* or *Aeli vetusto*, there can be no doubt that Milton was here deliberately using the sonnet form to do the work of Horace's tight stanzas; and not the whole of Shakespeare's or Petrarch's sonnets set alongside will show enough kinship with these sonnets of Milton to draw them away from their affinity with Horace. Such sonnets, too, as his addresses to Vane, Fairfax, and Cromwell are properly odes, and should be called odes, or at least odic sonnets.

Again, there is a class of poetry called "occasional verse," and such a poem as may be written on any trivial event or fancy cannot become a sonnet because it goes begging for a dress, and, conscious not only of nakedness but of leanness, steals a well-cut garment for disguise.

These examples may suffice, if it be noted first, that nothing forbids a true sonnet from having an epigrammatic, or odic, or occasional motive—and this last is very common; and secondly, that all these forms and others are found mixed in the sonnet with its true subject matter in all proportions.

Now not so many as half of Keats' sonnets can by any stretch of interpretation be called sonnets proper, if we consider their substance rather than their verse form. The greater number of them are occasional, reflective, or odic addresses or dedications, or poems on places and books. And these hybrids come thickest among the earlier poems, while the true sonnets predominate towards the end. Again, almost all the early sonnets are Italian in rhyme system, and all the later are Shakespearian; and if we pick out from them the twelve best poems, these will all be found to be true sonnets and eight of them on the Shakespearian model. Twelve is all that very high praise can be given to, and that number already encroaches on the second best; and if a next twelve be chosen, this would be made up almost equally of true sonnets and hybrids. From which it seems that these hybrid poems of Keats', though most of them contain lines which make us glad to possess and preserve them, are among his immature performances; and also that as he improved in composition he relinquished his foreign subject-matter, and the Italian rhyme system, and did his best work in the English manner.

There are ten very fine sonnets; they are—

"Much have I travelled."
"When I have fears."
"Come hither all sweet maidens."
"Four seasons."
"Bright star."
"O soft embalmer."
"I cry your mercy."
"As Hermes once."
"The day is gone."
"Time's sea."

And with these some might class for its easy and pleasant mastery—

"To one who hath been long in city pent."

And the sonnet "Why did I laugh to-night?" has been selected and admired by some critics: it seems to me to be turgid and capricious, and hence unsuccessful. But all the first ten are extremely fine—the first eight being nearly faultless—and must stand among the best in the language. And if we pass from them to the next in merit, there is a great fall. Such a list would contain *Spenser a jealous honourer*; *Many the wonders*; *Nymph of the downward smile*; *How many bards*; *Small busy flames*; *Keen fitful gusts*; *My spirit is too weak*; *Glory and loveliness*; and *The town the churchyard*; and there is not one of these which does not plainly fail, and that sometimes badly, in some part, though all have their points of excellence.[18]

Not to speak of the magnificence of the ten best sonnets (the 8th line of the first is below the mark; the final couplet of No. 2 is weak; and the 4th line of No. 9 requires much allowance), Keats' sonnets are generally distinguished by a total absence of the self-consciousness which is the common bane of sonnets, and has got them a bad name among honest folk; so that many lovers of poetry put Keats' sonnets next to Shakespeare's. They are free from effort and puzzle-headedness and pedantry, and when they do fall, they do not fall stiffly but negligently, and most of them are pleasant poems and grateful to the reader.

VIII. EPISTLES.

There are four *Epistles* written in ten-syllable couplets:—

1. To Geo. Felton Mathew (Nov. 1815).
2. To my brother George (Aug. 1816).
3. To Ch. Cowden Clarke (Sept. 1816).
4. To Reynolds (March 1818).

And with them may be grouped the two poems criticized earlier, that is the short *Endymion* and *Sleep and Poetry.*

Though there are good things in these *Epistles*, their execution is in every respect very poor, and they are in so far more like letters written in rhyme than poems in the form of letters, and they may all be taken with the apology which Keats sent with the fourth, to "excuse the unconnected subject and careless verse." The Epistle to Cowden Clarke is altogether far the worst, and though it has a rational argument, it is not worth defending from any condemnation for want of artistic form; but it is in my opinion wrong to include the other early epistles and poems in this judgment. In my previous analysis of two of these, I have pointed out their really solid construction, and the 1st, 2nd, and 4th of the *Epistles* are, I should say, quite as well built. Their "argument" is perfectly clear, and if the form of it escapes the reader's attention, that is due to the lightness of the imaginative touch and flight, which is a welcome escape from the conscious pedantries of form, and, so long as the sense is clear, a great merit. Indeed, if the expression of these *Epistles* were at all worthy of their framework, they would be models of what such epistles should be. Nos. 1 and 2 must be passed over here.

[18] Matthew Arnold selected eight sonnets; five are among the eight which I have set first: the other three are—*After dark vapours*; *Great spirits now*; *The poetry of the earth.*

No. 4 is of great interest. Its argument (though Keats himself calls the poem unconnected) is a very beautiful artistic movement of thought, just short of caprice, returning at the end with great force to the apparent first motive, which is suddenly revealed as being much weightier than at first allowed to appear. The heads are these:—Automatic capricious imaginations of all kinds, 1-12, very common; they may be beautiful, as a picture by Titian, described, -25; or like Claude's Enchanted Castle, described, -66. The wish that all our imaginings could take such colouring, &c., question why they cannot, -85. The poet shows himself haunted by a horrid mood, -end.

The passage l. 67 onwards is of importance with respect to Keats' method—

> "O that our dreamings all, of sleep or wake,
> Would all their colours from the sunset take:
> From something of *material sublime*," &c.

If this be compared with the passage which is contrasted with Wordsworth earlier ('Lo, I see afar, ...) there will be a mutual illustration of sense.

Keats also here, in a confession of failure, analyses his inability to express his ideas—

> "Imagination brought
> Beyond its proper bound, yet still confined,
> Lost in a sort of Purgatory blind,
> Cannot refer to any standard law
> Of either earth or heaven."

Also in this poem he plainly states that he does not consider his mind matured, nor able to teach, and that he is a prey to the moods of pessimism, but that he will not give way to them. He longs rather for the time when he shall arrive at "the love of good and ill," and speaks of it as his "award."

IX. LYRICAL POEMS.

If we include among the lyrical poems those written in seven-syllable couplets, we find three popular pieces, *Souls of Poets*, *Bards of Passion*, and *Ever let the fancy roam*. In a letter to his brother, January 1819, Keats writes: "These are specimens of a sort of rondeau which I think I shall become partial to, because you have one idea amplified with greater ease and more delight and freedom than in the sonnet." The theme is stated in the first four lines, and then, after an amplification without progress, these are used again in the last division to make a close by return, like a rondo in music; and the form seems good, simple, and attractive. These three poems have all of them the popular qualities of fluency and grace, and the statement of the subject is provocative of interest; yet, though the first sustains itself in a fine vein for six lines, there is little other merit either of thought or diction in the first two. Mr. M. Arnold chose these and excluded the *Fancy* from his selection, but there can be no doubt that this last is by far the best of the three. It is maintained throughout at a fair level, and the simple descriptions of nature, recalling *L'Allegro*, are often very beautiful; and in the last division there is a sensuous passage done in the fine Miltonic manner, where the eight-syllable line is introduced with great effect, descriptively of Jove's languor.

Of the five other poems in this measure there is none worthy of praise as a whole.

There are left now only the lyrical poems in stanza, and easily first, holding a unique place in literature, stands *La belle dame sans merci*. This occurs in a long journalistic letter from Keats to his brother in America, and is dated "Wednesday evening," that is, April 28, 1819. It seems as if he had composed it on that day, and written it down hastily from memory, so that he had to correct several mistakes afterwards; and, from the remarks appended to it, it looks as if he was at the time unaware of its great merit. It was not inserted in the *Lamia* volume, but first appeared through Leigh Hunt in the *Indicator* for May 10, 1820, and this version differs from that in Keats' letter in one or two points; and these may be corrections by Keats, but the original first line will certainly preserve the first version, which exists in Keats' own handwriting, as the favorite and accepted one. "*Wretched wight*," the correction, is cold and poor, and fatal to the tragic motive of the poem, and out of keeping with its heroic detail, whereas the original "*knight-at-arms*" gives the keynote of romance and of aloofness from real life, and the suggestion of armor is of the greatest value to the general coloring. It would be impertinence to praise this poem, which charms alike old and young: and it stands above the reach of criticism. For other reasons it is better not to criticize, "*In a drear-nighted December*," which, after a very long interval indeed, must be placed next. This poem is a great favorite, and perhaps deservedly so, both for its beauty and originality, but the latter quality proves expensive. And after this poem there is another gap, for if we mention the next best lyrics, we come to such poems as *Meg Merrilies*, and *Where be you going, you Devon maid*? which, as Lord Houghton printed it, omitting the second stanza, is successful; and *I had a dove*, which could only have been written by a poet; and *Walking in Scotland*, of which the obscurity and strangeness of the sentiment described make it noteworthy. Mrs. Owen quotes the Faery song *Shed no tear*! as worthy of Keats, but we wonder how it was that there are not more better lyrics. Keats, one would have thought, would have excelled in them, and we can only suppose that we have his odes instead.

Success in lyrical verse requires a delicately strict subjection of imagination to one purpose, and this was not a part of Keats' poetic instinct; and though when he came to learn it, he wrote as it would seem almost unconsciously one of the best lyrics in the world; yet it is not improbable that he would still have regarded lyrics as a tract where he might cast off restraint. The fact remains that, with the exception of *La belle dame*, he never brought all his genius to "spend its fury in a song."

X. "OTHO" AND "STEPHEN."

Otho the Great is contemporary with Lamia: it was written July-September 1819, and should therefore be among Keats' best work; but it is not, so that its failure must be specially accounted for: and it may, I think, be entirely laid to inexperience, and to the ugly and ill-shapen Elizabethan models to which Keats apparently looked in good faith for guidance; and among which, with their stagey fury, unnecessary confusions, rude manners, and occasional magnificences, his play might pass undistinguished. Unfortunately too this play turns on a question of maiden virtue, which he could not handle, and which he did not even choose for himself, for the plot was furnished him by a friend, who gave him the scenes across the table to versify or dramatize one by one—a most deadening situation. It is badly contrived: the antecedent conditions are very elaborate, and yet are never plainly stated; they have to be discovered from isolated, ill-managed and confused hints in the dialogue; so that the attention of an auditor, if it was not entirely put off by this riddle, would only be kept alive by a wish to come to a judgment of his guesses. The riddle, moreover, has no satisfactory solution. Then the scenes themselves are rather lacking in distinct dramatic point, independently of the uncertainty of the motive. But if these faults are not wholly due to Keats he must yet have the blame of the lack of moral import, and of the imperfect delineation of the characters, whose manners are not good, and who seem to take a conscious interest in the plot. The style has the faults of cold magnificence, occasional flatness and common expressions, with careless grammar, and the use of childish tricks for impromptu effect. In spite of all this, there is a succinctness and force about the whole, which forbid one to conclude that Keats would not have succeeded in drama: and though it is commonly said that he lacked the essential moral grasp, his letters seem to me to refute this, and his determination would have been sufficient assurance of success. In fact, the fragment of *Stephen*, which he began on his own lines after finishing *Otho*, already shows an advance. This is written in a style midway between

Marlowe and Shakespeare, and recalls the opening of the third part of *Henry VI.* The imitated magnificence is somewhat restless, but the narrative and purpose of the characters stand out fairly well amid the stir and freedom which was evidently the poet's aim.

It would be easy to quote from *Otho* some fine passages, and many fine lines and expressions, but they seem to be buried in a rubbish-heap from which one gladly turns back to the green tangle of *Endymion.*

XI. DICTION AND RHYTHM.

Keats' vocabulary, to judge by the impression that one gets from reading his poems, is rich, and his use of quite a large number of words that are not commonly found must be reckoned among the factors of his style. Mr. W. Arnold has made a special examination of these, and his remarks imply an objection to adjectives with the suffix *y*, like *bloomy and bowery*; but when these are formed from substantives they are regular enough. Adjectives thus formed from other adjectives—take *paly*, which should mean full of pales or palings,—are not on the same footing: to any one accustomed to Chaucer's verse they would sound more like old than new words, and they would be useful in versification, but they are also like baby-talk, and generally indefensible; it does not appear, however, that Keats laid himself open to any reproach in this particular. *Paly* had been used by other writers; and even with these words the test is their success, not their regularity. I never heard of any one objecting to Shakespeare's

> "I can call spirits from the *vasty* deep.'"

Indeed, what is in question is very much the same with the words as with the spirits, whether they will come when you do call for them.

Among Keats' inventions *spangly* does not look promising; but the passage in *Isabella*—

> "As when of healthful midnight sleep bereft,
> Thinking on rugged hours and fruitless toil,
> We put our eyes into a pillowy cleft,
> And see the *spangly* gloom froth up and boil,"

amply justifies the word, for which no other could be substituted: and it has been received into the language. So again the "*pipy* hemlock" in the Ode to Pan is admirable: on the other hand, "*boundly reverence*" defies interpretation: but the general result of Mr. Arnold's examination is that most of the strange words in Keats were taken from earlier writers. Readers of the poems cannot miss noting these: they are less likely to observe the exact nature of the class of epithets which most frequently recur; the chief group might, I think, be called languid, such as *quiet*, *sweet*, *fair*, *white*, *green*, *old*, *young*, *little*, and other such words as *tender*, *gentle*, *easy*, *fresh*, *pleasant*, most of these suggestive of comfort. Then the *melting*, *fainting*, *swimming*, *swooning*, and *panting* words are over-frequent. Words like *wild*, *dark*, *deep*, *strange*, *lone*, *mysterious*, &c., have a great deal to do, but they are not worked so hard as by Shelley. Keats has also a pretty steady recurrence of certain objects; he is as fond of *moss* and *eagles* as Shelley was, and *echoes*, *bees*, *marble*, *silver*, *dew*, *nests* and *weeds*,—and the list might be extended,—are too conspicuous. A great deal of the general insipidity and tedium of *Endymion* may be analyzed down to this. The over-frequent use which he makes of *tiptoe*—taken from Shakespeare—is very characteristic of his manner. But he outgrew all this, and if in his early poems he uses these words too frequently, yet he has also used them as well as they can be used. Some faults of his pronunciation, which have been called Cockneyisms, cannot be passed so easily. Thus *perhaps*, used as a monosyllable, is abominable: but this occurs only in the early poems. And he renounces in *Lamia* his pronunciation of *toward*, which he had hitherto used as a disyllable accented on the last, and comes round to the contracted pronunciation. This word, and words like *fire* and *lyre*, which he makes disyllables, often weaken his lines; for in disyllabic metres which admit elisions and trisyllabic feet, they will not readily, at least to my ear, sustain a whole foot of two syllables. Verse which allows such a line as this—

> "Ah desperate mortal! I even dared to press" (*End.* i. 661),

halts at the following—

> "And then, towards me, like a very maid" (i. 634).
> "Dearest Endymion, my entire love" (iii. 1022).
> "The lyre of his soul Aeolian tuned" (ii. 866).

But Keats also amended this later, though too late to destroy the effect of his example, and used these syllables[19] in *Hyperion* as Milton would have done—

> "Didst find a lyre all golden by thy side" (iii. 63).

Of the same kind is the exaggerated value which he gives to the semivowel *l*, in the following lines for example—

---

[19] Lyre is an unfortunate word to extend unduly. I have seen the following verse as motto for a song-book—

> "The lyres' voice is lovely everywhere."

"The dazz-l-ing sunrise; two sisters sweet,
Turn'd syllab-l-ing thus: Ah, Lycius bright."

He also, like Shelley, makes a trisyllable of *evening*.

There is another peculiarity common to Keats and Shelley, which should be noticed because it introduces an instability into Keats' rhythms. It is found in earlier writers, for instance, in this line from Shakespeare—

"Fair Jessica shall be my torch-bearer,"

where the accent of the last foot is not inverted, but the compound *torch-bearer*, which we pronounce with a stress both on the first and second syllables, carries no stress at all on the second, but perhaps a slight compensating stress or delay on the last. There are a great many words made in this way of a monosyllable and a disyllable, in which we now observe both the colliding accents; and if these words occur in disyllabic rhythms of alternate stress, with their first syllable in the regular stressed place, then the next foot will to our ears, trained as they have been by Milton, have its stress inverted. I think that this is not always intended by Keats: here are examples—

"A shów-monstèr about the streets of Prague."
"That cámp-mushroòm, dishonour of our house."
"Of béan-blossòms in heaven freshly shed."
"Or they might watch the qúoit-pitchèrs, intent."
"Of lóve-spanglès just off yon cape of trees."
"The poor folk of the séa-countrỳ I blest."
"Then came a conquering éarth-thundèr and rumbled."
"All deáth-shadòws, and glooms that overcast."
"Make not your rosary of yéw-berriès."

And the pronunciation in the following lines is probably caused by the same dislike of colliding accents in a compounded trisyllable—

"Look'd up; a cónflicting of shame and ruth."
"And strives in vain to únsettle and wield."

And thus no doubt—

"In a dreár-nightèd December."

We now read this line and most of the others with our changed accent, and we rather like the irregularity thus introduced into the verse.

There is, in fact, one line of Shelley which is particularly admired for a very beautiful rhythm, which he probably did not intend—

"And wild-roses and ivy serpentine,"

where Shelley, I should suppose, stressed *wild-roses* like *primroses*: in the same poem is

"There grew pied windflowers and violets."

And he has

"Swéet-basil and mígnonétte."

Bírde-maidèns, *quíck-silvèr*, *bírd-footèd*, *train-bearèr*, &c., and in the *Recollection are píne-forèst*, and *wóodpeckèr*, where the beautiful versification has, at least to my ear, a charm added to it by the extra license which our pronunciation introduces.

Whether these poets took this accent from the Elizabethans, or whether it really had lingered on, I do not know; in later poets it seems only an affectation; but it is a real source of uncertainty in Keats' verse, because he not only used the other pronunciation also, but he admitted the rhythmical inversions which that would introduce into the verses where it was apparently not intended.

And for this reason it would not do to decide this question merely on the assumption that Keats could not have intended the inversion of stress. He begins one sonnet with thc linc—

"How many bards gild the lapses of time,"

where the inversion of the third and fourth stresses is very musical and suitable to the exclamatory form of the sentence. Again, in *End.* i.—

"Young companies nimbly began dancing."

The inversion of the third and fifth stresses admirably pictures the dancers stepping on the scene: and such rhythms as

"Visions of all places; a bowery nook,"

show what a broad view he took of rhythm, and how melodiously his verse carries variety. And he was fond of inversion even of the fifth foot, *e.g.*—

"Guarding his forehead with her round elbow."
"Was in his plaited brow; yet his eyelids."
"Like vestal primroses, but dark velvet."
"Golden, or rainbow-sided, or purplish," &c.

And if these might be regarded as merely a grace snatched from the remembered cadences of old romance, yet he also uses this inversion deliberately with its full proper force of strangeness of suggestion in the following line—

"What it might mean. Perhaps, thought I, Morpheus,"

and for the irony of impossibility in

"Bright star, would I were stedfast as thou art,"

and in the following, where the strong enclitic accent has almost the effect of terror—

"Who comforts those she sees not, who knows not."

In one place at least in *Endymion* an inverted fifth foot is made to rhyme to a line with an extra-metrical syllable at the end of it: an uncomfortable effect common in Wyatt and writers of the time of Henry VIII. And in another place a rhythmical effect is sought by using Chaucer's license of omitting the first syllable of the line; for there is evidence that Keats intended this (Lett, xxxix.)—

"And the dull twanging bow-string, and the raft
Branch down sweeping from a tall ash top."

As there is not space in this essay to treat this subject thoroughly, I have chosen these few points as being of special interest. I may conclude by saying generally that Keats' rhythm, in spite of its variety, is easy and melodious rather than sonorous or powerful.

XII. GENERAL.

In these detached criticisms many of the main qualities of Keats' poetry have been incidentally brought out; there is one, as yet unmentioned, which claims the first place in a general description, and that is the very seal of his poetic birthright, the highest gift of all in poetry, that which sets poetry above the other arts; I mean the power of concentrating all the far-reaching resources of language on one point, so that a single and apparently effortless expression rejoices the aesthetic imagination at the moment when it is most expectant and exacting, and at the same time astonishes the intellect with a new aspect of truth. This is only found in the greatest poets, and is rare in them; and it is no doubt for the possession of this power that Keats has been often likened to Shakespeare, and very justly, for Shakespeare is of all poets the greatest master of it; the difference between them here is that Keats' intellect does not supply the second factor in the proportion or degree that Shakespeare does; indeed, it is chiefly when he is dealing with material and sensuous subjects that his poems afford illustrations; but these are, as far as they go, not only like Shakespeare, but often as good as Shakespeare when he happens to be confining himself to the same limited field. Examples from Shakespeare are such well-known sayings as these—

"My way of life
Is fain into the sear, the yellow leaf."—*Macbeth.*

"Lay not that nattering unction to your soul."—*Hamlet.*

"We are such stuff
As dreams are made on, and our little life
Is rounded with a sleep."—*Tempest.*

Examples from Keats are—

"The journey homeward to habitual self."

"Solitary thinkings; such as dodge
Conception to the very bourne of heaven."

"My sleep had been embroider'd with dim dreams."

In most of Keats' phrases of this sort there is a quality which makes them unlike Shakespeare; and if we should put into one group all those which are absolutely satisfactory, and then make a second group of those which are not so simply convincing, we should find in these last that the un-Shakespearian quality was more declared, and came out as something fanciful, or rather too vaguely or venturesomely suggestive; the whole phrase displaying its poetry rather than its meaning, and being in consequence less apt and masterly. This second group would contain many of the most admired lines of Keats, and these are very characteristic of him. Such are—

> "Those green-rob'd senators of mighty woods,
> Tall oaks,"

and—

> "How tiptoe Night holds back her dark-grey hood."

The *Revision of Hyperion* shows that Keats himself was dissatisfied with his *senators*; and one can see the reason without condemning the passage or approving its omission. Finally, there would be left a third group of such-like phrases which plainly miss the mark.

Closely allied to these imaginative phrases, and perhaps more characteristic of Keats and peculiar to him, are the short vivid pictures which may be called his masterpieces of word-painting, in which with a few words he contrives completely to finish a picture which is often of vast size. Good examples of this are the sestet of the *Leander sonnet*; the last four lines of the *Chapman's Homer*; the passage beginning *Golden his hair* in *Hyperion* ii. 371; and, to quote one from *Endymion*—

> "The woes of Troy, towers smothering o'er their blaze,
> Stiff-holden shields, far-piercing spears, keen blades,
> Struggling, and blood, and shrieks."

For its wealth in such rare strokes of descriptive imagination Keats' poetry must always take the very first rank; and it is his imaginative quality of phrase which sets him more than any other poet of his time in creative antagonism to the eighteenth-century writers; for it was not only foreign to their style, but incomprehensible and repugnant to their pseudo-classic taste, which preferred a "reasonable propriety of thought," such as Hume found to be lacking in Shakespeare, to the shadowy powers of imagination, however godlike.

The limitation of Keats' faculty in this excellence—which, if it may be ascribed wholly to his youth, amply justifies the sentiment of the opening lines of this essay—leads us on naturally to another of his chief characteristics, and that is his close relationship with common Nature: he is forever drawing his imagery from common things, which are for the first time represented as beautiful: and again in this we see his opposition to the eighteenth-century writers, who mainly contented themselves with conventional commonplaces for their natural imagery; whereas Keats discovers in the most usual objects either beauty or sources of delight or comfort, or sometimes even of imaginative horror, which are all new; and here his originality seems inexhaustible, and his wide poetic sympathies the strongest. Nor does he confine himself to matters of which he could have had much experience; he makes Nature the object of his imaginative faculty—Nature apart from man, or related to man as an enchantress to a dreamer. This is, I suppose, what he means when, comparing himself with Byron, he says, "There is this great difference between us: he describes what he sees,—I describe what I imagine. Mine is the hardest task: now see the immense difference."[20] Here he shows a vast wealth which makes his poems a mine of pleasure. *Endymion* is crowded to excess with a variety of these images, and as they came up in his mind in an endless stream to illustrate his ideas, the ideas sometimes fare rather badly; for though they were no doubt generally held firm in his own mind, they are yet drowned by the images of their objective presentation; until these themselves at last lose even their own virtue, and fatigue the reader, who feels like a sightseer in a gallery overcrowded with pictures, which by degrees he ceases to regard with attention.

And in this devotion to natural beauty lies, I believe, one true reason of Keats' failure in the delineation of human passion. The only passion delineated by Keats is the imaginative love of Nature, and human love is regarded by him as a part of this, and his lover is happy merely because admitted into communion with new forms of natural beauty. This, which appeared in theory in the explanation of the allegory of *Endymion*, is practically exposed in the 2nd stanza of the *Ode to Melancholy*, where, among the objects on which a sensitive mind is recommended to indulge its melancholy fit, the anger of his mistress is enumerated with roses, peonies, and rainbows, as a beautiful phenomenon, plainly without respect to its cause, meaning, or effect. And so in *Lamia*—

"He took delight
Luxurious in her sorrows, soft and new,"

and

"Fine was the mitigated fury."

How different is the parallel passage of Shakespeare, which at once occurs to one—

"O, what a deal of scorn looks beautiful
In the contempt and anger of his lip!"

This is not artistic admiration, but a lover's entire devotion.

---

[20] Letters, cxvi. p. 301.

In the criticism of *Endymion* we found a want of taste in Keats' idea of woman; we have now to add a charge of lack of true insight into human passion. If this was wholly due to the absence of awakening experience, it is at least unfortunate that in *Lamia*, in which from its date we might have expected something mature, he should have chosen so low a type. Though perhaps suggested by the original of his story, it was not necessary to it; and even if he preferred to have his snake-woman bad, there was every reason why Lycius' passion should have been of a higher type. How unworthy it is is shown in the description of their meeting and in the following sentiment—

> "But too short was their bliss
> To breed distrust and hate, that make the soft voice hiss."

This love is an association for mutual pleasure, the end of which is satiety and revulsion, and it is, I repeat, at least unfortunate that Keats, after he had known love, should, in his first attempt to delineate it, have been satisfied with so vulgar a type. The ideal passion in *Isabella* is insipid, and even in *The Eve of St. Agnes*, the passion, as expressed in stanzas xxxv.-xxxix., is at best of a conventional type, and has to have a good deal read into it by the light of the story.

But Keats' doctrine of beauty, which might be defended if it was spiritualized, which it never is by him, may often be reconciled with true feeling by the allowance which is due to his objective method; concerning this, as illustrations have been given (see pp. xxvi.-xxvii.), I shall say no more here except to repeat that Keats' imagery probably always followed, if it did not always clearly picture, some train of ideas; and when he says in the Ode *To Fanny*

> "My muse had wings,
> And ever ready was to take her course
> Whither I bent her force,
> Unintellectual, yet divine to me;—
> Divine, I say! What sea-bird o'er the sea
> Is a philosopher the while he goes
> Winging along where the great water throes?"

these words should not be taken as a disavowal of meaning in "those abstractions which were his only life," but as an apology for immaturity, and they must be interpreted in the light of his high idea of philosophy. Keats was conscious, like Virgil, of a double inclination. He said of himself, April 1818:[21] "I have been hovering for some time between an exquisite sense of the luxurious, and a love for philosophy.

[21] Letters, l.

Were I calculated for the former, I should be glad; but as I am not, I shall turn all my soul to the latter." This would be a strange variant of

"Me vero primum dulces ante omnia Musae,"

if we need suppose it to be anything more than an utterance of that contrarious mood so common to introspection: it is nevertheless evidence that Keats was unlikely to have depreciated the intellectual element of his art: but the intellectual element is always in league with emotion, and would have been, I imagine, considered by him as worthless in poetry without such mixture. In the *Epistle to Reynolds*, even the unpleasantness of the consideration of what we call the struggle for existence would, simply presented, have been flat and commonplace; but he shows it as a "horrid mood," by which he is haunted, and uses great skill and a wealth of contrasted beauty in introducing it under this enhanced aspect, "wreathing a flowery band spite of the unhealthy ways made for his searching;" and in calling his Muse unintellectual, he was no doubt uttering his reiterated impatience for more knowledge, the expression of which recurs so often in his poems and letters, that it is needless to quote any one, and which rises to a sort of consummation in the *Revision of Hyperion*, where it seems as if he had imagined himself to have at length attained to an insight of the mystery.

There is less opposition, it seems to me, between Keats' true instinct for ideal philosophy and his luxurious poetry (which seems rather its young expression), than between these on the one hand and his practical human qualities, as revealed by his letters, on the other. The bond of all was an unbroken and unflagging earnestness, which is so utterly unconscious and unobservant of itself as to be almost unmatched. It is always present in his poetry both for good and ill, in the spontaneous and felt quality of his epithets, and the absence of any barrier even, it would sometimes seem, of consideration or judgment between his mind and his pen. Whether this earnestness is the account of his failure in his purely comic freaks I do not know, but it may certainly account for his want of humor, for which, in spite of some traces in his letters, it does not appear to have left any room. The best of the letters are serious and full of good matter, a few are quite foolish, and a great number are written in a high-spirited jocular vein, which seems to be carelessly assumed for the double purpose of amusing his correspondent and relaxing his own mind. The chief charm in all of them is their unalloyed sincerity: there is nothing between the pen and the mind, not always even an effort or desire to write what should be worth reading: it is enough that it is he that writes, and his brother or friend that will read.

In spite of this earnestness and philosophy, it is certainly true that

Keats' mind was of a luxurious habit; and it must have been partly due to this temperament that he showed so little severity towards himself in the castigation of his poems, though that was, as I said before, chiefly caused by the prolific activity of his imagination, which was always providing him with fresh material to work on. In this respect he is above all poets an example of what is meant by inspiration: the mood which all artists require, covet, and find most rare was the common mood with him; and I should say that being amply supplied with this, what as an artist he most lacked was self-restraint and self-castigation,—which was indeed foreign to his luxurious temperament, unselfish and devoted to his art as he was,—the presence of which was most needful to watch, choose, and reject the images which crowded on him as he thought or wrote.

And it is thus that Keats' best period was when he fell under the influence and example of Milton. He was a great deal influenced by other poets, and had an unequaled power of reproducing not only the style of any writer whom he imitated, but the mental attitude which informed the style,[22] so that one is tempted to venture a bull of him, and say that if he had not been so original, he would have been only a plagiarist. But it was not until he came to rival Milton's epic that his originality seemed to be in danger; and no one would think of judging *Hyperion* by its likeness to *Paradise Lost*. If the two poems should be generally compared, though it is plain that Keats does not reach the sustained sonority and force of Milton (nor has he even shown as much skill in characterizing his divinities, whose elemental personalities would seem to have offered him a more interesting and poetically rich opportunity than the biblical devils did to Milton), yet in one respect he is in my opinion superior to Milton, and that is for a warmth in his poetry of inestimable worth. To give an example, where he describes Asia, he has

> "More thought than woe was in her dusky face,
> For she was prophesying of her glory."

Here there is a sympathetic touch in *dusky* which Milton would not have stopped to give, and it has the effect—at least it has to me—of warming the fine intellectual picture of Oriental slavery and metaphysics with an emotion that brings one at once into contact and sympathy with it.

So fragmentary and incomplete a treatise may break off abruptly. I began it with a due sense, as I thought, of responsibility, and with full

---

[22] This is not true of his earliest work. But see for example the sonnet *Time's Sea*, which might have been written by Shakespeare.

admiration for the poet: I find both increased at the end. I owe much to the kindness of friends, who have read my papers and offered suggestions; especially I may name Mrs. Margaret L. Woods, and my old friend Canon Dixon, whose remarks were of great service to me; but most of all I have to thank Mr. Ellis Wooldridge, without the promise of whose collaboration I should not have ventured on my task. In the qualitative analysis there is as much of his work as of my own, and I could not put my name to it without this acknowledgment.

Of the books which I have read, or in any way used, I have mentioned all in the notes except Lord Houghton's short memoir, and Mr. Coventry Patmore's Essay, and Mr. Buxton Forman's large edition, which last, on account of its careful text and numbered lines, I have trusted for all my references.

If my criticism should seem sometimes harsh, that is, I believe, due to its being given in plain terms, a manner which I prefer, because by obliging the writer to say definitely what he means, it makes his mistakes easy to point out, and in this way the true business of criticism may be advanced; nor do I know that, in work of this sort, criticism has any better function than to discriminate between the faults and merits of the best art: for it commonly happens, when any great artist comes to be generally admired, that his faults, being graced by his excellences, are confounded with them in the popular judgment, and being easy of imitation, are the points of his work which are most liable to be copied. Keats has had some such imitators, and would, I imagine, have been glad to be justified from them. And if I have read him rightly, he would be pleased, could he see it, at the universal recognition of his genius, and the utter rout of its traducers; but much more moved, stirred he would be to the depth of his great nature to know that he was understood, and that for the nobility of his character his name was loved and esteemed.

ROBERT BRIDGES

Yattendon, 1894.

P.S.—The statement in the text that Keats began *Hyperion* in November 1818, and worked at it as late as April 1819, finally discarding it in September 1819, is, I think, probable; but I do not wish it to be taken for more than an opinion. It seems possible that the poem may have been begun as long as two months earlier, and as much of it as there is may, in that case, have been done by January. This does not affect the sequence of his work; but a careless interpretation of his reference to *Hyperion* in the letter to Bailey of August 1819 would entirely mislead. I have not attempted to settle doubtful details of chronology, and do not wish to appear to have done so. This question of the exact date of *Hyperion* would take many pages by itself to exhibit and weigh the evidence.

The Poems

Imitation of Spenser

Now Morning from her orient chamber came,
And her first footsteps touched a verdant hill;
Crowning its lawny crest with amber flame,
Silv'ring the untainted gushes of its rill;
Which, pure from mossy beds, did down distill,
And after parting beds of simple flowers,
By many streams a little lake did fill,
Which round its marge reflected woven bowers,
And, in its middle space, a sky that never lowers.

There the king-fisher saw his plumage bright
Vying with fish of brilliant dye below;
Whose silken fins, and golden scalès light
Cast upward, through the waves, a ruby glow:
There saw the swan his neck of archèd snow,
And oared himself along with majesty;
Sparkled his jetty eyes; his feet did show
Beneath the waves like Afric's ebony,
And on his back a fay reclined voluptuously.

Ah! could I tell the wonders of an isle
That in that fairest lake had placèd been,
I could e'en Dido of her grief beguile;
Or rob from aged Lear his bitter teen:
For sure so fair a place was never seen,
Of all that ever charmed romantic eye:
It seemed an emerald in the silver sheen
Of the bright waters; or as when on high,
Through clouds of fleecy white, laughs the cerulean sky.

And all around it dipped luxuriously
Slopings of verdure through the glossy tide,
Which, as it were in gentle amity,
Rippled delighted up the flowery side;
As if to glean the ruddy tears, it tried,
Which fell profusely from the rose-tree stem!
Haply it was the workings of its pride,
In strife to throw upon the shore a gem
Outvying all the buds in Flora's diadem.

On Peace

O Peace! and dost thou with thy presence bless
  The dwellings of this war-surrounded Isle;
Soothing with placid brow our late distress,
  Making the triple kingdom brightly smile?
Joyful I hail thy presence; and I hail
  The sweet companions that await on thee;
Complete my joy—let not my first wish fail,
  Let the sweet mountain nymph thy favourite be,
With England's happiness proclaim Europa's liberty.
O Europe! let not sceptred tyrants see
  That thou must shelter in thy former state;
Keep thy chains burst, and boldly say thou art free;
  Give thy kings law—leave not uncurbed the great;
  So with the horrors past thou'lt win thy happier fate!

'*Fill for me a brimming bowl*'

'*What wondrous beauty*! *From this moment I efface from my mind all women.*' Terence [*Eunuch* II.3.296]

Fill for me a brimming bowl
And let me in it drown my soul:
But put therein some drug, designed
To banish Woman from my mind:
For I want not the stream inspiring
That heats the sense with lewd desiring,
But I want as deep a draught
As e'er from Lethe's waves was quaffed;
From my despairing breast to charm
The Image of the fairest form
That e'er my revelling eyes beheld,
That e'er my wandering fancy spelled.

'Tis vain! away I cannot chase
The melting softness of that face,
The beaminess of those bright eyes,
That breast—earth's only Paradise.

My sight will never more be blessed;
For all I see has lost its zest:
Nor with delight can I explore
The Classic page, the Muse's lore.

Had she but known how beat my heart,
And with one smile relieved its smart,
I should have felt a sweet relief,
I should have felt 'the joy of grief'.
Yet as a Tuscan 'mid the snow
Of Lapland thinks on sweet Arno,
Even so for ever shall she be
The Halo of my Memory.

To Lord Byron

Byron! how sweetly sad thy melody!
  Attuning still the soul to tenderness,
  As if soft Pity, with unusual stress,
Had touched her plaintive lute, and thou, being by,
Hadst caught the tones, nor suffered them to die.
  O'ershading sorrow doth not make thee less
  Delightful: thou thy griefs dost dress
With a bright halo, shining beamily,
As when a cloud a golden moon doth veil,
  Its sides are tinged with a resplendent glow,
Through the dark robe oft amber rays prevail,
  And like fair veins in sable marble flow;
Still warble, dying swan! still tell the tale,
  The enchanting tale, the tale of pleasing woe.

'As from the darkening gloom a silver dove'

As from the darkening gloom a silver dove
  Upsoars, and darts into the Eastern light,
  On pinions that naught moves but pure delight,
So fled thy soul into the realms above,
Regions of peace and everlasting love;
  Where happy spirits, crowned with circlets bright
  Of starry beam, and gloriously bedight,
Taste the high joy none but the blest can prove.
There thou or joinest the immortal quire
  In melodies that even Heaven fair
Fill with superior bliss, or, at desire
  Of the omnipotent Father, cleavest the air
On holy message sent—What pleasures higher?
  Wherefore does any grief our joy impair?

'Can death be sleep, when life is but a dream'

I

Can death be sleep, when life is but a dream,
And scenes of bliss pass as a phantom by?
The transient pleasures as a vision seem,
And yet we think the greatest pain's to die.

II

How strange it is that man on earth should roam,
And lead a life of woe, but not forsake
His rugged path; nor dare he view alone
His future doom which is but to awake.

To Chatterton

O Chatterton! how very sad thy fate!
Dear child of sorrow—son of misery!
How soon the film of death obscured that eye,
Whence Genius wildly flashed, and high debate.
How soon that voice, majestic and elate,
Melted in dying murmurs! Oh! how nigh
Was night to thy fair morning. Thou didst die
A half-blown flower which cold blasts amate.
But this is past: thou art among the stars
Of highest Heaven: to the rolling spheres
Thou sweetly singest: naught thy hymning mars,
Above the ingrate world and human fears.
On earth the good man base detraction bars
From thy fair name, and waters it with tears.

Written on the Day that Mr Leigh Hunt left Prison

What though, for showing truth to flattered state,
Kind Hunt was shut in prison, yet has he,
In his immortal spirit, been as free
As the sky-searching lark, and as elate.
Minion of grandeur! think you he did wait?
Think you he naught but prison walls did see,
Till, so unwilling, thou unturned'st the key?
Ah, no! far happier, nobler was his fate!
In Spenser's halls he strayed, and bowers fair,

Culling enchanted flowers; and he flew
With daring Milton through the fields of air:
To regions of his own his genius true
Took happy flights. Who shall his fame impair
When thou art dead, and all thy wretched crew?

To Hope

When by my solitary hearth I sit,
And hateful thoughts enwrap my soul in gloom;
When no fair dreams before my 'mind's eye' flit,
And the bare heath of life presents no bloom;
Sweet Hope, ethereal balm upon me shed,
And wave thy silver pinions o'er my head.

Whene'er I wander, at the fall of night,
Where woven boughs shut out the moon's bright ray,
Should sad Despondency my musings fright,
And frown, to drive fair Cheerfulness away,
Peep with the moon-beams through the leafy roof,
And keep that fiend Despondence far aloof.

Should Disappointment, parent of Despair,
Strive for her son to seize my careless heart;
When, like a cloud, he sits upon the air,
Preparing on his spell-bound prey to dart:
Chase him away, sweet Hope, with visage bright,
And fright him as the morning frightens night!

Whene'er the fate of those I hold most dear
Tells to my fearful breast a tale of sorrow,
O bright-eyed Hope, my morbid fancy cheer;
Let me awhile thy sweetest comforts borrow:
Thy heaven-born radiance around me shed,
And wave thy silver pinions o'er my head!

Should e'er unhappy love my bosom pain,
From cruel parents, or relentless fair;
O let me think it is not quite in vain
To sigh out sonnets to the midnight air!
Sweet Hope, ethereal balm upon me shed,
And wave thy silver pinions o'er my head!

In the long vista of the years to roll,
Let me not see our country's honour fade:
O let me see our land retain her soul,
Her pride, her freedom; and not freedom's shade.
From thy bright eyes unusual brightness shed—
Beneath thy pinions canopy my head!

Let me not see the patriot's high bequest,
Great Liberty! how great in plain attire!
With the base purple of a court oppressed,
Bowing her head, and ready to expire:
But let me see thee stoop from heaven on wings
That fill the skies with silver glitterings!

And as, in sparkling majesty, a star
Gilds the bright summit of some gloomy cloud;
Brightening the half-veiled face of heaven afar:
So, when dark thoughts my boding spirit shroud,
Sweet Hope, celestial influence round me shed,
Waving thy silver pinions o'er my head.

Ode to Apollo

In thy western halls of gold
When thou sittest in thy state,
Bards, that erst sublimely told
Heroic deeds, and sung of fate,
With fervour seize their adamantine lyres,
Whose chords are solid rays, and twinkle radiant fires.

There Homer with his nervous arms
Strikes the twanging harp of war,
And even the western splendour warms,
While the trumpets sound afar:
But, what creates the most intense surprise,
His soul looks out through renovated eyes.

Then, through thy Temple wide, melodious swells
The sweet majestic tone of Maro's lyre:
The soul delighted on each accent dwells,—
Enraptur'd dwells,—not daring to respire,
The while he tells of grief around a funeral pyre.

'Tis awful silence then again;
  Expectant stand the spheres;
  Breathless the laurelled peers,
Nor move, till ends the lofty strain,
Nor move till Milton's tuneful thunders cease,
And leave once more the ravished heavens in peace.

Thou biddest Shakespeare wave his hand,
  And quickly forward spring
The Passions—a terrific band—
  And each vibrates the string
That with its tyrant temper best accords,
While from their Master's lips pour forth the inspiring words.

A silver trumpet Spenser blows,
  And, as its martial notes to silence flee,
From a virgin chorus flows
  A hymn in praise of spotless Chastity.
'Tis still! Wild warblings from the Aeolian lyre
Enchantment softly breathe, and tremblingly expire.

Next thy Tasso's ardent numbers
  Float along the pleasèd air,
Calling youth from idle slumbers,
  Rousing them from Pleasure's lair:—
Then o'er the strings his fingers gently move,
And melt the soul to pity and to love.

But when *Thou* joinest with the Nine,
And all the powers of song combine,
  We listen here on earth:
The dying tones that fill the air,
And charm the ear of evening fair,
From thee, great God of Bards, receive their heavenly birth.

Lines Written on 29 May
The Anniversary of the Restoration of Charles the 2nd

Infatuate Britons, will you still proclaim
His memory, your direst, foulest shame?
  Nor patriots revere?

Ah! when I hear each traitorous lying bell,
'Tis gallant Sidney's, Russell's, Vane's sad knell,
 That pains my wounded ear.

To Some Ladies

What though, while the wonders of nature exploring,
 I cannot your light, mazy footsteps attend;
Nor listen to accents that, almost adoring,
 Bless Cynthia's face, the enthusiast's friend:

Yet over the steep, whence the mountain stream rushes,
 With you, kindest friends, in idea I muse—
Mark the clear tumbling crystal, its passionate gushes,
 Its spray that the wild flower kindly bedews.

Why linger you so, the wild labyrinth strolling?
 Why breathless, unable your bliss to declare?
Ah! you list to the nightingale's tender condoling,
 Responsive to sylphs, in the moon-beamy air.

'Tis mom, and the flowers with dew are yet drooping,
 I see you are treading the verge of the sea:
And now! ah, I see it—you just now are stooping
 To pick up the keep-sake intended for me.

If a cherub, on pinions of silver descending,
 Had brought me a gem from the fret-work of heaven;
And, smiles with his star-cheering voice sweetly blending,
 The blessing of Tighe had melodiously given;

It had not created a warmer emotion
 Than the present, fair nymphs, I was blessed with from you,
Than the shell, from the bright golden sands of the ocean
 Which the emerald waves at your feet gladly threw.

For, indeed, 'tis a sweet and peculiar pleasure
 (And blissful is he who such happiness finds),
To possess but a span of the hour of leisure,
 In elegant, pure, and aërial minds.

On Receiving a Curious Shell, and a Copy of Verses, from the Same Ladies

Hast thou from the caves of Golconda a gem,
Pure as the ice-drop that froze on the mountain?
Bright as the humming-bird's green diadem,
When it flutters in sunbeams that shine through a fountain?

Hast thou a goblet for dark sparkling wine?
That goblet right heavy, and massy, and gold?
And splendidly marked with the story divine
Of Armida the fair, and Rinaldo the bold?

Hast thou a steed with a mane richly flowing?
Hast thou a sword that thine enemy's smart is?
Hast thou a trumpet rich melodies blowing?
And wear'st thou the shield of the famed Britomartis?

What is it that hangs from thy shoulder, so brave,
Embroidered with many a spring-peering flower?
Is it a scarf that thy fair lady gave?
And hastest thou now to that fair lady's bower?

Ah! courteous Sir Knight, with large joy thou art crowned;
Full many the glories that brighten thy youth!
I will tell thee my blisses, which richly abound
In magical powers to bless, and to soothe.

On this scroll thou seest written in characters fair
A sunbeamy tale of a wreath, and a chain;
And, warrior, it nurtures the property rare
Of charming my mind from the trammels of pain.

This canopy mark: 'tis the work of a fay;
Beneath its rich shade did King Oberon languish,
When lovely Titania was far, far away,
And cruelly left him to sorrow, and anguish.

There, oft would he bring from his soft-sighing lute
Wild strains to which, spell-bound, the nightingales listened;
The wondering spirits of heaven were mute,
And tears 'mong the dewdrops of morning oft glistened.

In this little dome, all those melodies strange,
Soft, plaintive, and melting, for ever will sigh;
Nor e'er will the notes from their tenderness change;
Nor e'er will the music of Oberon die.

So, when I am in a voluptuous vein,
I pillow my head on the sweets of the rose,
And list to the tale of the wreath, and the chain,
Till its echoes depart; then I sink to repose.

Adieu, valiant Eric! with joy thou art crowned;
Full many the glories that brighten thy youth,
I too have my blisses, which richly abound
In magical powers, to bless and to soothe.

To Emma

O come, dearest Emma! the rose is full blown,
And the riches of Flora are lavishly strown,
The air is all softness, and crystal the streams,
And the West is resplendently clothèd in beams.

We will hasten, my fair, to the opening glades,
The quaintly carved seats, and the freshening shades,
Where the faeries are chanting their evening hymns,
And in the last sunbeam the sylph lightly swims.

And when thou art weary I'll find thee a bed
Of mosses and flowers to pillow thy head;
There, beauteous Emma, I'll sit at thy feet,
While my story of love I enraptured repeat.

So fondly I'll breathe, and so softly I'll sigh,
Thou wilt think that some amorous Zephyr is nigh—
Ah, no!—as I breathe, I will press thy fair knee,
And then thou wilt know that the sigh comes from me.

Then why, lovely girl, should we lose all these blisses?
That mortal's a fool who such happiness misses.
So smile acquiescence, and give me thy hand,
With love-looking eyes, and with voice sweetly bland.

Song

Tune—'*Julia to the Wood-Robin*'

Stay, ruby-breasted warbler, stay,
   And let me see thy sparkling eye,
Oh brush not yet the pearl-strung spray
   Nor bow thy pretty head to fly.

Stay while I tell thee, fluttering thing,
   That thou of love an emblem art,
Yes! patient plume thy little wing,
   Whilst I my thoughts to thee impart.

When summer nights the dews bestow,
   And summer suns enrich the day,
Thy notes the blossoms charm to blow,
   Each opes delighted at thy lay.

So when in youth the eye's dark glance
   Speaks pleasure from its circle bright,
The tones of love our joys enhance
   And make superior each delight.

And when bleak storms resistless rove,
   And every rural bliss destroy,
Nought comforts then the leafless grove
   But thy soft note—its only joy—

E'en so the words of love beguile
   When Pleasure's tree no longer bears,
And draw a soft endearing smile
   Amid the gloom of grief and tears.

'*Woman*! *when I behold thee flippant, vain*'

Woman! when I behold thee flippant, vain,
   Inconstant, childish, proud, and full of fancies;
   Without that modest softening that enhances
The downcast eye, repentant of the pain
That its mild light creates to heal again:
   E'en then, elate, my spirit leaps, and prances,
   E'en then my soul with exultation dances
For that to love, so long, I've dormant lain :

But when I see thee meek, and kind, and tender,
  Heavens! how desperately do I adore
Thy winning graces;—to be thy defender
  I hotly burn—to be a Calidore—
A very Red Cross Knight—a stout Leander—
  Might I be loved by thee like these of yore.

Light feet, dark violet eyes, and parted hair,
  Soft dimpled hands, white neck, and creamy breast,
  Are things on which the dazzled senses rest
Till the fond, fixèd eyes forget they stare.
From such fine pictures, heavens! I cannot dare
  To turn my admiration, though unpossessed
  They be of what is worthy,—though not dressed
In lovely modesty, and virtues rare.
Yet these I leave as thoughtless as a lark;
  These lures I straight forget,—e'en ere I dine,
Or thrice my palate moisten: but when I mark
  Such charms with mild intelligences shine,
My ear is open like a greedy shark,
  To catch the tunings of a voice divine.

Ah! who can e'er forget so fair a being?
  Who can forget her half-retiring sweets?
  God! she is like a milk-white lamb that bleats
For man's protection. Surely the All-seeing,
Who joys to see us with His gifts agreeing,
  Will never give him pinions, who intreats
  Such innocence to ruin,—who vilely cheats
A dove-like bosom. In truth there is no freeing
One's thoughts from such a beauty; when I hear
  A lay that once I saw her hand awake,
Her form seems floating palpable, and near;
  Had I e'er seen her from an arbour take
A dewy flower, oft would that hand appear,
  And o'er my eyes the trembling moisture shake.

'*O Solitude! if I must with thee dwell*'

O Solitude! if I must with thee dwell,
  Let it not be among the jumbled heap
  Of murky buildings; climb with me the steep—
Nature's observatory—whence the dell,
Its flowery slopes, its river's crystal swell,
  May seem a span; let me thy vigils keep

'Mongst boughs pavilioned, where the deer's swift leap
Startles the wild bee from the foxglove bell.
But though I'll gladly trace these scenes with thee,
Yet the sweet converse of an innocent mind,
Whose words are images of thoughts refined,
Is my soul's pleasure; and it sure must be
Almost the highest bliss of human-kind,
When to thy haunts two kindred spirits flee.

To George Felton Mathew

Sweet are the pleasures that to verse belong,
And doubly sweet a brotherhood in song;
Nor can remembrance, Mathew! bring to view
A fate more pleasing, a delight more true
Than that in which the brother Poets joyed,
Who with combinèd powers, their wit employed
To raise a trophy to the drama's muses.
The thought of this great partnership diffuses
Over the genius-loving heart, a feeling
Of all that's high, and great, and good, and healing.

Too partial friend! fain would I follow thee
Past each horizon of fine poesy;
Fain would I echo back each pleasant note
As o'er Sicilian seas, clear anthems float
'Mong the light skimming gondolas far parted,
Just when the sun his farewell beam has darted—
But 'tis impossible; far different cares
Beckon me sternly from soft 'Lydian airs',
And hold my faculties so long in thrall,
That I am oft in doubt whether at all
I shall again see Phoebus in the morning:
Or flushed Aurora in the roseate dawning!
Or a white Naiad in a rippling stream;
Or a rapt seraph in a moonlight beam;
Or again witness what with thee I've seen,
The dew by fairy feet swept from the green,
After a night of some quaint jubilee
Which every elf and fay had come to see:
When bright processions took their airy march
Beneath the curvèd moon's triumphal arch.

But might I now each passing moment give
To the coy muse, with me she would not live
In this dark city, nor would condescend
'Mid contradictions her delights to lend.
Should e'er the fine-eyed maid to me be kind,
Ah! surely it must be whene'er I find
Some flowery spot, sequestered, wild, romantic,
That often must have seen a poet frantic;
Where oaks, that erst the Druid knew, are growing,
And flowers, the glory of one day, are blowing;
Where the dark-leaved laburnum's drooping clusters
Reflect athwart the stream their yellow lustres,
And intertwined the cassia's arms unite,
With its own drooping buds, but very white;
Where on one side are covert branches hung,
'Mong which the nightingales have always sung
In leafy quiet: where to pry, aloof,
Atween the pillars of the sylvan roof,
Would be to find where violet beds were nestling,
And where the bee with cowslip bells was wrestling.
There must be too a ruin dark, and gloomy,
To say 'joy not too much in all that's bloomy'.

Yet this is vain—O Mathew, lend thy aid
To find a place where I may greet the maid—
Where we may soft humanity put on,
And sit and rhyme, and think on Chatterton;
And that warm-hearted Shakespeare sent to meet him
Four laurelled spirits, heaven-ward to entreat him.
With reverence would we speak of all the sages
Who have left streaks of light athwart their ages:
And thou shouldst moralize on Milton's blindness,
And mourn the fearful dearth of human kindness
To those who strove with the bright golden wing
Of genius, to flap away each sting
Thrown by the pitiless world. We next could tell
Of those who in the cause of freedom fell;
Of our own Alfred, of Helvetian Tell;
Of him whose name to ev'ry heart's a solace,
High-minded and unbending William Wallace.
While to the rugged north our musing turns
We well might drop a tear for him, and Burns.

Felton! without incitements such as these,
How vain for me the niggard Muse to tease:
For thee, she will thy every dwelling grace,
And make 'a sun-shine in a shady place':
For thou wast once a floweret blooming wild,
Close to the source, bright, pure, and undefiled,
Whence gush the streams of song: in happy hour
Came chaste Diana from her shady bower,
Just as the sun was from the east uprising;
And, as for him some gift she was devising,
Beheld thee, plucked thee, cast thee in the stream
To meet her glorious brother's greeting beam.
I marvel much that thou hast never told
How, from a flower, into a fish of gold
Apollo changed thee; how thou next didst seem
A black-eyed swan upon the widening stream;
And when thou first didst in that mirror trace
The placid features of a human face:
That thou hast never told thy travels strange,
And all the wonders of the mazy range
O'er pebbly crystal, and o'er golden sands,
Kissing thy daily food from Naiad's pearly hands.

To [*Mary Frogley*]

Hadst thou lived in days of old,
O what wonders had been told
Of thy lively countenance,
And thy humid eyes that dance
In the midst of their own brightness,
In the very fane of lightness.
Over which thine eyebrows, leaning,
Picture out each lovely meaning:
In a dainty bend they lie,
Like to streaks across the sky,
Or the feathers from a crow,
Fallen on a bed of snow.
Of thy dark hair that extends
Into many graceful bends:
As the leaves of hellebore
Turn to whence they sprung before
And behind each ample curl
Peeps the richness of a pearl.
Downward too flows many a tress

With a glossy waviness;
Full, and round like globes that rise
From the censer to the skies
Through sunny air. Add too, the sweetness
Of thy honeyed voice; the neatness
Of thine ankle lightly turned:
With those beauties, scarce discerned,
Kept with such sweet privacy,
That they seldom meet the eye
Of the little loves that fly
Round about with eager pry.
Saving when, with freshening lave,
Thou dipp'st them in the taintless wave;
Like twin water-lilies, born
In the coolness of the morn.
O, if thou hadst breathèd then,
Now the Muses had been ten.
Couldst thou wish for lineage higher
Than twin sister of Thalia?
At least for ever, evermore,
Will I call the Graces four.

Hadst thou lived when chivalry
Lifted up her lance on high,
Tell me what thou wouldst have been?
Ah! I see the silver sheen
Of thy broidered, floating vest
Covering half thine ivory breast;
Which, O heavens! I should see,
But that cruel destiny
Has placed a golden cuirass there;
Keeping secret what is fair.
Like sunbeams in a cloudlet nested
Thy locks in knightly casque are rested:
O'er which bend four milky plumes
Like the gentle lily's blooms
Springing from a costly vase.
See with what a stately pace
Comes thine alabaster steed;
Servant of heroic deed!
O'er his loins, his trappings glow
Like the northern lights on snow.
Mount his back! thy sword unsheathe!
Sign of the enchanter's death;
Bane of every wicked spell;

Silencer of dragon's yell.
Alas! thou this wilt never do—
Thou art an enchantress too,
And wilt surely never spill
Blood of those whose eyes can kill.

To —

Had I a man's fair form, then might my sighs
  Be echoed swiftly through that ivory shell
  Thine ear, and find thy gentle heart; so well
Would passion arm me for the enterprise:
But ah! I am no knight whose foeman dies;
  No cuirass glistens on my bosom's swell;
  I am no happy shepherd of the dell
Whose lips have trembled with a maiden's eyes.
Yet must I dote upon thee—call thee sweet,
  Sweeter by far than Hybla's honeyed roses
    When steeped in dew rich to intoxication.
Ah! I will taste that dew, for me 'tis meet,
  And when the moon her pallid face discloses,
    I'll gather some by spells, and incantation.

'Give me Women, Wine, and Snuff'

Give me Women, Wine, and Snuff
Until I cry out, 'Hold, enough!'
You may do so sans objection
Till the day of resurrection;
For, bless my beard, they aye shall be
My belovèd Trinity.

Specimen of an Induction to a Poem

Lo! I must tell a tale of chivalry;
For large white plumes are dancing in mine eye.
Not like the formal crest of latter days:
But bending in a thousand graceful ways—
So graceful, that it seems no mortal hand,
Or e'en the touch of Archimago's wand,
Could charm them into such an attitude.
We must think rather, that in playful mood,
Some mountain breeze had turned its chief delight,
To show this wonder of its gentle might.
Lo! I must tell a tale of chivalry;

For while I muse, the lance points slantingly
Athwart the morning air: some lady sweet,
Who cannot feel for cold her tender feet,
From the worn top of some old battlement
Hails it with tears, her stout defender sent:
And from her own pure self no joy dissembling,
Wraps round her ample robe with happy trembling.
Sometimes, when the good Knight his rest would take,
It is reflected, clearly, in a lake,
With the young ashen boughs, 'gainst which it rests,
And th' half-seen mossiness of linnets' nests.
Ah! shall I ever tell its cruelty,
When the fire flashes from a warrior's eye,
And his tremendous hand is grasping it,
And his dark brow for very wrath is knit?
Or when his spirit, with more calm intent,
Leaps to the honours of a tournament,
And makes the gazers round about the ring
Stare at the grandeur of the balancing?
No, no! this is far off:—then how shall I
Revive the dying tones of minstrelsy,
Which linger yet about lone gothic arches,
In dark green ivy, and among wild larches?
How sing the splendour of the revelries,
When butts of wine are drunk off to the lees?
And that bright lance, against the fretted wall,
Beneath the shade of stately banneral,
Is slung with shining cuirass, sword, and shield
Where ye may see a spur in bloody field?
Light-footed damsels move with gentle paces
Round the wide hall, and show their happy faces;
Or stand in courtly talk by fives and sevens,
Like those fair stars that twinkle in the heavens.
Yet must I tell a tale of chivalry—
Or wherefore comes that steed so proudly by?
Wherefore more proudly does the gentle Knight
Rein in the swelling of his ample might?

Spenser! thy brows are archèd, open, kind,
And come like a clear sun-rise to my mind;
And always does my heart with pleasure dance,
When I think on thy noble countenance:
Where never yet was aught more earthly seen
Than the pure freshness of thy laurels green.
Therefore, great bard, I not so fearfully

Call on thy gentle spirit to hover nigh
My daring steps: or if thy tender care,
Thus startled unaware,
Be jealous that the foot of other wight
Should madly follow that bright path of light
Traced by thy loved Libertas, he will speak,
And tell thee that my prayer is very meek;
That I will follow with due reverence,
And start with awe at mine own strange pretence.
Him thou wilt hear; so I will rest in hope
To see wide plains, fair trees and lawny slope,
The morn, the eve, the light, the shade, the flowers,
Clear streams, smooth lakes, and overlooking towers.

Calidore. A Fragment

Young Calidore is paddling o'er the lake,
His healthful spirit eager and awake
To feel the beauty of a silent eve,
Which seemed full loth this happy world to leave,
The light dwelt o'er the scene so lingeringly.
He bares his forehead to the cool blue sky,
And smiles at the far clearness all around,
Until his heart is well nigh over-wound,
And turns for calmness to the pleasant green
Of easy slopes, and shadowy trees that lean
So elegantly o'er the waters' brim
And show their blossoms trim.
Scarce can his clear and nimble eyesight follow
The freaks, and dartings of the black-winged swallow,
Delighting much, to see it half at rest,
Dip so refreshingly its wings, and breast
'Gainst the smooth surface, and to mark anon,
The widening circles into nothing gone.

And now the sharp keel of his little boat
Comes up with ripple, and with easy float,
And glides into a bed of water-lilies:
Broad-leaved are they and their white canopies
Are upward turned to catch the heavens' dew.
Near to a little island's point they grew;
Whence Calidore might have the goodliest view
Of this sweet spot of earth. The bowery shore
Went off in gentle windings to the hoar
And light blue mountains: but no breathing man

With a warm heart, and eye prepared to scan
Nature's clear beauty, could pass lightly by
Objects that looked out so invitingly
On either side. These, gentle Calidore
Greeted, as he had known them long before.
The sidelong view of swelling leafiness,
Which the glad setting sun in gold doth dress;
Whence ever and anon the jay outsprings,
And scales upon the beauty of its wings.
The lonely turret, shattered, and outworn,
Stands venerably proud—too proud to mourn
Its long lost grandeur: fir trees grow around,
Aye dropping their hard fruit upon the ground.
The little chapel with the cross above
Upholding wreaths of ivy; the white dove,
That on the window spreads his feathers light,
And seems from purple clouds to wing its flight.
Green tufted islands casting their soft shades
Across the lake; sequestered leafy glades,
That through the dimness of their twilight show
Large dock leaves, spiral foxgloves, or the glow
Of the wild cat's-eyes, or the silvery stems
Of delicate birch trees, or long grass which hems
A little brook. The youth had long been viewing
These pleasant things, and heaven was bedewing
The mountain flowers, when his glad senses caught
A trumpet's silver voice. Ah! it was fraught
With many joys for him. The warder's ken
Had found white coursers prancing in the glen:
Friends very dear to him he soon will see;
So pushes off his boat most eagerly,
And soon upon the lake he skims along,
Deaf to the nightingale's first undersong;
Nor minds he the white swans that dream so sweetly:
His spirit flies before him so completely.

And now he turns a jutting point of land,
Whence may be seen the castle gloomy, and grand:
Nor will a bee buzz round two swelling peaches,
Before the point of his light shallop reaches
Those marble steps that through the water dip:
Now over them he goes with hasty trip,
And scarcely stays to ope the folding doors:
Anon he leaps along the oaken floors
Of halls and corridors.

Delicious sounds! those little bright-eyed things
That float about the air on azure wings,
Had been less heartfelt by him than the clang
Of clattering hoofs. Into the court he sprang,
Just as two noble steeds, and palfreys twain,
Were slanting out their necks with loosened rein;
While from beneath the threatening portcullis
They brought their happy burthens. What a kiss,
What gentle squeeze he gave each lady's hand!
How tremblingly their delicate ankles spanned!
Into how sweet a trance his soul was gone,
While whisperings of affection
Made him delay to let their tender feet
Come to the earth. With an incline so sweet
From their low palfreys o'er his neck they bent:
And whether there were tears of languishment,
Or that the evening dew had pearled their tresses,
He feels a moisture on his cheek, and blesses
With lips that tremble, and with glistening eye,
All the soft luxury
That nestled in his arms. A dimpled hand,
Fair as some wonder out of fairy land,
Hung from his shoulder like the drooping flowers
Of whitest cassia, fresh from summer showers:
And this he fondled with his happy cheek
As if for joy he would no further seek—
When the kind voice of good Sir Clerimond
Came to his ear, like something from beyond
His present being: so he gently drew
His warm arms, thrilling now with pulses new,
From their sweet thrall, and forward gently bending,
Thanked heaven that his joy was never ending,
While 'gainst his forehead he devoutly pressed
A hand heaven made to succour the distressed;
A hand that from the world's bleak promontory
Had lifted Calidore for deeds of Glory.
Amid the pages, and the torches' glare,
There stood a knight, patting the flowing hair
Of his proud horse's mane. He was withal
A man of elegance, and stature tall,
So that the waving of his plumes would be
High as the berries of a wild ash tree,
Or as the wingèd cap of Mercury.
His armour was so dexterously wrought
In shape, that sure no living man had thought

It hard, and heavy steel, but that indeed
It was some glorious form, some splendid weed,
In which a spirit new come from the skies
Might live, and show itself to human eyes.
'Tis the far-famed, the brave Sir Gondibert,
Said the good man to Calidore alert;
While the young warrior with a step of grace
Came up—a courtly smile upon his face,
And mailèd hand held out, ready to greet
The large-eyed wonder and ambitious heat
Of the aspiring boy; who as he led
Those smiling ladies, often turned his head
To admire the visor arched so gracefully
Over a knightly brow; while they went by
The lamps that from the high-roofed hall were pendent,
And gave the steel a shining quite transcendent.

Soon in a pleasant chamber they are seated;
The sweet-lipped ladies have already greeted
All the green leaves that round the window clamber,
To show their purple stars, and bells of amber.
Sir Gondibert had doffed his shining steel,
Gladdening in the free and airy feel
Of a light mantle; and while Clerimond
Is looking round about him with a fond
And placid eye, young Calidore is burning
To hear of knightly deeds, and gallant spurning
Of all unworthiness, and how the strong of arm
Kept off dismay, and terror, and alarm
From lovely woman: while brimful of this,
He gave each damsel's hand so warm a kiss,
And had such manly ardour in his eye,
That each at other looked half-staringly;
And then their features started into smiles
Sweet as blue heavens o'er enchanted isles.

Softly the breezes from the forest came,
Softly they blew aside the taper's flame;
Clear was the song from Philomel's far bower;
Grateful the incense from the lime-tree flower;
Mysterious, wild, the far heard trumpet's tone;
Lovely the moon in ether, all alone:
Sweet too the converse of these happy mortals,
As that of busy spirits when the portals
Are closing in the west, or that soft humming

We hear around when Hesperus is coming.
Sweet be their sleep. ...

'To one who has been long in city pent'

To one who has been long in city pent,
'Tis very sweet to look into the fair
And open face of heaven—to breathe a prayer
Full in the smile of the blue firmament.
Who is more happy, when, with heart's content,
Fatigued he sinks into some pleasant lair
Of wavy grass, and reads a debonair
And gentle tale of love and languishment?
Returning home at evening, with an ear
Catching the notes of Philomel—an eye
Watching the sailing cloudlet's bright career,
He mourns that day so soon has glided by:
E'en like the passage of an angel's tear
That falls through the clear ether silently.

'O! how I love, on a fair summer's eve'

O! how I love, on a fair summer's eve,
When streams of light pour down the golden west,
And on the balmy zephyrs tranquil rest
The silver clouds, far—far away to leave
All meaner thoughts, and take a sweet reprieve
From little cares; to find, with easy quest,
A fragrant wild, with Nature's beauty dressed,
And there into delight my soul deceive.
There warm my breast with patriotic lore,
Musing on Milton's fate—on Sidney's bier—
Till their stern forms before my mind arise:
Perhaps on the wing of Poesy upsoar,
Full often dropping a delicious tear,
When some melodious sorrow spells mine eyes.

To a Friend who Sent me some Roses

As late I rambled in the happy fields—
What time the skylark shakes the tremulous dew
From his lush clover covert, when anew
Adventurous knights take up their dinted shields—
I saw the sweetest flower wild nature yields,
A fresh-blown musk-rose; 'twas the first that threw

Its sweets upon the summer: graceful it grew
As is the wand that queen Titania wields.
And, as I feasted on its fragrancy,
I thought the garden-rose it far excelled:
But when, O Wells! thy roses came to me
My sense with their deliciousness was spelled:
Soft voices had they, that with tender plea
Whispered of peace, and truth, and friendliness unquelled.

To my Brother George

Many the wonders I this day have seen:
The sun, when first he kissed away the tears
That filled the eyes of mom—the laurelled peers
Who from the feathery gold of evening lean—
The ocean with its vastness, its blue green,
Its ships, its rocks, its caves, its hopes, its fears—
Its voice mysterious, which whoso hears
Must think on what will be, and what has been.
E'en now, dear George, while this for you I write,
Cynthia is from her silken curtains peeping
So scantly, that it seems her bridal night,
And she her half-discovered revels keeping.
But what, without the social thought of thee,
Would be the wonders of the sky and sea?

To my Brother George

Full many a dreary hour have I passed,
My brain bewildered, and my mind o'ercast
With heaviness; in seasons when I've thought
No sphery strains by me could e'er be caught
From the blue dome, though I to dimness gaze
On the far depth where sheeted lightning plays;
Or, on the wavy grass outstretched supinely,
Pry 'mong the stars, to strive to think divinely:
That I should never hear Apollo's song,
Though feathery clouds were floating all along
The purple west, and, two bright streaks between,
The golden lyre itself were dimly seen:
That the still murmur of the honey bee
Would never teach a rural song to me:
That the bright glance from beauty's eyelids slanting
Would never make a lay of mine enchanting,
Or warm my breast with ardour to unfold

Some tale of love and arms in time of old.
But there are times, when those that love the bay,
Fly from all sorrowing far, far away;
A sudden glow comes on them, naught they see
In water, earth, or air, but poesy.
It has been said, dear George, and true I hold it,
(For knightly Spenser to Libertas told it,)
That when a Poet is in such a trance,
In air he sees white coursers paw, and prance,
Bestridden of gay knights, in gay apparel,
Who at each other tilt in playful quarrel,
And what we, ignorantly, sheet-lightning call,
Is the swift opening of their wide portal,
When the bright warder blows his trumpet clear,
Whose tones reach naught on earth but Poet's ear.
When these enchanted portals open wide,
And through the light the horsemen swiftly glide,
The Poet's eye can reach those golden halls,
And view the glory of their festivals:
Their ladies fair, that in the distance seem
Fit for the silvering of a seraph's dream;
Their rich brimmed goblets, that incessant run
Like the bright spots that move about the sun;
And, when upheld, the wine from each bright jar
Pours with the lustre of a falling star.
Yet further off, are dimly seen their bowers,
Of which, no mortal eye can reach the flowers—
And 'tis right just, for well Apollo knows
'Twould make the Poet quarrel with the rose.
All that's revealed from that far seat of blisses,
Is, the clear fountains' interchanging kisses,
As gracefully descending, light and thin,
Like silver streaks across a dolphin's fin,
When he upswimmeth from the coral caves,
And sports with half his tail above the waves.

These wonders strange he sees, and many more,
Whose head is pregnant with poetic lore.
Should he upon an evening ramble fare
With forehead to the soothing breezes bare,
Would he naught see but the dark, silent blue
With all its diamonds trembling through and through?
Or the coy moon, when in the waviness
Of whitest clouds she does her beauty dress,
And staidly paces higher up, and higher,

Like a sweet nun in holy-day attire?
Ah, yes! much more would start into his sight—
The revelries, and mysteries of night:
And should I ever see them, I will tell you
Such tales as needs must with amazement spell you.

These are the living pleasures of the bard:
But richer far posterity's award.
What does he murmur with his latest breath,
While his proud eye looks through the film of death?
'What though I leave this dull, and earthly mould,
Yet shall my spirit lofty converse hold
With after times. The patriot shall feel
My stern alarum, and unsheathe his steel;
Or, in the senate thunder out my numbers
To startle princes from their easy slumbers.
The sage will mingle with each moral theme
My happy thoughts sententious; he will teem
With lofty periods when my verses fire him,
And then I'll stoop from heaven to inspire him.
Lays have I left of such a dear delight
That maids will sing them on their bridal night.
Gay villagers, upon a mom of May,
When they have tired their gentle limbs with play,
And formed a snowy circle on the grass,
And plac'd in midst of all that lovely lass
Who chosen is their queen—with her fine head
Crownèd with flowers purple, white, and red:
For there the lily, and the musk-rose, sighing,
Are emblems true of hapless lovers dying.
Between her breasts, that never yet felt trouble,
A bunch of violets full blown, and double,
Serenely sleep: she from a casket takes
A little book and then a joy awakes
About each youthful heart, with stifled cries,
And rubbing of white hands, and sparkling eyes—
For she's to read a tale of hopes, and fears,
One that I fostered in my youthful years.
The pearls, that on each glistening circlet sleep,
Gush ever and anon with silent creep,
Lured by the innocent dimples. To sweet rest
Shall the dear babe, upon its mother's breast,
Be lulled with songs of mine. Fair world, adieu!
Thy dales, and hills, are fading from my view:
Swiftly I mount, upon wide spreading pinions,

Far from the narrow bounds of thy dominions.
Full joy I feel, while thus I cleave the air,
That my soft verse will charm thy daughters fair,
And warm thy sons!' Ah, my dear friend and brother,
Could I, at once, my mad ambition smother,
For tasting joys like these, sure I should be
Happier, and dearer to society.
At times, 'tis true, I've felt relief from pain
When some bright thought has darted through my brain:
Through all that day I've felt a greater pleasure
Than if I'd brought to light a hidden treasure.
As to my sonnets, though none else should heed them,
I feel delighted, still, that you should read them.
Of late, too, I have had much calm enjoyment,
Stretched on the grass at my best loved employment
Of scribbling lines for you. These things I thought
While, in my face, the freshest breeze I caught.
E'en now I'm pillowed on a bed of flowers
That crowns a lofty clift, which proudly towers
Above the ocean-waves. The stalks, and blades,
Chequer my tablet with their quivering shades.
On one side is a field of drooping oats,
Through which the poppies show their scarlet coats,
So pert and useless, that they bring to mind
The scarlet coats that pester human-kind.
And on the other side, outspread, is seen
Ocean's blue mantle streaked with purple, and green.
Now 'tis I see a canvassed ship, and now
Mark the bright silver curling round her prow.
I see the lark down-dropping to his nest
And the broad winged sea-gull never at rest;
For when no more he spreads his feathers free,
His breast is dancing on the restless sea.
Now I direct my eyes into the west,
Which at this moment is in sunbeams dressed:
Why westward turn? 'Twas but to say adieu!
'Twas but to kiss my hand, dear George, to you!

To Charles Cowden Clarke

Oft have you seen a swan superbly frowning,
And with proud breast his own white shadow crowning;
He slants his neck beneath the waters bright
So silently, it seems a beam of light
Come from the galaxy: anon he sports—

With outspread wings the Naiad Zephyr courts,
Or ruffles all the surface of the lake
In striving from its crystal face to take
Some diamond water drops, and them to treasure
In milky nest, and sip them off at leisure.
But not a moment can he there insure them,
Nor to such downy rest can he allure them;
For down they rush as though they would be free,
And drop like hours into eternity.

Just like that bird am I in loss of time,
Whene'er I venture on the stream of rhyme;
With shattered boat, oar snapped, and canvas rent
I slowly sail, scarce knowing my intent;
Still scooping up the water with my fingers,
In which a trembling diamond never lingers.
By this, friend Charles, you may full plainly see
Why I have never penned a line to thee:
Because my thoughts were never free, and clear,
And little fit to please a classic ear;
Because my wine was of too poor a savour
For one whose palate gladdens in the flavour
Of sparkling Helicon—small good it were
To take him to a desert rude, and bare,
Who had on Baiae's shore reclined at ease,
While Tasso's page was floating in a breeze
That gave soft music from Armida's bowers,
Mingled with fragrance from her rarest flowers:
Small good to one who had by Mulla's stream
Fondled the maidens with the breasts of cream;
Who had beheld Belphoebe in a brook,
And lovely Una in a leafy nook,
And Archimago leaning o'er his book:
Who had of all that's sweet tasted, and seen,
From silvery ripple, up to beauty's queen;
From the sequestered haunts of gay Titania,
To the blue dwelling of divine Urania:
One, who, of late, had ta'en sweet forest walks
With him who elegantly chats, and talks—
The wronged Libertas—who has told you stories
Of laurel chaplets, and Apollo's glories;
Of troops chivalrous prancing through a city,
And tearful ladies made for love, and pity:
With many else which I have never known.

Thus have I thought; and days on days have flown
Slowly, or rapidly—unwilling still
For you to try my dull, unlearned quill.
Nor should I now, but that I've known you long,
That you first taught me all the sweets of song:
The grand, the sweet, the terse, the free, the fine;
What swelled with pathos, and what right divine;
Spenserian vowels that elope with ease,
And float along like birds o'er summer seas;
Miltonian storms, and more, Miltonian tenderness;
Michael in arms, and more, meek Eve's fair slenderness.
Who read for me the sonnet swelling loudly
Up to its climax and then dying proudly?
Who found for me the grandeur of the ode,
Growing, like Atlas, stronger from its load?
Who let me taste that more than cordial dram,
The sharp, the rapier-pointed epigram?
Showed me that epic was of all the king,
Round, vast, and spanning all like Saturn's ring?
You too upheld the veil from Clio's beauty,
And pointed out the patriot's stem duty;
The might of Alfred, and the shaft of Tell;
The hand of Brutus, that so grandly fell
Upon a tyrant's head. Ah! had I never seen,
Or known your kindness, what might I have been?
What my enjoyments in my youthful years,
Bereft of all that now my life endears?
And can I e'er these benefits forget?
And can I e'er repay the friendly debt?
No, doubly no—yet should these rhymings please,
I shall roll on the grass with two-fold ease:
For I have long time been my fancy feeding
With hopes that you would one day think the reading
Of my rough verses not an hour misspent;
Should it e'er be so, what a rich content!

Some weeks have passed since last I saw the spires
In lucent Thames reflected—warm desires
To see the sun o'er-peep the eastern dimness,
And morning shadows streaking into slimness
Across the lawny fields, and pebbly water;
To mark the time as they grow broad, and shorter;
To feel the air that plays about the hills,
And sips its freshness from the little rills;
To see high, golden corn wave in the light

When Cynthia smiles upon a summer's night,
And peers among the cloudlets jet and white,
As though she were reclining in a bed
Of bean blossoms, in heaven freshly shed—
No sooner had I stepped into these pleasures
Than I began to think of rhymes and measures:
The air that floated by me seemed to say
'Write! thou wilt never have a better day.'
And so I did. When many lines I'd written,
Though with their grace I was not oversmitten,
Yet, as my hand was warm, I thought I'd better
Trust to my feelings, and write you a letter.
Such an attempt required an inspiration
Of a peculiar sort—a consummation—
Which, had I felt, these scribblings might have been
Verses from which the soul would never wean:
But many days have passed since last my heart
Was warmed luxuriously by divine Mozart,
By Arne delighted, or by Handel maddened,
Or by the song of Erin pierced and saddened,
What time you were before the music sitting,
And the rich notes to each sensation fitting.
Since I have walk'd with you through shady lanes
That freshly terminate in open plains,
And revell'd in a chat that ceasèd not
When at night-fall among your books we got:
No, nor when supper came, nor after that—
Nor when reluctantly I took my hat;
No, nor till cordially you shook my hand
Mid-way between our homes. Your accents bland
Still sounded in my ears, when I no more
Could hear your footsteps touch the gravelly floor.
Sometimes I lost them, and then found again;
You changed the footpath for the grassy plain.
In those still moments I have wished you joys
That well you know to honour—'Life's very toys
With him,' said I, 'will take a pleasant charm;
It cannot be that aught will work him harm.'
These thoughts now come o'er me with all their might—
Again I shake your hand—friend Charles, good night.

'How many bards gild the lapses of time!'

How many bards gild the lapses of time!
  A few of them have ever been the food
  Of my delighted fancy—I could brood
Over their beauties, earthly, or sublime:
And often, when I sit me down to rhyme,
  These will in throngs before my mind intrude:
  But no confusion, no disturbance rude
Do they occasion; 'tis a pleasing chime.
So the unnumbered sounds that evening store;
The songs of birds, the whispering of the leaves,
  The voice of waters, the great bell that heaves
With solemn sound, and thousand others more,
  That distance of recognizance bereaves,
Make pleasing music, and not wild uproar.

On First Looking into Chapman's Homer

Much have I travelled in the realms of gold,
  And many goodly states and kingdoms seen;
  Round many western islands have I been
Which bards in fealty to Apollo hold.
Oft of one wide expanse had I been told
  That deep-browed Homer ruled as his demesne;
  Yet did I never breathe its pure serene
Till I heard Chapman speak out loud and bold:
Then felt I like some watcher of the skies
  When a new planet swims into his ken;
Or like stout Cortez when with eagle eyes
  He stared at the Pacific—and all his men
Looked at each other with a wild surmise—
  Silent, upon a peak in Darien.

To a Young Lady who sent me a Laurel Crown

Fresh morning gusts have blown away all fear
  From my glad bosom: now from gloominess
  I mount for ever—not an atom less
Than the proud laurel shall content my bier.
No! by the eternal stars! or why sit here
  In the Sun's eye, and 'gainst my temples press
  Apollo's very leaves, woven to bless
By thy white fingers and thy spirit clear.

Lo! who dares say, 'Do this'? Who dares call down
   My will from its high purpose? Who say, 'Stand',
Or 'Go'? This very moment I would frown
   On abject Caesars—not the stoutest band
Of mailèd heroes should tear off my crown:
   Yet would I kneel and kiss thy gentle hand!

On Leaving some Friends at an Early Hour

Give me a golden pen, and let me lean
   On heaped up flowers, in regions clear, and far;
   Bring me a tablet whiter than a star,
Or hand of hymning angel, when 'tis seen
The silver strings of heavenly harp atween:
   And let there glide by many a pearly car,
   Pink robes, and wavy hair, and diamond jar,
And half-discovered wings, and glances keen.
The while let music wander round my ears,
   And as it reaches each delicious ending,
      Let me write down a line of glorious tone,
And full of many wonders of the spheres:
   For what a height my spirit is contending!
      'Tis not content so soon to be alone.

'*Keen, fitful gusts are whispering here and there*'

Keen, fitful gusts are whispering here and there
   Among the bushes half leafless, and dry;
   The stars look very cold about the sky,
And I have many miles on foot to fare.
Yet feel I little of the cool bleak air,
   Or of the dead leaves rustling drearily,
   Or of those silver lamps that burn on high,
Or of the distance from home's pleasant lair:
For I am brimful of the friendliness
   That in a little cottage I have found;
Of fair-haired Milton's eloquent distress,
   And all his love for gentle Lycid drowned;
Of lovely Laura in her light green dress,
   And faithful Petrarch gloriously crowned.

Addressed to Haydon

Highmindedness, a jealousy for good,
   A loving-kindness for the great man's fame,
   Dwells here and there with people of no name,
In noisome alley, and in pathless wood:
And where we think the truth least understood,
   Oft may be found a 'singleness of aim',
That ought to frighten into hooded shame
A money-mongering, pitiable brood.
How glorious this affection for the cause
   Of steadfast genius, toiling gallantly!
What when a stout unbending champion awes
   Envy, and Malice to their native sty?
Unnumbered souls breathe out a still applause,
   Proud to behold him in his country's eye.

To my Brothers

Small, busy flames play through the fresh-laid coals,
   And their faint cracklings o'er our silence creep
   Like whispers of the household gods that keep
A gentle empire o'er fraternal souls.
And while, for rhymes, I search around the poles,
   Your eyes are fixed, as in poetic sleep,
   Upon the lore so voluble and deep,
That aye at fall of night our care condoles.
This is your birth-day Tom, and I rejoice
   That thus it passes smoothly, quietly.
Many such eves of gently whispering noise
   May we together pass, and calmly try
What are this world's true joys—ere the great voice,
   From its fair face, shall bid our spirits fly.

Addressed to [*Haydon*]

Great spirits now on earth are sojourning;
   He of the cloud, the cataract, the lake,
   Who on Helvellyn's summit, wide awake,
Catches his freshness from Archangel's wing:
He of the rose, the violet, the spring,
   The social smile, the chain for Freedom's sake:
   And lo!—whose steadfastness would never take
A meaner sound than Raphael's whispering.

And other spirits there are standing apart
Upon the forehead of the age to come;
These, these will give the world another heart,
And other pulses. Hear ye not the hum
Of mighty workings?—
Listen awhile ye nations, and be dumb.

'I stood tip-toe upon a little hill'

'Places of nestling green for Poets made'
'The Story of Rimini'

I stood tip-toe upon a little hill,
The air was cooling, and so very still,
That the sweet buds which with a modest pride
Pull droopingly, in slanting curve aside,
Their scantly leaved, and finely tapering stems,
Had not yet lost those starry diadems
Caught from the early sobbing of the morn.
The clouds were pure and white as flocks new shorn,
And fresh from the clear brook; sweetly they slept
On the blue fields of heaven, and then there crept
A little noiseless noise among the leaves,
Born of the very sigh that silence heaves:
For not the faintest motion could be seen
Of all the shades that slanted o'er the green.
There was wide wandering for the greediest eye,
To peer about upon variety;
Far round the horizon's crystal air to skim,
And trace the dwindled edgings of its brim;
To picture out the quaint, and curious bending
Of a fresh woodland alley, never ending;
Or by the bowery clefts, and leafy shelves,
Guess where the jaunty streams refresh themselves.
I gazed awhile, and felt as light, and free
As though the fanning wings of Mercury
Had played upon my heels: I was light-hearted,
And many pleasures to my vision started;
So I straightway began to pluck a posy
Of luxuries bright, milky, soft and rosy.

A bush of May flowers with the bees about them;
Ah, sure no tasteful nook would be without them;
And let a lush laburnum oversweep them,
And let long grass grow round the roots to keep them

Moist, cool and green; and shade the violets,
That they may bind the moss in leafy nets.
A filbert hedge with wild briar overtwined,
And clumps of woodbine taking the soft wind
Upon their summer thrones; there too should be
The frequent chequer of a youngling tree,
That with a score of light green brethren shoots
From the quaint mossiness of agèd roots:
Round which is heard a spring-head of clear waters
Babbling so wildly of its lovely daughters
The spreading blue-bells—it may haply mourn
That such fair clusters should be rudely torn
From their fresh beds, and scattered thoughtlessly
By infant hands, left on the path to die.

Open afresh your round of starry folds,
Ye ardent marigolds!
Dry up the moisture from your golden lids,
For great Apollo bids
That in these days your praises should be sung
On many harps, which he has lately strung;
And when again your dewiness he kisses,
Tell him, I have you in my world of blisses:
So haply when I rove in some far vale,
His mighty voice may come upon the gale.

Here are sweet peas, on tip-toe for a flight:
With wings of gentle flush o'er delicate white,
And taper fingers catching at all things,
To bind them all about with tiny rings.

Linger awhile upon some bending planks
That lean against a streamlet's rushy banks,
And watch intently Nature's gentle doings:
They will be found softer than ring-dove's cooings.
How silent comes the water round that bend;
Not the minutest whisper does it send
To the o'erhanging sallows: blades of grass
Slowly across the chequered shadows pass—
Why, you might read two sonnets, ere they reach
To where the hurrying freshnesses aye preach
A natural sermon o'er their pebbly beds;
Where swarms of minnows show their little heads,
Staying their wavy bodies 'gainst the streams,
To taste the luxury of sunny beams

Tempered with coolness. How they ever wrestle
With their own sweet delight, and ever nestle
Their silver bellies on the pebbly sand.
If you but scantily hold out the hand,
That very instant not one will remain;
But turn your eye, and they are there again.
The ripples seem right glad to reach those cresses,
And cool themselves among the emerald tresses;
The while they cool themselves, they freshness give,
And moisture, that the bowery green may live:
So keeping up an interchange of favours,
Like good men in the truth of their behaviours.
Sometimes goldfinches one by one will drop
From low-hung branches; little space they stop;
But sip, and twitter, and their feathers sleek—
Then off at once, as in a wanton freak:
Or perhaps, to show their black, and golden wings,
Pausing upon their yellow flutterings.
Were I in such a place, I sure should pray
That naught less sweet might call my thoughts away,
Than the soft rustle of a maiden's gown
Fanning away the dandelion's down;
Than the light music of her nimble toes
Patting against the sorrel as she goes.
How she would start, and blush, thus to be caught
Playing in all her innocence of thought.
O let me lead her gently o'er the brook,
Watch her half-smiling lips, and downward look;
O let me for one moment touch her wrist;
Let me one moment to her breathing list;
And as she leaves me may she often turn
Her fair eyes looking through her locks aubùrn.
What next? A tuft of evening primroses,
O'er which the mind may hover till it dozes;
O'er which it well might take a pleasant sleep,
But that 'tis ever startled by the leap
Of buds into ripe flowers; or by the flitting
Of diverse moths, that aye their rest are quitting;
Or by the moon lifting her silver rim
Above a cloud, and with a gradual swim
Coming into the blue with all her light.
O Maker of sweet poets, dear delight
Of this fair world, and all its gentle livers;
Spangler of clouds, halo of crystal rivers,
Mingler with leaves, and dew and tumbling streams,

Closer of lovely eyes to lovely dreams,
Lover of loneliness, and wandering,
Of upcast eye, and tender pondering!
Thee must I praise above all other glories
That smile us on to tell delightful stories.
For what has made the sage or poet write
But the fair paradise of Nature's light?
In the calm grandeur of a sober line,
We see the waving of the mountain pine;
And when a tale is beautifully staid,
We feel the safety of a hawthorn glade:
When it is moving on luxurious wings,
The soul is lost in pleasant smotherings:
Fair dewy roses brush against our faces,
And flowering laurels spring from diamond vases;
O'er head we see the jasmine and sweet briar,
And bloomy grapes laughing from green attire;
While at our feet, the voice of crystal bubbles
Charms us at once away from all our troubles:
So that we feel uplifted from the world,
Walking upon the white clouds wreathed and curled.
So felt he, who first told, how Psyche went
On the smooth wind to realms of wonderment;
What Psyche felt, and Love, when their full lips
First touched; what amorous, and fondling nips
They gave each other's cheeks; with all their sighs,
And how they kissed each other's tremulous eyes;
The silver lamp—the ravishment—the wonder—
The darkness—loneliness—the fearful thunder;
Their woes gone by, and both to heaven upflown,
To bow for gratitude before Jove's throne.
So did he feel, who pulled the boughs aside,
That we might look into a forest wide,
To catch a glimpse of Fauns and Dryadès
Coming with softest rustle through the trees,
And garlands woven of flowers wild, and sweet,
Upheld on ivory wrists, or sporting feet:
Telling us how fair, trembling Syrinx fled
Arcadian Pan, with such a fearful dread.
Poor nymph—poor Pan—how he did weep to find,
Naught but a lovely sighing of the wind
Along the reedy stream; a half-heard strain,
Full of sweet desolation—balmy pain.

What first inspired a bard of old to sing
Narcissus pining o'er the untainted spring?
In some delicious ramble, he had found
A little space, with boughs all woven round;
And in the midst of all, a clearer pool
Than e'er reflected in its pleasant cool
The blue sky here, and there, serenely peeping
Through tendril wreaths fantastically creeping.
And on the bank a lonely flower he spied,
A meek and forlorn flower, with naught of pride,
Drooping its beauty o'er the watery clearness,
To woo its own sad image into nearness:
Deaf to light Zephyrus it would not move;
But still would seem to droop, to pine, to love.
So while the Poet stood in this sweet spot,
Some fainter gleamings o'er his fancy shot;
Nor was it long ere he had told the tale
Of young Narcissus, and sad Echo's bale.

Where had he been, from whose warm head out-flew
That sweetest of all songs, that ever new,
That aye refreshing, pure deliciousness,
Coming ever to bless
The wanderer by moonlight? to him bringing
Shapes from the invisible world, unearthly singing
From out the middle air, from flowery nests,
And from the pillowy silkiness that rests
Full in the speculation of the stars.
Ah! surely he had burst our mortal bars;
Into some wondrous region he had gone,
To search for thee, divine Endymion!

He was a Poet, sure a lover too,
Who stood on Latmos' top, what time there blew
Soft breezes from the myrtle vale below;
And brought in faintness solemn, sweet, and slow
A hymn from Dian's temple; while upswelling,
The incense went to her own starry dwelling.
But though her face was clear as infant's eyes,
Though she stood smiling o'er the sacrifice,
The Poet wept at her so piteous fate,
Wept that such beauty should be desolate:
So in fine wrath some golden sounds he won,
And gave meek Cynthia her Endymion.

Queen of the wide air! thou most lovely queen
Of all the brightness that mine eyes have seen!
As thou exceedest all things in thy shine,
So every tale, does this sweet tale of thine.
O for three words of honey, that I might
Tell but one wonder of thy bridal night!

Where distant ships do seem to show their keels,
Phoebus awhile delayed his mighty wheels,
And turned to smile upon thy bashful eyes,
Ere he his unseen pomp would solemnize.
The evening weather was so bright and clear,
That men of health were of unusual cheer;
Stepping like Homer at the trumpet's call,
Or young Apollo on the pedestal:
And lovely women were as fair and warm,
As Venus looking sideways in alarm.
The breezes were ethereal, and pure,
And crept through half-closed lattices to cure
The languid sick; it cooled their fevered sleep,
And soothed them into slumbers full and deep.
Soon they awoke clear-eyed: nor burnt with thirsting,
Nor with hot fingers, nor with temples bursting:
And springing up, they met the wondering sight
Of their dear friends, nigh foolish with delight;
Who feel their arms, and breasts, and kiss and stare,
And on their placid foreheads part the hair.
Young men, and maidens at each other gazed
With hands held back, and motionless, amazed
To see the brightness in each other's eyes;
And so they stood, filled with a sweet surprise,
Until their tongues were loosed in Poesy.
Therefore no lover did of anguish die:
But the soft numbers, in that moment spoken,
Made silken ties, that never may be broken.
Cynthia! I cannot tell the greater blisses,
That followed thine, and thy dear shepherd's kisses:
Was there a Poet born?—but now no more,
My wandering spirit must no further soar.—

Sleep and Poetry

'As I lay in my bed slepe full unmete
Was unto me, but why that I ne might
Rest I ne wist, for there rias earthly wight
[*As I suppose*] *had more of hertis ese*
Than I, for I n'ad sicknesse nor disese.'

Chaucer

What is more gentle than a wind in summer?
What is more soothing than the pretty hummer
That stays one moment in an open flower,
And buzzes cheerily from bower to bower?
What is more tranquil than a musk-rose blowing
In a green island, far from all men's knowing?
More healthful than the leafiness of dales?
More secret than a nest of nightingales?
More serene than Cordelia's countenance?
More full of visions than a high romance?
What, but thee Sleep? Soft closer of our eyes!
Low murmurer of tender lullabies!
Light hoverer around our happy pillows!
Wreather of poppy buds, and' weeping willows!
Silent entangler of a beauty's tresses!
Most happy listener! when the morning blesses
Thee for enlivening all the cheerful eyes
That glance so brightly at the new sun-rise.

But what is higher beyond thought than thee?
Fresher than berries of a mountain tree?
More strange, more beautiful, more smooth, more regal,
Than wings of swans, than doves, than dim-seen eagle?
What is it? And to what shall I compare it?
It has a glory, and naught else can share it:
The thought thereof is awful, sweet, and holy,
Chasing away all worldliness and folly;
Coming sometimes like fearful claps of thunder,
Or the low rumblings earth's regions under;
And sometimes like a gentle whispering
Of all the secrets of some wondrous thing
That breathes about us in the vacant air;
So that we look around with prying stare,
Perhaps to see shapes of light, aerial limning,
And catch soft floatings from a faint-heard hymning,

To see the laurel wreath, on high suspended,
That is to crown our name when life is ended.
Sometimes it gives a glory' to the voice,
And from the heart up-springs, 'Rejoice! Rejoice!'—
Sounds which will reach the Framer of all things,
And die away in ardent mutterings.

No one who once the glorious sun has seen,
And all the clouds, and felt his bosom clean
For his great Maker's presence, but must know
What 'tis I mean, and feel his being glow:
Therefore no insult will I give his spirit,
By telling what he sees from native merit.

O Poesy! for thee I hold my pen
That am not yet a glorious denizen
Of thy wide heaven—Should I rather kneel
Upon some mountain-top until I feel
A glowing splendour round about me hung,
And echo back the voice of thine own tongue?
O Poesy! for thee I grasp my pen
That am not yet a glorious denizen
Of thy wide heaven; yet, to my ardent prayer,
Yield from thy sanctuary some clear air,
Smoothed for intoxication by the breath
Of flowering bays, that I may die a death
Of luxury, and my young spirit follow
The morning sunbeams to the great Apollo
Like a fresh sacrifice; or, if I can bear
The o'erwhelming sweets, 'twill bring to me the fair
Visions of all places: a bowery nook
Will be elysium—an eternal book
Whence I may copy many a lovely saying
About the leaves, and flowers—about the playing
Of nymphs in woods, and fountains; and the shade
Keeping a silence round a sleeping maid;
And many a verse from so strange influence
That we must ever wonder how, and whence
It came. Also imaginings will hover
Round my fire-side, and haply there discover
Vistas of solemn beauty, where I'd wander
In happy silence, like the clear Meander
Through its lone vales; and where I found a spot
Of awfuller shade, or an enchanted grot,
Or a green hill o'erspread with chequered dress

Of flowers, and fearful from its loveliness,
Write on my tablets all that was permitted,
All that was for our human senses fitted.
Then the events of this wide world I'd seize
Like a strong giant, and my spirit tease
Till at its shoulders it should proudly see
Wings to find out an immortality.

Stop and consider! life is but a day;
A fragile dew-drop on its perilous way
From a tree's summit; a poor Indian's sleep
While his boat hastens to the monstrous steep
Of Montmorenci. Why so sad a moan?
Life is the rose's hope while yet unblown;
The reading of an ever-changing tale;
The light uplifting of a maiden's veil;
A pigeon tumbling in clear summer air;
A laughing school-boy, without grief or care,
Riding the springy branches of an elm.

O for ten years, that I may overwhelm
Myself in poesy; so I may do the deed
That my own soul has to itself decreed.
Then will I pass the countries that I see
In long perspective, and continually
Taste their pure fountains. First the realm I'll pass
Of Flora, and old Pan: sleep in the grass,
Feed upon apples red, and strawberries,
And choose each pleasure that my fancy sees;
Catch the white-handed nymphs in shady places,
To woo sweet kisses from averted faces—
Play with their fingers, touch their shoulders white
Into a pretty shrinking with a bite
As hard as lips can make it, till, agreed,
A lovely tale of human life we'll read.
And one will teach a tame dove how it best
May fan the cool air gently o'er my rest;
Another, bending o'er her nimble tread,
Will set a green robe floating round her head,
And still will dance with ever varied ease,
Smiling upon the flowers and the trees:
Another will entice me on, and on
Through almond blossoms and rich cinnamon;
Till in the bosom of a leafy world
We rest in silence, like two gems upcurled

In the recesses of a pearly shell.

And can I ever bid these joys farewell?
Yes, I must pass them for a nobler life,
Where I may find the agonies, the strife
Of human hearts—for lo! I see afar,
O'er-sailing the blue cragginess, a car
And steeds with streamy manes—the charioteer
Looks out upon the winds with glorious fear:
And now the numerous tramplings quiver lightly
Along a huge cloud's ridge; and now with sprightly
Wheel downward come they into fresher skies,
Tipped round with silver from the sun's bright eyes.
Still downward with capacious whirl they glide;
And now I see them on a green-hill's side
In breezy rest among the nodding stalks.
The charioteer with wondrous gesture talks
To the trees and mountains; and there soon appear
Shapes of delight, of mystery, and fear,
Passing along before a dusky space
Made by some mighty oaks: as they would chase
Some ever-fleeting music on they sweep.
Lo! how they murmur, laugh, and smile, and weep—
Some with upholden hand and mouth severe;
Some with their faces muffled to the ear
Between their arms; some, clear in youthful bloom,
Go glad and smilingly athwart the gloom;
Some looking back, and some with upward gaze;
Yes, thousands in a thousand different ways
Flit onward—now a lovely wreath of girls
Dancing their sleek hair into tangled curls;
And now broad wings. Most awfully intent
The driver of those steeds is forward bent,
And seems to listen: O that I might know
All that he writes with such a hurrying glow.
   The visions all are fled—the car is fled
Into the light of heaven, and in their stead
A sense of real things comes doubly strong,
And, like a muddy stream, would bear along
My soul to nothingness: but I will strive
Against all doubtings, and will keep alive
The thought of that same chariot, and the strange
Journey it went.
                    Is there so small a range
In the present strength of manhood, that the high

Imagination cannot freely fly
As she was wont of old? Prepare her steeds,
Paw up against the light, and do strange deeds
Upon the clouds? Has she not shown us all?
From the clear space of ether, to the small
Breath of new buds unfolding? From the meaning
Of Jove's large eye-brow, to the tender greening
Of April meadows? Here her altar shone,
E'en in this isle; and who could paragon
The fervid choir that lifted up a noise
Of harmony, to where it aye will poise
Its mighty self of convoluting sound,
Huge as a planet, and like that roll round,
Eternally around a dizzy void?
Ay, in those days the Muses were nigh cloyed
With honours; nor had any other care
Than to sing out and soothe their wavy hair.

Could all this be forgotten? Yes, a schism
Nurtured by foppery and barbarism,
Made great Apollo blush for this his land.
Men were thought wise who could not understand
His glories: with a puling infant's force
They swayed about upon a rocking horse,
And thought it Pegasus. Ah, dismal souled!
The winds of heaven blew, the ocean rolled
Its gathering waves—ye felt it not. The blue
Bared its eternal bosom, and the dew
Of summer nights collected still to make
The morning precious: beauty was awake!
Why were ye not awake? But ye were dead
To things ye knew not of—were closely wed
To musty laws lined out with wretched rule
And compass vile: so that ye taught a school
Of dolts to smooth, inlay, and clip, and fit,
Till, like the certain wands of Jacob's wit,
Their verses tallied. Easy was the task:
A thousand handicraftsmen wore the mask
Of Poesy. Ill-fated, impious race!
That blasphemed the bright Lyrist to his face,
And did not know it! No, they went about,
Holding a poor, decrepit standard out
Marked with most flimsy mottoes, and in large
The name of one Boileau!

O ye whose charge
It is to hover round our pleasant hills!
Whose congregated majesty so fills
My boundly reverence, that I cannot trace
Your hallowed names, in this unholy place,
So near those common folk—did not their shames
Affright you? Did our old lamenting Thames
Delight you? Did ye never cluster round
Delicious Avon, with a mournful sound,
And weep? Or did ye wholly bid adieu
To regions where no more the laurel grew?
Or did ye stay to give a welcoming
To some lone spirits who could proudly sing
Their youth away, and die? 'Twas even so.
But let me think away those times of woe:
Now 'tis a fairer season; ye have breathed
Rich benedictions o'er us; ye have wreathed
Fresh garlands: for sweet music has been heard
In many places—some has been upstirred
From out its crystal dwelling in a lake,
By a swan's ebon bill; from a thick brake,
Nested and quiet in a valley mild,
Bubbles a pipe—fine sounds are floating wild
About the earth: happy are ye and glad.

These things are doubtless: yet in truth we've had
Strange thunders from the potency of song;
Mingled indeed with what is sweet and strong,
From majesty: but in clear truth the themes
Are ugly clubs, the poets Polyphemes
Disturbing the grand sea. A drainless shower
Of light is Poesy; 'tis the supreme of power;
'Tis might half-slumbering on its own right arm.
The very archings of her eye-lids charm
A thousand willing agents to obey,
And still she governs with the mildest sway:
But strength alone, though of the Muses bom,
Is like a fallen angel: trees uptom,
Darkness, and worms, and shrouds, and sepulchres
Delight it; for it feeds upon the burrs,
And thorns of life; forgetting the great end
Of Poesy, that it should be a friend
To soothe the cares, and lift the thoughts of man.

Yet I rejoice: a myrtle fairer than
E'er grew in Paphos, from the bitter weeds
Lifts its sweet head into the air, and feeds
A silent space with ever sprouting green.
All tenderest birds there find a pleasant screen,
Creep through the shade with jaunty fluttering,
Nibble the little cuppèd flowers and sing.
Then let us clear away the choking thorns
From round its gentle stem; let the young fawns,
Yeaned in after times, when we are flown,
Find a fresh sward beneath it, overgrown
With simple flowers: let there nothing be
More boisterous than a lover's bended knee;
Naught more ungentle than the placid look
Of one who leans upon a closèd book;
Naught more untranquil than the grassy slopes
Between two hills. All hail delightful hopes!
As she was wont, th' imagination
Into most lovely labyrinths will be gone,
And they shall be accounted poet-kings
Who simply tell the most heart-easing things.
O may these joys be ripe before I die.

Will not some say that I presumptuously
Have spoken? that from hastening disgrace
'Twere better far to hide my foolish face?
That whining boyhood should with reverence bow
Ere the dread thunderbolt could reach? How!
If I do hide myself, it sure shall be
In the very fane, the light of Poesy:
If I do fall, at least I will be laid
Beneath the silence of a poplar shade;
And over me the grass shall be smooth-shaven;
And there shall be a kind memorial graven.
But off, Despondence! miserable bane!
They should not know thee, who, athirst to gain
A noble end, are thirsty every hour.
What though I am not wealthy in the dower
Of spanning wisdom; though I do not know
The shiftings of the mighty winds that blow
Hither and thither all the changing thoughts
Of man: though no great minist'ring reason sorts
Out the dark mysteries of human souls
To clear conceiving—yet there ever rolls

A vast idea before me, and I glean
Therefrom my liberty; thence too I've seen
The end and aim of Poesy. 'Tis clear
As any thing most true; as that the year
Is made of the four seasons—manifest
As a large cross, some old cathedral's crest,
Lifted to the white clouds. Therefore should I
Be but the essence of deformity,
A coward, did my very eye-lids wink
At speaking out what I have dared to think.
Ah! rather let me like a madman run
Over some precipice! let the hot sun
Melt my Dedalian wings, and drive me down
Convulsed and headlong! Stay! an inward frown
Of conscience bids me be more calm awhile.
An ocean dim, sprinkled with many an isle,
Spreads awfully before me. How much toil!
How many days! what desperate turmoil!
Ere I can have explored its widenesses.
Ah, what a task! upon my bended knees,
I could unsay those—no, impossible!
Impossible!

For sweet relief I'll dwell
On humbler thoughts, and let this strange assay
Begun in gentleness die so away.
E'en now all tumult from my bosom fades:
I turn full-hearted to the friendly aids
That smooth the path of honour; brotherhood,
And friendliness the nurse of mutual good.
The hearty grasp that sends a pleasant sonnet
Into the brain ere one can think upon it;
The silence when some rhymes are coming out;
And when they're come, the very pleasant rout:
The message certain to be done to-morrow—
'Tis perhaps as well that it should be to borrow
Some precious book from out its snug retreat,
To cluster round it when we next shall meet.
Scarce can I scribble on; for lovely airs
Are fluttering round the room like doves in pairs;
Many delights of that glad day recalling,
When first my senses caught their tender falling.
And with these airs come forms of elegance
Stooping their shoulders o'er a horse's prance,
Careless, and grand—fingers soft and round
Parting luxuriant curls—and the swift bound

Of Bacchus from his chariot, when his eye
Made Ariadne's cheek look blushingly.
Thus I remember all the pleasant flow
Of words at opening a portfolio.
Things such as these are ever harbingers
To trains of peaceful images: the stirs
Of a swan's neck unseen among the rushes;
A linnet starting all about the bushes;
A butterfly, with golden wings broad parted,
Nestling a rose, convulsed as though it smarted
With over-pleasure—many, many more,
Might I indulge at large in all my store
Of luxuries: yet I must not forget
Sleep, quiet with his poppy coronet,
For what there may be worthy in these rhymes
I partly owe to him: and thus, the chimes
Of friendly voices had just given place
To as sweet a silence, when I 'gan retrace
The pleasant day, upon a couch at ease.
It was a poet's house who keeps the keys
Of Pleasure's temple. Round about were hung
The glorious features of the bards who sung
In other ages—cold and sacred busts
Smiled at each other. Happy he who trusts
To clear Futurity his darling fame!
Then there were fauns and satyrs taking aim
At swelling apples with a frisky leap
And reaching fingers, 'mid a luscious heap
Of vine leaves. Then there rose to view a fane
Of liny marble, and thereto a train
Of nymphs approaching fairly o'er the sward:
One, loveliest, holding her white hand toward
The dazzling sun-rise: two sisters sweet
Bending their graceful figures till they meet
Over the trippings of a little child:
And some are hearing, eagerly, the wild
Thrilling liquidity of dewy piping.
See, in another picture, nymphs are wiping
Cherishingly Diana's timorous limbs—
A fold of lawny mantle dabbling swims
At the bath's edge, and keeps a gentle motion
With the subsiding crystal, as when ocean
Heaves calmly its broad swelling smoothness o'er
Its rocky marge, and balances once more
The patient weeds, that now unshent by foam

Feel all about their undulating home.

Sappho's meek head was there half smiling down
At nothing; just as though the earnest frown
Of over-thinking had that moment gone
From off her brow, and left her all alone.

Great Alfred's too, with anxious, pitying eyes,
As if he always listened to the sighs
Of the goaded world; and Kosciusko's worn
By horrid sufferance—mightily forlorn.

Petrarch, outstepping from the shady green,
Starts at the sight of Laura; nor can wean
His eyes from her sweet face. Most happy they!
For over them was seen a free display
Of out-spread wings, and from between them shone
The face of Poesy: from off her throne
She overlooked things that I scarce could tell.
The very sense of where I was might well
Keep Sleep aloof: but more than that there came
Thought after thought to nourish up the flame
Within my breast; so that the morning light
Surprised me even from a sleepless night;
And up I rose refreshed, and glad, and gay,
Resolving to begin that very day
These lines; and howsoever they be done,
I leave them as a father does his son.

Written in Disgust of Vulgar Superstition

The church bells toll a melancholy round,
   Calling the people to some other prayers,
   Some other gloominess, more dreadful cares,
More hearkening to the sermon's horrid sound.
Surely the mind of man is closely bound
   In some black spell; seeing that each one tears
   Himself from fireside joys, and Lydian airs,
And converse high of those with glory crowned.
Still, still they toll, and I should feel a damp—
   A chill as from a tomb—did I not know
That they are dying like an outburnt lamp;
   That 'tis their sighing, wailing ere they go
   Into oblivion—that fresh flowers will grow,
And many glories of immortal stamp.

On the Grasshopper and Cricket

The poetry of earth is never dead:
When all the birds are faint with the hot sun,
And hide in cooling trees, a voice will run
From hedge to hedge about the new-mown mead—
That is the Grasshopper's. He takes the lead
In summer luxury; he has never done
With his delights, for when tired out with fun
He rests at ease beneath some pleasant weed.
The poetry of earth is ceasing never:
On a lone winter evening, when the frost
Has wrought a silence, from the stove there shrills
The Cricket's song, in warmth increasing ever,
And seems to one in drowsiness half lost,
The Grasshopper's among some grassy hills.

To Kosciusko

Good Kosciusko, thy great name alone
Is a full harvest whence to reap high feeling;'
It comes upon us like the glorious pealing
Of the wide spheres—an everlasting tone.
And now it tells me, that in worlds unknown,
The names of heroes burst from clouds concealing,
And change to harmonies, for ever stealing
Through cloudless blue, and round each silver throne.
It tells me too, that on a happy day,
When some good spirit walks upon the earth,
Thy name with Alfred's and the great of yore
Gently commingling, gives tremendous birth
To a loud hymn, that sounds far, far away
To where the great God lives for evermore.

To G[*eorgiana*] *A*[*ugusta*] *W*[*ylie*]

Nymph of the downward smile, and sidelong glance,
In what diviner moments of the day
Art thou most lovely?—When gone far astray
Into the labyrinths of sweet utterance?
Or when serenely wandering in a trance
Of sober thought?—Or when starting away,
With careless robe, to meet the morning ray,
Thou spar'st the flowers in thy mazy dance?

Haply 'tis when thy ruby lips part sweetly,
And so remain, because thou listenest:
But thou to please wert nurtured so completely
That I can never tell what mood is best.
I shall as soon pronounce which Grace more neatly
Trips it before Apollo than the rest.

'*Happy is England! I could be content*'

Happy is England! I could be content
To see no other verdure than its own;
To feel no other breezes than are blown
Through its tall woods with high romances blent:
Yet do I sometimes feel a languishment
For skies Italian, and an inward groan
To sit upon an Alp as on a throne,
And half forget what world or worldling meant.
Happy is England, sweet her artless daughters;
Enough their simple loveliness for me,
Enough their whitest arms in silence clinging:
Yet do I often warmly burn to see
Beauties of deeper glance, and hear their singing,
And float with them about the summer waters.

'*After dark vapours have oppressed our plains*'

After dark vapours have oppressed our plains
For a long dreary season, comes a day
Born of the gentle South, and clears away
From the sick heavens all unseemly stains.
The anxious month, relieving from its pains,
Takes as a long-lost right the feel of May,
The eyelids with the passing coolness play,
Like rose leaves with the drip of summer rains.
And calmest thoughts come round us—as of leaves
Budding—fruit ripening in stillness—autumn suns
Smiling at eve upon the quiet sheaves—
Sweet Sappho's cheek—a sleeping infant's breath—
The gradual sand that through an hour-glass runs—
A woodland rivulet—a Poet's death.

To Leigh Hunt, Esq.

Glory and loveliness have passed away;
For if we wander out in early morn,
No wreathèd incense do we see upborne
Into the east, to meet the smiling day:
No crowd of nymphs soft voiced and young, and gay,
In woven baskets bringing ears of com,
Roses, and pinks, and violets, to adorn
The shrine of Flora in her early May.
But there are left delights as high as these,
And I shall ever bless my destiny,
That in a time, when under pleasant trees
Pan is no longer sought, I feel a free,
A leafy luxury, seeing I could please
With these poor offerings, a man like thee.

Written on a Blank Space at the End of Chaucer's Tale of The Floure and the Leafe

This pleasant tale is like a little copse:
The honeyed lines do freshly interlace
To keep the reader in so sweet a place,
So that he here and there full-hearted stops;
And oftentimes he feels the dewy drops
Come cool and suddenly against his face,
And by the wandering melody may trace
Which way the tender-leggèd linnet hops.
Oh! what a power has white simplicity!
What mighty power has this gentle story!
I that do ever feel athirst for glory
Could at this moment be content to lie
Meekly upon the grass, as those whose sobbings
Were heard of none beside the mournful robins.

On Receiving a Laurel Crown from Leigh Hunt

Minutes are flying swiftly, and as yet
Nothing unearthly has enticed my brain
Into a delphic labyrinth—I would fain
Catch an immortal thought to pay the debt
I owe to the kind poet who has set
Upon my ambitious head a glorious gain.
Two bending laurel sprigs—'tis nearly pain

To be conscious of such a coronet.
Still time is fleeting, and no dream arises
  Gorgeous as I would have it; only I see
A trampling down of what the world most prizes,
  Turbans and crowns, and blank regality—
And then I run into most wild surmises
  Of all the many glories that may be.

To the Ladies who Saw Me Crowned

What is there in the universal Earth
  More lovely than a wreath from the bay tree?
  Haply a halo round the moon—a glee
Circling from three sweet pair of lips in mirth;
And haply you will say the dewy birth
  Of morning roses—ripplings tenderly
  Spread by the halcyon's breath upon the sea—
But these comparisons are nothing worth.
Then is there nothing in the world so fair?
  The silvery tears of April? Youth of May?
Or June that breathes out life for butterflies?
  No—none of these can from my favourite bear
Away the palm—yet shall it ever pay
  Due reverence to your most sovereign eyes.

Ode to Apollo

  God of the golden bow,
    And of the golden lyre,
  And of the golden hair,
    And of the golden fire,
      Charioteer
      Round the patient year,
    Where—where slept thine ire,
When like a blank idiot I put on thy wreath,
    Thy laurel, thy glory,
    The light of thy story,
Or was I a worm—too low-creeping, for death?
    O Delphic Apollo!

  The Thunderer grasped and grasped,
    The Thunderer frowned and frowned;
  The eagle's feathery mane
    For wrath became stiffened—the sound
      Of breeding thunder

Went drowsily under,
Muttering to be unbound.
O why didst thou pity, and beg for a worm?
Why touch thy soft lute
Till the thunder was mute,
Why was I not crush'd—such a pitiful germ?
O Delphic Apollo!

The Pleiades were up,
Watching the silent air;
The seeds and roots in Earth
Were swelling for summer fare;
The Ocean, its neighbour,
Was at his old labour,
When, who—who did dare
To tie for a moment thy plant round his brow,
And grin and look proudly,
And blaspheme so loudly,
And live for that honour, to stoop to thee now?
O Delphic Apollo!

On Seeing the Elgin Marbles

My spirit is too weak—mortality
Weighs heavily on me like unwilling sleep,
And each imagined pinnacle and steep
Of godlike hardship, tells me I must die
Like a sick Eagle looking at the sky.
Yet 'tis a gentle luxury to weep
That I have not the cloudy winds to keep
Fresh for the opening of the morning's eye.
Such dim-conceivèd glories of the brain
Bring round the heart an undescribable feud;
So do these wonders a most dizzy pain,
That mingles Grecian grandeur with the rude
Wasting of old Time—with a billowy main—
A sun—a shadow of a magnitude.

To B. R. Haydon, with a Sonnet Written on Seeing the Elgin Marbles

Haydon! forgive me that I cannot speak
Definitively on these mighty things;
Forgive me that I have not Eagle's wings—
That what I want I know not where to seek:
And think that I would not be over-meek

In rolling out up-followed thunderings,
Even to the steep of Heliconian springs,
Were I of ample strength for such a freak—
Think too, that all those numbers should be thine;
Whose else? In this who touch thy vesture's hem?
For when men stared at what was most divine
With browless idiotism—o'erwise phlegm—
Thou hadst beheld the Hesperian shine
Of their star in the East, and gone to worship them.

On The Story of Rimini

Who loves to peer up at the morning sun,
With half-shut eyes and comfortable cheek,
Let him, with this sweet tale, full often seek
For meadows where the little rivers run;
Who loves to linger with that brightest one
Of Heaven—Hesperus—let him lowly speak
These numbers to the night, and starlight meek,
Or moon, if that her hunting be begun.
He who knows these delights, and too is prone
To moralise upon a smile or tear,
Will find at once a region of his own,
A bower for his spirit, and will steer
To alleys, where the fir-tree drops its cone,
Where robins hop, and fallen leaves are sear.

On a Leander Gem which Miss Reynolds, my Kind Friend, Gave Me

Come hither all sweet maidens soberly,
Down-looking—ay, and with a chastened light
Hid in the fringes of your eyelids white,
And meekly let your fair hands joined be.
Are ye so gentle that ye could not see,
Untouched, a victim of your beauty bright—
Sinking away to his young spirit's night,
Sinking bewildered 'mid the dreary sea:
'Tis young Leander toiling to his death.
Nigh swooning, he doth purse his weary lips
For Hero's cheek, and smiles against her smile.
O horrid dream! see how his body dips
Dead-heavy; arms and shoulders gleam awhile:
He's gone: up bubbles all his amorous breath!

On the Sea

It keeps eternal whisperings around
  Desolate shores, and with its mighty swell
  Gluts twice ten thousand caverns, till the spell
Of Hecate leaves them their old shadowy sound.
Often 'tis in such gentle temper found,
  That scarcely will the very smallest shell
  Be moved for days from where it sometime fell,
When last the winds of Heaven were unbound.
Oh ye! who have your eye-balls vexed and tired,
  Feast them upon the wideness of the Sea—
    Oh ye! whose ears are dinned with uproar rude,
  Or fed too much with cloying melody—
    Sit ye near some old cavern's mouth and brood
Until ye start, as if the sea-nymphs quired!

Lines

    Unfelt, unheard, unseen,
    I've left my little queen,
Her languid arms in silver slumber lying:
    Ah! through their nestling touch,
    Who—who could tell how much
There is for madness—cruel, or complying?

    Those faery lids how sleek!
    Those lips how moist!—they speak,
In ripest quiet, shadows of sweet sounds:
    Into my fancy's ear
    Melting a burden dear,
How 'Love doth know no fullness nor no bounds.'

    True!—tender monitors!
    I bend unto your laws:
This sweetest day for dalliance was born!
    So, without more ado,
    I'll feel my heaven anew,
For all the blushing of the hasty morn.

Stanzas

I

You say you love; but with a voice
Chaster than a nun's, who singeth
The soft Vespers to herself
While the chime-bell ringeth—
O love me truly!

II

You say you love; but with a smile
Cold as sunrise in September,
As you were Saint Cupid's nun,
And kept his weeks of Ember.
O love me truly!

III

You say you love—but then your lips
Coral tinted teach no blisses
More than coral in the sea—
They never pout for kisses—
O love me truly!

IV

You say you love; but then your hand
No soft squeeze for squeeze retumeth,
It is like a statue's, dead—
While mine for passion burneth—
O love me truly!

V

O breathe a word or two of fire!
Smile, as if those words should burn me,
Squeeze as lovers should—O kiss
And in thy heart inurn me!
O love me truly!

'Hither, hither, love'

Hither, hither, love—
  'Tis a shady mead—
Hither, hither, love,
  Let us feed and feed!

Hither, hither, sweet—
  'Tis a cowslip bed—
Hither, hither, sweet!
  'Tis with dew bespread!

Hither, hither, dear—
  By the breath of life—
Hither, hither, dear!
  Be the summer's wife!

Though one moment's pleasure
  In one moment flies,
Though the passion's treasure
  In one moment dies;

Yet it has not passed—
  Think how near, how near!—
And while it doth last,
  Think how dear, how dear!

Hither, hither, hither,
  Love this boon has sent—
If I die and wither
  I shall die content.

Lines Rhymed in a Letter Received (by J. H. Reynolds) From Oxford

    The Gothic looks solemn—
    The plain Doric column
Supports an old Bishop and crosier;
    The mouldering arch,
    Shaded o'er by a larch
Stands next door to Wilson the Hosier.

Vicè—that is, by turns—
O'er pale faces mourns
The black-tassled trencher and common hat;
The chantry boy sings,
The steeple bell rings,
And as for the Chancellor—*dominat.*

There are plenty of trees,
And plenty of ease,
And plenty of fat deer for parsons;
And when it is venison,
Short is the benison—
Then each on a leg or thigh fastens.

'*Think not of it, sweet one, so—*'

Think not of it, sweet one, so—
Give it not a tear;
Sigh thou mayst, and bid it go
Any, any where.

Do not look so sad, sweet one—
Sad and fadingly;
Shed one drop, then it is gone,
O 'twas born to die.

Still so pale? then, dearest, weep—
Weep, I'll count the tears,
And each one shall be a bliss
For thee in after years.

Brighter has it left thine eyes
Than a sunny rill;
And thy whispering melodies
Are tenderer still.

Yet—as all things mourn awhile
At fleeting blisses,
E'en let us too! but be our dirge
A dirge of kisses.

Endymion: *A Poetic Romance*

'*The stretched metre of an antique song*'

Inscribed to the memory of
Thomas Chatterton

BOOK I

A thing of beauty is a joy for ever:
Its loveliness increases; it will never
Pass into nothingness; but still will keep
A bower quiet for us, and a sleep
Full of sweet dreams, and health, and quiet breathing.
Therefore, on every morrow, are we wreathing
A flowery band to bind us to the earth,
Spite of despondence, of the inhuman dearth
Of noble natures, of the gloomy days,
Of all the unhealthy and o'er-darkened ways
Made for our searching: yes, in spite of all,
Some shape of beauty moves away the pall
From our dark spirits. Such the sun, the moon,
Trees old and young, sprouting a shady boon
For simple sheep; and such are daffodils
With the green world they live in; and clear rills
That for themselves a cooling covert make
'Gainst the hot season; the mid forest brake,
Rich with a sprinkling of fair musk-rose blooms:
And such too is the grandeur of the dooms
We have imagined for the mighty dead;
All lovely tales that we have heard or read:
An endless fountain of immortal drink,
Pouring unto us from the heaven's brink.

Nor do we merely feel these essences
For one short hour; no, even as the trees
That whisper round a temple become soon
Dear as the temple's self, so does the moon,
The passion poesy, glories infinite,
Haunt us till they become a cheering light
Unto our souls, and bound to us so fast,
That, whether there be shine, or gloom o'ercast,
They alway must be with us, or we die.

Therefore, 'tis with full happiness that I
Will trace the story of Endymion.
The very music of the name has gone
Into my being, and each pleasant scene
Is growing fresh before me as the green
Of our own vallies: so I will begin
Now while I cannot hear the city's din;
Now while the early budders are just new,
And run in mazes of the youngest hue
About old forests; while the willow trails
Its delicate amber; and the dairy pails
Bring home increase of milk. And, as the year
Grows lush in juicy stalks, I'll smoothly steer
My little boat, for many quiet hours,
With streams that deepen freshly into bowers.
Many and many a verse I hope to write,
Before the daisies, vermeil rimm'd and white,
Hide in deep herbage; and ere yet the bees
Hum about globes of clover and sweet peas,
I must be near the middle of my story.
O may no wintry season, bare and hoary,
See it half finished: but let Autumn bold,
With universal tinge of sober gold,
Be all about me when I make an end.
And now at once, adventuresome, I send
My herald thought into a wilderness:
There let its trumpet blow, and quickly dress
My uncertain path with green, that I may speed
Easily onward, thorough flowers and weed.

Upon the sides of Latmos was outspread
A mighty forest; for the moist earth fed
So plenteously all weed-hidden roots
Into o'er-hanging boughs, and precious fruits.
And it had gloomy shades, sequestered deep,
Where no man went; and if from shepherd's keep
A lamb strayed far a-down those inmost glens,
Never again saw he the happy pens
Whither his brethren, bleating with content,
Over the hills at every nightfall went.
Among the shepherds, 'twas believèd ever,
That not one fleecy lamb which thus did sever
From the white flock, but pass'd unworried
By angry wolf, or pard with prying head,
Until it came to some unfooted plains

Where fed the herds of Pan: ay great his gains
Who thus one lamb did lose. Paths there were many,
Winding through palmy fern, and rushes fenny,
And ivy banks; all leading pleasantly
To a wide lawn, whence one could only see
Stems thronging all around between the swell
Of turf and slanting branches: who could tell
The freshness of the space of heaven above,
Edg'd round with dark tree tops? through which a dove
Would often beat its wings, and often too
A little cloud would move across the blue.

Full in the middle of this pleasantness
There stood a marble altar, with a tress
Of flowers budded newly; and the dew
Had taken fairy phantasies to strew
Daisies upon the sacred sward last eve,
And so the dawnèd light in pomp receive.
For 'twas the morn: Apollo's upward fire
Made every eastern cloud a silvery pyre
Of brightness so unsullied, that therein
A melancholy spirit well might win
Oblivion, and melt out his essence fine
Into the winds: rain-scented eglantine
Gave temperate sweets to that well-wooing sun;
The lark was lost in him; cold springs had run
To warm their chilliest bubbles in the grass;
Man's voice was on the mountains; and the mass
Of nature's lives and wonders puls'd tenfold,
To feel this sun-rise and its glories old.

Now while the silent workings of the dawn
Were busiest, into that self-same lawn
All suddenly, with joyful cries, there sped
A troop of little children garlanded;
Who gathering round the altar, seemed to pry
Earnestly round as wishing to espy
Some folk of holiday: nor had they waited
For many moments, ere their ears were sated
With a faint breath of music, which ev'n then
Fill'd out its voice, and died away again.
Within a little space again it gave
Its airy swellings, with a gentle wave,
To light-hung leaves, in smoothest echoes breaking
Through copse-clad vallies,—ere their death, o'ertaking

The surgy murmurs of the lonely sea.

And now, as deep into the wood as we
Might mark a lynx's eye, there glimmered light
Fair faces and a rush of garments white,
Plainer and plainer shewing, till at last
Into the widest alley they all past,
Making directly for the woodland altar.
O kindly muse! let not my weak tongue faulter
In telling of this goodly company,
Of their old piety, and of their glee:
But let a portion of ethereal dew
Fall on my head, and presently unmew
My soul; that I may dare, in wayfaring,
To stammer where old Chaucer used to sing.

Leading the way, young damsels danced along,
Bearing the burden of a shepherd song;
Each having a white wicker over brimm'd
With April's tender younglings: next, well trimm'd,
A crowd of shepherds with as sunburnt looks
As may be read of in Arcadian books;
Such as sat listening round Apollo's pipe,
When the great deity, for earth too ripe,
Let his divinity o'er-flowing die
In music, through the vales of Thessaly:
Some idly trail'd their sheep-hooks on the ground,
And some kept up a shrilly mellow sound
With ebon-tippèd flutes: close after these,
Now coming from beneath the forest trees,
A venerable priest full soberly,
Begirt with ministring looks: alway his eye
Stedfast upon the matted turf he kept,
And after him his sacred vestments swept.
From his right hand there swung a vase, milk-white,
Of mingled wine, out-sparkling generous light;
And in his left he held a basket full
Of all sweet herbs that searching eye could cull:
Wild thyme, and valley-lilies whiter still
Than Leda's love, and cresses from the rill.
His agèd head, crownèd with beechen wreath,
Seem'd like a poll of ivy in the teeth
Of winter hoar. Then came another crowd
Of shepherds, lifting in due time aloud
Their share of the ditty. After them appear'd,

Up-followed by a multitude that rear'd
Their voices to the clouds, a fair wrought car,
Easily rolling so as scarce to mar
The freedom of three steeds of dapple brown:
Who stood therein did seem of great renown
Among the throng. His youth was fully blown,
Shewing like Ganymede to manhood grown;
And, for those simple times, his garments were
A chieftain king's: beneath his breast, half bare,
Was hung a silver bugle, and between
His nervy knees there lay a boar-spear keen.
A smile was on his countenance; he seem'd,
To common lookers on, like one who dream'd
Of idleness in groves Elysian:
But there were some who feelingly could scan
A lurking trouble in his nether lip,
And see that oftentimes the reins would slip
Through his forgotten hands: then would they sigh,
And think of yellow leaves, of owlets cry,
Of logs piled solemnly.—Ah, well-a-day,
Why should our young Endymion pine away!
   Soon the assembly, in a circle rang'd,
Stood silent round the shrine: each look was chang'd
To sudden veneration: women meek
Beckon'd their sons to silence; while each cheek
Of virgin bloom paled gently for slight fear.
Endymion too, without a forest peer,
Stood, wan, and pale, and with an awèd face,
Among his brothers of the mountain chase.
In midst of all, the venerable priest
Eyed them with joy from greatest to the least,
And, after lifting up his agèd hands,
Thus spake he: "Men of Latmos! shepherd bands!
Whose care it is to guard a thousand flocks:
Whether descended from beneath the rocks
That overtop your mountains; whether come
From vallies where the pipe is never dumb;
Or from your swelling downs, where sweet air stirs
Blue hare-bells lightly, and where prickly furze
Buds lavish gold; or ye, whose precious charge
Nibble their fill at ocean's very marge,
Whose mellow reeds are touch'd with sounds forlorn
By the dim echoes of old Triton's horn:
Mothers and wives! who day by day prepare
The scrip, with needments, for the mountain air;

And all ye gentle girls who foster up
Udderless lambs, and in a little cup
Will put choice honey for a favoured youth:
Yea, every one attend! for in good truth
Our vows are wanting to our great god Pan.
Are not our lowing heifers sleeker than
Night-swollen mushrooms? Are not our wide plains
Speckled with countless fleeces? Have not rains
Green'd over April's lap? No howling sad
Sickens our fearful ewes; and we have had
Great bounty from Endymion our lord.
The earth is glad: the merry lark has pour'd
His early song against yon breezy sky,
That spreads so clear o'er our solemnity."
Thus ending, on the shrine he heap'd a spire
Of teeming sweets, enkindling sacred fire;
Anon he stain'd the thick and spongy sod
With wine, in honour of the shepherd-god.
Now while the earth was drinking it, and while
Bay leaves were crackling in the fragrant pile,
And gummy frankincense was sparkling bright
'Neath smothering parsley, and a hazy light
Spread greyly eastward, thus a chorus sang:

"O thou, whose mighty palace roof doth hang
From jagged trunks, and overshadoweth
Eternal whispers, glooms, the birth, life, death
Of unseen flowers in heavy peacefulness;
Who lov'st to see the hamadryads dress
Their ruffled locks where meeting hazels darken;
And through whole solemn hours dost sit, and hearken
The dreary melody of bedded reeds—
In desolate places, where dank moisture breeds
The pipy hemlock to strange overgrowth;
Bethinking thee, how melancholy loth
Thou wast to lose fair Syrinx—do thou now,
By thy love's milky brow!
By all the trembling mazes that she ran,
Hear us, great Pan!

"O thou, for whose soul-soothing quiet, turtles
Passion their voices cooingly 'mong myrtles,
What time thou wanderest at eventide
Through sunny meadows, that outskirt the side
Of thine enmossèd realms: O thou, to whom

Broad leavèd fig trees even now foredoom
Their ripen'd fruitage; yellow girted bees
Their golden honeycombs; our village leas
Their fairest blossom'd beans and poppied corn;
The chuckling linnet its five young unborn,
To sing for thee; low creeping strawberries
Their summer coolness; pent up butterflies
Their freckled wings; yea, the fresh budding year
All its completions—be quickly near,
By every wind that nods the mountain pine,
O forester divine!

"Thou, to whom every fawn and satyr flies
For willing service; whether to surprise
The squatted hare while in half sleeping fit;
Or upward ragged precipices flit
To save poor lambkins from the eagle's maw;
Or by mysterious enticement draw
Bewildered shepherds to their path again;
Or to tread breathless round the frothy main,
And gather up all fancifullest shells
For thee to tumble into Naiads' cells,
And, being hidden, laugh at their out-peeping;
Or to delight thee with fantastic leaping,
The while they pelt each other on the crown
With silvery oak apples, and fir cones brown—
By all the echoes that about thee ring,
Hear us, O satyr king!

"O Hearkener to the loud clapping shears,
While ever and anon to his shorn peers
A ram goes bleating: Winder of the horn,
When snouted wild-boars routing tender corn
Anger our huntsman: Breather round our farms,
To keep off mildews, and all weather harms:
Strange ministrant of undescribèd sounds,
That come a swooning over hollow grounds,
And wither drearily on barren moors:
Dread opener of the mysterious doors
Leading to universal knowledge—see,
Great son of Dryope,
The many that are come to pay their vows
With leaves about their brows!

"Be still the unimaginable lodge
For solitary thinkings; such as dodge
Conception to the very bourne of heaven,
Then leave the naked brain: be still the leaven,
That spreading in this dull and clodded earth
Gives it a touch ethereal—a new birth:
Be still a symbol of immensity;
A firmament reflected in a sea;
An element filling the space between;
An unknown—but no more: we humbly screen
With uplift hands our foreheads, lowly bending,
And giving out a shout most heaven rending,
Conjure thee to receive our humble Pæan,
Upon thy Mount Lycean!"

Even while they brought the burden to a close,
A shout from the whole multitude arose,
That lingered in the air like dying rolls
Of abrupt thunder, when Ionian shoals
Of dolphins bob their noses through the brine.
Meantime, on shady levels, mossy fine,
Young companies nimbly began dancing
To the swift treble pipe, and humming string.
Aye, those fair living forms swam heavenly
To tunes forgotten—out of memory:
Fair creatures! whose young childrens' children bred
Thermopylæ its heroes—not yet dead,
But in old marbles ever beautiful.
High genitors, unconscious did they cull
Time's sweet first-fruits—they danc'd to weariness,
And then in quiet circles did they press
The hillock turf, and caught the latter end
Of some strange history, potent to send
A young mind from its bodily tenement.
Or they might watch the quoit-pitchers, intent
On either side; pitying the sad death
Of Hyacinthus, when the cruel breath
Of Zephyr slew him,—Zephyr penitent,
Who now, ere Phœbus mounts the firmament,
Fondles the flower amid the sobbing rain.
The archers too, upon a wider plain,
Beside the feathery whizzing of the shaft,
And the dull twanging bowstring, and the raft
Branch down sweeping from a tall ash top,

Call'd up a thousand thoughts to envelope
Those who would watch. Perhaps, the trembling knee
And frantic gape of lonely Niobe,
Poor, lonely Niobe! when her lovely young
Were dead and gone, and her caressing tongue
Lay a lost thing upon her paly lip,
And very, very deadliness did nip
Her motherly cheeks. Arous'd from this sad mood
By one, who at a distance loud halloo'd,
Uplifting his strong bow into the air,
Many might after brighter visions stare:
After the Argonauts, in blind amaze
Tossing about on Neptune's restless ways,
Until, from the horizon's vaulted side,
There shot a golden splendour far and wide,
Spangling those million poutings of the brine
With quivering ore: 'twas even an awful shine
From the exaltation of Apollo's bow;
A heavenly beacon in their dreary woe.
Who thus were ripe for high contemplating,
Might turn their steps towards the sober ring
Where sat Endymion and the aged priest
'Mong shepherds gone in eld, whose looks increas'd
The silvery setting of their mortal star.
There they discours'd upon the fragile bar
That keeps us from our homes ethereal;
And what our duties there: to nightly call
Vesper, the beauty-crest of summer weather;
To summon all the downiest clouds together
For the sun's purple couch; to emulate
In ministring the potent rule of fate
With speed of fire-tailèd exhalations;
To tint her pallid cheek with bloom, who cons
Sweet poesy by moonlight: besides these,
A world of other unguess'd offices.
Anon they wander'd, by divine converse,
Into Elysium; vieing to rehearse
Each one his own anticipated bliss.
One felt heart-certain that he could not miss
His quick gone love, among fair blossom'd boughs,
Where every zephyr-sigh pouts, and endows
Her lips with music for the welcoming.
Another wish'd, mid that eternal spring,
To meet his rosy child, with feathery sails,
Sweeping, eye-earnestly, through almond vales:

Who, suddenly, should stoop through the smooth wind,
And with the balmiest leaves his temples bind;
And, ever after, through those regions be
His messenger, his little Mercury,
Some were athirst in soul to see again
Their fellow huntsmen o'er the wide champaign
In times long past; to sit with them, and talk
Of all the chances in their earthly walk;
Comparing, joyfully, their plenteous stores
Of happiness, to when upon the moors,
Benighted, close they huddled from the cold,
And shar'd their famish'd scrips. Thus all out-told
Their fond imaginations,—saving him
Whose eyelids curtain'd up their jewels dim,
Endymion: yet hourly had he striven
To hide the cankering venom, that had riven
His fainting recollections. Now indeed
His senses had swoon'd off: he did not heed
The sudden silence, or the whispers low,
Or the old eyes dissolving at his woe,
Or anxious calls, or close of trembling palms,
Or maiden's sigh, that grief itself embalms:
But in the self-same fixèd trance he kept,
Like one who on the earth had never stept.
Aye, even as dead-still as a marble man,
Frozen in that old tale Arabian.

Who whispers him so pantingly and close?
Peona, his sweet sister: of all those,
His friends, the dearest. Hushing signs she made,
And breath'd a sister's sorrow to persuade
A yielding up, a cradling on her care.
Her eloquence did breathe away the curse:
She led him, like some midnight spirit nurse
Of happy changes in emphatic dreams,
Along a path between two little streams,—
Guarding his forehead, with her round elbow,
From low-grown branches, and his footsteps slow
From stumbling over stumps and hillocks small;
Until they came to where these streamlets fall,
With mingled bubblings and a gentle rush,
Into a river, clear, brimful, and flush
With crystal mocking of the trees and sky.
A little shallop, floating there hard by,
Pointed its beak over the fringed bank;

And soon it lightly dipt, and rose, and sank,
And dipt again, with the young couple's weight,—
Peona guiding, through the water straight,
Towards a bowery island opposite;
Which gaining presently, she steerèd light
Into a shady, fresh, and ripply cove,
Where nested was an arbour, overwove
By many a summer's silent fingering;
To whose cool bosom she was used to bring
Her playmates, with their needle broidery,
And minstrel memories of times gone by.

So she was gently glad to see him laid
Under her favourite bower's quiet shade,
On her own couch, new made of flower leaves,
Dried carefully on the cooler side of sheaves
When last the sun his autumn tresses shook,
And the tann'd harvesters rich armfuls took.
Soon was he quieted to slumbrous rest:
But, ere it crept upon him, he had prest
Peona's busy hand against his lips,
And still, a sleeping, held her finger-tips
In tender pressure. And as a willow keeps
A patient watch over the stream that creeps
Windingly by it, so the quiet maid
Held her in peace: so that a whispering blade
Of grass, a wailful gnat, a bee bustling
Down in the blue-bells, or a wren light rustling
Among sere leaves and twigs, might all be heard.

O magic sleep! O comfortable bird,
That broodest o'er the troubled sea of the mind
Till it is hush'd and smooth! O unconfin'd
Restraint! imprisoned liberty! great key
To golden palaces, strange minstrelsy,
Fountains grotesque, new trees, bespangled caves,
Echoing grottos, full of tumbling waves
And moonlight; aye, to all the mazy world
Of silvery enchantment!—who, upfurl'd
Beneath thy drowsy wing a triple hour,
But renovates and lives?—Thus, in the bower,
Endymion was calm'd to life again.
Opening his eyelids with a healthier brain,
He said: "I feel this thine endearing love
All through my bosom: thou art as a dove

Trembling its closèd eyes and sleekèd wings
About me; and the pearliest dew not brings
Such morning incense from the fields of May,
As do those brighter drops that twinkling stray
From those kind eyes,—the very home and haunt
Of sisterly affection. Can I want
Aught else, aught nearer heaven, than such tears?
Yet dry them up, in bidding hence all fears
That, any longer, I will pass my days
Alone and sad. No, I will once more raise
My voice upon the mountain-heights; once more
Make my horn parley from their foreheads hoar:
Again my trooping hounds their tongues shall loll
Around the breathèd boar: again I'll poll
The fair-grown yew tree, for a chosen bow:
And, when the pleasant sun is getting low,
Again I'll linger in a sloping mead
To hear the speckled thrushes, and see feed
Our idle sheep. So be thou cheerèd sweet,
And, if thy lute is here, softly intreat
My soul to keep in its resolvèd course."

Hereat Peona, in their silver source,
Shut her pure sorrow drops with glad exclaim,
And took a lute, from which there pulsing came
A lively prelude, fashioning the way
In which her voice should wander. 'Twas a lay
More subtle cadenced, more forest wild
Than Dryope's lone lulling of her child;
And nothing since has floated in the air
So mournful strange. Surely some influence rare
Went, spiritual, through the damsel's hand;
For still, with Delphic emphasis, she spann'd
The quick invisible strings, even though she saw
Endymion's spirit melt away and thaw
Before the deep intoxication.
But soon she came, with sudden burst, upon
Her self-possession—swung the lute aside,
And earnestly said: "Brother, 'tis vain to hide
That thou dost know of things mysterious,
Immortal, starry; such alone could thus
Weigh down thy nature. Hast thou sinn'd in aught
Offensive to the heavenly powers? Caught
A Paphian dove upon a message sent?
Thy deathful bow against some deer-herd bent,

Sacred to Dian? Haply, thou hast seen
Her naked limbs among the alders green;
And that, alas! is death. No, I can trace
Something more high perplexing in thy face!"

Endymion look'd at her, and press'd her hand,
And said, "Art thou so pale, who wast so bland
And merry in our meadows? How is this?
Tell me thine ailment: tell me all amiss!—
Ah! thou hast been unhappy at the change
Wrought suddenly in me. What indeed more strange?
Or more complete to overwhelm surmise?
Ambition is no sluggard: 'tis no prize,
That toiling years would put within my grasp,
That I have sigh'd for: with so deadly gasp
No man e'er panted for a mortal love.
So all have set my heavier grief above
These things which happen. Rightly have they done:
I, who still saw the horizontal sun
Heave his broad shoulder o'er the edge of the world,
Out-facing Lucifer, and then had hurl'd
My spear aloft, as signal for the chace—
I, who, for very sport of heart, would race
With my own steed from Araby; pluck down
A vulture from his towery perching; frown
A lion into growling, loth retire—
To lose, at once, all my toil breeding fire,
And sink thus low! but I will ease my breast
Of secret grief, here in this bowery nest.

"This river does not see the naked sky,
Till it begins to progress silverly
Around the western border of the wood,
Whence, from a certain spot, its winding flood
Seems at the distance like a crescent moon:
And in that nook, the very pride of June,
Had I been used to pass my weary eves;
The rather for the sun unwilling leaves
So dear a picture of his sovereign power,
And I could witness his most kingly hour,
When he doth lighten up the golden reins,
And paces leisurely down amber plains
His snorting four. Now when his chariot last
Its beams against the zodiac-lion cast,
There blossom'd suddenly a magic bed

Of sacred ditamy, and poppies red:
At which I wondered greatly, knowing well
That but one night had wrought this flowery spell;
And, sitting down close by, began to muse
What it might mean. Perhaps, thought I, Morpheus,
In passing here, his owlet pinions shook;
Or, it may be, ere matron Night uptook
Her ebon urn, young Mercury, by stealth,
Had dipt his rod in it: such garland wealth
Came not by common growth. Thus on I thought,
Until my head was dizzy and distraught.
Moreover, through the dancing poppies stole
A breeze, most softly lulling to my soul;
And shaping visions all about my sight
Of colours, wings, and bursts of spangly light;
The which became more strange, and strange, and dim,
And then were gulph'd in a tumultuous swim:
And then I fell asleep. Ah, can I tell
The enchantment that afterwards befel?
Yet it was but a dream: yet such a dream
That never tongue, although it overteem
With mellow utterance, like a cavern spring,
Could figure out and to conception bring
All I beheld and felt. Methought I lay
Watching the zenith, where the milky way
Among the stars in virgin splendour pours;
And travelling my eye, until the doors
Of heaven appear'd to open for my flight,
I became loth and fearful to alight
From such high soaring by a downward glance:
So kept me stedfast in that airy trance,
Spreading imaginary pinions wide.
When, presently, the stars began to glide,
And faint away, before my eager view:
At which I sigh'd that I could not pursue,
And dropt my vision to the horizon's verge;
And lo! from opening clouds, I saw emerge
The loveliest moon, that ever silver'd o'er
A shell for Neptune's goblet: she did soar
So passionately bright, my dazzled soul
Commingling with her argent spheres did roll
Through clear and cloudy, even when she went
At last into a dark and vapoury tent—
Whereat, methought, the lidless-eyèd train
Of planets all were in the blue again.

To commune with those orbs, once more I rais'd
My sight right upward: but it was quite dazed
By a bright something, sailing down apace,
Making me quickly veil my eyes and face:
Again I look'd, and, O ye deities,
Who from Olympus watch our destinies!
Whence that completed form of all completeness?
Whence came that high perfection of all sweetness?
Speak, stubborn earth, and tell me where, O where
Hast thou a symbol of her golden hair?
Not oat-sheaves drooping in the western sun;
Not—thy soft hand, fair sister! let me shun
Such follying before thee—yet she had,
Indeed, locks bright enough to make me mad;
And they were simply gordian'd up and braided,
Leaving, in naked comeliness, unshaded,
Her pearl round ears, white neck, and orbed brow;
The which were blended in, I know not how,
With such a paradise of lips and eyes,
Blush-tinted cheeks, half smiles, and faintest sighs,
That, when I think thereon, my spirit clings
And plays about its fancy, till the stings
Of human neighbourhood envenom all.
Unto what awful power shall I call?
To what high fane?—Ah! see her hovering feet,
More bluely vein'd, more soft, more whitely sweet
Than those of sea-born Venus, when she rose
From out her cradle shell. The wind out-blows
Her scarf into a fluttering pavilion;
'Tis blue, and over-spangled with a million
Of little eyes, as though thou wert to shed,
Over the darkest, lushest blue-bell bed,
Handfuls of daisies."—"Endymion, how strange!
Dream within dream!"—"She took an airy range,
And then, towards me, like a very maid,
Came blushing, waning, willing, and afraid,
And press'd me by the hand: Ah! 'twas too much;
Methought I fainted at the charmèd touch,
Yet held my recollection, even as one
Who dives three fathoms where the waters run
Gurgling in beds of coral: for anon,
I felt upmounted in that region
Where falling stars dart their artillery forth,
And eagles struggle with the buffeting north
That balances the heavy meteor-stone;—

Felt too, I was not fearful, nor alone,
But lapp'd and lull'd along the dangerous sky.
Soon, as it seem'd, we left our journeying high,
And straightway into frightful eddies swoop'd;
Such as ay muster where grey time has scoop'd
Huge dens and caverns in a mountain's side:
There hollow sounds arous'd me, and I sigh'd
To faint once more by looking on my bliss—
I was distracted; madly did I kiss
The wooing arms which held me, and did give
My eyes at once to death: but 'twas to live,
To take in draughts of life from the gold fount
Of kind and passionate looks; to count, and count
The moments, by some greedy help that seem'd
A second self, that each might be redeem'd
And plunder'd of its load of blessedness.
Ah, desperate mortal! I ev'n dar'd to press
Her very cheek against my crowned lip,
And, at that moment, felt my body dip
Into a warmer air: a moment more,
Our feet were soft in flowers. There was store
Of newest joys upon that alp. Sometimes
A scent of violets, and blossoming limes,
Loiter'd around us; then of honey cells,
Made delicate from all white-flower bells;
And once, above the edges of our nest,
An arch face peep'd,—an Oread as I guess'd.

"Why did I dream that sleep o'er-power'd me
In midst of all this heaven? Why not see,
Far off, the shadows of his pinions dark,
And stare them from me? But no, like a spark
That needs must die, although its little beam
Reflects upon a diamond, my sweet dream
Fell into nothing—into stupid sleep.
And so it was, until a gentle creep,
A careful moving caught my waking ears,
And up I started: Ah! my sighs, my tears,
My clenchèd hands;—for lo! the poppies hung
Dew-dabbled on their stalks, the ouzel sung
A heavy ditty, and the sullen day
Had chidden herald Hesperus away,
With leaden looks: the solitary breeze
Bluster'd, and slept, and its wild self did teaze
With wayward melancholy; and I thought,

Mark me, Peona! that sometimes it brought
Faint fare-thee-wells, and sigh-shrillèd adieus!—
Away I wander'd—all the pleasant hues
Of heaven and earth had faded: deepest shades
Were deepest dungeons; heaths and sunny glades
Were full of pestilent light; our taintless rills
Seem'd sooty, and o'er-spread with upturn'd gills
Of dying fish; the vermeil rose had blown
In frightful scarlet, and its thorns out-grown
Like spiked aloe. If an innocent bird
Before my heedless footsteps stirr'd, and stirr'd
In little journeys, I beheld in it
A disguis'd demon, missionèd to knit
My soul with under darkness; to entice
My stumblings down some monstrous precipice:
Therefore I eager followed, and did curse
The disappointment. Time, that agèd nurse,
Rock'd me to patience. Now, thank gentle heaven!
These things, with all their comfortings, are given
To my down-sunken hours, and with thee,
Sweet sister, help to stem the ebbing sea
Of weary life."
Thus ended he, and both
Sat silent: for the maid was very loth
To answer; feeling well that breathèd words
Would all be lost, unheard, and vain as swords
Against the enchasèd crocodile, or leaps
Of grasshoppers against the sun. She weeps,
And wonders; struggles to devise some blame;
To put on such a look as would say, *Shame
On this poor weakness*! but, for all her strife,
She could as soon have crush'd away the life
From a sick dove. At length, to break the pause,
She said with trembling chance: "Is this the cause?
This all? Yet it is strange, and sad, alas!
That one who through this middle earth should pass
Most like a sojourning demi-god, and leave
His name upon the harp-string, should achieve
No higher bard than simple maidenhood,
Singing alone, and fearfully,—how the blood
Left his young cheek; and how he used to stray
He knew not where; and how he would say, *nay*,
If any said 'twas love: and yet 'twas love;
What could it be but love? How a ring-dove
Let fall a sprig of yew tree in his path;

And how he died: and then, that love doth scathe,
The gentle heart, as northern blasts do roses;
And then the ballad of his sad life closes
With sighs, and an alas!—Endymion!
Be rather in the trumpet's mouth,—anon
Among the winds at large—that all may hearken!
Although, before the crystal heavens darken,
I watch and dote upon the silver lakes
Pictur'd in western cloudiness, that takes
The semblance of gold rocks and bright gold sands,
Islands, and creeks, and amber-fretted strands
With horses prancing o'er them, palaces
And towers of amethyst,—would I so tease
My pleasant days, because I could not mount
Into those regions? The Morphean fount
Of that fine element that visions, dreams,
And fitful whims of sleep are made of, streams
Into its airy channels with so subtle,
So thin a breathing, not the spider's shuttle,
Circled a million times within the space
Of a swallow's nest-door, could delay a trace,
A tinting of its quality: how light
Must dreams themselves be; seeing they're more slight
Than the mere nothing that engenders them!
Then wherefore sully the entrusted gem
Of high and noble life with thoughts so sick?
Why pierce high-fronted honour to the quick
For nothing but a dream?" Hereat the youth
Look'd up: a conflicting of shame and ruth
Was in his plaited brow: yet, his eyelids
Widened a little, as when Zephyr bids
A little breeze to creep between the fans
Of careless butterflies: amid his pains
He seem'd to taste a drop of manna-dew,
Full palatable; and a colour grew
Upon his cheek, while thus he lifeful spake.

"Peona! ever have I long'd to slake
My thirst for the world's praises: nothing base,
No merely slumberous phantasm, could unlace
The stubborn canvas for my voyage prepar'd—
Though now 'tis tatter'd; leaving my bark bar'd
And sullenly drifting: yet my higher hope
Is of too wide, too rainbow-large a scope,
To fret at myriads of earthly wrecks.

Wherein lies happiness? In that which becks
Our ready minds to fellowship divine,
A fellowship with essence; till we shine,
Full alchemiz'd, and free of space. Behold
The clear religion of heaven! Fold
A rose leaf round thy finger's taperness,
And soothe thy lips: hist, when the airy stress
Of music's kiss impregnates the free winds,
And with a sympathetic touch unbinds
Eolian magic from their lucid wombs:
Then old songs waken from enclouded tombs;
Old ditties sigh above their father's grave;
Ghosts of melodious prophecyings rave
Round every spot were trod Apollo's foot;
Bronze clarions awake, and faintly bruit,
Where long ago a giant battle was;
And, from the turf, a lullaby doth pass
In every place where infant Orpheus slept.
Feel we these things?—that moment have we stept
Into a sort of oneness, and our state
Is like a floating spirit's. But there are
Richer entanglements, enthralments far
More self-destroying, leading, by degrees,
To the chief intensity: the crown of these
Is made of love and friendship, and sits high
Upon the forehead of humanity.
All its more ponderous and bulky worth
Is friendship, whence there ever issues forth
A steady splendour; but at the tip-top,
There hangs by unseen film, an orbèd drop
Of light, and that is love: its influence,
Thrown in our eyes, genders a novel sense,
At which we start and fret; till in the end,
Melting into its radiance, we blend,
Mingle, and so become a part of it,—
Nor with aught else can our souls interknit
So wingedly: when we combine therewith,
Life's self is nourish'd by its proper pith,
And we are nurtured like a pelican brood.
Aye, so delicious is the unsating food,
That men, who might have tower'd in the van
Of all the congregated world, to fan
And winnow from the coming step of time
All chaff of custom, wipe away all slime
Left by men-slugs and human serpentry,

Have been content to let occasion die,
Whilst they did sleep in love's elysium.
And, truly, I would rather be struck dumb,
Than speak against this ardent listlessness:
For I have ever thought that it might bless
The world with benefits unknowingly;
As does the nightingale, up-perchèd high,
And cloister'd among cool and bunchèd leaves—
She sings but to her love, nor e'er conceives
How tiptoe Night holds back her dark-grey hood.
Just so may love, although 'tis understood
The mere commingling of passionate breath,
Produce more than our searching witnesseth:
What I know not: but who, of men, can tell
That flowers would bloom, or that green fruit would swell
To melting pulp, that fish would have bright mail,
The earth its dower of river, wood, and vale,
The meadows runnels, runnels pebble-stones,
The seed its harvest, or the lute its tones,
Tones ravishment, or ravishment its sweet,
If human souls did never kiss and greet?

"Now, if this earthly love has power to make
Men's being mortal, immortal; to shake
Ambition from their memories, and brim
Their measure of content; what merest whim,
Seems all this poor endeavour after fame,
To one, who keeps within his stedfast aim
A love immortal, an immortal too.
Look not so wilder'd; for these things are true,
And never can be born of atomies
That buzz about our slumbers, like brain-flies,
Leaving us fancy-sick. No, no, I'm sure,
My restless spirit never could endure
To brood so long upon one luxury,
Unless it did, though fearfully, espy
A hope beyond the shadow of a dream.
My sayings will the less obscurèd seem,
When I have told thee how my waking sight
Has made me scruple whether that same night
Was pass'd in dreaming. Hearken, sweet Peona!
Beyond the matron-temple of Latona,
Which we should see but for these darkening boughs,
Lies a deep hollow, from whose ragged brows
Bushes and trees do lean all round athwart,

And meet so nearly, that with wings outraught,
And spreaded tail, a vulture could not glide
Past them, but he must brush on every side.
Some moulder'd steps lead into this cool cell,
Far as the slabbèd margin of a well,
Whose patient level peeps its crystal eye
Right upward, through the bushes, to the sky.
Oft have I brought thee flowers, on their stalks set
Like vestal primroses, but dark velvet
Edges them round, and they have golden pits:
'Twas there I got them, from the gaps and slits
In a mossy stone, that sometimes was my seat,
When all above was faint with mid-day heat.
And there in strife no burning thoughts to heed,
I'd bubble up the water through a reed;
So reaching back to boy-hood: make me ships
Of moulted feathers, touchwood, alder chips,
With leaves stuck in them; and the Neptune be
Of their petty ocean. Oftener, heavily,
When love-lorn hours had left me less a child,
I sat contemplating the figures wild
Of o'er-head clouds melting the mirror through.
Upon a day, while thus I watch'd, by flew
A cloudy Cupid, with his bow and quiver;
So plainly character'd, no breeze would shiver
The happy chance: so happy, I was fain
To follow it upon the open plain,
And, therefore, was just going; when, behold!
A wonder, fair as any I have told—
The same bright face I tasted in my sleep,
Smiling in the clear well. My heart did leap
Through the cool depth.—It moved as if to flee—
I started up, when lo! refreshfully,
There came upon my face, in plenteous showers,
Dew-drops, and dewy buds, and leaves, and flowers,
Wrapping all objects from my smothered sight,
Bathing my spirit in a new delight.
Aye, such a breathless honey-feel of bliss
Alone preserved me from the drear abyss
Of death, for the fair form had gone again.
Pleasure is oft a visitant; but pain
Clings cruelly to us, like the gnawing sloth
On the deer's tender haunches: late, and loth,
'Tis scar'd away by slow returning pleasure.
How sickening, how dark the dreadful leisure

Of weary days, made deeper exquisite,
By a fore-knowledge of unslumbrous night!
Like sorrow came upon me, heavier still,
Than when I wander'd from the poppy hill:
And a whole age of lingering moments crept
Sluggishly by, ere more contentment swept
Away at once the deadly yellow spleen.
Yes, thrice have I this fair enchantment seen;
Once more been tortured with renewèd life.
When last the wintry gusts gave over strife
With the conquering sun of spring, and left the skies
Warm and serene, but yet with moistened eyes
In pity of the shatter'd infant buds,—
That time thou didst adorn, with amber studs,
My hunting cap, because I laugh'd and smil'd,
Chatted with thee, and many days exil'd
All torment from my breast;—'twas even then,
Straying about, yet, coop'd up in the den
Of helpless discontent,—hurling my lance
From place to place, and following at chance,
At last, by hap, through some young trees it struck,
And, plashing among bedded pebbles, stuck
In the middle of a brook,—whose silver ramble
Down twenty little falls, through reeds and bramble,
Tracing along, it brought me to a cave,
Whence it ran brightly forth, and white did lave
The nether sides of mossy stones and rock,—
'Mong which it gurgled blythe adieus, to mock
Its own sweet grief at parting. Overhead,
Hung a lush scene of drooping weeds, and spread
Thick, as to curtain up some wood-nymph's home.
"Ah! impious mortal, whither do I roam?"
Said I, low voic'd: "Ah, whither! 'Tis the grot
Of Proserpine, when Hell, obscure and hot,
Doth her resign; and where her tender hands
She dabbles, on the cool and sluicy sands:
Or 'tis the cell of Echo, where she sits,
And babbles thorough silence, till her wits
Are gone in tender madness, and anon,
Faints into sleep, with many a dying tone
Of sadness. O that she would take my vows,
And breathe them sighingly among the boughs,
To sue her gentle ears for whose fair head,
Daily, I pluck sweet flowerets from their bed,
And weave them dyingly—send honey-whispers

Round every leaf, that all those gentle lispers
May sigh my love unto her pitying!
O charitable echo! hear, and sing
This ditty to her!—tell her"—so I stay'd
My foolish tongue, and listening, half afraid,
Stood stupefied with my own empty folly,
And blushing for the freaks of melancholy.
Salt tears were coming, when I heard my name
Most fondly lipp'd, and then these accents came:
"Endymion! the cave is secreter
Than the isle of Delos. Echo hence shall stir
No sighs but sigh-warm kisses, or light noise
Of thy combing hand, the while it travelling cloys
And trembles through my labyrinthine hair."
At that oppress'd I hurried in.—Ah! where
Are those swift moments? Whither are they fled?
I'll smile no more, Peona; nor will wed
Sorrow the way to death; but patiently
Bear up against it: so farewel, sad sigh;
And come instead demurest meditation,
To occupy me wholly, and to fashion
My pilgrimage for the world's dusky brink.
No more will I count over, link by link,
My chain of grief: no longer strive to find
A half-forgetfulness in mountain wind
Blustering about my ears: aye, thou shalt see,
Dearest of sisters, what my life shall be;
What a calm round of hours shall make my days.
There is a paly flame of hope that plays
Where'er I look: but yet, I'll say 'tis naught—
And here I bid it die. Have not I caught,
Already, a more healthy countenance?
By this the sun is setting; we may chance
Meet some of our near-dwellers with my car."

This said, he rose, faint-smiling like a star
Through autumn mists, and took Peona's hand:
They stept into the boat, and launch'd from land.

BOOK II

O sovereign power of love! O grief! O balm!
All records, saving thine, come cool, and calm,
And shadowy, through the mist of passed years:
For others, good or bad, hatred and tears
Have become indolent; but touching thine,
One sigh doth echo, one poor sob doth pine,
One kiss brings honey-dew from buried days.
The woes of Troy, towers smothering o'er their blaze,
Stiff-holden shields, far-piercing spears, keen blades,
Struggling, and blood, and shrieks—all dimly fades
Into some backward corner of the brain;
Yet, in our very souls, we feel amain
The close of Troilus and Cressid sweet.
Hence, pageant history! hence, gilded cheat!
Swart planet in the universe of deeds!
Wide sea, that one continuous murmur breeds
Along the pebbled shore of memory!
Many old rotten-timber'd boats there be
Upon thy vaporous bosom, magnified
To goodly vessels; many a sail of pride,
And golden keel'd, is left unlaunch'd and dry.
But wherefore this? What care, though owl did fly
About the great Athenian admiral's mast?
What care, though striding Alexander past
The Indus with his Macedonian numbers?
Though old Ulysses tortured from his slumbers
The glutted Cyclops, what care?—Juliet leaning
Amid her window-flowers,—sighing,—weaning
Tenderly her fancy from its maiden snow,
Doth more avail than these: the silver flow
Of Hero's tears, the swoon of Imogen,
Fair Pastorella in the bandit's den,
Are things to brood on with more ardency
Than the death-day of empires. Fearfully
Must such conviction come upon his head,
Who, thus far, discontent, has dared to tread,
Without one muse's smile, or kind behest,
The path of love and poesy. But rest,
In chaffing restlessness, is yet more drear
Than to be crush'd, in striving to uprear
Love's standard on the battlements of song.
So once more days and nights aid me along,

Like legion'd soldiers.

Brain-sick shepherd prince,
What promise hast thou faithful guarded since
The day of sacrifice? Or, have new sorrows
Come with the constant dawn upon thy morrows?
Alas! 'tis his old grief. For many days,
Has he been wandering in uncertain ways:
Through wilderness, and woods of mossèd oaks;
Counting his woe-worn minutes, by the strokes
Of the lone woodcutter; and listening still,
Hour after hour, to each lush-leavèd rill.
Now he is sitting by a shady spring,
And elbow-deep with feverous fingering
Stems the upbursting cold: a wild rose tree
Pavilions him in bloom, and he doth see
A bud which snares his fancy: lo! but now
He plucks it, dips its stalk in the water: how!
It swells, it buds, it flowers beneath his sight;
And, in the middle, there is softly pight
A golden butterfly; upon whose wings
There must be surely character'd strange things,
For with wide eye he wonders, and smiles oft.

Lightly this little herald flew aloft,
Follow'd by glad Endymion's claspèd hands:
Onward it flies. From languor's sullen bands
His limbs are loos'd, and eager, on he hies
Dazzled to trace it in the sunny skies.
It seem'd he flew, the way so easy was;
And like a new-born spirit did he pass
Through the green evening quiet in the sun,
O'er many a heath, through many a woodland dun,
Through buried paths, where sleepy twilight dreams
The summer time away. One track unseams
A wooded cleft, and, far away, the blue
Of ocean fades upon him; then, anew,
He sinks adown a solitary glen,
Where there was never sound of mortal men,
Saving, perhaps, some snow-light cadences
Melting to silence, when upon the breeze
Some holy bark let forth an anthem sweet,
To cheer itself to Delphi. Still his feet
Went swift beneath the merry-wingèd guide,
Until it reached a splashing fountain's side

That, near a cavern's mouth, for ever pour'd
Unto the temperate air: then high it soar'd,
And, downward, suddenly began to dip,
As if, athirst with so much toil, 'twould sip
The crystal spout-head: so it did, with touch
Most delicate, as though afraid to smutch
Even with mealy gold the waters clear.
But, at that very touch, to disappear
So fairy-quick, was strange! Bewilderèd,
Endymion sought around, and shook each bed
Of covert flowers in vain; and then he flung
Himself along the grass. What gentle tongue,
What whisperer disturb'd his gloomy rest?
It was a nymph uprisen to the breast
In the fountain's pebbly margin, and she stood
'Mong lilies, like the youngest of the brood.
To him her dripping hand she softly kist,
And anxiously began to plait and twist
Her ringlets round her fingers, saying: "Youth!
Too long, alas, hast thou starv'd on the ruth,
The bitterness of love: too long indeed,
Seeing thou art so gentle. Could I weed
Thy soul of care, by heavens, I would offer
All the bright riches of my crystal coffer
To Amphitrite; all my clear-eyed fish,
Golden, or rainbow-sided, or purplish,
Vermilion-tail'd, or finn'd with silvery gauze;
Yea, or my veinèd pebble-floor, that draws
A virgin light to the deep; my grotto-sands
Tawny and gold, ooz'd slowly from far lands
By my diligent springs; my level lilies, shells,
My charming rod, my potent river spells;
Yes, every thing, even to the pearly cup
Meander gave me,—for I bubbled up
To fainting creatures in a desert wild.
But woe is me, I am but as a child
To gladden thee; and all I dare to say,
Is, that I pity thee; that on this day
I've been thy guide; that thou must wander far
In other regions, past the scanty bar
To mortal steps, before thou cans't be ta'en
From every wasting sigh, from every pain,
Into the gentle bosom of thy love.
Why it is thus, one knows in heaven above:
But, a poor Naiad, I guess not. Farewel!

I have a ditty for my hollow cell."

Hereat, she vanished from Endymion's gaze,
Who brooded o'er the water in amaze:
The dashing fount pour'd on, and where its pool
Lay, half asleep, in grass and rushes cool,
Quick waterflies and gnats were sporting still,
And fish were dimpling, as if good nor ill
Had fallen out that hour. The wanderer,
Holding his forehead, to keep off the burr
Of smothering fancies, patiently sat down;
And, while beneath the evening's sleepy frown
Glow-worms began to trim their starry lamps,
Thus breath'd he to himself: "Whoso encamps
To take a fancied city of delight,
O what a wretch is he! and when 'tis his,
After long toil and travelling, to miss
The kernel of his hopes, how more than vile:
Yet, for him there's refreshment even in toil;
Another city doth he set about,
Free from the smallest pebble-head of doubt
That he will seize on trickling honey-combs:
Alas, he finds them dry; and then he foams,
And onward to another city speeds.
But this is human life: the war, the deeds,
The disappointment, the anxiety,
Imagination's struggles, far and nigh,
All human; bearing in themselves this good,
That they are still the air, the subtle food,
To make us feel existence, and to shew
How quiet death is. Where soil is men grow,
Whether to weeds or flowers; but for me,
There is no depth to strike in: I can see
Nought earthly worth my compassing; so stand
Upon a misty, jutting head of land—
Alone? No, no; and by the Orphean lute,
When mad Eurydice is listening to't;
I'd rather stand upon this misty peak,
With not a thing to sigh for, or to seek,
But the soft shadow of my thrice-seen love,
Than be—I care not what. O meekest dove
Of heaven! O Cynthia, ten-times bright and fair!
From thy blue throne, now filling all the air,
Glance but one little beam of temper'd light
Into my bosom, that the dreadful might

And tyranny of love be somewhat scar'd!
Yet do not so, sweet queen; one torment spar'd,
Would give a pang to jealous misery,
Worse than the torment's self: but rather tie
Large wings upon my shoulders, and point out
My love's far dwelling. Though the playful rout
Of Cupids shun thee, too divine art thou,
Too keen in beauty, for thy silver prow
Not to have dipp'd in love's most gentle stream.
O be propitious, nor severely deem
My madness impious; for, by all the stars
That tend thy bidding, I do think the bars
That kept my spirit in are burst—that I
Am sailing with thee through the dizzy sky!
How beautiful thou art! The world how deep!
How tremulous-dazzlingly the wheels sweep
Around their axle! Then these gleaming reins,
How lithe! When this thy chariot attains
Its airy goal, haply some bower veils
Those twilight eyes?—Those eyes!—my spirit fails—
Dear goddess, help! or the wide-gaping air
Will gulph me—help!"—At this with madden'd stare,
And lifted hands, and trembling lips he stood;
Like old Deucalion mountain'd o'er the flood,
Or blind Orion hungry for the morn.
And, but from the deep cavern there was borne
A voice, he had been froze to senseless stone;
Nor sigh of his, nor plaint, nor passion'd moan
Had more been heard. Thus swell'd it forth: "Descend,
Young mountaineer! descend where alleys bend
Into the sparry hollows of the world!
Oft hast thou seen bolts of the thunder hurl'd
As from thy threshold; day by day hast been
A little lower than the chilly sheen
Of icy pinnacles, and dipp'dst thine arms
Into the deadening ether that still charms
Their marble being: now, as deep profound
As those are high, descend! He ne'er is crown'd
With immortality, who fears to follow
Where airy voices lead: so through the hollow,
The silent mysteries of earth, descend!"

He heard but the last words, nor could contend
One moment in reflection: for he fled
Into the fearful deep, to hide his head

From the clear moon, the trees, and coming madness.

'Twas far too strange, and wonderful for sadness;
Sharpening, by degrees, his appetite
To dive into the deepest. Dark, nor light,
The region; nor bright, nor sombre wholly,
But mingled up; a gleaming melancholy;
A dusky empire and its diadems;
One faint eternal eventide of gems.
Aye, millions sparkled on a vein of gold,
Along whose track the prince quick footsteps told,
With all its lines abrupt and angular:
Out-shooting sometimes, like a meteor-star,
Through a vast antre; then the metal woof,
Like Vulcan's rainbow, with some monstrous roof
Curves hugely: now, far in the deep abyss,
It seems an angry lightning, and doth hiss
Fancy into belief: anon it leads
Through winding passages, where sameness breeds
Vexing conceptions of some sudden change;
Whether to silver grots, or giant range
Of sapphire columns, or fantastic bridge
Athwart a flood of crystal. On a ridge
Now fareth he, that o'er the vast beneath
Towers like an ocean-cliff, and whence he seeth
A hundred waterfalls, whose voices come
But as the murmuring surge. Chilly and numb
His bosom grew, when first he, far away,
Descried an orbèd diamond, set to fray
Old darkness from his throne: 'twas like the sun
Uprisen o'er chaos: and with such a stun
Came the amazement, that, absorb'd in it,
He saw not fiercer wonders—past the wit
Of any spirit to tell, but one of those
Who, when this planet's sphering time doth close,
Will be its high remembrancers: who they?
The mighty ones who have made eternal day
For Greece and England. While astonishment
With deep-drawn sighs was quieting, he went
Into a marble gallery, passing through
A mimic temple, so complete and true
In sacred custom, that he well nigh fear'd
To search it inwards; whence far off appear'd,
Through a long pillar'd vista, a fair shrine,
And, just beyond, on light tiptoe divine,

A quiver'd Dian. Stepping awfully,
The youth approach'd; oft turning his veil'd eye
Down sidelong aisles, and into niches old.
And when, more near against the marble cold
He had touch'd his forehead, he began to thread
All courts and passages, where silence dead
Rous'd by his whispering footsteps murmured faint:
And long he travers'd to and fro, to acquaint
Himself with every mystery, and awe;
Till, weary, he sat down before the maw
Of a wide outlet, fathomless and dim
To wild uncertainty and shadows grim.
There, when new wonders ceas'd to float before,
And thoughts of self came on, how crude and sore
The journey homeward to habitual self!
A mad-pursuing of the fog-born elf,
Whose flitting lantern, through rude nettle-briar,
Cheats us into a swamp, into a fire,
Into the bosom of a hated thing.

What misery most drowningly doth sing
In lone Endymion's ear, now he has caught
The goal of consciousness? Ah, 'tis the thought,
The deadly feel of solitude: for lo!
He cannot see the heavens, nor the flow
Of rivers, nor hill-flowers running wild
In pink and purple chequer, nor, up-pil'd,
The cloudy rack slow journeying in the west,
Like herded elephants; nor felt, nor prest
Cool grass, nor tasted the fresh slumberous air;
But far from such companionship to wear
An unknown time, surcharg'd with grief, away,
Was now his lot. And must he patient stay,
Tracing fantastic figures with his spear?
"No!" exclaimed he, "why should I tarry here?"
No! loudly echoed times innumerable.
At which he straightway started, and 'gan tell
His paces back into the temple's chief;
Warming and growing strong in the belief
Of help from Dian: so that when again
He caught her airy form, thus did he plain,
Moving more near the while. "O Haunter chaste
Of river sides, and woods, and heathy waste,
Where with thy silver bow and arrows keen
Art thou now forested? O woodland Queen,

What smoothest air thy smoother forehead woos?
Where dost thou listen to the wide halloos
Of thy disparted nymphs? Through what dark tree
Glimmers thy crescent? Wheresoe'er it be,
'Tis in the breath of heaven: thou dost taste
Freedom as none can taste it, nor dost waste
Thy loveliness in dismal elements;
But, finding in our green earth sweet contents,
There livest blissfully. Ah, if to thee
It feels Elysian, how rich to me,
An exil'd mortal, sounds its pleasant name!
Within my breast there lives a choking flame—
O let me cool it among the zephyr-boughs!
A homeward fever parches up my tongue—
O let me slake it at the running springs!
Upon my car a noisy nothing rings—
O let me once more hear the linnet's note!
Before mine eyes thick films and shadows float—
O let me 'noint them with the heaven's light!
Dost thou now lave thy feet and ankles white?
O think how sweet to me the freshening sluice!
Dost thou now please thy thirst with berry-juice?
O think how this dry palate would rejoice!
If in soft slumber thou dost hear my voice,
O think how I should love a bed of flowers!—
Young goddess! let me see my native bowers!
Deliver me from this rapacious deep!"

Thus ending loudly, as he would o'erleap
His destiny, alert he stood: but when
Obstinate silence came heavily again,
Feeling about for its old couch of space
And airy cradle, lowly bow'd his face
Desponding, o'er the marble floor's cold thrill.
But 'twas not long; for, sweeter than the rill
To its old channel, or a swollen tide
To margin sallows, were the leaves he spied,
And flowers, and wreaths, and ready myrtle crowns
Up heaping through the slab: refreshment drowns
Itself, and strives its own delights to hide—
Nor in one spot alone; the floral pride
In a long whispering birth enchanted grew
Before his footsteps; as when heav'd anew
Old ocean rolls a lengthened wave to the shore,
Down whose green back the short-liv'd foam, all hoar,

Bursts gradual, with a wayward indolence.

Increasing still in heart, and pleasant sense,
Upon his fairy journey on he hastes;
So anxious for the end, he scarcely wastes
One moment with his hand among the sweets:
Onward he goes—he stops—his bosom beats
As plainly in his ear, as the faint charm
Of which the throbs were born. This still alarm,
This sleepy music, forc'd him walk tiptoe:
For it came more softly than the east could blow
Arion's magic to the Atlantic isles;
Or than the west, made jealous by the smiles
Of thron'd Apollo, could breathe back the lyre
To seas Ionian and Tyrian.

O did he ever live, that lonely man,
Who lov'd—and music slew not? 'Tis the pest
Of love, that fairest joys give most unrest;
That things of delicate and tenderest worth
Are swallow'd all, and made a searèd dearth,
By one consuming flame: it doth immerse
And suffocate true blessings in a curse.
Half-happy, by comparison of bliss,
Is miserable. 'Twas even so with this
Dew-dropping melody, in the Carian's ear;
First heaven, then hell, and then forgotten clear,
Vanish'd in elemental passion.

And down some swart abysm he had gone,
Had not a heavenly guide benignant led
To where thick myrtle branches, 'gainst his head
Brushing, awakened: then the sounds again
Went noiseless as a passing noontide rain
Over a bower, where little space he stood;
For as the sunset peeps into a wood
So saw he panting light, and towards it went
Through winding alleys; and lo, wonderment!
Upon soft verdure saw, one here, one there,
Cupids a slumbering on their pinions fair.

After a thousand mazes overgone,
At last, with sudden step, he came upon
A chamber, myrtle wall'd, embowered high,
Full of light, incense, tender minstrelsy,

And more of beautiful and strange beside:
For on a silken couch of rosy pride,
In midst of all, there lay a sleeping youth
Of fondest beauty; fonder, in fair sooth,
Than sighs could fathom, or contentment reach:
And coverlids gold-tinted like the peach,
Or ripe October's faded marigolds,
Fell sleek about him in a thousand folds—
Not hiding up an Apollonian curve
Of neck and shoulder, nor the tenting swerve
Of knee from knee, nor ankles pointing light;
But rather, giving them to the fillèd sight
Officiously. Sideway his face repos'd
On one white arm, and tenderly unclos'd,
By tenderest pressure, a faint damask mouth
To slumbery pout; just as the morning south
Disparts a dew-lipp'd rose. Above his head,
Four lily stalks did their white honours wed
To make a coronal; and round him grew
All tendrils green, of every bloom and hue,
Together intertwin'd and trammel'd fresh:
The vine of glossy sprout; the ivy mesh,
Shading its Ethiop berries; and woodbine,
Of velvet leaves and bugle-blooms divine;
Convolvulus in streakèd vases flush;
The creeper, mellowing for an autumn blush;
And virgin's bower, trailing airily;
With others of the sisterhood. Hard by,
Stood serene Cupids watching silently.
One, kneeling to a lyre, touch'd the strings,
Muffling to death the pathos with his wings;
And, ever and anon, uprose to look
At the youth's slumber; while another took
A willow-bough, distilling odorous dew,
And shook it on his hair; another flew
In through the woven roof, and fluttering-wise
Rain'd violets upon his sleeping eyes.

At these enchantments, and yet many more,
The breathless Latmian wonder'd o'er and o'er;
Until, impatient in embarrassment,
He forthright pass'd, and lightly treading went
To that same feather'd lyrist, who straightway,
Smiling, thus whisper'd: "Though from upper day
Thou art a wanderer, and thy presence here

Might seem unholy, be of happy cheer!
For 'tis the nicest touch of human honour,
When some ethereal and high-favouring donor
Presents immortal bowers to mortal sense;
As now 'tis done to thee, Endymion. Hence
Was I in no wise startled. So recline
Upon these living flowers. Here is wine,
Alive with sparkles—never, I aver,
Since Ariadne was a vintager,
So cool a purple: taste these juicy pears,
Sent me by sad Vertumnus, when his fears
Were high about Pomona: here is cream,
Deepening to richness from a snowy gleam;
Sweeter than that nurse Amalthea skimm'd
For the boy Jupiter: and here, undimm'd
By any touch, a bunch of blooming plums
Ready to melt between an infant's gums:
And here is manna pick'd from Syrian trees,
In starlight, by the three Hesperides.
Feast on, and meanwhile I will let thee know
Of all these things around us." He did so,
Still brooding o'er the cadence of his lyre;
And thus: "I need not any hearing tire
By telling how the sea-born goddess pin'd
For a mortal youth, and how she strove to bind
Him all in all unto her doting self.
Who would not be so prison'd? but, fond elf,
He was content to let her amorous plea
Faint through his careless arms; content to see
An unseiz'd heaven dying at his feet;
Content, O fool! to make a cold retreat,
When on the pleasant grass such love, lovelorn,
Lay sorrowing; when every tear was born
Of diverse passion; when her lips and eyes
Were clos'd in sullen moisture, and quick sighs
Came vex'd and pettish through her nostrils small.
Hush! no exclaim—yet, justly mightst thou call
Curses upon his head.—I was half glad,
But my poor mistress went distract and mad,
When the boar tusk'd him: so away she flew
To Jove's high throne, and by her plainings drew
Immortal tear-drops down the thunderer's beard;
Whereon, it was decreed he should be rear'd
Each summer time to life. Lo! this is he,
That same Adonis, safe in the privacy

Of this still region all his winter-sleep.
Aye, sleep; for when our love-sick queen did weep
Over his wanèd corse, the tremulous shower
Heal'd up the wound, and, with a balmy power,
Medicined death to a lengthened drowsiness:
The which she fills with visions, and doth dress
In all this quiet luxury; and hath set
Us young immortals, without any let,
To watch his slumber through. 'Tis well nigh pass'd,
Even to a moment's filling up, and fast
She scuds with summer breezes, to pant through
The first long kiss, warm firstling, to renew
Embower'd sports in Cytherea's isle.
Look! how those wingèd listeners all this while
Stand anxious: see! behold!"—This clamant word
Broke through the careful silence; for they heard
A rustling noise of leaves, and out there flutter'd
Pigeons and doves: Adonis something mutter'd,
The while one hand, that erst upon his thigh
Lay dormant, mov'd convuls'd and gradually
Up to his forehead. Then there was a hum
Of sudden voices, echoing, "Come! come!
Arise! awake! Clear summer has forth walk'd
Unto the clover-sward, and she has talk'd
Full soothingly to every nested finch:
Rise, Cupids! or we'll give the blue-bell pinch
To your dimpled arms. Once more sweet life begin!"
At this, from every side they hurried in,
Rubbing their sleepy eyes with lazy wrists,
And doubling over head their little fists
In backward yawns. But all were soon alive:
For as delicious wine doth, sparkling, dive
In nectar'd clouds and curls through water fair,
So from the arbour roof down swell'd an air
Odorous and enlivening; making all
To laugh, and play, and sing, and loudly call
For their sweet queen: when lo! the wreathèd green
Disparted, and far upward could be seen
Blue heaven, and a silver car, air-borne,
Whose silent wheels, fresh wet from clouds of morn,
Spun off a drizzling dew,—which falling chill
On soft Adonis' shoulders, made him still
Nestle and turn uneasily about.
Soon were the white doves plain, with necks stretch'd out,
And silken traces lighten'd in descent;

And soon, returning from love's banishment,
Queen Venus leaning downward open arm'd:
Her shadow fell upon his breast, and charm'd
A tumult to his heart, and a new life
Into his eyes. Ah, miserable strife,
But for her comforting! unhappy sight,
But meeting her blue orbs! Who, who can write
Of these first minutes? The unchariest muse
To embracements warm as theirs makes coy excuse.

O it has ruffled every spirit there,
Saving love's self, who stands superb to share
The general gladness: awfully he stands;
A sovereign quell is in his waving hands;
No sight can bear the lightning of his bow;
His quiver is mysterious, none can know
What themselves think of it; from forth his eyes
There darts strange light of varied hues and dyes:
A scowl is sometimes on his brow, but who
Look full upon it feel anon the blue
Of his fair eyes run liquid through their souls.
Endymion feels it, and no more controls
The burning prayer within him; so, bent low,
He had begun a plaining of his woe.
But Venus, bending forward, said: "My child,
Favour this gentle youth; his days are wild
With love—he—but alas! too well I see
Thou know'st the deepness of his misery.
Ah, smile not so, my son: I tell thee true,
That when through heavy hours I used to rue
The endless sleep of this new-born Adon',
This stranger ay I pitied. For upon
A dreary morning once I fled away
Into the breezy clouds, to weep and pray
For this my love: for vexing Mars had teaz'd
Me even to tears: thence, when a little eas'd,
Down-looking, vacant, through a hazy wood,
I saw this youth as he despairing stood:
Those same dark curls blown vagrant in the wind;
Those same full fringèd lids a constant blind
Over his sullen eyes: I saw him throw
Himself on wither'd leaves, even as though
Death had come sudden; for no jot he mov'd,
Yet mutter'd wildly. I could hear he lov'd
Some fair immortal, and that his embrace

Had zoned her through the night. There is no trace
Of this in heaven: I have mark'd each cheek,
And find it is the vainest thing to seek;
And that of all things 'tis kept secretest.
Endymion! one day thou wilt be blest:
So still obey the guiding hand that fends
Thee safely through these wonders for sweet ends.
'Tis a concealment needful in extreme;
And if I guess'd not so, the sunny beam
Thou shouldst mount up to with me. Now adieu!
Here must we leave thee."—At these words up flew
The impatient doves, up rose the floating car,
Up went the hum celestial. High afar
The Latmian saw them minish into nought;
And, when all were clear vanish'd, still he caught
A vivid lightning from that dreadful bow.
When all was darkened, with Etnean throe
The earth clos'd—gave a solitary moan—
And left him once again in twilight lone.

He did not rave, he did not stare aghast,
For all those visions were o'ergone, and past,
And he in loneliness: he felt assur'd
Of happy times, when all he had endur'd
Would seem a feather to the mighty prize.
So, with unusual gladness, on he hies
Through caves, and palaces of mottled ore,
Gold dome, and crystal wall, and turquois floor,
Black polish'd porticos of awful shade,
And, at the last, a diamond balustrade,
Leading afar past wild magnificence,
Spiral through ruggedest loopholes, and thence
Stretching across a void, then guiding o'er
Enormous chasms, where, all foam and roar,
Streams subterranean tease their granite beds;
Then heighten'd just above the silvery heads
Of a thousand fountains, so that he could dash
The waters with his spear; but at the splash,
Done heedlessly, those spouting columns rose
Sudden a poplar's height, and 'gan to enclose
His diamond path with fretwork, streaming round
Alive, and dazzling cool, and with a sound,
Haply, like dolphin tumults, when sweet shells
Welcome the float of Thetis. Long he dwells
On this delight; for, every minute's space,

The streams with changèd magic interlace:
Sometimes like delicatest lattices,
Cover'd with crystal vines; then weeping trees,
Moving about as in a gentle wind,
Which, in a wink, to watery gauze refin'd,
Pour'd into shapes of curtain'd canopies,
Spangled, and rich with liquid broideries
Of flowers, peacocks, swans, and naiads fair.
Swifter than lightning went these wonders rare;
And then the water, into stubborn streams
Collecting, mimick'd the wrought oaken beams,
Pillars, and frieze, and high fantastic roof,
Of those dusk places in times far aloof
Cathedrals call'd. He bade a loth farewel
To these founts Protean, passing gulph, and dell,
And torrent, and ten thousand jutting shapes,
Half seen through deepest gloom, and griesly gapes,
Blackening on every side, and overhead
A vaulted dome like Heaven's, far bespread
With starlight gems: aye, all so huge and strange,
The solitary felt a hurried change
Working within him into something dreary,—
Vex'd like a morning eagle, lost, and weary,
And purblind amid foggy, midnight wolds.
But he revives at once: for who beholds
New sudden things, nor casts his mental slough?
Forth from a rugged arch, in the dusk below,
Came mother Cybele! alone—alone—
In sombre chariot; dark foldings thrown
About her majesty, and front death-pale,
With turrets crowned. Four manèd lions hale
The sluggish wheels; solemn their toothèd maws,
Their surly eyes brow-hidden, heavy paws
Uplifted drowsily, and nervy tails
Cowering their tawny brushes. Silent sails
This shadowy queen athwart, and faints away
In another gloomy arch.
                                        Wherefore delay,
Young traveller, in such a mournful place?
Art thou wayworn, or canst not further trace
The diamond path? And does it indeed end
Abrupt in middle air? Yet earthward bend
Thy forehead, and to Jupiter cloud-borne
Call ardently! He was indeed wayworn;
Abrupt, in middle air, his way was lost;

To cloud-borne Jove he bowed, and there crost
Towards him a large eagle, 'twixt whose wings,
Without one impious word, himself he flings,
Committed to the darkness and the gloom:
Down, down, uncertain to what pleasant doom,
Swift as a fathoming plummet down he fell
Through unknown things; till exhaled asphodel,
And rose, with spicy fannings interbreath'd,
Came swelling forth where little caves were wreath'd
So thick with leaves and mosses, that they seem'd
Large honey-combs of green, and freshly teem'd
With airs delicious. In the greenest nook
The eagle landed him, and farewel took.

It was a jasmine bower, all bestrewn
With golden moss. His every sense had grown
Ethereal for pleasure; 'bove his head
Flew a delight half-graspable; his tread
Was Hesperean; to his capable ears
Silence was music from the holy spheres;
A dewy luxury was in his eyes;
The little flowers felt his pleasant sighs
And stirr'd them faintly. Verdant cave and cell
He wander'd through, oft wondering at such swell
Of sudden exaltation: but, "Alas!
Said he, "will all this gush of feeling pass
Away in solitude? And must they wane,
Like melodies upon a sandy plain,
Without an echo? Then shall I be left
So sad, so melancholy, so bereft!
Yet still I feel immortal! O my love,
My breath of life, where art thou? High above,
Dancing before the morning gates of heaven?
Or keeping watch among those starry seven,
Old Atlas' children? Art a maid of the waters,
One of shell-winding Triton's bright-hair'd daughters?
Or art, impossible! a nymph of Dian's,
Weaving a coronal of tender scions
For very idleness? Where'er thou art,
Methinks it now is at my will to start
Into thine arms; to scare Aurora's train,
And snatch thee from the morning; o'er the main
To scud like a wild bird, and take thee off
From thy sea-foamy cradle; or to doff
Thy shepherd vest, and woo thee mid fresh leaves.

No, no, too eagerly my soul deceives
Its powerless self: I know this cannot be.
O let me then by some sweet dreaming flee
To her entrancements: hither sleep awhile!
Hither most gentle sleep! and soothing foil
For some few hours the coming solitude."

Thus spake he, and that moment felt endued
With power to dream deliciously; so wound
Through a dim passage, searching till he found
The smoothest mossy bed and deepest, where
He threw himself, and just into the air
Stretching his indolent arms, he took, O bliss!
A naked waist: "Fair Cupid, whence is this?"
A well-known voice sigh'd, "Sweetest, here am I!"
At which soft ravishment, with doating cry
They trembled to each other.—Helicon!
O fountain'd hill! Old Homer's Helicon!
That thou wouldst spout a little streamlet o'er
These sorry pages; then the verse would soar
And sing above this gentle pair, like lark
Over his nested young: but all is dark
Around thine agèd top, and thy clear fount
Exhales in mists to heaven. Aye, the count
Of mighty Poets is made up; the scroll
Is folded by the Muses; the bright roll
Is in Apollo's hand: our dazèd eyes
Have seen a new tinge in the western skies:
The world has done its duty. Yet, oh yet,
Although the sun of poesy is set,
These lovers did embrace, and we must weep
That there is no old power left to steep
A quill immortal in their joyous tears.
Long time in silence did their anxious fears
Question that thus it was; long time they lay
Fondling and kissing every doubt away;
Long time ere soft caressing sobs began
To mellow into words, and then there ran
Two bubbling springs of talk from their sweet lips.
"O known Unknown! from whom my being sips
Such darling essence, wherefore may I not
Be ever in these arms? in this sweet spot
Pillow my chin for ever? ever press
These toying hands and kiss their smooth excess?
Why not for ever and for ever feel

That breath about my eyes? Ah, thou wilt steal
Away from me again, indeed, indeed—
Thou wilt be gone away, and wilt not heed
My lonely madness. Speak, my kindest fair!
Is—is it to be so? No! Who will dare
To pluck thee from me? And, of thine own will,
Full well I feel thou wouldst not leave me. Still
Let me entwine thee surer, surer—now
How can we part? Elysium! who art thou?
Who, that thou canst not be for ever here,
Or lift me with thee to some starry sphere?
Enchantress! tell me by this soft embrace,
By the most soft completion of thy face,
Those lips, O slippery blisses, twinkling eyes,
And by these tenderest, milky sovereignties—
These tenderest, and by the nectar-wine,
The passion"—"O lov'd Ida the divine!
Endymion! dearest! Ah, unhappy me!
His soul will 'scape us—O felicity!
How he does love me! His poor temples beat
To the very tune of love—how sweet, sweet, sweet.
Revive, dear youth, or I shall faint and die;
Revive, or these soft hours will hurry by
In trancèd dulness; speak, and let that spell
Affright this lethargy! I cannot quell
Its heavy pressure, and will press at least
My lips to thine, that they may richly feast
Until we taste the life of love again.
What! dost thou move? dost kiss? O bliss! O pain!
I love thee, youth, more than I can conceive;
And so long absence from thee doth bereave
My soul of any rest: yet must I hence:
Yet, can I not to starry eminence
Uplift thee; nor for very shame can own
Myself to thee. Ah, dearest, do not groan
Or thou wilt force me from this secrecy,
And I must blush in heaven. O that I
Had done it already; that the dreadful smiles
At my lost brightness, my impassion'd wiles,
Had wanèd from Olympus' solemn height,
And from all serious Gods; that our delight
Was quite forgotten, save of us alone!
And wherefore so ashamed? 'Tis but to atone
For endless pleasure, by some coward blushes:
Yet must I be a coward!—Honour rushes

Too palpable before me—the sad look
Of Jove—Minerva's start—no bosom shook
With awe of purity—no Cupid pinion
In reverence veiled—my crystalline dominion
Half lost, and all old hymns made nullity!
But what is this to love? O I could fly
With thee into the ken of heavenly powers,
So thou wouldst thus, for many sequent hours,
Press me so sweetly. Now I swear at once
That I am wise, that Pallas is a dunce—
Perhaps her love like mine is but unknown—
O I do think that I have been alone
In chastity: yes, Pallas has been sighing,
While every eye saw me my hair uptying
With fingers cool as aspen leaves. Sweet love,
I was as vague as solitary dove,
Nor knew that nests were built. Now a soft kiss—
Aye, by that kiss, I vow an endless bliss,
An immortality of passion's thine:
Ere long I will exalt thee to the shine
Of heaven ambrosial; and we will shade
Ourselves whole summers by a river glade;
And I will tell thee stories of the sky,
And breathe thee whispers of its minstrelsy.
My happy love will overwing all bounds!
O let me melt into thee; let the sounds
Of our close voices marry at their birth;
Let us entwine hoveringly—O dearth
Of human words! roughness of mortal speech!
Lispings empyrean will I sometime teach
Thine honied tongue—lute-breathings, which I gasp
To have thee understand, now while I clasp
Thee thus, and weep for fondness—I am pain'd,
Endymion: woe! woe! is grief contain'd
In the very deeps of pleasure, my sole life?"—
Hereat, with many sobs, her gentle strife
Melted into a languor. He return'd
Entranced vows and tears.

Ye who have yearn'd
With too much passion, will here stay and pity,
For the mere sake of truth; as 'tis a ditty
Not of these days, but long ago 'twas told
By a cavern wind unto a forest old;
And then the forest told it in a dream

To a sleeping lake, whose cool and level gleam
A poet caught as he was journeying
To Phœbus' shrine; and in it he did fling
His weary limbs, bathing an hour's space,
And after, straight in that inspirèd place
He sang the story up into the air,
Giving it universal freedom. There
Has it been ever sounding for those ears
Whose tips are glowing hot. The legend cheers
Yon sentinel stars; and he who listens to it
Must surely be self-doomed or he will rue it:
For quenchless burnings come upon the heart,
Made fiercer by a fear lest any part
Should be engulfèd in the eddying wind.
As much as here is penn'd doth always find
A resting place, thus much comes clear and plain;
Anon the strange voice is upon the wane—
And 'tis but echo'd from departing sound,
That the fair visitant at last unwound
Her gentle limbs, and left the youth asleep.—
Thus the tradition of the gusty deep.

Now turn we to our former chroniclers.—
Endymion awoke, that grief of hers
Sweet paining on his ear: he sickly guess'd
How lone he was once more, and sadly press'd
His empty arms together, hung his head,
And most forlorn upon that widow'd bed
Sat silently. Love's madness he had known:
Often with more than tortured lion's groan
Moanings had burst from him; but now that rage
Had pass'd away: no longer did he wage
A rough-voic'd war against the dooming stars.
No, he had felt too much for such harsh jars:
The lyre of his soul Aeolian tun'd
Forgot all violence, and but commun'd
With melancholy thought: O he had swoon'd
Drunken from pleasure's nipple; and his love
Henceforth was dove-like.—Loth was he to move
From the imprinted couch, and when he did,
'Twas with slow, languid paces, and face hid
In muffling hands. So temper'd, out he stray'd
Half seeing visions that might have dismay'd
Alecto's serpents; ravishments more keen
Than Hermes' pipe, when anxious he did lean

Over eclipsing eyes: and at the last
It was a sounding grotto, vaulted, vast,
O'er studded with a thousand, thousand pearls,
And crimson mouthèd shells with stubborn curls,
Of every shape and size, even to the bulk
In which whales arbour close, to brood and sulk
Against an endless storm. Moreover too,
Fish-semblances, of green and azure hue,
Ready to snort their streams. In this cool wonder
Endymion sat down, and 'gan to ponder
On all his life: his youth, up to the day
When 'mid acclaim, and feasts, and garlands gay,
He stept upon his shepherd throne: the look
Of his white palace in wild forest nook,
And all the revels he had lorded there:
Each tender maiden whom he once thought fair,
With every friend and fellow-woodlander—
Pass'd like a dream before him. Then the spur
Of the old bards to mighty deeds: his plans
To nurse the golden age 'mong shepherd clans:
That wondrous night: the great Pan-festival:
His sister's sorrow; and his wanderings all,
Until into the earth's deep maw he rush'd:
Then all its buried magic, till it flush'd
High with excessive love. "And now," thought he,
"How long must I remain in jeopardy
Of blank amazements that amaze no more?
Now I have tasted her sweet soul to the core
All other depths are shallow: essences,
Once spiritual, are like muddy lees,
Meant but to fertilize my earthly root,
And make my branches lift a golden fruit
Into the bloom of heaven: other light,
Though it be quick and sharp enough to blight
The Olympian eagle's vision, is dark,
Dark as the parentage of chaos. Hark!
My silent thoughts are echoing from these shells;
Or they are but the ghosts, the dying swells
Of noises far away?—list!"—Hereupon
He kept an anxious ear. The humming tone
Came louder, and behold, there as he lay,
On either side outgush'd, with misty spray,
A copious spring; and both together dash'd
Swift, mad, fantastic round the rocks, and lash'd
Among the conchs and shells of the lofty grot,

Leaving a trickling dew. At last they shot
Down from the ceiling's height, pouring a noise
As of some breathless racers whose hopes poize
Upon the last few steps, and with spent force
Along the ground they took a winding course.
Endymion follow'd—for it seem'd that one
Ever pursued, the other strove to shun—
Follow'd their languid mazes, till well nigh
He had left thinking of the mystery,—
And was now rapt in tender hoverings
Over the vanish'd bliss. Ah! what is it sings
His dream away? What melodies are these?
They sound as through the whispering of trees,
Not native in such barren vaults. Give ear!

"O Arethusa, peerless nymph! why fear
Such tenderness as mine? Great Dian, why,
Why didst thou hear her prayer? O that I
Were rippling round her dainty fairness now,
Circling about her waist, and striving how
To entice her to a dive! then stealing in
Between her luscious lips and eyelids thin.
O that her shining hair was in the sun,
And I distilling from it thence to run
In amorous rillets down her shrinking form!
To linger on her lily shoulders, warm
Between her kissing breasts, and every charm
Touch raptur'd!—See how painfully I flow:
Fair maid, be pitiful to my great woe.
Stay, stay thy weary course, and let me lead,
A happy wooer, to the flowery mead
Where all that beauty snar'd me."—"Cruel god,
Desist! or my offended mistress' nod
Will stagnate all thy fountains:—tease me not
With syren words—Ah, have I really got
Such power to madden thee? And is it true—
Away, away, or I shall dearly rue
My very thoughts: in mercy then away,
Kindest Alpheus, for should I obey
My own dear will, 'twould be a deadly bane."—
"O, Oread-Queen! would that thou hadst a pain
Like this of mine, then would I fearless turn
And be a criminal."—"Alas, I burn,
I shudder—gentle river, get thee hence.
Alpheus! thou enchanter! every sense

Of mine was once made perfect in these woods.
Fresh breezes, bowery lawns, and innocent floods,
Ripe fruits, and lonely couch, contentment gave;
But ever since I heedlessly did lave
In thy deceitful stream, a panting glow
Grew strong within me: wherefore serve me so,
And call it love? Alas, 'twas cruelty.
Not once more did I close my happy eyes
Amid the thrush's song. Away! Avaunt!
O 'twas a cruel thing."—"Now thou dost taunt
So softly, Arethusa, that I think
If thou wast playing on my shady brink,
Thou wouldst bathe once again. Innocent maid!
Stifle thine heart no more:—nor be afraid
Of angry powers: there are deities
Will shade us with their wings. Those fitful sighs
'Tis almost death to hear: O let me pour
A dewy balm upon them!—fear no more,
Sweet Arethusa! Dian's self must feel
Sometimes these very pangs. Dear maiden, steal
Blushing into my soul, and let us fly
These dreary caverns for the open sky.
I will delight thee all my winding course,
From the green sea up to my hidden source
About Arcadian forests; and will shew
The channels where my coolest waters flow
Through mossy rocks; where, 'mid exuberant green,
I roam in pleasant darkness, more unseen
Than Saturn in his exile; where I brim
Round flowery islands, and take thence a skim
Of mealy sweets, which myriads of bees
Buzz from their honied wings: and thou shouldst please
Thyself to choose the richest, where we might
Be incense-pillow'd every summer night.
Doff all sad fears, thou white deliciousness,
And let us be thus comforted; unless
Thou couldst rejoice to see my hopeless stream
Hurry distracted from Sol's temperate beam,
And pour to death along some hungry sands."—
"What can I do, Alpheus? Dian stands
Severe before me: persecuting fate!
Unhappy Arethusa! thou wast late
A huntress free in"—At this, sudden fell
Those two sad streams adown a fearful dell.
The Latmian listen'd, but he heard no more,

Save echo, faint repeating o'er and o'er
The name of Arethusa. On the verge
Of that dark gulph he wept, and said: "I urge
Thee, gentle Goddess of my pilgrimage,
By our eternal hopes, to soothe, to assuage,
If thou art powerful, these lovers pains;
And make them happy in some happy plains.

He turn'd—there was a whelming sound—he stept,
There was a cooler light; and so he kept
Towards it by a sandy path, and lo!
More suddenly than doth a moment go,
The visions of the earth were gone and fled—
He saw the giant sea above his head.

BOOK III

There are who lord it o'er their fellow-men
With most prevailing tinsel: who unpen
Their baaing vanities, to browse away
The comfortable green and juicy hay
From human pastures; or, O torturing fact!
Who, through an idiot blink, will see unpack'd
Fire-branded foxes to sear up and singe
Our gold and ripe-ear'd hopes. With not one tinge
Of sanctuary splendour, not a sight
Able to face an owl's, they still are dight
By the blear-eyed nations in empurpled vests,
And crowns, and turbans. With unladen breasts,
Save of blown self-applause, they proudly mount
To their spirit's perch, their being's high account,
Their tiptop nothings, their dull skies, their thrones—
Amid the fierce intoxicating tones
Of trumpets, shoutings, and belabour'd drums,
And sudden cannon. All! how all this hums,
In wakeful ears, like uproar past and gone—
Like thunder clouds that spake to Babylon,
And set those old Chaldeans to their tasks.—
Are then regalities all gilded masks?
No, there are thronèd seats unscalable
But by a patient wing, a constant spell,
Or by ethereal things that, unconfin'd,
Can make a ladder of the eternal wind,
And poise about in cloudy thunder-tents
To watch the abysm-birth of elements.

Aye, 'bove the withering of old-lipp'd Fate
A thousand Powers keep religious state,
In water, fiery realm, and airy bourne;
And, silent as a consecrated urn,
Hold sphery sessions for a season due.
Yet few of these far majesties, ah, few!
Have bared their operations to this globe—
Few, who with gorgeous pageantry enrobe
Our piece of heaven—whose benevolence
Shakes hand with our own Ceres; every sense
Filling with spiritual sweets to plenitude,
As bees gorge full their cells. And, by the feud
'Twixt Nothing and Creation, I here swear,
Eterne Apollo! that thy Sister fair
Is of all these the gentlier-mightiest.
When thy gold breath is misting in the west,
She unobservèd steals unto her throne,
And there she sits most meek and most alone;
As if she had not pomp subservient;
As if thine eye, high Poet! was not bent
Towards her with the Muses in thine heart;
As if the ministring stars kept not apart,
Waiting for silver-footed messages.
O Moon! the oldest shades 'mong oldest trees
Feel palpitations when thou lookest in:
O Moon! old boughs lisp forth a holier din
The while they feel thine airy fellowship.
Thou dost bless every where, with silver lip
Kissing dead things to life. The sleeping kine,
Couched in thy brightness, dream of fields divine:
Innumerable mountains rise, and rise,
Ambitious for the hallowing of thine eyes;
And yet thy benediction passeth not
One obscure hiding-place, one little spot
Where pleasure may be sent: the nested wren
Has thy fair face within its tranquil ken,
And from beneath a sheltering ivy leaf
Takes glimpses of thee; thou art a relief
To the poor patient oyster, where it sleeps
Within its pearly house.—The mighty deeps,
The monstrous sea is thine—the myriad sea!
O Moon! far-spooming Ocean bows to thee,
And Tellus feels his forehead's cumbrous load.

Cynthia! where art thou now? What far abode
Of green or silvery bower doth enshrine
Such utmost beauty? Alas, thou dost pine
For one as sorrowful: thy cheek is pale
For one whose cheek is pale: thou dost bewail
His tears, who weeps for thee. Where dost thou sigh?
Ah! surely that light peeps from Vesper's eye,
Or what a thing is love! 'Tis She, but lo!
How chang'd, how full of ache, how gone in woe!
She dies at the thinnest cloud; her loveliness
Is wan on Neptune's blue: yet there's a stress
Of love-spangles, just off yon cape of trees,
Dancing upon the waves, as if to please
The curly foam with amorous influence.
O, not so idle: for down-glancing thence
She fathoms eddies, and runs wild about
O'erwhelming water-courses; scaring out
The thorny sharks from hiding-holes, and fright'ning
Their savage eyes with unaccustomed lightning.
Where will the splendor be content to reach?
O love! how potent hast thou been to teach
Strange journeyings! Wherever beauty dwells,
In gulf or aerie, mountains or deep dells,
In light, in gloom, in star or blazing sun,
Thou pointest out the way, and straight 'tis won.
Amid his toil thou gav'st Leander breath;
Thou leddest Orpheus through the gleams of death;
Thou madest Pluto bear thin element;
And now, O wingèd Chieftain! them hast sent
A moon-beam to the deep, deep water-world,
To find Endymion.
On gold sand impearl'd
With lily shells, and pebbles milky white,
Poor Cynthia greeted him, and sooth'd her light
Against his pallid face: he felt the charm
To breathlessness, and suddenly a warm
Of his heart's blood: 'twas very sweet; he stay'd
His wandering steps, and half-entranced laid
His head upon a tuft of straggling weeds,
To taste the gentle moon, and freshening beads,
Lashed from the crystal roof by fishes' tails.
And so he kept, until the rosy veils
Mantling the east, by Aurora's peering hand
Were lifted from the water's breast, and faun'd

Into sweet air; and sober'd morning came
Meekly through billows:—when like taper-flame
Left sudden by a dallying breath of air,
He rose in silence, and once more 'gan fare
Along his fated way.
                                        Far had he roam'd,
With nothing save the hollow vast, that foam'd
Above, around, and at his feet; save things
More dead than Morpheus' imaginings:
Old rusted anchors, helmets, breast-plates large
Of gone sea-warriors; brazen beaks and targe;
Rudders that for a hundred years had lost
The sway of human hand; gold vase emboss'd
With long-forgotten story, and wherein
No reveller had ever dipp'd a chin
But those of Saturn's vintage; mouldering scrolls,
Writ in the tongue of heaven, by those souls
Who first were on the earth; and sculptures rude
In ponderous stone, developing the mood
Of ancient Nox;—then skeletons of man,
Of beast, behemoth, and leviathan,
And elephant, and eagle, and huge jaw
Of nameless monster. A cold leaden awe
These secrets struck into him; and unless
Dian had chaced away that heaviness,
He might have died: but now, with cheered feel,
He onward kept; wooing these thoughts to steal
About the labyrinth in his soul of love.

"What is there in thee, Moon! that thou shouldst move
My heart so potently? When yet a child
I oft have dried my tears when thou hast smil'd.
Thou seem'dst my sister: hand in hand we went
From eve to morn across the firmament.
No apples would I gather from the tree,
Till thou hadst cool'd their cheeks deliciously:
No tumbling water ever spake romance,
But when my eyes with thine thereon could dance:
No woods were green enough, no bower divine,
Until thou liftedst up thine eyelids fine:
In sowing time ne'er would I dibble take,
Or drop a seed, till thou wast wide awake;
And, in the summer tide of blossoming,
No one but thee hath heard me blithly sing
And mesh my dewy flowers all the night.

No melody was like a passing spright
If it went not to solemnize thy reign.
Yes, in my boyhood, every joy and pain
By thee were fashion'd to the self-same end;
And as I grew in years, still didst thou blend
With all my ardours: thou wast the deep glen;
Thou wast the mountain-top—the sage's pen—
The poet's harp—the voice of friends—the sun;
Thou wast the river—thou wast glory won;
Thou wast my clarion's blast—thou wast my steed—
My goblet full of wine—my topmost deed:—
Thou wast the charm of women, lovely Moon!
O what a wild and harmonizèd tune
My spirit struck from all the beautiful!
On some bright essence could I lean, and lull
Myself to immortality: I prest
Nature's soft pillow in a wakeful rest.
But, gentle Orb! there came a nearer bliss—
My strange love came—Felicity's abyss!
She came, and thou didst fade, and fade away—
Yet not entirely; no, thy starry sway
Has been an under-passion to this hour.
Now I begin to feel thine orby power
Is coming fresh upon me: O be kind,
Keep back thine influence, and do not blind
My sovereign vision.—Dearest love, forgive
That I can think away from thee and live!—
Pardon me, airy planet, that I prize
One thought beyond thine argent luxuries!
How far beyond!" At this a surpris'd start
Frosted the springing verdure of his heart;
For as he lifted up his eyes to swear
How his own goddess was past all things fair,
He saw far in the concave green of the sea
An old man sitting calm and peacefully.
Upon a weeded rock this old man sat,
And his white hair was awful, and a mat
Of weeds were cold beneath his cold thin feet;
And, ample as the largest winding-sheet,
A cloak of blue wrapp'd up his agèd bones,
O'erwrought with symbols by the deepest groans
Of ambitious magic: every ocean-form
Was woven in with black distinctness; storm,
And calm, and whispering, and hideous roar
Were emblem'd in the woof; with every shape

That skims, or dives, or sleeps, 'twixt cape and cape.
The gulphing whale was like a dot in the spell,
Yet look upon it, and 'twould size and swell
To its huge self; and the minutest fish
Would pass the very hardest gazer's wish,
And shew his little eye's anatomy.
Then there was pictur'd the regality
Of Neptune; and the sea nymphs round his state,
In beauteous vassalage, look up and wait.
Beside this old man lay a pearly wand,
And in his lap a book, the which he conn'd
So stedfastly, that the new denizen
Had time to keep him in amazèd ken,
To mark these shadowings, and stand in awe.
The old man rais'd his hoary head and saw
The wilder'd stranger—seeming not to see,
His features were so lifeless. Suddenly
He woke as from a trance; his snow-white brows
Went arching up, and like two magic ploughs
Furrow'd deep wrinkles in his forehead large,
Which kept as fixedly as rocky marge,
Till round his wither'd lips had gone a smile.
Then up he rose, like one whose tedious toil
Had watch'd for years in forlorn hermitage,
Who had not from mid-life to utmost age
Eas'd in one accent his o'er-burden'd soul,
Even to the trees. He rose: he grasp'd his stole,
With convuls'd clenches waving it abroad,
And in a voice of solemn joy, that aw'd
Echo into oblivion, he said:—

"Thou art the man! Now shall I lay my head
In peace upon my watery pillow: now
Sleep will come smoothly to my weary brow.
O Jove! I shall be young again, be young!
O shell-borne Neptune, I am pierc'd and stung
With new-born life! What shall I do? Where go,
When I have cast this serpent-skin of woe?—
I'll swim to the syrens, and one moment listen
Their melodies, and see their long hair glisten;
Anon upon that giant's arm I'll be,
That writhes about the roots of Sicily:
To northern seas I'll in a twinkling sail,
And mount upon the snortings of a whale
To some black cloud; thence down I'll madly sweep

On forkèd lightning, to the deepest deep,
Where through some sucking pool I will be hurl'd
With rapture to the other side of the world!
O, I am full of gladness! Sisters three,
I bow full hearted to your old decree!
Yes, every god be thank'd, and power benign,
For I no more shall wither, droop, and pine.
Thou art the man!" Endymion started back
Dismay'd; and, like a wretch from whom the rack
Tortures hot breath, and speech of agony,
Mutter'd: "What lonely death am I to die
In this cold region? Will he let me freeze,
And float my brittle limbs o'er polar seas?
Or will he touch me with his searing hand,
And leave a black memorial on the sand?
Or tear me piece-meal with a bony saw,
And keep me as a chosen food to draw
His magian fish through hated fire and flame?
O misery of hell! resistless, tame,
Am I to be burnt up? No, I will shout,
Until the gods through heaven's blue look out!—
O Tartarus! but some few days agone
Her soft arms were entwining me, and on
Her voice I hung like fruit among green leaves:
Her lips were all my own, and—ah, ripe sheaves
Of happiness! ye on the stubble droop,
But never may be garner'd. I must stoop
My head, and kiss death's foot. Love! love, farewel!
Is there no hope from thee? This horrid spell
Would melt at thy sweet breath.—By Dian's hind
Feeding from her white fingers, on the wind
I see thy streaming hair! and now, by Pan,
I care not for this old mysterious man!"

He spake, and walking to that agèd form,
Look'd high defiance. Lo! his heart 'gan warm
With pity, for the grey-hair'd creature wept.
Had he then wrong'd a heart where sorrow kept?
Had he, though blindly contumelious, brought
Rheum to kind eyes, a sting to human thought,
Convulsion to a mouth of many years?
He had in truth; and he was ripe for tears.
The penitent shower fell, as down he knelt
Before that care-worn sage, who trembling felt
About his large dark locks, and faultering spake:

"Arise, good youth, for sacred Phœbus' sake!
I know thine inmost bosom, and I feel
A very brother's yearning for thee steal
Into mine own: for why? thou openest
The prison gates that have so long opprest
My weary watching. Though thou know'st it not,
Thou art commission'd to this fated spot
For great enfranchisement. O weep no more;
I am a friend to love, to loves of yore:
Aye, hadst thou never lov'd an unknown power,
I had been grieving at this joyous hour.
But even now most miserable old,
I saw thee, and my blood no longer cold
Gave mighty pulses: in this tottering case
Grew a new heart, which at this moment plays
As dancingly as thine. Be not afraid,
For thou shalt hear this secret all display'd,
Now as we speed towards our joyous task."

So saying, this young soul in age's mask
Went forward with the Carian side by side:
Resuming quickly thus; while ocean's tide
Hung swollen at their backs, and jewel'd sands
Took silently their foot-prints:

"My soul stands
Now past the midway from mortality,
And so I can prepare without a sigh
To tell thee briefly all my joy and pain.
I was a fisher once, upon this main,
And my boat danc'd in every creek and bay;
Rough billows were my home by night and day,—
The sea-gulls not more constant; for I had
No housing from the storm and tempests mad,
But hollow rocks,—and they were palaces
Of silent happiness, of slumberous ease:
Long years of misery have told me so.
Aye, thus it was one thousand years ago.
One thousand years!—Is it then possible
To look so plainly through them? to dispel
A thousand years with backward glance sublime?
To breathe away as 'twere all scummy slime
From off a crystal pool, to see its deep,
And one's own image from the bottom peep?
Yes: now I am no longer wretched thrall,

My long captivity and moanings all
Are but a slime, a thin-pervading scum,
The which I breathe away, and thronging come
Like things of yesterday my youthful pleasures.

"I touch'd no lute, I sang not, trod no measures:
I was a lonely youth on desert shores.
My sports were lonely, 'mid continuous roars,
And craggy isles, and sea-mew's plaintive cry
Plaining discrepant between sea and sky.
Dolphins were still my playmates; shapes unseen
Would let me feel their scales of gold and green,
Nor be my desolation; and, full oft,
When a dread waterspout had rear'd aloft
Its hungry hugeness, seeming ready ripe
To burst with hoarsest thunderings, and wipe
My life away like a vast sponge of fate,
Some friendly monster, pitying my sad state,
Has dived to its foundations, gulph'd it down,
And left me tossing safely. But the crown
Of all my life was utmost quietude:
More did I love to lie in cavern rude,
Keeping in wait whole days for Neptune's voice,
And if it came at last, hark, and rejoice!
There blush'd no summer eve but I would steer
My skiff along green shelving coasts, to hear
The shepherd's pipe come clear from aery steep,
Mingled with ceaseless bleatings of his sheep:
And never was a day of summer shine,
But I beheld its birth upon the brine:
For I would watch all night to see unfold
Heaven's gates, and Æthon snort his morning gold
Wide o'er the swelling streams: and constantly
At brim of day-tide, on some grassy lea,
My nets would be spread out, and I at rest.
The poor folk of the sea-country I blest
With daily boon of fish most delicate:
They knew not whence this bounty, and elate
Would strew sweet flowers on a sterile beach.

"Why was I not contented? Wherefore reach
At things which, but for thee, O Latmian!
Had been my dreary death? Fool! I began
To feel distemper'd longings: to desire
The utmost privilege that ocean's sire

Could grant in benediction: to be free
Of all his kingdom. Long in misery
I wasted, ere in one extremest fit
I plung'd for life or death. To interknit
One's senses with so dense a breathing stuff
Might seem a work of pain; so not enough
Can I admire how crystal-smooth it felt,
And buoyant round my limbs. At first I dwelt
Whole days and days in sheer astonishment;
Forgetful utterly of self-intent;
Moving but with the mighty ebb and flow.
Then, like a new fledg'd bird that first doth shew
His spreaded feathers to the morrow chill,
I tried in fear the pinions of my will.
'Twas freedom! and at once I visited
The ceaseless wonders of this ocean-bed.
No need to tell thee of them, for I see
That thou hast been a witness—it must be—
For these I know thou canst not feel a drouth,
By the melancholy corners of that mouth.
So I will in my story straightway pass
To more immediate matter. Woe, alas!
That love should be my bane! Ah, Scylla fair!
Why did poor Glaucus ever—ever dare
To sue thee to his heart? Kind stranger-youth!
I lov'd her to the very white of truth,
And she would not conceive it. Timid thing!
She fled me swift as sea-bird on the wing,
Round every isle, and point, and promontory,
From where large Hercules wound up his story
Far as Egyptian Nile. My passion grew
The more, the more I saw her dainty hue
Gleam delicately through the azure clear:
Until 'twas too fierce agony to bear;
And in that agony, across my grief
It flash'd, that Circe might find some relief—
Cruel enchantress! So above the water
I rear'd my head, and look'd for Phœbus' daughter.
Ææa's isle was wondering at the moon:—
It seem'd to whirl around me, and a swoon
Left me dead-drifting to that fatal power.

"When I awoke, 'twas in a twilight bower;
Just when the light of morn, with hum of bees,
Stole through its verdurous matting of fresh trees.

How sweet, and sweeter! for I heard a lyre,
And over it a sighing voice expire.
It ceased—I caught light footsteps; and anon
The fairest face that morn e'er look'd upon
Push'd through a screen of roses. Starry Jove!
With tears, and smiles, and honey-words she wove
A net whose thraldom was more bliss than all
The range of flower'd Elysium. Thus did fall
The dew of her rich speech: "Ah! Art awake?
O let me hear thee speak, for Cupid's sake!
I am so oppress'd with joy! Why, I have shed
An urn of tears, as though thou wert cold dead;
And now I find thee living, I will pour
From these devoted eyes their silver store,
Until exhausted of the latest drop,
So it will pleasure thee, and force thee stop
Here, that I too may live: but if beyond
Such cool and sorrowful offerings, thou art fond
Of soothing warmth, of dalliance supreme;
If thou art ripe to taste a long love dream;
If smiles, if dimples, tongues for ardour mute,
Hang in thy vision like a tempting fruit,
O let me pluck it for thee." Thus she link'd
Her charming syllables, till indistinct
Their music came to my o'er-sweeten'd soul;
And then she hover'd over me, and stole
So near, that if no nearer it had been
This furrow'd visage thou hadst never seen.

"Young man of Latmos! thus particular
Am I, that thou may'st plainly see how far
This fierce temptation went: and thou may'st not
Exclaim, How then, was Scylla quite forgot?

"Who could resist? Who in this universe?
She did so breathe ambrosia; so immerse
My fine existence in a golden clime.
She took me like a child of suckling time,
And cradled me in roses. Thus condemn'd,
The current of my former life was stemm'd,
And to this arbitrary queen of sense
I bow'd a trancèd vassal: nor would thence
Have mov'd, even though Amphion's harp had woo'd
Me back to Scylla o'er the billows rude.
For as Apollo each eve doth devise

A new appareling for western skies;
So every eve, nay every spendthrift hour
Shed balmy consciousness within that bower.
And I was free of haunts umbrageous;
Could wander in the mazy forest-house
Of squirrels, foxes shy, and antler'd deer,
And birds from coverts innermost and drear
Warbling for very joy mellifluous sorrow—
To me new born delights!

"Now let me borrow,
For moments few, a temperament as stern
As Pluto's sceptre, that my words not burn
These uttering lips, while I in calm speech tell
How specious heaven was changed to real hell.

"One morn she left me sleeping: half awake
I sought for her smooth arms and lips, to slake
My greedy thirst with nectarous camel-draughts;
But she was gone. Whereat the barbèd shafts
Of disappointment stuck in me so sore,
That out I ran and search'd the forest o'er.
Wandering about in pine and cedar gloom
Damp awe assail'd me; for there 'gan to boom
A sound of moan, an agony of sound,
Sepulchral from the distance all around.
Then came a conquering earth-thunder, and rumbled
That fierce complain to silence: while I stumbled
Down a precipitous path, as if impell'd.
I came to a dark valley.—Groanings swell'd
Poisonous about my ears, and louder grew,
The nearer I approach'd a flame's gaunt blue,
That glar'd before me through a thorny brake.
This fire, like the eye of gordian snake,
Bewitch'd me towards; and I soon was near
A sight too fearful for the feel of fear:
In thicket hid I curs'd the haggard scene—
The banquet of my arms, my arbour queen,
Seated upon an uptorn forest root;
And all around her shapes, wizard and brute,
Laughing, and wailing, groveling, serpenting,
Shewing tooth, tusk, and venom-bag, and sting!
O such deformities! Old Charon's self,
Should he give up awhile his penny pelf,
And take a dream 'mong rushes Stygian,

It could not be so phantasied. Fierce, wan,
And tyrannizing was the lady's look,
As over them a gnarled staff she shook.
Oft-times upon the sudden she laugh'd out,
And from a basket emptied to the rout
Clusters of grapes, the which they raven'd quick
And roar'd for more; with many a hungry lick
About their shaggy jaws. Avenging, slow,
Anon she took a branch of mistletoe,
And emptied on't a black dull-gurgling phial:
Groan'd one and all, as if some piercing trial
Was sharpening for their pitiable bones.
She lifted up the charm: appealing groans
From their poor breasts went sueing to her ear
In vain; remorseless as an infant's bier
She whisk'd against their eyes the sooty oil.
Whereat was heard a noise of painful toil,
Increasing gradual to a tempest rage,
Shrieks, yells, and groans of torture-pilgrimage;
Until their grievèd bodies 'gan to bloat
And puff from the tail's end to stifled throat:
Then was appalling silence: then a sight
More wildering than all that hoarse affright;
For the whole herd, as by a whirlwind writhen,
Went through the dismal air like one huge Python
Antagonizing Boreas,—and so vanish'd.
Yet there was not a breath of wind: she banish'd
These phantoms with a nod. Lo! from the dark
Came waggish fauns, and nymphs, and satyrs stark,
With dancing and loud revelry,—and went
Swifter than centaurs after rapine bent.—
Sighing an elephant appear'd and bow'd
Before the fierce witch, speaking thus aloud
In human accent: "Potent goddess! chief
Of pains resistless! make my being brief,
Or let me from this heavy prison fly:
Or give me to the air, or let me die!
I sue not for my happy crown again;
I sue not for my phalanx on the plain;
I sue not for my lone, my widow'd wife;
I sue not for my ruddy drops of life,
My children fair, my lovely girls and boys!
I will forget them; I will pass these joys;
Ask nought so heavenward, so too—too high:
Only I pray, as fairest boon, to die,

Or be deliver'd from this cumbrous flesh,
From this gross, detestable, filthy mesh,
And merely given to the cold bleak air.
Have mercy, Goddess! Circe, feel my prayer!"

"That curst magician's name fell icy numb
Upon my wild conjecturing: truth had come
Naked and sabre-like against my heart.
I saw a fury whetting a death-dart;
And my slain spirit, overwrought with fright,
Fainted away in that dark lair of night.
Think, my deliverer, how desolate
My waking must have been! disgust, and hate,
And terrors manifold divided me
A spoil amongst them. I prepar'd to flee
Into the dungeon core of that wild wood:
I fled three days—when lo! before me stood
Glaring the angry witch. O Dis, even now,
A clammy dew is beading on my brow,
At mere remembering her pale laugh, and curse.
'Ha! ha! Sir Dainty! there must be a nurse
Made of rose leaves and thistledown, express,
To cradle thee my sweet, and lull thee: yes,
I am too flinty-hard for thy nice touch:
My tenderest squeeze is but a giant's clutch.
So, fairy-thing, it shall have lullabies
Unheard of yet; and it shall still its cries
Upon some breast more lily-feminine.
Oh, no—it shall not pine, and pine, and pine
More than one pretty, trifling thousand years;
And then 'twere pity, but fate's gentle shears
Cut short its immortality. Sea-flirt!
Young dove of the waters! truly I'll not hurt
One hair of thine: see how I weep and sigh,
That our heart-broken parting is so nigh.
And must we part? Ah, yes, it must be so.
Yet ere thou leavest me in utter woe,
Let me sob over thee my last adieus,
And speak a blessing: Mark me! Thou hast thews
Immortal, for thou art of heavenly race:
But such a love is mine, that here I chase
Eternally away from thee all bloom
Of youth, and destine thee towards a tomb.
Hence shalt thou quickly to the watery vast;
And there, ere many days be overpast,

Disabled age shall seize thee; and even then
Thou shalt not go the way of agèd men;
But live and wither, cripple and still breathe
Ten hundred years: which gone, I then bequeath
Thy fragile bones to unknown burial.
Adieu, sweet love, adieu!'—As shot stars fall,
She fled ere I could groan for mercy. Stung
And poisoned was my spirit: despair sung
A war-song of defiance 'gainst all hell.
A hand was at my shoulder to compel
My sullen steps; another 'fore my eyes
Moved on with pointed finger. In this guise
Enforcèd, at the last by ocean's foam
I found me; by my fresh, my native home.
Its tempering coolness, to my life akin,
Came salutary as I waded in;
And, with a blind voluptuous rage, I gave
Battle to the swollen billow-ridge, and drave
Large froth before me, while there yet remain'd
Hale strength, nor from my bones all marrow drain'd.

"Young lover, I must weep—such hellish spite
With dry cheek who can tell? While thus my might
Proving upon this element, dismay'd,
Upon a dead thing's face my hand I laid;
I look'd—'twas Scylla! Cursèd, cursèd Circe!
O vulture-witch, hast never heard of mercy?
Could not thy harshest vengeance be content,
But thou must nip this tender innocent
Because I lov'd her?—Cold, O cold indeed
Were her fair limbs, and like a common weed
The sea-swell took her hair. Dead as she was
I clung about her waist, nor ceas'd to pass
Fleet as an arrow through unfathom'd brine,
Until there shone a fabric crystalline,
Ribb'd and inlaid with coral, pebble, and pearl.
Headlong I darted; at one eager swirl
Gain'd its bright portal, enter'd, and behold!
'Twas vast, and desolate, and icy-cold;
And all around—But wherefore this to thee
Who in few minutes more thyself shalt see?—
I left poor Scylla in a niche and fled.
My fever'd parchings up, my scathing dread
Met palsy half way: soon these limbs became
Gaunt, wither'd, sapless, feeble, cramp'd, and lame.

"Now let me pass a cruel, cruel space,
Without one hope, without one faintest trace
Of mitigation, or redeeming bubble
Of colour'd phantasy; for I fear 'twould trouble
Thy brain to loss of reason: and next tell
How a restoring chance came down to quell
One half of the witch in me.

"On a day,
Sitting upon a rock above the spray,
I saw grow up from the horizon's brink
A gallant vessel: soon she seem'd to sink
Away from me again, as though her course
Had been resum'd in spite of hindering force—
So vanish'd: and not long, before arose
Dark clouds, and muttering of winds morose.
Old Eolus would stifle his mad spleen,
But could not: therefore all the billows green
Toss'd up the silver spume against the clouds.
The tempest came: I saw that vessel's shrouds
In perilous bustle; while upon the deck
Stood trembling creatures. I beheld the wreck;
The final gulphing; the poor struggling souls:
I heard their cries amid loud thunder-rolls.
O they had all been sav'd but crazèd eld
Annull'd my vigorous cravings: and thus quell'd
And curb'd, think on't, O Latmian! did I sit
Writhing with pity, and a cursing fit
Against that hell-born Circe. The crew had gone,
By one and one, to pale oblivion;
And I was gazing on the surges prone,
With many a scalding tear and many a groan,
When at my feet emerg'd an old man's hand,
Grasping this scroll, and this same slender wand.
I knelt with pain—reached out my hand—had grasp'd
These treasures—touch'd the knuckles—they unclasp'd—
I caught a finger: but the downward weight
O'erpowered me—it sank. Then 'gan abate
The storm, and through chill aguish gloom outburst
The comfortable sun. I was athirst
To search the book, and in the warming air
Parted its dripping leaves with eager care.
Strange matters did it treat of, and drew on
My soul page after page, till well-nigh won

Into forgetfulness; when, stupefied,
I read these words, and read again, and tried
My eyes against the heavens, and read again.
O what a load of misery and pain
Each Atlas-line bore off!—a shine of hope
Came gold around me, cheering me to cope
Strenuous with hellish tyranny. Attend!
For thou hast brought their promise to an end.

"*In the wide sea there lives a forlorn wretch,*
Doom'd with enfeeblèd carcase to outstretch
His loath'd existence through ten centuries,
And then to die alone. Who can devise
A total opposition? No one. So
One million times ocean must ebb and flow,
And he oppressèd. Yet he shall not die,
These things accomplish'd:—If he utterly
Scans all the depths of magic, and expounds
The meanings of all motions, shapes, and sounds;
If he explores all forms and substances
Straight homeward to their symbol-essences;
He shall not die. Moreover, and in chief,
He must pursue this task of joy and grief
Most piously;—all lovers tempest-tost,
And in the savage overwhelming lost,
He shall deposit side by side, until
Time's creeping shall the dreary space fulfil:
Which done, and all these labours ripened,
A youth, by heavenly power lov'd and led,
Shall stand before him; whom he shall direct
How to consummate all. The youth elect
Must do the thing, or both will be destroy'd."

"Then," cried the young Endymion, overjoy'd,
"We are twin brothers in this destiny!
Say, I intreat thee, what achievement high
Is, in this restless world, for me reserv'd.
What! if from thee my wandering feet had swerv'd,
Had we both perish'd?"—"Look!" the sage replied,
"Dost thou not mark a gleaming through the tide,
Of divers brilliances? 'tis the edifice
I told thee of, where lovely Scylla lies;
And where I have enshrinèd piously
All lovers, whom fell storms have doom'd to die
Throughout my bondage." Thus discoursing, on

They went till unobscur'd the porches shone;
Which hurryingly they gain'd, and enter'd straight.
Sure never since king Neptune held his state
Was seen such wonder underneath the stars.
Turn to some level plain where haughty Mars
Has legion'd all his battle; and behold
How every soldier, with firm foot, doth hold
His even breast: see, many steelèd squares,
And rigid ranks of iron—whence who dares
One step? Imagine further, line by line,
These warrior thousands on the field supine:—
So in that crystal place, in silent rows,
Poor lovers lay at rest from joys and woes.—
The stranger from the mountains, breathless, trac'd
Such thousands of shut eyes in order plac'd;
Such ranges of white feet, and patient lips
All ruddy,—for here death no blossom nips.
He mark'd their brows and foreheads; saw their hair
Put sleekly on one side with nicest care;
And each one's gentle wrists, with reverence,
Put cross-wise to its heart.

"Let us commence,"
Whisper'd the guide, stuttering with joy, "even now."
He spake, and, trembling like an aspen-bough,
Began to tear his scroll in pieces small,
Uttering the while some mumblings funeral.
He tore it into pieces small as snow
That drifts unfeather'd when bleak northerns blow;
And having done it, took his dark blue cloak
And bound it round Endymion: then struck
His wand against the empty air times nine.—
"What more there is to do, young man, is thine:
But first a little patience; first undo
This tangled thread, and wind it to a clue.
Ah, gentle! 'tis as weak as spider's skein;
And shouldst thou break it—What, is it done so clean?
A power overshadows thee! Oh, brave!
The spite of hell is tumbling to its grave.
Here is a shell; 'tis pearly blank to me,
Nor mark'd with any sign or charactery—
Canst thou read aught? O read for pity's sake!
Olympus! we are safe! Now, Carian, break
This wand against yon lyre on the pedestal."

'Twas done: and straight with sudden swell and fall
Sweet music breath'd her soul away, and sigh'd
A lullaby to silence.—"Youth! now strew
These mincèd leaves on me, and passing through
Those files of dead, scatter the same around,
And thou wilt see the issue."

'Mid the sound
Of flutes and viols, ravishing his heart,
Endymion from Glaucus stood apart,
And scatter'd in his face some fragments light.
How lightning-swift the change! a youthful wight
Smiling beneath a coral diadem,
Out-sparkling sudden like an upturn'd gem,
Appear'd, and, stepping to a beauteous corse,
Kneel'd down beside it, and with tenderest force
Press'd its cold hand, and wept,—and Scylla sigh'd!
Endymion, with quick hand, the charm applied—
The nymph arose: he left them to their joy,
And onward went upon his high employ,
Showering those powerful fragments on the dead.
And, as he pass'd, each lifted up its head,
As doth a flower at Apollo's touch.
Death felt it to his inwards: 'twas too much:
Death fell a weeping in his charnel-house.
The Latmian persever'd along, and thus
All were re-animated. There arose
A noise of harmony, pulses and throes
Of gladness in the air—while many, who
Had died in mutual arms devout and true,
Sprang to each other madly; and the rest
Felt a high certainty of being blest.
They gaz'd upon Endymion. Enchantment
Grew drunken, and would have its head and bent.
Delicious symphonies, like airy flowers,
Budded, and swell'd, and, full-blown, shed full showers
Of light, soft, unseen leaves of sounds divine.
The two deliverers tasted a pure wine
Of happiness, from fairy-press ooz'd out.
Speechless they eyed each other, and about
The fair assembly wander'd to and fro,
Distracted with the richest overflow
Of joy that ever pour'd from heaven.

"Away!"
Shouted the new born god; "Follow, and pay
Our piety to Neptunus supreme!"—
Then Scylla, blushing sweetly from her dream,
They led on first, bent to her meek surprise,
Though portal columns of a giant size,
Into the vaulted, boundless emerald.
Joyous all follow'd, as the leader call'd,
Down marble steps; pouring as easily
As hour-glass sand,—and fast, as you might see
Swallows obeying the south summer's call,
Or swans upon a gentle waterfall.

Thus went that beautiful multitude, nor far,
Ere from among some rocks of glittering spar,
Just within ken, they saw descending thick
Another multitude. Whereat more quick
Moved either host. On a wide sand they met,
And of those numbers every eye was wet;
For each their old love found. A murmuring rose,
Like what was never heard in all the throes
Of wind and waters: 'tis past human wit
To tell; 'tis dizziness to think of it.

This mighty consummation made, the host
Mov'd on for many a league; and gain'd, and lost
Huge sea-marks; vanward swelling in array,
And from the rear diminishing away,—
Till a faint dawn surpris'd them. Glaucus cried,
"Behold! behold, the palace of his pride!
God Neptune's palaces!" With noise increas'd,
They shoulder'd on towards that brightening east.
At every onward step proud domes arose
In prospect,—diamond gleams, and golden glows
Of amber 'gainst their faces levelling.
Joyous, and many as the leaves in spring,
Still onward; still the splendour gradual swell'd.
Rich opal domes were seen, on high upheld
By jasper pillars, letting through their shafts
A blush of coral. Copious wonder-draughts
Each gazer drank; and deeper drank more near:
For what poor mortals fragment up, as mere
As marble was there lavish, to the vast
Of one fair palace, that far far surpass'd,

Even for common bulk, those olden three,
Memphis, and Babylon, and Nineveh.

As large, as bright, as colour'd as the bow
Of Iris, when unfading it doth shew
Beyond a silvery shower, was the arch
Through which this Paphian army took its march,
Into the outer courts of Neptune's state:
Whence could be seen, direct, a golden gate,
To which the leaders sped; but not half raught
Ere it burst open swift as fairy thought,
And made those dazzlèd thousands veil their eyes
Like callow eagles at the first sunrise.
Soon with an eagle nativeness their gaze
Ripe from hue-golden swoons took all the blaze,
And then, behold! large Neptune on his throne
Of emerald deep: yet not exalt alone;
At his right hand stood wingèd Love, and on
His left sat smiling Beauty's paragon.

Far as the mariner on highest mast
Can see all round upon the calmèd vast,
So wide was Neptune's hall: and as the blue
Doth vault the waters, so the waters drew
Their doming curtains, high, magnificent,
Aw'd from the throne aloof;—and when storm-rent
Disclos'd the thunder-gloomings in Jove's air;
But sooth'd as now, flash'd sudden everywhere,
Noiseless, sub-marine cloudlets, glittering
Death to a human eye: for there did spring
From natural west, and east, and south, and north,
A light as of four sunsets, blazing forth
A gold-green zenith 'bove the Sea-God's head.
Of lucid depth the floor, and far outspread
As breezeless lake, on which the slim canoe
Of feather'd Indian darts about, as through
The delicatest air: air verily,
But for the portraiture of clouds and sky:
This palace floor breath-air,—but for the amaze
Of deep-seen wonders motionless,—and blaze
Of the dome pomp, reflected in extremes,
Globing a golden sphere.

They stood in dreams
Till Triton blew his horn. The palace rang;
The Nereids danc'd; the Syrens faintly sang;
And the great Sea-King bow'd his dripping head.
Then Love took wing, and from his pinions shed
On all the multitude a nectarous dew.
The ooze-born Goddess beckonèd and drew
Fair Scylla and her guides to conference;
And when they reach'd the thronèd eminence
She kist the sea-nymph's cheek,—who sat her down
A toying with the doves. Then,—"Mighty crown
And sceptre of this kingdom!" Venus said,
"Thy vows were on a time to Nais paid:
Behold!"—Two copious tear-drops instant fell
From the God's large eyes; he smil'd delectable,
And over Glaucus held his blessing hands.—
"Endymion! Ah! still wandering in the bands
Of love? Now this is cruel. Since the hour
I met thee in earth's bosom, all my power
Have I put forth to serve thee. What, not yet
Escap'd from dull mortality's harsh net?
A little patience, youth! 'twill not be long,
Or I am skilless quite: an idle tongue,
A humid eye, and steps luxurious,
Where these are new and strange, are ominous.
Aye, I have seen these signs in one of heaven,
When others were all blind; and were I given
To utter secrets, haply I might say
Some pleasant words:—but Love will have his day.
So wait awhile expectant. Pr'ythee soon,
Even in the passing of thine honey-moon,
Visit my Cytherea: thou wilt find
Cupid well-natured, my Adonis kind;
And pray persuade with thee—Ah, I have done,
All blisses be upon thee, my sweet son!"—
Thus the fair goddess: while Endymion
Knelt to receive those accents halcyon.
Meantime a glorious revelry began
Before the Water-Monarch. Nectar ran
In courteous fountains to all cups outreach'd;
And plunder'd vines, teeming exhaustless, pleach'd
New growth about each shell and pendent lyre;
The which, in disentangling for their fire,
Pull'd down fresh foliage and coverture

For dainty toying. Cupid, empire-sure,
Flutter'd and laugh'd, and oft-times through the throng
Made a delighted way. Then dance, and song,
And garlanding grew wild; and pleasure reign'd.
In harmless tendril they each other chain'd,
And strove who should be smother'd deepest in
Fresh crush of leaves.

O 'tis a very sin
For one so weak to venture his poor verse
In such a place as this. O do not curse,
High Muses! let him hurry to the ending.

All suddenly were silent. A soft blending
Of dulcet instruments came charmingly;
And then a hymn.

"King of the stormy sea!
Brother of Jove, and co-inheritor
Of elements! Eternally before
Thee the waves awful bow. Fast, stubborn rock,
At thy fear'd trident shrinking, doth unlock
Its deep foundations, hissing into foam.
All mountain-rivers lost, in the wide home
Of thy capacious bosom ever flow.
Thou frownest, and old Eolus thy foe
Skulks to his cavern, 'mid the gruff complaint
Of all his rebel tempests. Dark clouds faint
When, from thy diadem, a silver gleam
Slants over blue dominion. Thy bright team
Gulphs in the morning light, and scuds along
To bring thee nearer to that golden song
Apollo singeth, while his chariot
Waits at the doors of heaven. Thou art not
For scenes like this: an empire stern hast thou;
And it hath furrow'd that large front: yet now,
As newly come of heaven, dost thou sit
To blend and interknit
Subduèd majesty with this glad time.
O shell-borne King sublime!
We lay our hearts before thee evermore—
We sing, and we adore!

"Breathe softly, flutes;
Be tender of your strings, ye soothing lutes;
Nor be the trumpet heard! O vain, O vain;
Not flowers budding in an April rain,
Nor breath of sleeping dove, nor river's flow,—
No, nor the Eolian twang of Love's own bow,
Can mingle music fit for the soft ear
Of goddess Cytherea!
Yet deign, white Queen of Beauty, thy fair eyes
On our souls' sacrifice.

"Bright-wingèd Child!
Who has another care when thou hast smil'd?
Unfortunates on earth, we see at last
All death-shadows, and glooms that overcast
Our spirits, fann'd away by thy light pinions.
O sweetest essence! sweetest of all minions!
God of warm pulses, and dishevell'd hair,
And panting bosoms bare!
Dear unseen light in darkness! eclipser
Of light in light! delicious poisoner!
Thy venom'd goblet will we quaff until
We fill—we fill!
And by thy Mother's lips—"

Was heard no more
For clamour, when the golden palace door
Opened again, and from without, in shone
A new magnificence. On oozy throne
Smooth-moving came Oceanus the old,
To take a latest glimpse at his sheep-fold,
Before he went into his quiet cave
To muse for ever—Then a lucid wave,
Scoop'd from its trembling sisters of mid-sea,
Afloat, and pillowing up the majesty
Of Doris, and the Egean seer, her spouse—
Next, on a dolphin, clad in laurel boughs,
Theban Amphion leaning on his lute:
His fingers went across it—All were mute
To gaze on Amphitrite, queen of pearls,
And Thetis pearly too.
The palace whirls
Around giddy Endymion; seeing he
Was there far strayèd from mortality.

He could not bear it—shut his eyes in vain;
Imagination gave a dizzier pain.
"O I shall die! sweet Venus, be my stay!
Where is my lovely mistress? Well-away!
I die—I hear her voice—I feel my wing—"
At Neptune's feet he sank. A sudden ring
Of Nereids were about him, in kind strife
To usher back his spirit into life:
But still he slept. At last they interwove
Their cradling arms, and purpos'd to convey
Towards a crystal bower far away.

Lo! while slow carried through the pitying crowd,
To his inward senses these words spake aloud;
Written in star-light on the dark above:
"*Dearest Endymion! my entire love!*
How have I dwelt in fear of fate: 'tis done—
Immortal bliss for me too hast thou won.
Arise then! for the hen-dove shall not hatch
Her ready eggs, before I'll kissing snatch
Thee into endless heaven. Awake! awake!"

The youth at once arose: a placid lake
Came quiet to his eyes; and forest green,
Cooler than all the wonders he had seen,
Lull'd with its simple song his fluttering breast.
How happy once again in grassy nest!

BOOK IV

Muse of my native land! loftiest Muse!
O first-born on the mountains! by the hues
Of heaven on the spiritual air begot:
Long didst thou sit alone in northern grot,
While yet our England was a wolfish den;
Before our forests heard the talk of men;
Before the first of Druids was a child;—
Long didst thou sit amid our regions wild
Rapt in a deep prophetic solitude.
There came an eastern voice of solemn mood:—
Yet wast thou patient. Then sang forth the Nine,
Apollo's garland:—yet didst thou divine
Such home-bred glory, that they cry'd in vain,
"Come hither, Sister of the Island!" Plain
Spake fair Ausonia; and once more she spake

A higher summons:—still didst thou betake
Thee to thy native hopes. O thou hast won
A full accomplishment! The thing is done,
Which undone, these our latter days had risen
On barren souls. Great Muse, thou know'st what prison,
Of flesh and bone, curbs, and confines, and frets
Our spirit's wings: despondency besets
Our pillows; and the fresh to-morrow morn
Seems to give forth its light in very scorn
Of our dull, uninspired, snail-pacèd lives.
Long have I said, how happy he who shrives
To thee! But then I thought on poets gone,
And could not pray:—nor can I now—so on
I move to the end in lowliness of heart.—

"Ah, woe is me! that I should fondly part
From my dear native land! Ah, foolish maid!
Glad was the hour, when, with thee, myriads bade
Adieu to Ganges and their pleasant fields!
To one so friendless the clear freshet yields
A bitter coolness; the ripe grape is sour:
Yet I would have, great gods! but one short hour
Of native air—let me but die at home."

Endymion to heaven's airy dome
Was offering up a hecatomb of vows,
When these words reach'd him. Whereupon he bows
His head through thorny-green entanglement
Of underwood, and to the sound is bent,
Anxious as hind towards her hidden fawn.

"Is no one near to help me? No fair dawn
Of life from charitable voice? No sweet saying
To set my dull and sadden'd spirit playing?
No hand to toy with mine? No lips so sweet
That I may worship them? No eyelids meet
To twinkle on my bosom? No one dies
Before me, till from these enslaving eyes
Redemption sparkles!—I am sad and lost."

Thou, Carian lord, hadst better have been tost
Into a whirlpool. Vanish into air,
Warm mountaineer! for canst thou only bear
A woman's sigh alone and in distress?
See not her charms! Is Phœbe passionless?

Phœbe is fairer far—O gaze no more:—
Yet if thou wilt behold all beauty's store,
Behold her panting in the forest grass!
Do not those curls of glossy jet surpass
For tenderness the arms so idly lain
Amongst them? Feelest not a kindred pain,
To see such lovely eyes in swimming search
After some warm delight, that seems to perch
Dovelike in the dim cell lying beyond
Their upper lids?—Hist!

"O for Hermes' wand,
To touch this flower into human shape!
That woodland Hyacinthus could escape
From his green prison, and here kneeling down
Call me his queen, his second life's fair crown!
Ah me, how I could love!—My soul doth melt
For the unhappy youth—Love! I have felt
So faint a kindness, such a meek surrender
To what my own full thoughts had made too tender,
That but for tears my life had fled away!—
Ye deaf and senseless minutes of the day,
And thou, old forest, hold ye this for true,
There is no lightning, no authentic dew
But in the eye of love: there's not a sound,
Melodious howsoever, can confound
The heavens and earth in one to such a death
As doth the voice of love: there's not a breath
Will mingle kindly with the meadow air,
Till it has panted round, and stolen a share
Of passion from the heart!"—

Upon a bough
He leant, wretched. He surely cannot now
Thirst for another love: O impious,
That he can even dream upon it thus!—
Thought he, "Why am I not as are the dead,
Since to a woe like this I have been led
Through the dark earth, and through the wondrous sea?
Goddess! I love thee not the less: from thee
By Juno's smile I turn not—no, no, no—
While the great waters are at ebb and flow.—
I have a triple soul! O fond pretence—
For both, for both my love is so immense,
I feel my heart is cut in twain for them."

And so he groan'd, as one by beauty slain.
The lady's heart beat quick, and he could see
Her gentle bosom heave tumultuously.
He sprang from his green covert: there she lay,
Sweet as a muskrose upon new-made hay;
With all her limbs on tremble, and her eyes
Shut softly up alive. To speak he tries.
"Fair damsel, pity me! forgive that I
Thus violate thy bower's sanctity!
O pardon me, for I am full of grief—
Grief born of thee, young angel! fairest thief!
Who stolen hast away the wings wherewith
I was to top the heavens. Dear maid, sith
Thou art my executioner, and I feel
Loving and hatred, misery and weal,
Will in a few short hours be nothing to me,
And all my story that much passion slew me;
Do smile upon the evening of my days:
And, for my tortur'd brain begins to craze,
Be thou my nurse; and let me understand
How dying I shall kiss that lily hand.—
Dost weep for me? Then should I be content.
Scowl on, ye fates! until the firmament
Out-blackens Erebus, and the full-cavern'd earth
Crumbles into itself. By the cloud girth
Of Jove, those tears have given me a thirst
To meet oblivion."—As her heart would burst
The maiden sobb'd awhile, and then replied:
"Why must such desolation betide
As that thou speakest of? Are not these green nooks
Empty of all misfortune? Do the brooks
Utter a gorgon voice? Does yonder thrush,
Schooling its half-fledg'd little ones to brush
About the dewy forest, whisper tales?—
Speak not of grief, young stranger, or cold snails
Will slime the rose to night. Though if thou wilt,
Methinks 'twould be a guilt—a very guilt—
Not to companion thee, and sigh away
The light—the dusk—the dark—till break of day!"
"Dear lady," said Endymion, "'tis past:
I love thee! and my days can never last.
That I may pass in patience still speak:
Let me have music dying, and I seek
No more delight—I bid adieu to all.

Didst thou not after other climates call,
And murmur about Indian streams?"—Then she,
Sitting beneath the midmost forest tree,
For pity sang this roundelay—

"O Sorrow,
Why dost borrow
The natural hue of health, from vermeil lips?—
To give maiden blushes
To the white rose bushes?
Or is it thy dewy hand the daisy tips?

"O Sorrow,
Why dost borrow
The lustrous passion from a falcon-eye?—
To give the glow-worm light?
Or, on a moonless night,
To tinge, on syren shores, the salt sea-spry?

"O Sorrow,
Why dost borrow
The mellow ditties from a mourning tongue?—
To give at evening pale
Unto the nightingale,
That thou mayst listen the cold dews among?

"O Sorrow,
Why dost borrow
Heart's lightness from the merriment of May?—
A lover would not tread
A cowslip on the head,
Though he should dance from eve till peep of day—
Nor any drooping flower
Held sacred for thy bower,
Wherever he may sport himself and play.

"To Sorrow,
I bade good-morrow,
And thought to leave her far away behind;
But cheerly, cheerly,
She loves me dearly;
She is so constant to me, and so kind:
I would deceive her
And so leave her,
But ah! she is so constant and so kind.

"Beneath my palm trees, by the river side,
I sat a weeping: in the whole world wide
There was no one to ask me why I wept,—
　　And so I kept
Brimming the water-lily cups with tears
　　Cold as my fears.

"Beneath my palm trees, by the river side,
I sat a weeping: what enamour'd bride,
Cheated by shadowy wooer from the clouds,
　　But hides and shrouds
Beneath dark palm trees by a river side?

"And as I sat, over the light blue hills
There came a noise of revellers: the rills
Into the wide stream came of purple hue—
　　'Twas Bacchus and his crew!
The earnest trumpet spake, and silver thrills
From kissing cymbals made a merry din—
　　'Twas Bacchus and his kin!
Like to a moving vintage down they came,
Crown'd with green leaves, and faces all on flame;
All madly dancing through the pleasant valley,
　　To scare thee, Melancholy!
O then, O then, thou wast a simple name!
And I forgot thee, as the berried holly
By shepherds is forgotten, when, in June,
Tall chesnuts keep away the sun and moon:—
　　I rush'd into the folly!

"Within his car, aloft, young Bacchus stood,
Trifling his ivy-dart, in dancing mood,
　　With sidelong laughing;
And little rills of crimson wine imbrued
His plump white arms, and shoulders, enough white
　　For Venus' pearly bite:
And near him rode Silenus on his ass,
Pelted with flowers as he on did pass
　　Tipsily quaffing.

"Whence came ye, merry Damsels! whence came ye!
So many, and so many, and such glee?
Why have ye left your bowers desolate,
　　Your lutes, and gentler fate?—

'We follow Bacchus! Bacchus on the wing,
A conquering!
Bacchus, young Bacchus! good or ill betide,
We dance before him thorough kingdoms wide:—
Come hither, lady fair, and joined be
To our wild minstrelsy!'

"Whence came ye, jolly Satyrs! whence came ye!
So many, and so many, and such glee?
Why have ye left your forest haunts, why left
Your nuts in oak-tree cleft?—
'For wine, for wine we left our kernel tree;
For wine we left our heath, and yellow brooms,
And cold mushrooms;
For wine we follow Bacchus through the earth;
Great God of breathless cups and chirping mirth!—
Come hither, lady fair, and joined be
To our mad minstrelsy!'

"Over wide streams and mountains great we went,
And, save when Bacchus kept his ivy tent,
Onward the tiger and the leopard pants,
With Asian elephants:
Onward these myriads—with song and dance,
With zebras striped, and sleek Arabians' prance,
Web-footed alligators, crocodiles,
Bearing upon their scaly backs, in files,
Plump infant laughers mimicking the coil
Of seamen, and stout galley-rowers' toil:
With toying oars and silken sails they glide,
Nor care for wind and tide.

"Mounted on panthers' furs and lions' manes,
From rear to van they scour about the plains;
A three days' journey in a moment done:
And always, at the rising of the sun,
About the wilds they hunt with spear and horn,
On spleenful unicorn.

"I saw Osirian Egypt kneel adown
Before the vine-wreath crown!
I saw parch'd Abyssinia rouse and sing
To the silver cymbals' ring!
I saw the whelming vintage hotly pierce
Old Tartary the fierce!

The kings of Inde their jewel-sceptres vail,
And from their treasures scatter pearled hail;
Great Brahma from his mystic heaven groans,
And all his priesthood moans;
Before young Bacchus' eye-wink turning pale.—
Into these regions came I following him,
Sick hearted, weary—so I took a whim
To stray away into these forests drear
    Alone, without a peer:
And I have told thee all thou mayest hear.
    "Young stranger!
    I've been a ranger
In search of pleasure throughout every clime:
    Alas, 'tis not for me!
    Bewitch'd I sure must be,
To lose in grieving all my maiden prime.

    "Come then, Sorrow!
    Sweetest Sorrow!
Like an own babe I nurse thee on my breast:
    I thought to leave thee
    And deceive thee,
But now of all the world I love thee best.

    "There is not one,
    No, no, not one
But thee to comfort a poor lonely maid;
    Thou art her mother,
    And her brother,
Her playmate, and her wooer in the shade."

O what a sigh she gave in finishing,
And look, quite dead to every worldly thing!
Endymion could not speak, but gazed on her;
And listened to the wind that now did stir
About the crispèd oaks full drearily,
Yet with as sweet a softness as might be
Remember'd from its velvet summer song.
At last he said: "Poor lady, how thus long
Have I been able to endure that voice?
Fair Melody! kind Syren! I've no choice;
I must be thy sad servant evermore:
I cannot choose but kneel here and adore.
Alas, I must not think—by Phœbe, no!
Let me not think, soft Angel! shall it be so?

Say, beautifullest, shall I never think?
O thou could'st foster me beyond the brink
Of recollection! make my watchful care
Close up its bloodshot eyes, nor see despair!
Do gently murder half my soul, and I
Shall feel the other half so utterly!—
I'm giddy at that cheek so fair and smooth;
O let it blush so ever! let it soothe
My madness! let it mantle rosy-warm
With the tinge of love, panting in safe alarm.—
This cannot be thy hand, and yet it is;
And this is sure thine other softling—this
Thine own fair bosom, and I am so near!
Wilt fall asleep? O let me sip that tear!
And whisper one sweet word that I may know
This is this world—sweet dewy blossom!"—"*Woe*!
Woe! *Woe to that Endymion*! *Where is he*?—"
Even these words went echoing dismally
Through the wide forest—a most fearful tone,
Like one repenting in his latest moan;
And while it died away a shade pass'd by,
As of a thunder cloud. When arrows fly
Through the thick branches, poor ring-doves sleek forth
Their timid necks and tremble; so these both
Leant to each other trembling, and sat so
Waiting for some destruction—when lo,
Foot-feather'd Mercury appear'd sublime
Beyond the tall tree tops; and in less time
Than shoots the slanted hail-storm, down he dropt
Towards the ground; but rested not, nor stopt
One moment from his home: only the sward
He with his wand light touch'd, and heavenward
Swifter than sight was gone—even before
The teeming earth a sudden witness bore
Of his swift magic. Diving swans appear
Above the crystal circlings white and clear;
And catch the cheated eye in wild surprise,
How they can dive in sight and unseen rise—
So from the turf outsprang two steeds jet-black,
Each with large dark blue wings upon his back.
The youth of Caria plac'd the lovely dame
On one, and felt himself in spleen to tame
The other's fierceness. Through the air they flew,
High as the eagles. Like two drops of dew
Exhal'd to Phœbus' lips, away they are gone,

Far from the earth away—unseen, alone,
Among cool clouds and winds, but that the free,
The buoyant life of song can floating be
Above their heads, and follow them untir'd.—
Muse of my native land, am I inspir'd?
This is the giddy air, and I must spread
Wide pinions to keep here; nor do I dread
Or height, or depth, or width, or any chance
Precipitous: I have beneath my glance
Those towering horses and their mournful freight.
Could I thus sail, and see, and thus await
Fearless for power of thought, without thine aid?—

There is a sleepy dusk, an odorous shade
From some approaching wonder, and behold
Those wingèd steeds, with snorting nostrils bold
Snuff at its faint extreme, and seem to tire,
Dying to embers from their native fire!

There curl'd a purple mist around them; soon,
It seem'd as when around the pale new moon
Sad Zephyr droops the clouds like weeping willow:
'Twas Sleep slow journeying with head on pillow.
For the first time, since he came nigh dead born
From the old womb of night, his cave forlorn
Had he left more forlorn; for the first time,
He felt aloof the day and morning's prime—
Because into his depth Cimmerian
There came a dream, shewing how a young man,
Ere a lean bat could plump its wintery skin,
Would at high Jove's empyreal footstool win
An immortality, and how espouse
Jove's daughter, and be reckon'd of his house.
Now was he slumbering towards heaven's gate,
That he might at the threshold one hour wait
To hear the marriage melodies, and then
Sink downward to his dusky cave again.
His litter of smooth semilucent mist,
Diversely ting'd with rose and amethyst,
Puzzled those eyes that for the centre sought;
And scarcely for one moment could be caught
His sluggish form reposing motionless.
Those two on wingèd steeds, with all the stress
Of vision search'd for him, as one would look
Athwart the sallows of a river nook

To catch a glance at silver throated eels,—
Or from old Skiddaw's top, when fog conceals
His rugged forehead in a mantle pale,
With an eye-guess towards some pleasant vale
Descry a favourite hamlet faint and far.

These raven horses, though they foster'd are
Of earth's splenetic fire, dully drop
Their full-veined ears, nostrils blood wide, and stop;
Upon the spiritless mist have they outspread
Their ample feathers, are in slumber dead,—
And on those pinions, level in mid air,
Endymion sleepeth and the lady fair.
Slowly they sail, slowly as icy isle
Upon a calm sea drifting: and meanwhile
The mournful wanderer dreams. Behold! he walks
On heaven's pavement; brotherly he talks
To divine powers: from his hand full fain
Juno's proud birds are pecking pearly grain:
He tries the nerve of Phœbus' golden bow,
And asketh where the golden apples grow:
Upon his arm he braces Pallas' shield,
And strives in vain to unsettle and wield
A Jovian thunderbolt: arch Hebe brings
A full-brimm'd goblet, dances lightly, sings
And tantalizes long; at last he drinks,
And lost in pleasure at her feet he sinks,
Touching with dazzled lips her starlight hand.
He blows a bugle,—an ethereal band
Are visible above: the Seasons four,—
Green-kyrtled Spring, flush Summer, golden store
In Autumn's sickle, Winter frosty hoar,
Join dance with shadowy Hours; while still the blast,
In swells unmitigated, still doth last
To sway their floating morris. "Whose is this?
Whose bugle?" he inquires: they smile—"O Dis!
Why is this mortal here? Dost thou not know
Its mistress' lips? Not thou?—'Tis Dian's: lo!
She rises crescented!" He looks, 'tis she,
His very goddess: good-bye earth, and sea,
And air, and pains, and care, and suffering;
Good-bye to all but love! Then doth he spring
Towards her, and awakes—and, strange, o'erhead,
Of those same fragrant exhalations bred,
Beheld awake his very dream: the gods

Stood smiling; merry Hebe laughs and nods;
And Phœbe bends towards him crescented.
O state perplexing! On the pinion bed,
Too well awake, he feels the panting side
Of his delicious lady. He who died
For soaring too audacious in the sun,
Where that same treacherous wax began to run,
Felt not more tongue-tied than Endymion.
His heart leapt up as to its rightful throne,
To that fair shadow'd passion puls'd its way—
Ah, what perplexity! Ah, well a day!
So fond, so beauteous was his bed-fellow,
He could not help but kiss her: then he grew
Awhile forgetful of all beauty save
Young Phœbe's, golden hair'd; and so 'gan crave
Forgiveness: yet he turn'd once more to look
At the sweet sleeper,—all his soul was shook,—
She press'd his hand in slumber; so once more
He could not help but kiss her and adore.
At this the shadow wept, melting away.
The Latmian started up: "Bright goddess, stay!
Search my most hidden breast! By truth's own tongue,
I have no dædale heart: why is it wrung
To desperation? Is there nought for me,
Upon the bourne of bliss, but misery?"

These words awoke the stranger of dark tresses:
Her dawning love-look rapt Endymion blesses
With 'haviour soft. Sleep yawned from underneath.
"Thou swan of Ganges, let us no more breathe
This murky phantasm! thou contented seem'st
Pillow'd in lovely idleness, nor dream'st
What horrors may discomfort thee and me.
Ah, shouldst thou die from my heart-treachery!—
Yet did she merely weep—her gentle soul
Hath no revenge in it: as it is whole
In tenderness, would I were whole in love!
Can I prize thee, fair maid, till price above,
Even when I feel as true as innocence?
I do, I do.—What is this soul then? Whence
Came it? It does not seem my own, and I
Have no self-passion or identity.
Some fearful end must be: where, where is it?
By Nemesis, I see my spirit flit
Alone about the dark—Forgive me, sweet:

Shall we away?" He rous'd the steeds: they beat
Their wings chivàlrous into the clear air,
Leaving old Sleep within his vapoury lair.

The good-night blush of eve was waning slow,
And Vesper, risen star, began to throe
In the dusk heavens silvery, when they
Thus sprang direct towards the Galaxy.
Nor did speed hinder converse soft and strange—
Eternal oaths and vows they interchange,
In such wise, in such temper, so aloof
Up in the winds, beneath a starry roof,
So witless of their doom, that verily
'Tis well nigh past man's search their hearts to see;
Whether they wept, or laugh'd, or griev'd, or toy'd—
Most like with joy gone mad, with sorrow cloy'd.

Full facing their swift flight, from ebon streak,
The moon put forth a little diamond peak,
No bigger than an unobserved star,
Or tiny point of fairy scymetar;
Bright signal that she only stoop'd to tie
Her silver sandals, ere deliciously
She bow'd into the heavens her timid head.
Slowly she rose, as though she would have fled,
While to his lady meek the Carian turn'd,
To mark if her dark eyes had yet discern'd
This beauty in its birth—Despair! despair!
He saw her body fading gaunt and spare
In the cold moonshine. Straight he seiz'd her wrist;
It melted from his grasp: her hand he kiss'd,
And, horror! kiss'd his own—he was alone.
Her steed a little higher soar'd, and then
Dropt hawkwise to the earth.

There lies a den,
Beyond the seeming confines of the space
Made for the soul to wander in and trace
Its own existence, of remotest glooms.
Dark regions are around it, where the tombs
Of buried griefs the spirit sees, but scarce
One hour doth linger weeping, for the pierce
Of new-born woe it feels more inly smart:
And in these regions many a venom'd dart
At random flies; they are the proper home

Of every ill: the man is yet to come
Who hath not journeyed in this native hell.
But few have ever felt how calm and well
Sleep may be had in that deep den of all.
There anguish does not sting; nor pleasure pall:
Woe-hurricanes beat ever at the gate,
Yet all is still within and desolate.
Beset with plainful gusts, within ye hear
No sound so loud as when on curtain'd bier
The death-watch tick is stifled. Enter none
Who strive therefore: on the sudden it is won.
Just when the sufferer begins to burn,
Then it is free to him; and from an urn,
Still fed by melting ice, he takes a draught—
Young Semele such richness never quaft
In her maternal longing. Happy gloom!
Dark Paradise! where pale becomes the bloom
Of health by duc; where silence dreariest
Is most articulate; where hopes infest;
Where those eyes are the brightest far that keep
Their lids shut longest in a drcamless sleep.
O happy spirit-home! O wondrous soul!
Pregnant with such a den to save the whole
In thine own depth. Hail, gentle Carian!
For, never since thy griefs and woes began,
Hast thou felt so content: a grievous feud
Hath let thee to this Cave of Quietude.
Aye, his lull'd soul was there, although upbornc
With dangerous speed: and so he did not mourn
Because he knew not whither he was going.
So happy was he, not the aerial blowing
Of trumpets at clear parley from the east
Could rouse from that fine relish, that high feast.
They stung the feather'd horse: with fierce alarm
He flapp'd towards the sound. Alas, no charm
Could lift Endymion's head, or he had view'd
A skyey mask, a pinion'd multitude,—
And silvery was its passing: voices sweet
Warbling the while as if to lull and greet
The wanderer in his path. Thus warbled they,
While past the vision went in bright array.

"Who, who from Dian's feast would be away?
For all the golden bowers of the day
Are empty left? Who, who away would be

From Cynthia's wedding and festivity?
Not Hesperus: lo! upon his silver wings
He leans away for highest heaven and sings,
Snapping his lucid fingers merrily!—
Ah, Zephyrus! art here, and Flora too!
Ye tender bibbers of the rain and dew,
Young playmates of the rose and daffodil,
Be careful, ere ye enter in, to fill
    Your baskets high
With fennel green, and balm, and golden pines,
Savory, latter-mint, and columbines,
Cool parsley, basil sweet, and sunny thyme;
Yea, every flower and leaf of every clime,
All gather'd in the dewy morning: hie
    Away! fly, fly!—
Crystalline brother of the belt of heaven,
Aquarius! to whom king Jove has given
Two liquid pulse streams 'stead of feather'd wings,
Two fan-like fountains,—thine illuminings
    For Dian play:
Dissolve the frozen purity of air;
Let thy white shoulders silvery and bare
Shew cold through watery pinions; make more bright
The Star-Queen's crescent on her marriage night:
    Haste, haste away!—
Castor has tamed the planet Lion, see!
And of the Bear has Pollux mastery:
A third is in the race! who is the third,
Speeding away swift as the eagle bird?
    The ramping Centaur!
The Lion's mane's on end: the Bear how fierce!
The Centaur's arrow ready seems to pierce
Some enemy: far forth his bow is bent
Into the blue of heaven. He'll be shent,
    Pale unrelentor,
When he shall hear the wedding lutes a playing.—
Andromeda! sweet woman! why delaying
So timidly among the stars: come hither!
Join this bright throng, and nimbly follow whither
    They all are going.
Danae's Son, before Jove newly bow'd,
Has wept for thee, calling to Jove aloud.
Thee, gentle lady, did he disenthral:
Ye shall for ever live and love, for all
    Thy tears are flowing.—

By Daphne's fright, behold Apollo!—"
More
Endymion heard not: down his steed him bore,
Prone to the green head of a misty hill.

His first touch of the earth went nigh to kill.
"Alas!" said he, "were I but always borne
Through dangerous winds, had but my footsteps worn
A path in hell, for ever would I bless
Horrors which nourish an uneasiness
For my own sullen conquering: to him
Who lives beyond earth's boundary, grief is dim,
Sorrow is but a shadow: now I see
The grass; I feel the solid ground—Ah, me!
It is thy voice—divinest! Where?—who? who
Left thee so quiet on this bed of dew?
Behold upon this happy earth we are;
Let us ay love each other; let us fare
On forest-fruits, and never, never go
Among the abodes of mortals here below,
Or be by phantoms duped. O destiny!
Into a labyrinth now my soul would fly,
But with thy beauty will I deaden it.
Where didst thou melt too? By thee will I sit
For ever: let our fate stop here—a kid
I on this spot will offer: Pan will bid
Us live in peace, in love and peace among
His forest wildernesses. I have clung
To nothing, lov'd a nothing, nothing seen
Or felt but a great dream! O I have been
Presumptuous against love, against the sky,
Against all elements, against the tie
Of mortals each to each, against the blooms
Of flowers, rush of rivers, and the tombs
Of heroes gone! Against his proper glory
Has my own soul conspired: so my story
Will I to children utter, and repent.
There never liv'd a mortal man, who bent
His appetite beyond his natural sphere,
But starv'd and died. My sweetest Indian, here,
Here will I kneel, for thou redeemèd hast
My life from too thin breathing: gone and past
Are cloudy phantasms. Caverns lone, farewel!
And air of visions, and the monstrous swell
Of visionary seas! No, never more

Shall airy voices cheat me to the shore
Of tangled wonder, breathless and aghast.
Adieu, my daintiest Dream! although so vast
My love is still for thee. The hour may come
When we shall meet in pure elysium.
On earth I may not love thee; and therefore
Doves will I offer up, and sweetest store
All through the teeming year: so thou wilt shine
On me, and on this damsel fair of mine,
And bless our simple lives. My Indian bliss!
My river-lily bud! one human kiss!
One sigh of real breath—one gentle squeeze,
Warm as a dove's nest among summer trees,
And warm with dew at ooze from living blood!
Whither didst melt? Ah, what of that!—all good
We'll talk about—no more of dreaming.—Now,
Where shall our dwelling be? Under the brow
Of some steep mossy hill, where ivy dun
Would hide us up, although spring leaves were none;
And where dark yew trees, as we rustle through,
Will drop their scarlet berry cups of dew?
O thou wouldst joy to live in such a place;
Dusk for our loves, yet light enough to grace
Those gentle limbs on mossy bed reclin'd:
For by one step the blue sky shouldst thou find,
And by another, in deep dell below,
See, through the trees, a little river go
All in its mid-day gold and glimmering.
Honey from out the gnarlèd hive I'll bring,
And apples, wan with sweetness, gather thee,—
Cresses that grow where no man may them see,
And sorrel untorn by the dew-claw'd stag:
Pipes will I fashion of the syrinx flag,
That thou mayst always know whither I roam,
When it shall please thee in our quiet home
To listen and think of love. Still let me speak;
Still let me dive into the joy I seek,—
For yet the past doth prison me. The rill,
Thou haply mayst delight in, will I fill
With fairy fishes from the mountain tarn,
And thou shall feed them from the squirrel's barn.
Its bottom will I strew with amber shells,
And pebbles blue from deep enchanted wells.
Its sides I'll plant with dew-sweet eglantine,
And honeysuckles full of clear bee-wine.

I will entice this crystal rill to trace
Love's silver name upon the meadow's face.
I'll kneel to Vesta, for a flame of fire;
And to god Phœbus, for a golden lyre;
To Empress Dian, for a hunting spear;
To Vesper, for a taper silver-clear,
That I may see thy beauty through the night;
To Flora, and a nightingale shall light
Tame on thy finger; to the River-gods,
And they shall bring thee taper fishing-rods
Of gold, and lines of Naiads' long bright tress.
Heaven shield thee for thine utter loveliness!
Thy mossy footstool shall the altar be
'Fore which I'll bend, bending, dear love, to thee:
Those lips shall be my Delphos, and shall speak
Laws to my footsteps, colour to my cheek,
Trembling or stedfastness to this same voice,
And of three sweetest pleasurings the choice:
And that affectionate light, those diamond things,
Those eyes, those passions, those supreme pearl springs,
Shall be my grief, or twinkle me to pleasure.
Say, is not bliss within our perfect seizure?
O that I could not doubt?"

The mountaineer
Thus strove by fancies vain and crude to clear
His briar'd path to some tranquillity.
It gave bright gladness to his lady's eye,
And yet the tears she wept were tears of sorrow;
Answering thus, just as the golden morrow
Beam'd upward from the vallies of the east:
"O that the flutter of this heart had ceas'd,
Or the sweet name of love had pass'd away.
Young feathor'd tyrant! by a swift decay
Wilt thou devote this body to the earth:
And I do think that at my very birth
I lisp'd thy blooming titles inwardly;
For at the first, first dawn and thought of thee,
With uplift hands I blest the stars of heaven.
Art thou not cruel? Ever have I striven
To think thee kind, but ah, it will not do!
When yet a child, I heard that kisses drew
Favour from thee, and so I gave and gave
To the void air, bidding them find out love:
But when I came to feel how far above

All fancy, pride, and fickle maidenhood,
All earthly pleasure, all imagin'd good,
Was the warm tremble of a devout kiss,—
Even then, that moment, at the thought of this,
Fainting I fell into a bed of flowers,
And languish'd there three days. Ye milder powers,
Am I not cruelly wrong'd? Believe, believe
Me, dear Endymion, were I to weave
With my own fancies garlands of sweet life,
Thou shouldst be one of all. Ah, bitter strife!
I may not be thy love: I am forbidden—
Indeed I am—thwarted, affrighted, chidden,
By things I trembled at, and gorgon wrath.
Twice hast thou ask'd whither I went: henceforth
Ask me no more! I may not utter it,
Nor may I be thy love. We might commit
Ourselves at once to vengeance; we might die;
We might embrace and die: voluptuous thought!
Enlarge not to my hunger, or I'm caught
In trammels of perverse deliciousness.
No, no, that shall not be: thee will I bless,
And bid a long adieu."

The Carian
No word return'd: both lovelorn, silent, wan,
Into the vallies green together went.
Far wandering, they were perforce content
To sit beneath a fair lone beechen tree;
Nor at each other gaz'd, but heavily
Por'd on its hazle cirque of shedded leaves.

Endymion! unhappy! it nigh grieves
Me to behold thee thus in last extreme:
Ensky'd ere this, but truly that I deem
Truth the best music in a first-born song.
Thy lute-voic'd brother will I sing ere long,
And thou shall aid—hast thou not aided me?
Yes, moonlight Emperor! felicity
Has been thy meed for many thousand years;
Yet often have I, on the brink of tears,
Mourn'd as if yet thou wert a forester;—
Forgetting the old tale.

He did not stir
His eyes from the dead leaves, or one small pulse
Of joy he might have felt. The spirit culls
Unfaded amaranth, when wild it strays
Through the old garden-ground of boyish days.
A little onward ran the very stream
By which he took his first soft poppy dream;
And on the very bark 'gainst which he leant
A crescent he had carv'd, and round it spent
His skill in little stars. The teeming tree
Had swollen and green'd the pious charactery,
But not ta'en out. Why, there was not a slope
Up which he had not fear'd the antelope;
And not a tree, beneath whose rooty shade
He had not with his tamed leopards play'd;
Nor could an arrow light, or javelin,
Fly in the air where his had never been—
And yet he knew it not.

O treachery!
Why does his lady smile, pleasing her eye
With all his sorrowing? He sees her not.
But who so stares on him? His sister sure!
Peona of the woods!—Can she endure—
Impossible—how dearly they embrace!
His lady smiles; delight is in her face;
It is no treachery.
"Dear brother mine!
Endymion, weep not so! Why shouldst thou pine
When all great Latmos so exalt will be?
Thank the great gods, and look not bitterly;
And speak not one pale word, and sigh no more.
Sure I will not believe thou hast such store
Of grief, to last thee to my kiss again.
Thou surely canst not bear a mind in pain,
Come hand in hand with one so beautiful.
Be happy both of you! for I will pull
The flowers of autumn for your coronals.
Pan's holy priest for young Endymion calls;
And when he is restor'd, thou, fairest dame,
Shalt be our queen. Now, is it not a shame
To see ye thus,—not very, very sad?
Perhaps ye are too happy to be glad:
O feel as if it were a common day;

Free-voic'd as one who never was away.
No tongue shall ask, whence come ye? but ye shall
Be gods of your own rest imperial.
Not even I, for one whole month, will pry
Into the hours that have pass'd us by,
Since in my arbour I did sing to thee.
O Hermes! on this very night will be
A hymning up to Cynthia, queen of light;
For the soothsayers old saw yesternight
Good visions in the air,—whence will befal,
As say these sages, health perpetual
To shepherds and their flocks; and furthermore,
In Dian's face they read the gentle lore:
Therefore for her these vesper-carols are.
Our friends will all be there from nigh and far.
Many upon thy death have ditties made;
And many, even now, their foreheads shade
With cypress, on a day of sacrifice.
New singing for our maids shalt thou devise,
And pluck the sorrow from our huntsmen's brows.
Tell me, my lady-queen, how to espouse
This wayward brother to his rightful joys!
His eyes are on thee bent, as thou didst poise
His fate most goddess-like. Help me, I pray,
To lure—Endymion, dear brother, say
What ails thee?" He could bear no more, and so
Bent his soul fiercely like a spiritual bow,
And twang'd it inwardly, and calmly said:
"I would have thee my only friend, sweet maid!
My only visitor! not ignorant though,
That those deceptions which for pleasure go
'Mong men, are pleasures real as real may be:
But there are higher ones I may not see,
If impiously an earthly realm I take.
Since I saw thee, I have been wide awake
Night after night, and day by day, until
Of the empyrean I have drunk my fill.
Let it content thee, Sister, seeing me
More happy than betides mortality.
A hermit young, I'll live in mossy cave,
Where thou alone shalt come to me, and lave
Thy spirit in the wonders I shall tell.
Through me the shepherd realm shall prosper well;
For to thy tongue will I all health confide.
And, for my sake, let this young maid abide

With thee as a dear sister. Thou alone,
Peona, mayst return to me. I own
This may sound strangely: but when, dearest girl,
Thou seest it for my happiness, no pearl
Will trespass down those cheeks. Companion fair!
Wilt be content to dwell with her, to share
This sister's love with me?" Like one resign'd
And bent by circumstance, and thereby blind
In self-commitment, thus that meek unknown:
"Aye, but a buzzing by my ears has flown,
Of jubilee to Dian:—truth I heard!
Well then, I see there is no little bird,
Tender soever, but is Jove's own care.
Long have I sought for rest, and, unaware,
Behold I find it! so exalted too!
So after my own heart! I knew, I knew
There was a place untenanted in it:
In that same void white Chastity shall sit,
And monitor me nightly to lone slumber.
With sanest lips I vow me to the number
Of Dian's sisterhood; and, kind lady,
With thy good help, this very night shall see
My future days to her fane consecrate."

As feels a dreamer what doth most create
His own particular fright, so these three felt:
Or like one who, in after ages, knelt
To Lucifer or Baal, when he'd pine
After a little sleep: or when in mine
Far under-ground, a sleeper meets his friends
Who know him not. Each diligently bends
Towards common thoughts and things for very fear;
Striving their ghastly malady to cheer,
By thinking it a thing of yes and no,
That housewives talk of. But the spirit-blow
Was struck, and all were dreamers. At the last
Endymion said: "Are not our fates all cast?
Why stand we here? Adieu, ye tender pair!
Adieu!" Whereat those maidens, with wild stare,
Walk'd dizzily away. Painèd and hot
His eyes went after them, until they got
Near to a cypress grove, whose deadly maw,
In one swift moment, would what then he saw
Engulph for ever. "Stay!" he cried, "ah, stay!
Turn, damsels! hist! one word I have to say.

Sweet Indian, I would see thee once again.
It is a thing I dote on: so I'd fain,
Peona, ye should hand in hand repair
Into those holy groves, that silent are
Behind great Dian's temple. I'll be yon,
At vesper's earliest twinkle—they are gone—
But once, once, once again—" At this he press'd
His hands against his face, and then did rest
His head upon a mossy hillock green,
And so remain'd as he a corpse had been
All the long day; save when he scantly lifted
His eyes abroad, to see how shadows shifted
With the slow move of time,—sluggish and weary
Until the poplar tops, in journey dreary,
Had reach'd the river's brim. Then up he rose,
And, slowly as that very river flows,
Walk'd towards the temple grove with this lament:
"Why such a golden eve? The breeze is sent
Careful and soft, that not a leaf may fall
Before the serene father of them all
Bows down his summer head below the west.
Now am I of breath, speech, and speed possest,
But at the setting I must bid adieu
To her for the last time. Night will strew
On the damp grass myriads of lingering leaves,
And with them shall I die; nor much it grieves
To die, when summer dies on the cold sward.
Why, I have been a butterfly, a lord
Of flowers, garlands, love-knots, silly posies,
Groves, meadows, melodies, and arbour roses;
My kingdom's at its death, and just it is
That I should die with it: so in all this
We miscal grief, bale, sorrow, heartbreak, woe,
What is there to plain of? By Titan's foe
I am but rightly serv'd." So saying, he
Tripp'd lightly on, in sort of deathful glee;
Laughing at the clear stream and setting sun,
As though they jests had been: nor had he done
His laugh at nature's holy countenance,
Until that grove appear'd, as if perchance,
And then his tongue with sober seemlihed
Gave utterance as he entered: "Ha!" I said,
"King of the butterflies; but by this gloom,
And by old Rhadamanthus' tongue of doom,
This dusk religion, pomp of solitude,

And the Promethean clay by thief endued,
By old Saturnus' forelock, by his head
Shook with eternal palsy, I did wed
Myself to things of light from infancy;
And thus to be cast out, thus lorn to die,
Is sure enough to make a mortal man
Grow impious." So he inwardly began
On things for which no wording can be found;
Deeper and deeper sinking, until drown'd
Beyond the reach of music: for the choir
Of Cynthia he heard not, though rough briar
Nor muffling thicket interpos'd to dull
The vesper hymn, far swollen, soft and full,
Through the dark pillars of those sylvan aisles.
He saw not the two maidens, nor their smiles,
Wan as primroses gather'd at midnight
By chilly finger'd spring. "Unhappy wight!
Endymion!" said Peona, "we are here!
What wouldst thou ere we all are laid on bier?"
Then he embrac'd her, and his lady's hand
Press'd, saying: "Sister, I would have command,
If it were heaven's will, on our sad fate."
At which that dark-eyed stranger stood elate
And said, in a new voice, but sweet as love,
To Endymion's amaze: "By Cupid's dove,
And so thou shalt! and by the lily truth
Of my own breast thou shalt, beloved youth!"
And as she spake, into her face there came
Light, as reflected from a silver flame:
Her long black hair swell'd ampler, in display
Full golden; in her eyes a brighter day
Dawn'd blue and full of love. Aye, he beheld
Phœbe, his passion! joyous she upheld
Her lucid bow, continuing thus: "Drear, drear
Has our delaying been; but foolish fear
Withheld me first; and then decrees of fate;
And then 'twas fit that from this mortal state
Thou shouldst, my love, by some unlook'd for change
Be spiritualiz'd. Peona, we shall range
These forests, and to thee they safe shall be
As was thy cradle; hither shalt thou flee
To meet us many a time." Next Cynthia bright
Peona kiss'd, and bless'd with fair good night:
Her brother kiss'd her too, and knelt adown
Before his goddess, in a blissful swoon.

She gave her fair hands to him, and behold,
Before three swiftest kisses he had told,
They vanish'd far away!—Peona went
Home through the gloomy wood in wonderment.

'*In drear nighted December*'

I

In drear nighted December,
Too happy, happy tree,
Thy branches ne'er remember
Their green felicity—
The north cannot undo them
With a sleety whistle through them
Nor frozen thawings glue them
From budding at the prime.

II

In drear-nighted December,
Too happy, happy brook,
Thy bubblings ne'er remember
Apollo's summer look;
But with a sweet forgetting,
They stay their crystal fretting,
Never, never petting
About the frozen time.

III

Ah! would 'twere so with many
A gentle girl and boy—
But were there ever any
Writh'd not of passed joy?
The feel of not to feel it,
When there is none to heal it
Nor numbed sense to steel it,
Was never said in rhyme.

Nebuchadnezzar's Dream

Before he went to live with owls and bats,
Nebuchadnezzar had an ugly dream,
Worse than a housewife's, when she thinks her cream
Made a naumachia for mice and rats:
So scared, he sent for that "good kind of cats,"
Young Daniel, who did straightway pluck the beam
From out his eye, and said—"I do not deem
Your sceptre worth a straw, your cushions old door mats."
A horrid nightmare, similar somewhat,
Of late has haunted a most valiant crew
Of loggerheads and chapmen;—we are told
That any Daniel, though he be a sot,
Can make their lying lips turn pale of hue,
By drawing out—"Ye are that head of gold!"

Apollo to the Graces

APOLLO
Which of the fairest three
Today will ride with me?
My steeds are all pawing on the thresholds of Morn:
Which of the fairest three
Today will ride with me?
Across the gold Autumn's whole kingdoms of corn?

THE GRACES *all answer*
I will, I—I—I—
O young Apollo let me fly along with thee,
I will, I—I—I—
The many, many wonders see—
I—I—I—I—
And thy lyre shall never have a slackened string.
I—I—I—I—
Thro' the whole day will sing.

To Mrs Reynolds's Cat

Cat! who hast passed thy grand climacteric,
How many mice and rats hast in thy days
Destroyed? How many tit-bits stolen? Gaze
With those bright languid segments green, and prick
Those velvet ears—but prithee do not stick

Thy latent talons in me, and up-raise
Thy gentle mew, and tell me all thy frays
Of fish and mice, and rats and tender chick.
Nay, look not down, nor lick thy dainty wrists—
For all thy wheezy asthma, and for all
Thy tail's tip is nicked off, and though the fists
Of many a maid have given thee many a maul,
Still is that fur as soft as when the lists
In youth thou enteredst on glass-bottled wall.

On seeing a Lock of Milton's Hair. Ode

Chief of organic Numbers!
Old Scholar of the Spheres!
Thy spirit never slumbers,
But rolls about our ears
For ever and for ever.
O, what a mad endeavour
Worketh he
Who, to thy sacred and ennobled hearse,
Would offer a burnt sacrifice of verse
And Melody!

How heavenward thou soundedst
Live Temple of sweet noise;
And discord unconfoundedst:
Giving delight new joys,
And Pleasure nobler pinions—
O where are thy Dominions!
Lend thine ear
To a young delian oath—aye, by thy soul,
By all that from thy mortal Lips did roll;
And by the Kernel of thine earthly Love,
Beauty, in things on earth and things above,
I swear!
When every childish fashion
Has vanish'd from my rhyme
Will I grey-gone in passion
Give to an after-time
Hymning and harmony
Of thee, and of thy Words and of thy Life:
But vain is now the bruning and the strife—
Pangs are in vain—until I grow high-rife
With Old Philosophy
And mad with glimpses at futurity!

For many years my offerings must be hush'd:
   When I do speak I'll think upon this hour,
Because I feel my forehead hot and flush'd,
   Even at the simplest vassal of thy Power,—
      A Lock of thy bright hair!
      Sudden it came,
And I was startled when I heard thy name
      Coupled so unaware—
Yet, at the moment, temperate was my blood:
Methought I had beheld it from the flood.

On Sitting Down to Read King Lear Once Again

O golden tongued Romance, with serene lute!
   Fair plumèd Syren, Queen of far-away!
   Leave melodizing on this wintry day,
Shut up thine olden pages, and be mute:
Adieu! for once again the fierce dispute
   Betwixt damnation and impassion'd clay
   Must I burn through; once more humbly assay
The bitter-sweet of this Shakespearian fruit.
Chief Poet! and ye clouds of Albion,
   Begetters of our deep eternal theme!
When through the old oak Forest I am gone,
   Let me not wander in a barren dream,
But when I am consumèd in the fire,
Give me new Phoenix wings to fly at my desire.

When I have Fears that I may cease to be

When I have fears that I may cease to be
   Before my pen has glean'd my teeming brain,
Before high pil'd books, in charact'ry,
   Hold like rich garners the full-ripen'd grain;
When I behold, upon the night's starr'd face,
   Huge cloudy symbols of a high romance,
And feel that I may never live to trace
   Their shadows, with the magic hand of chance;
And when I feel, fair creature of an hour!
   That I shall never look upon thee more,
Never have relish in the faery power
   Of unreflecting love;—then on the shore
Of the wide world I stand alone, and think,
Till Love and Fame to nothingness do sink.

'O blush not so! O blush not so!'

I

O blush not so! O blush not so!
Or I shall think you knowing;
And if you smile the blushing while,
Then maidenheads are going.

II

There's a blush for want, and a blush for shan't,
And a blush for having done it;
There's a blush for thought, and a blush for nought,
And a blush for just begun it.

III

O sigh not so! O sigh not so!
For it sounds of Eve's sweet pippin;
By these loosen'd lips you have tasted the pips
And fought in an amorous nipping.

IV

Will you play once more at nice-cut-core,
For it only will last our youth out,
And we have the prime of the kissing time,
We have not one sweet tooth out.

V

There's a sigh for aye, and a sigh for nay,
And a sigh for "I can't bear it!"
O what can be done, shall we stay or run?
O cut the sweet apple and share it!

'Hence Burgundy, Claret, and Port'

Hence Burgundy, Claret, and Port,
Away with old Hock and Madeira,
Too couthly ye are for my sport;
There's a beverage brighter and clearer.
Instead of a pitiful rummer,

My wine overbrims a whole summer;
   My bowl is the sky,
   And I drink at my eye,
   Till I feel in the brain
   A Delphian pain—
Then follow, my Caius! then follow!
   On the green of the hill
   We will drink our fill
   Of golden sunshine,
   Till our brains intcrtwine
With the glory and grace of Apollo!

'*God of the meridian*'

God of the meridian,
   And of the East and West,
To thee my soul is flown,
   And my body is earthward pressed.
It is an awful mission,
A terrible division,
And leaves a gulf austere
To be filled with worldly fear.
Ay, when the soul is fled
To high above our head,
Affrighted do we gaze
After its airy maze,
As doth a mother wild,
When her young infant child
Is in an eagle's claws—
And is not this the cause
Of madness ?—God of Song,
Thou bearest me along
Through sights I scarce can bear:
O let me, let me share
With the hot lyre and thee,
The staid Philosophy.
Temper my lonely hours,
And let me see thy bowers
More unalarmed!

Robin Hood

TO A FRIEND

No! those days are gone away,
And their hours are old and grey,
And their minutes buried all
Under the down-trodden pall
Of the leaves of many years;
Many times have winter's shears,
Frozen North, and chilling East,
Sounded tempests to the feast
Of the forest's whispering fleeces,
Since men knew nor rent nor leases.

No, the bugle sounds no more,
And the twanging bow no more;
Silent is the ivory shrill
Past the heath and up the hill;
There is no mid-forest laugh,
Where lone Echo gives the half
To some wight, amazed to hear
Jesting, deep in forest drear.

On the fairest time of June
You may go, with sun or moon,
Or the seven stars to light you,
Or the polar ray to right you;
But you never may behold
Little John, or Robin bold;
Never one, of all the clan,
Thrumming on an empty can
Some old hunting ditty, while
He doth his green way beguile
To fair hostess Merriment,
Down beside the pasture Trent;
For he left the merry tale
Messenger for spicy ale.

Gone, the merry morris din;
Gone, the song of Gamelyn;
Gone, the tough-belted outlaw
Idling in the 'grene shawe';
All are gone away and past!

And if Robin should be cast
Sudden from his turfed grave,
And if Marian should have
Once again her forest days,
She would weep, and he would craze.
He would swear, for all his oaks,
Fallen beneath the dockyard strokes,
Have rotted on the briny seas;
She would weep that her wild bees
Sang not to her—strange! that honey
Can't be got without hard money I

So it is—yet let us sing,
Honour to the old bow-string!
Honour to the bugle-horn!
Honour to the woods unshorn!
Honour to the Lincoln green!
Honour to the archer keen!
Honour to tight little John,
And the horse he rode upon!
Honour to bold Robin Hood,
Sleeping in the underwood!
Honour to maid Marian,
And to all the Sherwood-clan!
Though their days have hurried by
Let us two a burden try.

Lines on the Mermaid Tavern

Souls of Poets dead and gone,
What Elysium have ye known,
Happy field or mossy cavern,
Choicer than the Mermaid Tavern?
Have ye tippled drink more fine
Than mine host's Canary wine?
Or are fruits of Paradise
Sweeter than those dainty pies
Of venison ? O generous food!
Dressed as though bold Robin Hood
Would, with his maid Marian,
Sup and bowse from horn and can.

I have heard that on a day
Mine host's sign-board flew away,
Nobody knew whither, till

An astrologer's old quill
To a sheepskin gave the story,
Said he saw you in your glory,
Underneath a new-old sign
Sipping beverage divine,
And pledging with contented smack
The Mermaid in the Zodiac.

Souls of Poets dead and gone,
What Elysium have ye known,
Happy field or mossy cavern,
Choicer than the Mermaid Tavern?

*To—**

Time's sea hath been five years at its slow ebb,
Long hours have to and fro let creep the sand,
Since I was tangled in thy beauty's web,
And snared by the ungloving of thy hand.
And yet I never look on midnight sky,
But I behold thine eyes' well-memoried light;
I cannot look upon the rose's dye,
But to thy cheek my soul doth take its flight;
I cannot look on any budding flower,
But my fond ear, in fancy at thy lips,
And hearkening for a love-sound, doth devour
Its sweets in the wrong sense:—Thou dost eclipse
Every delight with sweet remembering,
And grief unto my darling joys dost bring.

* A lady whom he saw for some few moments at Vauxhall.

To the Nile

Son of the old moon-mountains African!
Chief of the pyramid and crocodile!
We call thee fruitful, and, that very while,
A desert fills our seeing's inward span.
Nurse of swart nations since the world began,

Art thou so fruitful? or dost thou beguile
Such men to honour thee, who, worn with toil,
Rest for a space 'twixt Cairo and Decan?
O may dark fancies err! They surely do.
'Tis ignorance that makes a barren waste

Of all beyond itself. Thou dost bedew
   Green rushes like our rivers, and dost taste
The pleasant sun-rise. Green isles hast thou too,
And to the sea as happily dost haste.

‘*Spenser! a jealous honourer of thine*’

Spenser! a jealous honourer of thine,
   A forester deep in thy midmost trees,
Did last eve ask my promise to refine
   Some English that might strive thine ear to please.
But, Elfin Poet, ’tis impossible
   For an inhabitant of wintry earth
To rise like Phoebus with a golden quell,
   Fire-winged, and make a morning in his mirth.
It is impossible to escape from toil
   O’ the sudden and receive thy spiriting:
The flower must drink the nature of the soil
   Before it can put forth its blossoming.
Be with me in the summer days and I
Will for thine honour and his pleasure try.

‘*Blue! ’Tis the life of heaven, the domain*’

ANSWER TO A SONNET ENDING THUS:

Dark eyes are dearer far
Than orbs that mock the hyacinthine bell—
J. H. Reynolds

Blue! ’Tis the life of heaven, the domain
   Of Cynthia, the wide palace of the sun,
The tent of Hesperus, and all his train,
   The bosomer of clouds, gold, grey and dun.
Blue! ’Tis the life of waters—Ocean
   And all its vassal streams, pools numberless,
May rage, and foam, and fret, but never can
   Subside, if not to dark blue nativeness.
Blue! Gentle cousin to the forest-green,
   Married to green in all the sweetest flowers—
Forget-me-not, the blue-bell, and, that queen
   Of secrecy, the violet. What strange powers
Hast thou, as a mere shadow! But how great,
When in an eye thou art, alive with fate!

'O thou whose face hath felt the Winter's wind'

[*Letter to J. H. Reynolds, 19 February 1818*: '…I had no Idea but of the Morning and the Thrush said I was right—seeming to say…']

'O thou whose face hath felt the Winter's wind,
  Whose eye has seen the snow-clouds hung in mist,
  And the black elm tops, 'mong the freezing stars,
  To thee the spring will be a harvest-time.
O thou, whose only book has been the light
  Of supreme darkness which thou feddest on
  Night after night when Phoebus was away,
  To thee the Spring shall be a triple morn.
O fret not after knowledge—I have none,
  And yet my song comes native with the warmth.
O fret not after knowledge—I have none,
  And yet the Evening listens. He who saddens
At thought of idleness cannot be idle,
And he's awake who thinks himself asleep.'

Sonnet to A[*ubrey*] *G*[*eorge*] *S*[*pencer*]

ON READING HIS ADMIRABLE VERSES IN THIS (MISS REYNOLDS'S) ALBUM, ON EITHER SIDE OF THE FOLLOWING ATTEMPT TO PAY SMALL TRIBUTE THERETO

Where didst thou find, young Bard, thy sounding lyre?
  Where the bland accent, and the tender tone?
A-sitting snugly by thy parlour fire?
  Or didst thou with Apollo pick a bone?
The Muse will have a crow to pick with me
  For thus assaying in thy brightening path:
Who, that with his own brace of eyes can see,
  Unthunderstruck beholds thy gentle wrath?
Who from a pot of stout e'er blew the froth
Into the bosom of the wandering wind,
  Light as the powder on the back of moth,
But drank thy muses with a grateful mind?
  Yea, unto thee beldams drink metheglin
  And annisies, and carraway, and gin.

Extracts from an Opera

I

O! were I one of the Olympian twelve,
Their godships should pass this into a law—
That when a man doth set himself in toil
After some beauty veiled far away,
Each step he took should make his lady's hand
More soft, more white, and her fair cheek more fair;
And for each briar-berry he might eat,
A kiss should bud upon the tree of love,
And pulp and ripen richer every hour,
To melt away upon the traveller's lips.

II. DAISY'S SONG

1

The sun, with his great eye,
Sees not so much as I;
And the moon, all silver-proud,
Might as well be in a cloud.

2

And O the spring—the spring!
I lead the life of a king!
Couched in the teeming grass,
I spy each pretty lass.

3

I look where no one dares,
And I stare where no one stares,
And when the night is nigh,
Lambs bleat my lullaby.

III. FOLLY'S SONG

When wedding fiddles are a-playing,
          Huzza for folly O!
And when maidens go a-maying,
          Huzza, etc.
When a milk-pail is upset,
          Huzza, etc.
And the clothes left in the wet,
          Huzza, etc.
When the barrel's set abroach,
          Huzza, etc.
When Kate Eyebrow keeps a coach,
          Huzza, etc.
When the pig is over-roasted,
          Huzza, etc.
And the cheese is over-toasted,
          Huzza, etc.
When Sir Snap is with his lawyer,
          Huzza, etc.
And Miss Chip has kissed the sawyer,
          Huzza, etc.

IV.

O, I am frightened with most hateful thoughts!
Perhaps her voice is not a nightingale's,
Perhaps her teeth are not the fairest pearl;
Her eye-lashes may be, for aught I know,
Not longer than the may-fly's small fan-horns;
There may not be one dimple on her hand—
And freckles many. Ah! a careless nurse,
In haste to teach the little thing to walk,
May have crumped up a pair of Dian's legs
And warped the ivory of a Juno's neck.

V. SONG

1

The stranger lighted from his steed,
   And ere he spake a word,
He seized my lady's lily hand,
   And kissed it all unheard.

2

The stranger walked into the hall,
 And ere he spake a word,
He kissed my lady's cherry lips,
 And kissed 'em all unheard.

3

The stranger walked into the bower—
 But my lady first did go:
Ay, hand in hand into the bower,
 Where my lord's roses blow.

4

My lady's maid had a silken scarf,
 And a golden ring had she,
And a kiss from the stranger, as off he went
 Again on his fair palfrey.

VI

Asleep! O sleep a little while, white pearl!
And let me kneel, and let me pray to thee,
And let me call Heaven's blessing on thine eyes,
And let me breathe into the happy air,
That doth enfold and touch thee all about,
Vows of my slavery, my giving up,
My sudden adoration, my great love!

The Human Seasons

Four seasons fill the measure of the year;
 There are four seasons in the mind of man.
He has his lusty Spring, when fancy clear
 Takes in all beauty with an easy span.
He has his Summer, when luxuriously
 Spring's honeyed cud of youthful thought he loves
To ruminate, and by such dreaming nigh
 His nearest unto heaven. Quiet coves
His soul has in its Autumn, when his wings
 He furleth close; contented so to look
On mists in idleness—to let fair things

Pass by unheeded as a threshold brook.
He has his Winter too of pale misfeature,
Or else he would forego his mortal nature.

'*For there's Bishop's Teign*'

I

For there's Bishop's Teign
And King's Teign
And Coomb at the clear Teign head—
Where close by the stream.
You may have your cream
All spread upon barley bread.

II

There's Arch Brook
And there's Larch Brook
Both turning many a mill;
And cooling the drouth
Of the salmon's mouth,
And fattening his silver gill.

III

There is Wild Wood,
A mild hood
To the sheep on the lea o' the down,
Where the golden furze,
With its green, thin spurs,
Doth catch at the maiden's gown.

IV

There is Newton Marsh
With its spear grass harsh—
A pleasant summer level
Where the maidens sweet
Of the Market Street
Do meet in the dusk to revel.

V

There's the barton rich
With dyke and ditch
And hedge for the thrush to live in,
And the hollow tree
For the buzzing bee
And a bank for the wasp to hive in.

VI

And O, and O,
The daisies blow
And the primroses are wakened,
And violet white
Sits in silver plight,
And the green bud's as long as the spike end.

VII

Then who would go
Into dark Soho,
And chatter with dacked-haired critics,
When he can stay
For the new-mown hay,
And startle the dappled prickets?

'*Where be ye going, you Devon maid*'?

I

Where be ye going, you Devon maid?
And what have ye there i' the basket?
Ye tight little fairy, just fresh from the dairy,
Will ye give me some cream if I ask it?

II

I love your meads, and I love your flowers,
And I love your junkets mainly,
But 'hind the door I love kissing more,
O look not so disdainly.

III

I love your hills, and I love your dales,
  And I love your flocks a-bleating—
But O, on the heather to lie together,
  With both our hearts a-beating!

IV

I'll put your basket all safe in a *nook*,
  And your shawl I hang up *on this willow*,
And we will sigh in the daisy's eye
  And kiss on a grass-green pillow.

'*Over the hill and over the dale*'

Over the hill and over the dale,
And over the bourn to Dawlish—
Where gingerbread wives have a scanty sale
And gingerbread nuts are smallish.

Rantipole Betty she ran down a hill
And kicked up her petticoats fairly.
Says I, 'I'll be Jack if you will be Jill.'
So she sat on the grass debonairly.

'Here's somebody coming, here's somebody coming!'
Says I, ''Tis the wind at a parley.'
So without any fuss, any hawing and humming,
She lay on the grass debonairly.

'Here's somebody here, and here's somebody *there*!
Says I, 'Hold your tongue, you young gipsy.'
So she held her tongue and lay plump and fair,
And dead as a Venus tipsy.

O who wouldn't hie to Dawlish fair,
O who wouldn't stop in a meadow?
O [who] would not rumple the daisies there,
And make the wild fern for a bed do?

To J. H. Reynolds, Esq.

Dear Reynolds, as last night I lay in bed,
There came before my eyes that wonted thread
Of shapes, and shadows, and remembrances,
That every other minute vex and please:
Things all disjointed come from North and South—
Two witch's eyes above a cherub's mouth,
Voltaire with casque and shield and habergeon,
And Alexander with his nightcap on,
Old Socrates a-tying his cravat,
And Hazlitt playing with Miss Edgeworth's cat,
And Junius Brutus, pretty well so so,
Making the best of's way towards Soho.

Few are there who escape these visitings—
Perhaps one or two whose lives have patient wings,
And through whose curtains peeps no hellish nose,
No wild-boar tushes, and no mermaid's toes;
But flowers bursting out with lusty pride,
And young Aeolian harps personified,
Some, Titian colours touched into real life—
The sacrifice goes on; the pontiff knife
Gloams in the sun, the milk-white heifer lows,
The pipes go shrilly, the libation flows;
A white sail shows above the green-head cliff,
Moves round the point, and throws her anchor stiff.
The mariners join hymn with those on land.

You know the Enchanted Castle—it doth stand
Upon a rock, on the border of a lake,
Nested in trees, which all do seem to shake
From some old magic like Urganda's sword.
O Phoebus! that I had thy sacred word
To show this castle, in fair dreaming wise,
Unto my friend, while sick and ill he lies!

You know it well enough, where it doth seem
A mossy place, a Merlin's Hall, a dream.
You know the clear lake, and the little isles,
The mountains blue, and cold near-neighbour rills,
All which elsewhere are but half animate;
Here do they look alive to love and hate,
To smiles and frowns; they Ipeem a lifted mound
Above some giant, pulsing uhderground.

Part of the building was a chosen see,
Built by a banished santon of Chaldee;
The other part, two thousand years from him,
Was built by Cuthbert de Saint Aldebrim;
Then there's a little wing, far from the sun,
Built by a Lapland witch turned maudlin nun;
And many other juts of agèd stone
Founded with many a mason-devil's groan.

The doors all look as if they oped themselves,
The windows as if latched by fays and elves,
And from them comes a silver flash of light,
As from the westward of a summer's night;
Or like a beauteous woman's large blue eyes
Gone mad through olden songs and poesies—

See! what is coming from the distance dim!
A golden galley all in silken trim!
Three rows of oars are lightening, moment-whiles,
Into the verdurous bosoms of those isles.
Towards the shade, under the castle wall,
It comes in silence—now 'tis hidden all.
The clarion sounds, and from a postern-grate
An echo of sweet music doth create
A fear in the poor herdsman, who doth bring
His beasts to trouble the enchanted spring.
He tells of the sweet music, and the spot,
To all his friends—and they believe him not.

O that our dreamings all, of sleep or wake,
Would all their colours from the sunset take,
From something of material sublime,
Rather than shadow our own soul's daytime
In the dark void of night. For in the world
We jostle—but my flag is not unfurled

On the admiral staff—and to philosophize
I dare not yet! O, never will the prize,
High reason, and the lore of good and ill,
Be my award! Things cannot to the will
Be settled, but they tease us out of thought.
Or is it that imagination brought
Beyond its proper bound, yet still confined,
Lost in a sort of purgatory blind,
Cannot refer to any standard law
Of either earth or heaven? It is a flaw
In happiness, to see beyond our bourne—
It forces us in summer skies to mourn;
It spoils the singing of the nightingale.

Dear Reynolds, I have a mysterious tale,
And cannot speak it. The first page I read
Upon a lampit rock of green seaweed
Among the breakers. 'Twas a quiet eve;
The rocks were silent, the wide sea did weave
An untumultuous fringe of silver foam
Along the flat brown sand. I was at home
And should have been most happy—but I saw
Too far into the sea, where every maw
The greater on the less feeds evermore.—
But I saw too distinct into the core
Of an eternal fierce destruction,
And so from happiness I far was gone.
Still am I sick of it; and though, today,
I've gathered young spring-leaves, and flowers gay
Of periwinkle and wild strawberry,
Still do I that most fierce destruction see—
The shark at savage prey, the hawk at pounce,
The gentle robin, like a pard or ounce,
Ravening a worm.—Away, ye horrid moods!
Moods of one's mind! You know I hate them well,
You know I'd sooner be a clapping bell
To some Kamchatkan missionary church,
Than with these horrid moods be left in lurch.
Do you get health—and Tom the same—I'll dance,
And from detested moods in new romance
Take refuge. Of bad lines a centaine dose
Is sure enough—and so 'here follows prose'…

To J[*ames*] *R*[*ice*]

O that a week could be an age, and we
Felt parting and warm meeting every week,
Then one poor year a thousand years would be,
The flush of welcome ever on the cheek:
So could we live long life in little space,
So time itself would be annihilate,
So a day's journey in oblivious haze
To serve our joys would lengthen and dilate.
O to arrive each Monday mom from Ind!
To land each Tuesday from the rich Levant!
In little time a host of joys to bind,
And keep our souls in one eternal pant!
This mom, my friend, and yester-evening taught
Me how to harbour such a happy thought.

Isabella; *or*, *The Pot of Basil*

I

Fair Isabel, poor simple Isabel!
Lorenzo, a young palmer in Love's eye!
They could not in the self-same mansion dwell
Without some stir of heart, some malady;
They could not sit at meals but feel how well
It soothed each to be the other by;
They could not, sure, beneath the same roof sleep
But to each other dream, and nightly weep.

II

With every mom their love grew tenderer,
With every eve deeper and tenderer still;
He might not in house, field, or garden stir,
But her full shape would all his seeing fill;
And his continual voice was pleasanter
To her than noise of trees or hidden rill;
Her lute-string gave an echo of his name,
She spoilt her half-done broidery with the same.

III

He knew whose gentle hand was at the latch
  Before the door had given her to his eyes;
And from her chamber-window he would catch
  Her beauty farther than the falcon spies;
And constant as her vespers would he watch,
  Because her face was turned to the same skies;
And with sick longing all the night outwear,
To hear her morning-step upon the stair.

IV

A whole long month of May in this sad plight
  Made their cheeks paler by the break of June:
'To-morrow will I bow to my delight,
  To-morrow will I ask my lady's boon.'
'O may I never see another night,
  Lorenzo, if thy lips breathe not love's tune.'
So spake they to their pillows; but, alas,
Honeyless days and days did he let pass—

V

Until sweet Isabella's untouched cheek
  Fell sick within the rose's just domain,
Fell thin as a young mother's, who doth seek
  By every lull to cool her infant's pain:
'How ill she is,' said he, 'I may not speak,
  And yet I will, and tell my love all plain:
If looks speak love-laws, I will drink her tears,
And at the least 'twill startle off her cares.'

VI

So said he one fair morning, and all day
  His heart beat awfully against his side;
And to his heart he inwardly did pray
  For power to speak; but still the ruddy tide
Stifled his voice, and pulsed resolve away—
  Fevered his high conceit of such a bride,
Yet brought him to the meekness of a child:
Alas! when passion is both meek and wild!

VII

So once more he had waked and anguishèd
  A dreary night of love and misery,
If Isabel's quick eye had not been wed
  To every symbol on his forehead high.
She saw it waxing very pale and dead,
  And straight all flushed; so, lispèd tenderly,
'Lorenzo!'—here she ceased her timid quest,
But in her tone and look he read the rest.

VIII

'O Isabella, I can half-perceive
  That I may speak my grief into thine ear.
If thou didst ever anything believe,
  Believe how I love thee, believe how near
My soul is to its doom: I would not grieve
  Thy hand by unwelcome pressing, would not fear
Thine eyes by gazing; but I cannot live
Another night, and not my passion shrive.

IX

'Love! thou art leading me from wintry cold,
  Lady! thou leadest me to summer clime,
And I must taste the blossoms that unfold
  In its ripe warmth this gracious morning time.'
So said, his erewhile timid lips grew bold,
  And poesied with hers in dewy rhyme:
Great bliss was with them, and great happiness
Grew, like a lusty flower, in June's caress.

X

Parting they seemed to tread upon the air,
  Twin roses by the zephyr blown apart
Only to meet again more close, and share
  The inward fragrance of each other's heart.
She, to her chamber gone, a ditty fair
  Sang, of delicious love and honeyed dart;
He with light steps went up a western hill,
And bade the sun farewell, and joyed his fill.

XI

All close they met again, before the dusk
Had taken from the stars its pleasant veil,
All close they met, all eves, before the dusk
Had taken from the stars its pleasant veil,
Close in a bower of hyacinth and musk,
Unknown of any, free from whispering tale.
Ah! better had it been for ever so,
Than idle ears should pleasure in their woe.

XII

Were they unhappy then?—It cannot be—
Too many tears for lovers have been shed,
Too many sighs give we to them in fee,
Too much of pity after they are dead,
Too many doleful stories do we see,
Whose matter in bright gold were best be read;
Except in such a page where Theseus' spouse
Over the pathless waves towards him bows.

XIII

But, for the general award of love,
The little sweet doth kill much bitterness;
Though Dido silent is in under-grove,
And Isabella's was a great distress,
Though young Lorenzo in warm Indian clove
Was not embalmed, this truth is not the less—
Even bees, the little almsmen of spring-bowers,
Know there is richest juice in poison-flowers.

XIV

With her two brothers this fair lady dwelt,
Enrichèd from ancestral merchandise,
And for them many a weary hand did swelt
In torchèd mines and noisy factories,
And many once proud-quivered loins did melt
In blood from stinging whip—with hollow eyes
Many all day in dazzling river stood,
To take the rich-ored driftings of the flood.

XV

For them the Ceylon diver held his breath,
And went all naked to the hungry shark;
For them his ears gushed blood; for them in death
The seal on the cold ice with piteous bark
Lay full of darts; for them alone did seethe
A thousand men in troubles wide and dark:
Half-ignorant, they turned an easy wheel,
That set sharp racks at work to pinch and peel.

XVI

Why were they proud? Because their marble founts
Gushed with more pride than do a wretch's tears?
Why were they proud? Because fair orange-mounts
Were of more soft ascent than lazar stairs?—
Why were they proud? Because red-lined accounts
Were richer than the songs of Grecian years?—
Why were they proud? again we ask aloud,
Why in the name of Glory were they proud?

XVII

Yet were these Florentines as self-retired
In hungry pride and gainful cowardice,
As two close Hebrews in that land inspired,
Paled in and vineyarded from beggar-spies—
The hawks of ship-mast forests—the untired
And panniered mules for ducats and old lies—
Quick cat's-paws on the generous stray-away—
Great wits in Spanish, Tuscan, and Malay.

XVIII

How was it these same ledger-men could spy
Fair Isabella in her downy nest?
How could they find out in Lorenzo's eye
A straying from his toil? Hot Egypt's pest
Into their vision covetous and sly!
How could these money-bags see east and west?—
Yet so they did—and every dealer fair
Must see behind, as doth the hunted hare.

XIX

O eloquent and famed Boccaccio!
   Of thee we now should ask forgiving boon,
And of thy spicy myrtles as they blow,
   And of thy roses amorous of the moon,
And of thy lilies, that do paler grow
   Now they can no more hear thy gittern's tune,
For venturing syllables that ill beseem
The quiet glooms of such a piteous theme.

XX

Grant thou a pardon here, and then the tale
   Shall move on soberly, as it is meet;
There is no other crime, no mad assail
   To make old prose in modern rhyme more sweet:
But it is done—succeed the verse or fail—
   To honour thee, and thy gone spirit greet,
To stead thee as a verse in English tongue,
An echo of thee in the north wind sung.

XXI

These brethren having found by many signs
   What love Lorenzo for their sister had,
And how she loved him too, each unconfines
   His bitter thoughts to other, well nigh mad
That he, the servant of their trade designs,
   Should in their sister's love be blithe and glad,
When 'twas their plan to coax her by degrees
To some high noble and his olive-trees.

XXII

And many a jealous conference had they,
   And many times they bit their lips alone,
Before they fixed upon a surest way
   To make the youngster for his crime atone;
And at the last, these men of cruel clay
   Cut Mercy with a sharp knife to the bone,
For they resolvèd in some forest dim
To kill Lorenzo, and there bury him.

XXIII

So on a pleasant morning, as he leant
  Into the sunrise, o'er the balustrade
Of the garden-terrace, towards him they bent
  Their footing through the dews; and to him said,
'You seem there in the quiet of content,
  Lorenzo, and we are most loth to invade
Calm speculation; but if you are wise,
Bestride your steed while cold is in the skies.

XXIV

'To-day we purpose, ay, this hour we mount
  To spur three leagues towards the Apennine;
Come down, we pray thee, ere the hot sun count
  His dewy rosary on the eglantine.'
Lorenzo, courteously as he was wont,
  Bowed a fair greeting to these serpents' whine;
And went in haste, to get in readiness,
With belt, and spur, and bracing huntsman's dress.

XXV

And as he to the court-yard passed along,
  Each third step did he pause, and listened oft
If he could hear his lady's matin-song,
  Or the light whisper of her footstep soft;
And as he thus over his passion hung,
  He heard a laugh full musical aloft,
When, looking up, he saw her features bright
Smile through an in-door lattice, all delight.

XXVI

'Love, Isabel!' said he, 'I was in pain
  Lest I should miss to bid thee a good morrow:
Ah! what if I should lose thee, when so fain
  I am to stifle all the heavy sorrow
Of a poor three hours' absence? but we'll gain
  Out of the amorous dark what day doth borrow.
Good bye! I'll soon be back.' 'Good bye!' said she—
And as he went she chanted merrily.

XXVII

So the two brothers and their murdered man
Rode past fair Florence, to where Amo's stream
Gurgles through straitened banks, and still doth fan
Itself with dancing bulrush, and the bream
Keeps head against the freshets. Sick and wan
The brothers' faces in the ford did seem,
Lorenzo's flush with love.—They passed the water
Into a forest quiet for the slaughter.

XXVIII

There was Lorenzo slain and buried in,
There in that forest did his great love cease.
Ah! when a soul doth thus its freedom win,
It aches in loneliness—is ill at peace
As the break-covert blood-hounds of such sin.
They dipped their swords in the water, and did tease
Their horses homeward, with convulsed spur,
Each richer by his being a murderer.

XXIX

They told their sister how, with sudden speed,
Lorenzo had ta'en ship for foreign lands,
Because of some great urgency and need
In their affairs, requiring trusty hands.
Poor girl! put on thy stifling widow's weed,
And 'scape at once from Hope's accursed bands;
Today thou wilt not see him, nor tomorrow,
And the next day will be a day of sorrow.

XXX

She weeps alone for pleasures not to be;
Sorely she wept until the night came on,
And then, instead of love, O misery!
She brooded o'er the luxury alone:
His image in the dusk she seemed to see,
And to the silence made a gentle moan,
Spreading her perfect arms upon the air,
And on her couch low murmuring 'Where? O where?'

XXXI

But Selfishness, Love's cousin, held not long
Its fiery vigil in her single breast.
She fretted for the golden hour, and hung
Upon the time with feverish unrest—
Not long—for soon into her heart a throng
Of higher occupants, a richer zest,
Came tragic—passion not to be subdued,
And sorrow for her love in travels rude.

XXXII

In the mid days of autumn, on their eves
The breath of Winter comes from far away,
And the sick west continually bereaves
Of some gold tinge, and plays a roundelay
Of death among the bushes and the leaves,
To make all bare before he dares to stray
From his north cavern. So sweet Isabel
By gradual decay from beauty fell,

XXXIII

Because Lorenzo came not. Oftentimes
She asked her brothers, with an eye all pale,
Striving to be itself, what dungeon climes
Could keep him off so long? They spake a tale
Time after time, to quiet her. Their crimes
Came on them, like a smoke from Hinnom's vale
And every night in dreams they groaned aloud,
To see their sister in her snowy shroud.

XXXIV

And she had died in drowsy ignorance,
But for a thing more deadly dark than all.
It came like a fierce potion, drunk by chance,
Which saves a sick man from the feathered pall
For some few gasping moments; like a lance,
Waking an Indian from his cloudy hall
With cruel pierce, and bringing him again
Sense of the gnawing fire at heart and brain.

XXXV

It was a vision.—In the drowsy gloom,
   The dull of midnight, at her couch's foot
Lorenzo stood, and wept: the forest tomb
   Had marred his glossy hair which once could shoot
Lustre into the sun, and put cold doom
   Upon his lips, and taken the soft lute
From his lorn voice, and past his loamèd ears
Had made a miry channel for his tears.

XXXVI

Strange sound it was, when the pale shadow spake;
   For there was striving, in its piteous tongue,
To speak as when on earth it was awake,
   And Isabella on its music hung.
Languor there was in it, and tremulous shake,
   As in a palsied Druid's harp unstrung;
And through it moaned a ghostly under-song,
Like hoarse night-gusts sepulchral briars among.

XXXVII

Its eyes, though wild, were still all dewy bright
   With love, and kept all phantom fear aloof
From the poor girl by magic of their light,
   The while it did unthread the horrid woof
Of the late darkened time—the murderous spite
   Of pride and avarice, the dark pine roof
In the forest, and the sodden turfed dell,
Where, without any word, from stabs he fell.

XXXVIII

Saying moreover, 'Isabel, my sweet!
   Red whortle-berries droop above my head,
And a large flint-stone weighs upon my feet;
   Around me beeches and high chestnuts shed
Their leaves and prickly nuts; a sheep-fold bleat
   Comes from beyond the river to my bed:
Go, shed one tear upon my heather-bloom,
And it shall comfort me within the tomb.

XXXIX

'I am a shadow now, alas! alas!
  Upon the skirts of human-nature dwelling
Alone. I chant alone the holy mass,
  While little sounds of life are round me knelling,
And glossy bees at noon do fieldward pass,
  And many a chapel bell the hour is telling,
Paining me through: those sounds grow strange to me,
And thou art distant in humanity.

XL

'I know what was, I feel full well what is,
  And I should rage, if spirits could go mad;
Though I forget the taste of earthly bliss,
  That paleness warms my grave, as though I had
A seraph chosen from the bright abyss
  To be my spouse: thy paleness makes me glad;
Thy beauty grows upon me, and I feel
A greater love through all my essence steal.'

XLI

The Spirit mourn'd 'Adieu!'—dissolved, and left
  The atom darkness in a slow turmoil;
As when of healthful midnight sleep bereft,
  Thinking on rugged hours and fruitless toil,
We put our eyes into a pillowy cleft,
  And see the spangly gloom froth up and boil:
It made sad Isabella's eyelids ache,
And in the dawn she started up awake—

XLII

'Ha! ha!' said she, 'I knew not this hard life,
  I thought the worst was simple misery;
I thought some Fate with pleasure or with strife
  Portioned us—happy days, or else to die;
But there is crime—a brother's bloody knife!
  Sweet Spirit, thou hast schooled my infancy:
I'll visit thee for this, and kiss thine eyes,
And greet thee morn and even in the skies.'

XLIII

When the full morning came, she had devised
How she might secret to the forest hie;
How she might find the clay, so dearly prized,
And sing to it one latest lullaby;
How her short absence might be unsurmised,
While she the inmost of the dream would try.
Resolved, she took with her an agèd nurse,
And went into that dismal forest-hearse.

XLIV

See, as they creep along the river side,
How she doth whisper to that agèd dame,
And, after looking round the champaign wide,
Shows her a knife.—'What feverous hectic flame
Burns in thee, child?—What good can thee betide,
That thou shouldst smile again?' The evening came,
And they had found Lorenzo's earthy bed—
The flint was there, the berries at his head.

XLV

Who hath not loitered in a green church-yard,
And let his spirit, like a demon-mole,
Work through the clayey soil and gravel hard,
To see skull, coffined bones, and funeral stole;
Pitying each form that hungry Death hath marred
And filling it once more with human soul?
Ah! this is holiday to what was felt
When Isabella by Lorenzo knelt.

XLVI

She gazed into the fresh-thrown mould, as though
One glance did fully all its secrets tell;
Clearly she saw, as other eyes would know
Pale limbs at bottom of a crystal well;
Upon the murderous spot she seemed to grow,
Like to a native lily of the dell—
Then with her knife, all sudden, she began
To dig more fervently than misers can.

XLVII

Soon she turned up a soilèd glove, whereon
  Her silk had played in purple phantasies,
She kissed it with a lip more chill than stone,
  And put it in her bosom, where it dries
And freezes utterly unto the bone
  Those dainties made to still an infant's cries:
Then 'gan she work again, nor stayed her care,
But to throw back at times her veiling hair.

XLVIII

That old nurse stood beside her wondering,
  Until her heart felt pity to the core
At sight of such a dismal labouring,
  And so she kneelèd, with her locks all hoar,
And put her lean hands to the horrid thing.
  Three hours they laboured at this travail sore—
At last they felt the kernel of the grave,
And Isabella did not stamp and rave.

XLIX

Ah! wherefore all this wormy circumstance?
  Why linger at the yawning tomb so long?
O for the gentleness of old Romance,
  The simple plaining of a minstrel's song!
Fair reader, at the old tale take a glance,
  For here, in truth, it doth not well belong
To speak—O turn thee to the very tale,
And taste the music of that vision pale.

L

With duller steel than the Persèan sword
  They cut away no formless monster's head,
But one, whose gentleness did well accord
  With death, as life. The ancient harps have said,
Love never dies, but lives, immortal Lord:
  If Love impersonate was ever dead,
Pale Isabella kissed it, and low moaned.
'Twas Love—cold, dead indeed, but not dethroned.

LI

In anxious secrecy they took it home,
  And then the prize was all for Isabel.
She calmed its wild hair with a golden comb,
  And all around each eye's sepulchral cell
Pointed each fringèd lash; the smearèd loam
  With tears, as chilly as a dripping well,
She drenched away—and still she combed, and kept
Sighing all day—and still she kissed, and wept.

LII

Then in a silken scarf—sweet with the dews
  Of precious flowers plucked in Araby,
And divine liquids come with odorous ooze
  Through the cold serpent-pipe refreshfully—
She wrapped it up; and for its tomb did choose
  A garden-pot, wherein she laid it by,
And covered it with mould, and o'er it set
Sweet basil, which her tears kept ever wet.

LIII

And she forgot the stars, the moon, and sun,
  And she forgot the blue above the trees,
And she forgot the dells where waters run,
  And she forgot the chilly autumn breeze;
She had no knowledge when the day was done,
  And the new morn she saw not, but in peace
Hung over her sweet basil evermore,
And moistened it with tears unto the core.

LIV

And so she ever fed it with thin tears,
  Whence thick, and green, and beautiful it grew,
So that it smelt more balmy than its peers
  Of basil-tufts in Florence; for it drew
Nurture besides, and life, from human fears,
  From the fast mouldering head there shut from view
So that the jewel, safely casketed,
Came forth, and in perfumèd leafits spread.

LV

O Melancholy, linger here awhile!
  O Music, Music, breathe despondingly!
O Echo, Echo, from some sombre isle,
  Unknown, Lethean, sigh to us—O sigh!
Spirits in grief, lift up your heads, and smile.
  Lift up your heads, sweet Spirits, heavily,
And make a pale light in your cypress glooms,
Tinting with silver wan your marble tombs.

LVI

Moan hither, all ye syllables of woe,
  From the deep throat of sad Melpomene!
Through bronzèd lyre in tragic order go,
  And touch the strings into a mystery;
Sound mournfully upon the winds and low;
  For simple Isabel is soon to be
Among the dead. She withers, like a palm
Cut by an Indian for its juicy balm.

LVII

O leave the palm to wither by itself;
  Let not quick Winter chill its dying hour!—
It may not be—those Baälites of pelf,
  Her brethren, noted the continual shower
From her dead eyes; and many a curious elf,
  Among her kindred, wondered that such dower
Of youth and beauty should be thrown aside
By one marked out to be a Noble's bride.

LVIII

And, furthermore, her brethren wondered much
  Why she sat drooping by the basil green,
And why it flourished, as by magic touch.
  Greatly they wondered what the thing might mean:
They could not surely give belief, that such
  A very nothing would have power to wean
Her from her own fair youth, and pleasures gay,
And even remembrance of her love's delay.

LIX

Therefore they watched a time when they might sift
This hidden whim; and long they watched in vain:
For seldom did she go to chapel-shrift,
And seldom felt she any hunger-pain;
And when she left, she hurried back, as swift
As bird on wing to breast its eggs again;
And, patient as a hen-bird, sat her there
Beside her basil, weeping through her hair.

LX

Yet they contrived to steal the basil-pot,
And to examine it in secret place.
The thing was vile with green and livid spot,
And yet they knew it was Lorenzo's face:
The guerdon of their murder they had got,
And so left Florence in a moment's space,
Never to turn again. Away they went,
With blood upon their heads, to banishment.

LXI

O Melancholy, turn thine eyes away!
O Music, Music, breathe despondingly!
O Echo, Echo, on some other day,
From isles Lethean, sigh to us—O sigh!
Spirits of grief, sing not your 'Well-a-way!'
For Isabel, sweet Isabel, will die—
Will die a death too lone and incomplete,
Now they have ta'en away her basil sweet.

LXII

Piteous she looked on dead and senseless things,
Asking for her lost basil amorously;
And with melodious chuckle in the strings
Of her lorn voice, she oftentimes would cry
After the pilgrim in his wanderings,
To ask him where her basil was, and why
'Twas hid from her: 'For cruel 'tis,' said she,
To steal my basil-pot away from me.'

LXIII

And so she pined, and so she died forlorn,
  Imploring for her basil to the last.
No heart was there in Florence but did mourn
  In pity of her love, so overcast.
And a sad ditty on this story born
  From mouth to mouth through all the country passed:
Still is the burthen sung—'O cruelty,
To steal my basil-pot away from me!'

To Homer

Standing aloof in giant ignorance,
  Of thee I hear and of the Cyclades,
As one who sits ashore and longs perchance
  To visit dolphin-coral in deep seas.
So wast thou blind!—but then the veil was rent,
  For Jove uncurtained Heaven to let thee live,
And Neptune made for thee a spumy tent,
  And Pan made sing for thee his forest-hive;
Ay, on the shores of darkness there is light,
  And precipices show untrodden green;
There is a budding morrow in midnight;
  There is a triple sight in blindness keen;
Such seeing hadst thou, as it once befell
To Dian, Queen of Earth, and Heaven, and Hell.

Ode to May. Fragment

Mother of Hermes! and still youthful Maia!
    May I sing to thee
As thou wast hymnèd on the shores of Baiae?
    Or may I woo thee
In earlier Sicilian? or thy smiles
Seek as they once were sought, in Grecian isles,
By bards who died content in pleasant sward,
  Leaving great verse unto a little clan?
O, give me their old vigour, and unheard
  Save of the quiet primrose, and the span
    Of Heaven and few ears,
Rounded by thee, my song should die away
    Content as theirs,
Rich in the simple worship of a day.

Acrostic

Give me your patience, sister, while I frame
Exact in capitals your golden name,
Or sue the fair Apollo, and he will
Rouse from his heavy slumber and instill
Great love in me for thee and Poesy.
Imagine not that greatest mastery
And kingdom over all the realms of verse
Nears more to Heaven in aught than when we nurse,
And surety give, to love and brotherhood.

Anthropophagi in Othello's mood,
Ulysses stormed, and his enchanted belt
Glow with the Muse, but they are never felt
Unbosomed so and so eternal made,
Such tender incense in their laurel shade,
To all the regent sisters of the Nine,
As this poor offering to you, sister mine.

Kind sister! ay, this third name says you are.
Enchanted has it been the Lord knows where.
And may it taste to you like good old wine,
Take you to real happiness and give
Sons, daughters and a home like honeyed hive.

'Sweet, sweet is the greeting of eyes'

Sweet, sweet is the greeting of eyes,
And sweet is the voice in its greeting,
When adieus have grown old and goodbyes
Fade away where old Time is retreating.

Warm the nerve of a welcoming hand,
And earnest a kiss on the brow,
When we meet over sea and o'er land
Where furrows are new to the plough.

On Visiting the Tomb of Burns

The town, the churchyard, and the setting sun,
  The clouds, the trees, the rounded hills all seem,
  Though beautiful, cold—strange—as in a dream
I dreamèd long ago. Now new begun

The short-lived, paly summer is but won
  From winter's ague, for one hour's gleam;
  Through sapphire-warm, their stars do never beam—
All is cold Beauty; pain is never done
For who has mind to relish, Minos-w'ise,
  The real of Beauty, free from that dead hue
    Fickly imagination and sick pride
  Cast wan upon it! Burns! with honour due
    I have oft honoured thee. Great shadow, hide
Thy face! I sin against thy native skies.

'*Old Meg she was a gipsy*'

Old Meg she was a gipsy,
  And lived upon the moors,
Her bed it was the brown heath turf,
  And her house was out of doors.

Her apples were swart blackberries,
  Her currants pods o' broom,
Her wine was dew o' the wild white rose,
  Her book a churchyard tomb.

Her brothers were the craggy hills,
  Her sisters larchen trees—
Alone with her great family
  She lived as she did please.

No breakfast had she many a mom,
  No dinner many a noon,
And 'stead of supper she would stare
  Full hard against the moon.

But every mom of woodbine fresh
  She made her garlanding,
And every night the dark glen yew
  She wove, and she would sing.

And with her fingers old and brown
  She plaited mats o' rushes,
And gave them to the cottagers
  She met among the bushes.

Old Meg was brave as Margaret Queen
   And tall as Amazon,
An old red blanket cloak she wore,
   A chip-hat had she on.
God rest her agèd bones somewhere—
   She died full long agone!

A Song about Myself

I

There was a naughty boy,
   A naughty boy was he,
He would not stop at home,
   He could not quiet be—
      He took
      In his knapsack
      A book
      Full of vowels
      And a shirt
      With some towels—
      A slight cap
      For night-cap—
      A hair brush,
      Comb ditto,
      New stockings,
      For old ones
      Would split O!
      This knapsack
      Tight at's back
      He rivetted close
   And followed his nose
      To the North,
      To the North,
   And followed his nose
      To the North.

II

There was a naughty boy
   And a naughty boy was he,
For nothing would he do
   But scribble poetry—
      He took

An inkstand
In his hand
And a pen
Big as ten
In the other
And away
In a pother
He ran
To the mountains
And fountains
And ghostès
And postès
And witches
And ditches,
And wrote
In his coat
When the weather
Was cool—
Fear of gout—
And without
When the weather
Was warm.
Och, the charm
When we choose
To follow one's nose
To the North,
To the North,
To follow one's nose
To the North!

III

There was a naughty boy
And a naughty boy was he,
He kept little fishes
In washing tubs three
In spite
Of the might
Of the maid,
Nor afraid
Of his granny-good,
He often would
Hurly burly
Get up early
And go,

By hook or crook,
To the brook
And bring home
Miller's thumb,
Tittlebat
Not over fat,
Minnows small
As the stall
Of a glove,
Not above
The size
Of a nice
Little baby's
Little finger—
O he made
('Twas his trade)
Of fish a pretty kettle,
A kettle—
A kettle,
Of fish a pretty kettle,
A kettle!

IV

There was a naughty boy,
And a naughty boy was he,
He ran away to Scotland
The people for to see—
There he found
That the ground
Was as hard,
That a yard
Was as long,
That a song
Was as merry,
That a cherry
Was as red,
That lead
Was as weighty,
That fourscore
Was as eighty,
That a door
Was as wooden
As in England—
So he stood in his shoes

And he wondered,
He wondered,
He stood in his
Shoes and he wondered.

'Ah! ken ye what I met the day'

Ah! ken ye what I met the day
Out oure the mountains,
A-coming down by craggis grey
An mossie fountains?
Ah! goud-haired Marie yeve I pray
Ane minute's guessing,
For that I met upon the way
Is past expressing.
As I stood where a rocky brig
A torrent crosses,
I spied upon a misty rig
A troup o' horses—
And as they trotted down the glen
I sped to meet them
To see if I might know the men
To stop and greet them.
First Willie on his sleek mare came
At canting gallop—
His long hair rustled like a flame
On board a shallop.
Then came his brother Rab and then
Young Peggy's mither
And Peggy too—adown the glen
They went togither.
I saw her wrappit in her hood
Fra wind and raining—
Her cheek was flush wi' timid blood
Twixt growth and waning.
She turn'd her dazèd head full oft
For thence her brithers
Came riding with her bridegroom soft
An mony ithers.
Young Tam came up an' eyed me quick
With reddened cheek.
Braw Tam was daffèd like a chick—
He could na speak.
Ah! Marie they are all gane hame
Through blustering weather,

An' every heart is full on flame
An' light as feather.
Ah! Marie they are all gone hame
Fra happy wedding,
Whilst I—Ah! is it not a shame?—
Sad tears am shedding.

To Ailsa Rock

Hearken, thou craggy ocean pyramid!
Give answer by thy voice, the sea-fowls' screams!
When were thy shoulders mantled in huge streams?
When from the sun was thy broad forehead hid?
How long is't since the mighty power bid
Thee heave to airy sleep from fathom dreams?
Sleep in the lap of thunder or sunbeams,
Or when grey clouds are thy cold coverlid?
Thou answer'st not; for thou art dead asleep.
Thy life is but two dead eternities—
The last in air, the former in the deep,
First with the whales, last with the eagle-skies.
Drowned wast thou till an earthquake made thee steep,
Another cannot wake thy giant size!

'*This mortal body of a thousand days*'

This mortal body of a thousand days
Now fills, O Burns, a space in thine own room,
Where thou didst dream alone on budded bays,
Happy and thoughtless of thy day of doom!
My pulse is warm with thine own barley-bree,
My head is light with pledging a great soul,
My eyes are wandering, and I cannot see,
Fancy is dead and drunken at its goal:
Yet can I stamp my foot upon thy floor,
Yet can I ope thy window-sash to find
The meadow thou hast trampèd o'er and o'er,
Yet can I think of thee till thought is blind,
Yet can I gulp a bumper to thy name—
O smile among the shades, for this is fame!

'All gentle folks who owe a grudge'

All gentle folks who owe a grudge
To any living thing,
Open your ears and stay your trudge
Whilst I in dudgeon sing.

The gad-fly he hath stung me sore—
O may he ne'er sting you I
But we have many a horrid bore
He may sting black and blue.

Has any here an old grey mare
With three legs all her store?
O put it to her buttocks bare
And straight she'll run on four.

Has any here a lawyer suit
Of 1743?
Take lawyer's nose and put it to't
And you the end will see.

Is there a man in Parliament
Dumbfoundered in his speech?
O let his neighbour make a rent
And put one in his breech.

O Lowther, how much better thou
Hadst figured t'other day,
When to the folks thou mad'st a bow
And hadst no more to say,

If lucky gad-fly had but ta'en
His seat upon thine arse,
And put thee to a little pain
To save thee from a worse.

Better than Southey it had been,
Better than Mr D—,
Better than Wordsworth too, I ween,
Better than Mr V—.

Forgive me pray, good people all,
For deviating so.
In spirit sure I had a call—
And now I on will go.

Has any here a daughter fair
Too fond of reading novels,
Too apt to fall in love with care
And charming Mister Lovels?

O put a gad-fly to that thing
She keeps so white and pert—
I mean the finger for the ring,
And it will breed a Wert.

Has any here a pious spouse
Who seven times a day
Scolds as King David prayed, to chouse
And have her holy way?

O let a gad-fly's little sting
Persuade her sacred tongue
That noises are a common thing,
But that her bell has rung.

And as this is the *summum bo-*
num of all conquering,
leave withouten wordès mo
The gad-fly's little sting.

'*Of late two dainties were before me placed*'

Of late two dainties were before me placed,
Sweet, holy, pure, sacred and innocent,
From the ninth sphere benignly sent
That Gods might know my own particular taste.
First the soft bagpipe mourned with zealous haste,
The Stranger next, with head on bosom bent,
Sighed; rueful again the piteous bagpipe went,
Again the Stranger sighings fresh did waste.
O Bagpipe, thou didst steal my heart away—
O Stranger, thou my nerves from pipe didst charm—
O Bagpipe, thou didst re-assert thy sway—
Again, thou Stranger gav'st me fresh alarm!

Alas! I could not choose. Ah! my poor heart,
Mumchance art thou with both obliged to part.

Lines Written in the Highlands after a Visit to Burns's Country

There is a joy in footing slow across a silent plain,
Where patriot battle has been fought when glory had the gain;
There is a pleasure on the heath where Druids old have been,
Where mantles grey have rustled by and swept the nettles green;
There is a joy in every spot made known by times of old,
New to the feet, although the tale a hundred times be told;
There is a deeper joy than all, more solemn in the heart,
More parching to the tongue than all, of more divine a smart,
When weary steps forget themselves upon a pleasant turf,
Upon hot sand, or flinty road, or sea-shore iron scurf,
Toward the castle or the cot, where long ago was born
One who was great through mortal days, and died of fame unshorn.
Light heather-bells may tremble then, but they are far away;
Wood-lark may sing from sandy fern, the sun may hear his lay;
Runnels may kiss the grass on shelves and shallows clear,
But their low voices are not heard, though come on travels drear;
Blood-red the sun may set behind black mountain peaks;
Blue tides may sluice and drench their time in caves and weedy creeks;
Eagles may seem to sleep wing-wide upon the air;
Ring-doves may fly convulsed across to some high-cedared lair;
But the forgotten eye is still fast wedded to the ground,
As palmer's that, with weariness, mid-desert shrine hath found.
At such a time the soul's a child, in childhood is the brain;
Forgotten is the worldly heart—alone, it beats in vain.
Ay, if a madman could have leave to pass a healthful day
To tell his forehead's swoon and faint when first began decay,
He might make tremble many a man whose spirit had gone forth
To find a bard's low cradle-place about the silent North!
Scanty the hour and few the steps beyond the bourn of care,
Beyond the sweet and bitter world—beyond it unaware;
Scanty the hour and few the steps, because a longer stay
Would bar return, and make a man forget his mortal way.
O horrible! to lose the sight of well-remembered face,
Of brother's eyes, of sister's brow, constant to every place,
Filling the air, as on we move, with portraiture intense,
More warm than those heroic tints that fill a painter's sense,
When shapes of old come striding by, and visages of old,
Locks shining black, hair scanty grey, and passions manifold.
No, no, that horror cannot be, for at the cable's length
Man feels the gentle anchor pull and gladdens in its strength—

One hour, half-idiot, he stands by mossy waterfall,
But in the very next he reads his soul's memorial.
He reads it on the mountain's height, where chance he may sit down
Upon rough marble diadem, that hill's eternal crown.
Yet be the anchor e'er so fast, room is there for a prayer.
That man may never lose his mind on mountains bleak and bare;
That he may stray league after league some great birth-place to find,
And keep his vision clear from speck, his inward sight unblind.

On Visiting Staffa

Not Aladdin magian
Ever such a work began;
Not the wizard of the Dee
Ever such a dream could see;
Not St John, in Patmos' Isle,
In the passion of his toil,
When he saw the churches seven,
Golden aisled, built up in heaven,
Gazed at such a rugged wonder.
As I stood its roofing under,
Lo! I saw one sleeping there,
On the marble cold and bare,
While the surges wash'd his feet,
And his garments white did beat
Drenched about the sombre rocks.
On his neck his well-grown locks,
Lifted dry above the main,
Were upon the curl again.
'What is this? and what art thou?'
Whispered I, and touched his brow.
'What art thou? and what is this?'
Whispered I, and strove to kiss
The spirit's hand, to wake his eyes.
Up he started in a trice:
'I am Lycidas,' said he,
'Famed in funeral minstrelsy!
This was architected thus
By the great Oceanus!—
Here his mighty waters play
Hollow organs all the day;
Here by turns his dolphins all,
Finny palmers great and small,
Come to pay devotion due—
Each a mouth of pearls must strew.

Many a mortal of these days,
Dares to pass our sacred ways,
Dares to touch audaciously
This Cathedral of the Sea!
I have been the pontiff-priest
Where the waters never rest,
Where a fledgy sea-bird choir
Soars for ever; holy fire
I have hid from mortal man;
Proteus is my sacristan.
But the dulled eye of mortal
Hath passed beyond the rocky portal;
So for ever will I leave
Such a taint, and soon unweave
All the magic of the place.
'Tis now free to stupid face,
To cutters and to fashion boats,
To cravats and to petticoats.
The great sea shall war it down,
For its fame shall not be blown
At every farthing quadrille dance.'
So saying, with a Spirit's glance
He dived...

'*Read me a lesson, Muse, and speak it loud*'

Read me a lesson, Muse, and speak it loud
  Upon the top of Nevis, blind in mist!
I look into the chasms, and a shroud
  Vapourous doth hide them; just so much I wist
Mankind do know of Hell. I look o'erhead,
  And there is sullen mist; even so much
Mankind can tell of Heaven. Mist is spread
  Before the earth, beneath me—even such,
Even so vague is man's sight of himself.
  Here are the craggy stones beneath my feet—
Thus much I know, that, a poor witless elf,
  I tread on them, that all my eye doth meet
Is mist and crag, not only on this height,
  But in the world of thought and mental might.

'Upon my life, Sir Nevis, I am piqued'

MRS C.
Upon my life, Sir Nevis, I am piqued
That I have so far panted tugged and reeked
To do an honour to your old bald pate
And now am sitting on you just to bate,
Without your paying me one compliment.
Alas, 'tis so with all, when our intent
Is plain, and in the eye of all mankind
We fair ones show a preference, too blind I
You gentlemen immediately turn tail—
O let me then my hapless fate bewail!
Ungrateful baldpate, have I not disdained
The pleasant valleys, have I not, mad-brained,
Deserted all my pickles and preserves,
My china closet too—with wretched nerves
To boot—say, wretched ingrate, have I not
Left my soft cushion chair and caudle pot?
'Tis true I had no corns—no! thank the fates,
My shoemaker was always Mr Bates.
And if not Mr Bates, why I'm not old I
Still dumb, ungrateful Nevis—still so cold!

(Here the lady took some more whiskey and was putting even more to her lips when she dashed [it] to the ground for the mountain began to grumble—which continued for a few minutes, before he thus began,)

BEN NEVIS
What whining bit of tongue and mouth thus dares
Disturb my slumber of a thousand years?
Even so long my sleep has been secure—
And to be so awaked I'll not endure.
O, pain!—for since the eagle's earliest scream
I've had a damned confounded ugly dream,
A nightmare sure. What, Madam, was it you?
It cannot be! My old eyes are not true!
Red Crag, my spectacles! Now let me see!
Good Heavens, Lady, how the gemini
Did you get here? O I shall split my sides!
I shall earthquake—

MRS C.

Sweet Nevis, do not quake, for though I love
Your honest Countenance all things above,
Truly I should not like to be conveyed
So far into your bosom—gentle maid
Loves not too rough a treatment, gentle Sir—
Pray thee be calm and do not quake nor stir,
No, not a stone, or I shall go in fits—

BEN NEVIS

I must—I shall! I meet not such tit-bits—
I meet not such sweet creatures every day!
By my old night-cap, night-cap night and day,
I must have one sweet buss—I must and shall!
Red Crag!—What, Madam, can you then repent
Of all the toil and vigour you have spent
To see Ben Nevis and to touch his nose?
Red Crag, I say! O I must have you close!
Red Crag, there lies beneath my farthest toe
A vein of sulphur—go, dear Red Crag, go—
And rub your flinty back against it. Budge!
Dear Madam, I must kiss you, faith I must!
I must embrace you with my dearest gust!
Blockhead, d'ye hear—Blockhead, I'll make her feel—
There lies beneath my east leg's northern heel
A cave of young earth dragons—well, my boy,
Go thither quick and so complete my joy.
Take you a bundle of the largest pines
And, where the sun on fiercest phosphor shines,
Fire them and ram them in the dragons' nest,
Then will the dragons fry and fizz their best,
Until ten thousand now no bigger than
Poor alligators—poor things of one span—
Will each one swell to twice ten times the size
Of northern whale. Then for the tender prize—
The moment then—for then will Red Crag rub
His flinty back—and I shall kiss and snub
And press my dainty morsel to my breast.
Blockhead, make haste!
O Muses weep the rest—
The lady fainted, and he thought her dead,
So pulled the clouds again about his head,
And went to sleep again—soon she was roused
By her affrighted servants. Next day housed

Safe on the lowly ground she blessed her fate
That fainting fit was not delayed too late.

Stanzas on some Skulls in Beauly Abbey, near Inverness

'*I shed no tears*;
Deep thought, or awful vision, I had none;
By thousand petty fancies I was crossed.'
Wordsworth

'*And mocked the dead bones that lay scattered by*'
Shakespeare

[Written in collaboration with Charles Brown. Keats's contributions are given in roman type.]

I

In silent barren Synod met,
Within those roofless walls where yet
The shafted arch and carvèd fret
Cling to the ruin,
The brethren's skulls mourn, dewy wet,
Their creed's undoing.

II

The mitred ones of Nice and Trent
Were not so tongue-tied—no, they went
Hot to their Councils, scarce content
With orthodoxy;
But ye, poor tongueless things, were meant
To speak by proxy.

III

Your chronicles no more exist,
Since Knox, the revolutionist,
Destroyed the work of every fist
That scrawled black letter.
Well! I'm a craniologist
And may do better.

IV

This skull-cap wore the cowl from sloth
Or discontent, perhaps from both,
And yet one day, against his oath,
He tried escaping,
For men, though idle, may be loth
To live on gaping.

V

A toper this! he plied his glass
More strictly than he said the Mass,
And loved to see a tempting lass
Come to confession,
Letting her absolution pass
O'er fresh transgression.

VI

This crawled through life in feebleness,
Boasting he never knew excess,
Cursing those crimes he scarce could guess,
Or feel but faintly,
With prayers that Heaven would come to bless
Men so unsaintly.

VII

Here's a true Churchman! he'd affect
Much charity, and ne'er neglect
To pray for mercy on th' elect,
But thought no evil
In sending heathen, Turk and sect
All to the Devil!

VIII

Poor skull, thy fingers set ablaze,
With silver Saint in golden rays,
The holy missal. Thou didst craze
'Mid bead and spangle,
While others passed their idle days
In coil and wrangle.

IX

Long time this sconce a helmet wore,
But sickness smites the conscience sore;
He broke his sword, and hither bore
His gear and plunder,
Took to the cowl—then raved and swore
At his damned blunder!

X

This lily-coloured skull, with all
The teeth complete, so white and small,
Belonged to one whose early pall
A lover shaded;
He died ere superstition's gall
His heart invaded.

XI

Ha! here is 'undivulgèd crime!'
Despair forbade his soul to climb
Beyond this world, this mortal time
Of fevered sadness,
Until their monkish pantomime
Dazzled his madness!

XII

A younger brother this! A man
Aspiring as a Tartar Khan,
But, curbed and baffled, he began
The trade of frightening.
It smacked of power!—and here he ran
To deal Heaven's lightning.

XIII

This idiot-skull belonged to one,
A buried miser's only son,
Who, penitent, ere he'd begun
To taste of pleasure,
And hoping Heaven's dread wrath to shun,
Gave Hell his treasure.

XIV

Here is the forehead of an ape,
A robber's mark—and near the nape
That bone, fie on't, bears just the shape
Of carnal passion;
Ah! he was one for theft and rape,
In monkish fashion!

XV

This was the Porter!—he could sing,
Or dance, or play, do anything,
And what the friars bade him bring,
They ne'er were balked of
(Matters not worth remembering
And seldom talked of).

XVI

Enough! why need I further pore?
This corner holds at least a score,
And yonder twice as many more
Of Reverend Brothers;
'Tis the same story o'er and o'er—
They're like the others!

Translated from Ronsard

Nature withheld Cassandra in the skies,
For more adornment, a full thousand years;
She took their cream of Beauty, fairest dyes,
And shaped and tinted her above all peers:
Meanwhile Love kept her dearly with his wings,
And underneath their shadow filled her eyes
With such a richness that the cloudy Kings
Of high Olympus uttered slavish sighs.
When from the Heavens I saw her first descend,
My heart took fire, and only burning pains…
They were my pleasures—they my Life's sad end;
Love poured her beauty into my warm veins…

'Tis "the witching time of night"

'Tis 'the witching time of night',
Orbed is the moon and bright,
And the stars they glisten, glisten,
Seeming with bright eyes to listen—
    For what listen they?
For a song and for a charm,
See they glisten in alarm,
And the moon is waxing warm
    To hear what I shall say.
Moon! keep wide thy golden ears -
Hearken, stars! and hearken, spheres!
Hearken, thou eternal sky!
I sing an infant's lullaby,
    A pretty lullaby.
Listen, listen, listen, listen,
Glisten, glisten, glisten, glisten,
    And hear my lullaby!
Though the rushes that will make
Its cradle still are in the lake;
Though the linen then that will be
Its swathe, is on the cotton tree;
Though the woollen that will keep
It warm is on the silly sheep—
Listen, stars' light, listen, listen,
Glisten, glisten, glisten, glisten,
    And hear my lullaby!
Child, I see thee! Child, I've found thee
Midst of the quiet all around thee!
Child, I see thee! Child, I spy thee!
And thy mother sweet is nigh thee!
Child, I know thee! Child no more,
But a Poet evermore!
See, see, the lyre, the lyre,
In a flame of fire,
Upon the little cradle's top
Flaring, flaring, flaring,
Past the eyesight's bearing.
Awake it from its sleep,
And see if it can keep
Its eyes upon the blaze—
    Amaze, amaze!
It stares, it stares, it stares,

It dares what no one dares!
It lifts its little hand into the flame
Unharmed, and on the strings
Paddles a little tune, and sings,
With dumb endeavour sweetly—
Bard art thou completely!
    Little child
    O' th' western wild,
Bard art thou completely!
Sweetly with dumb endeavour,
A Poet now or never,
    Little child
    O' the western wild,
A Poet now or never!

'*Welcome joy, and welcome sorrow*'

'*Under the flag*
Of each his faction, they to battle bring
Their embryon atoms.'
Milton

Welcome joy, and welcome sorrow,
  Lethe's weed and Hermes' feather;
Come today, and come tomorrow,
  I do love you both together!
  I love to mark sad faces in fair weather,
And hear a merry laugh amid the thunder.
  Fair and foul I love together:
  Meadows sweet where flames burn under,
  And a giggle at a wonder;
  Visage sage at pantomime;
  Funeral, and steeple-chime;
  Infant playing with a skull;
  Morning fair, and stormwrecked hull;
  Nightshade with the woodbine kissing;
  Serpents in red roses hissing;
  Cleopatra regal-dressed
  With the aspics at her breast
  Dancing music, music sad,
  Both together, sane and mad;
  Muses bright and Muses pale;
  Sombre Saturn, Momus hale.
  Laugh and sigh, and laugh again—
  O the sweetness of the pain!

Muses bright, and Muses pale,
Bare your faces of the veil!
Let me see! and let me write
Of the day and of the night—
Both together. Let me slake
All my thirst for sweet heart-ache!
Let my bower be of yew,
Interwreathed with myrtles new,
Pines and lime-trees full in bloom,
And my couch a low grass tomb.

Song

I

Spirit here that reignest!
Spirit here that painest!
Spirit here that burnest!
Spirit here that moumest!
Spirit! I bow
My forehead low,
Enshaded with thy pinions!
Spirit! I look
All passion-struck
Into thy pale dominions!

II

Spirit here that laughest!
Spirit there that quaffest!
Spirit here that dancest!
Noble soul that prancest!
Spirit! with thee
I join in the glee,
A-nudging the elbow of Momus!
Spirit! I flush
With a Bacchanal blush
Just fresh from the banquet of Comus.

'Where's the Poet? Show him, show him'

Where's the Poet? Show him! show him,
Muses nine, that I may know him!
'Tis the man who with a man
Is an equal, be he king,

Or poorest of the beggar-clan,
  Or any other wondrous thing
A man may be 'twixt ape and Plato.
  'Tis the man who with a bird,
Wren or eagle, finds his way to
  All its instincts. He hath heard
The lion's roaring, and can tell
  What his horny throat expresseth,
And to him the tiger's yell
  Comes articulate and presseth
On his ear like mother-tongue...

Fragment of the 'Castle Builder'

CASTLE BUILDER

In short, convince you that however wise
You may have grown from convent libraries,
I have, by many yards at least, been carding
A longer skein of wit in Convent Garden.

BERNARDINE

A very Eden that same place must be!
Pray what demesne? Whose lordship's legacy?
What, have you convents in that Gothic isle?
Pray pardon me, I cannot help but smile.

CASTLE BUILDER

Sir, Convent Garden is a monstrous beast:
From morning, four o'clock, to twelve at noon,
It swallows cabbages without a spoon,
And then, from twelve till two, this Eden made is
A promenade for cooks and ancient ladies;
And then for supper, 'stead of soup and poaches,
It swallows chairmen, damns, and Hackney coaches.
In short, Sir, 'tis a very place for monks,
For it containeth twenty thousand punks,
Which any man may number for his sport,
By following fat elbows up a court...
In such like nonsense would I pass an hour
With random friar, or rake upon his tour,
Or one of few of that imperial host
Who came unmaimèd from the Russian frost.
To-night I'll have my friar—let me think
About my room—I'll have it in the pink.
It should be rich and sombre, and the moon,

Just in its mid-life in the midst of June,
Should look through four large windows and display
Clear, but for golden fishes in the way,
Their glassy diamonding on Turkish floor.
The tapers keep aside, an hour and more,
To see what else the moon alone can show;
While the night-breeze doth softly let us know
My terrace is well bowered with oranges.
Upon the floor the dullest spirit sees
A guitar-ribband and a lady's glove
Beside a crumple-leavèd tale of love;
A tambour-frame, with Venus sleeping there,
All finished but some ringlets of her hair;
A viol, bowstrings tom, cross-wise upon
A glorious folio of Anacreon;
A skull upon a mat of roses lying,
Inked purple with a song concerning dying;
An hour-glass on the turn, amid the trails
Of passion-flower—just in time there sails
A cloud across the moon—the lights bring in!
And see what more my fantasy can win.
It is a gorgeous room, but somewhat sad;
The draperies are so, as though they had
Been made for Cleopatra's winding-sheet;
And opposite the steadfast eye doth meet
A spacious looking-glass, upon whose face,
In letters raven-sombre, you may trace
Old 'Mene, Mene, Tekel, Upharsin'.
Greek busts and statuary have ever been
Held, by the finest spirits, fitter far
Than vase grotesque and Siamesian jar;
Therefore 'tis sure a want of Attic taste
That I should rather love a Gothic waste
Of eyesight on cinque-coloured potter's clay,
Than on the marble fairness of old Greece.
My table-coverlets of Jason's fleece
And black Numidian sheep-wool should be wrought,
Gold, black, and heavy, from the Lama brought.
My ebon sofa should delicious be
With down from Leda's cygnet progeny.
My pictures all Salvator's, save a few
Of Titian's portraiture, and one, though new,
Of Haydon's in its fresh magnificence.
My wine—O good! 'tis here at my desire,
And I must sit to supper with my friar.

'And what is love? It is a doll dressed up'

And what is love? It is a doll dressed up
For idleness to cosset, nurse, and dandle;
A thing of soft misnomers, so divine
That silly youth doth think to make itself
Divine by loving, and so goes on
Yawning and doting a whole summer long,
Till Miss's comb is made a pearl tiara,
And common Wellingtons turn Romeo boots;
Till Cleopatra lives at Number Seven,
And Antony resides in Brunswick Square.
Fools! if some passions high have warmed the world,
If queens and soldiers have played deep for hearts,
It is no reason why such agonies
Should be more common than the growth of weeds.
Fools! make me whole again that weighty pearl
The queen of Egypt melted, and I'll say
That ye may love in spite of beaver hats.

Hyperion. A Fragment

BOOK I

Deep in the shady sadness of a vale
Far sunken from the healthy breath of mom,
Far from the fiery noon, and eve's one star,
Sat grey-haired Saturn, quiet as a stone,
Still as the silence round about his lair;
Forest on forest hung above his head
Like cloud on cloud. No stir of air was there,
Not so much life as on a summer's day
Robs not one light seed from the feathered grass,
But where the dead leaf fell, there did it rest.
A stream went voiceless by, still deadened more
By reason of his fallen divinity
Spreading a shade: the Naiad 'mid her reeds
Pressed her cold finger closer to her lips.

Along the margin-sand large foot-marks went,
No further than to where his feet had strayed,
And slept there since. Upon the sodden ground
His old right hand lay nerveless, listless, dead,
Unsceptred; and his realmless eyes were closed;

While his bowed head seemed listening to the Earth,
His ancient mother, for some comfort yet.

It seemed no force could wake him from his place;
But there came one, who with a kindred hand
Touched his wide shoulders, after bending low
With reverence, though to one who knew it not.
She was a Goddess of the infant world;
By her in stature the tall Amazon
Had stood a pigmy's height: she would have ta'en
Achilles by the hair and bent his neck;
Or with a finger stayed Ixion's wheel.
Her face was large as that of Memphian sphinx,
Pedestalled haply in a palace court,
When sages looked to Egypt for their lore.
But O! how unlike marble was that face,
How beautiful, if sorrow had not made
Sorrow more beautiful than Beauty's self.
There was a listening fear in her regard,
As if calamity had but begun;
As if the vanward clouds of evil days
Had spent their malice, and the sullen rear
Was with its storèd thunder labouring up.
One hand she pressed upon that aching spot
Where beats the human heart, as if just there,
Though an immortal, she felt cruel pain;
The other upon Saturn's bended neck
She laid, and to the level of his ear
Leaning with parted lips, some words she spake
In solemn tenor and deep organ tone—
Some mourning words, which in our feeble tongue
Would come in these like accents (O how frail
To that large utterance of the early Gods!):
'Saturn, look up!—though wherefore, poor old King?
I have no comfort for thee, no, not one:
I cannot say, "O wherefore sleepest thou? "
For heaven is parted from thee, and the earth
Knows thee not, thus afflicted, for a God;
And ocean too, with all its solemn noise,
Has from thy sceptre passed; and all the air
Is emptied of thine hoary majesty.
Thy thunder, conscious of the new command,
Rumbles reluctant o'er our fallen house;
And thy sharp lightning in unpractised hands
Scorches and burns our once serene domain.

O aching time! O moments big as years!
All as ye pass swell out the monstrous truth,
And press it so upon our weary griefs
That unbelief has not a space to breathe.
Saturn, sleep on—O thoughtless, why did I
Thus violate thy slumbrous solitude?
Why should I ope thy melancholy eyes?
Saturn, sleep on, while at thy feet I weep!'

As when, upon a trancèd summer-night,
Those green-robed senators of mighty woods,
Tall oaks, branch-charmèd by the earnest stars,
Dream, and so dream all night without a stir,
Save from one gradual solitary gust
Which comes upon the silence, and dies off,
As if the ebbing air had but one wave;
So came these words and went; the while in tears
She touched her fair large forehead to the ground,
Just where her falling hair might be outspread
A soft and silken mat for Saturn's feet.
One moon, with alteration slow, had shed
Her silver seasons four upon the night,
And still these two were postured motionless,
Like natural sculpture in cathedral cavern;
The frozen God still couchant on the earth,
And the sad Goddess weeping at his feet:
Until at length old Saturn lifted up
His faded eyes, and saw his kingdom gone,
And all the gloom and sorrow of the place,
And that fair kneeling Goddess; and then spake,
As with a palsied tongue, and while his beard
Shook horrid with such aspen-malady:
'O tender spouse of gold Hyperion,
Thea, I feel thee ere I see thy face;
Look up, and let me see our doom in it;
Look up, and tell me if this feeble shape
Is Saturn's; tell me, if thou hear'st the voice
Of Saturn; tell me, if this wrinkling brow,
Naked and bare of its great diadem,
Peers like the front of Saturn. Who had power
To make me desolate? whence came the strength?
How was it nurtured to such bursting forth,
While Fate seemed strangled in my nervous grasp?
But it is so; and I am smothered up,
And buried from all godlike exercise

Of influence benign on planets pale,
Of admonitions to the winds and seas,
Of peaceful sway above man's harvesting,
And all those acts which Deity supreme
Doth ease its heart of love in.—I am gone
Away from my own bosom; I have left
My strong identity, my real self,
Somewhere between the throne and where I sit
Here on this spot of earth. Search, Thea, search!
Open thine eyes eterne, and sphere them round
Upon all space—space starred, and lorn of light;
Space regioned with life-air; and barren void;
Spaces of fire, and all the yawn of hell.
Search, Thea, search! and tell me, if thou seest
A certain shape or shadow, making way
With wings or chariot fierce to repossess
A heaven he lost erewhile: it must—it must
Be of ripe progress: Saturn must be King.
Yes, there must be a golden victory;
There must be Gods thrown down, and trumpets blown
Of triumph calm, and hymns of festival
Upon the gold clouds metropolitan,
Voices of soft proclaim, and silver stir
Of strings in hollow shells; and there shall be
Beautiful things made new, for the surprise
Of the sky-children. I will give command:
Thea! Thea! Thea! where is Saturn?'

This passion lifted him upon his feet,
And made his hands to struggle in the air,
His Druid locks to shake and ooze with sweat,
His eyes to fever out, his voice to cease.
He stood, and heard not Thea's sobbing deep;
A little time, and then again he snatched
Utterance thus: 'But cannot I create?
Cannot I form? Cannot I fashion forth
Another world, another universe,
To overbear and crumble this to naught?
Where is another Chaos? Where?'—That word
Found way unto Olympus, and made quake
The rebel three. Thea was startled up,
And in her bearing was a sort of hope,
As thus she quick-voiced spake, yet full of awe.

'This cheers our fallen house: come to our friends,
O Saturn! come away, and give them heart.
I know the covert, for thence came I hither.'
Thus brief; then with beseeching eyes she went
With backward footing through the shade a space:
He followed, and she turned to lead the way
Through agèd boughs, that yielded like the mist
Which eagles cleave up-mounting from their nest.

Meanwhile in other realms big tears were shed,
More sorrow like to this, and such like woe,
Too huge for mortal tongue or pen of scribe.
The Titans fierce, self-hid, or prison-bound,
Groaned for the old allegiance once more,
And listened in sharp pain for Saturn's voice.
But one of the whole mammoth-brood still kept
His sovereignty, and rule, and majesty—
Blazing Hyperion on his orbèd fire
Still sat, still snuffed the incense, teeming up
From man to the sun's God—yet unsecure:
For as among us mortals omens drear
Fright and perplex, so also shuddered he—
Not at dog's howl, or gloom-bird's hated screech,
Or the familiar visiting of one
Upon the first toll of his passing-bell,
Or prophesyings of the midnight lamp;
But horrors, portioned to a giant nerve,
Oft made Hyperion ache. His palace bright
Bastioned with pyramids of glowing gold,
And touched with shade of bronzèd obelisks,
Glared a blood-red through all its thousand courts,
Arches, and domes, and fiery galleries;
And all its curtains of Aurorian clouds
Flushed angerly, while sometimes eagle's wings,
Unseen before by Gods or wondering men,
Darkened the place, and neighing steeds were heard,
Not heard before by Gods or wondering men.
Also, when he would taste the spicy wreaths
Of incense, breathed aloft from sacred hills,
Instead of sweets, his ample palate took
Savour of poisonous brass and metal sick:
And so, when harboured in the sleepy west,
After the full completion of fair day,
For rest divine upon exalted couch

And slumber in the arms of melody,
He paced away the pleasant hours of ease
With stride colossal, on from hall to hall;
While far within each aisle and deep recess,
His wingèd minions in close clusters stood,
Amazed and full of fear; like anxious men
Who on wide plains gather in panting troops,
When earthquakes jar their battlements and towers.
Even now, while Saturn, roused from icy trance,
Went step for step with Thea through the woods,
Hyperion, leaving twilight in the rear,
Came slope upon the threshold of the west;
Then, as was wont, his palace-door flew ope
In smoothest silence, save what solemn tubes,
Blown by the serious Zephyrs, gave of sweet
And wandering sounds, slow-breathèd melodies—
And like a rose in vermeil tint and shape,
In fragrance soft, and coolness to the eye,
That inlet to severe magnificence
Stood full blown, for the God to enter in.

He entered, but he entered full of wrath;
His flaming robes streamed out beyond his heels,
And gave a roar, as if of earthly fire,
That scared away the meek ethereal Hours
And made their dove-wings tremble. On he flared,
From stately nave to nave, from vault to vault,
Through bowers of fragrant and enwreathèd light,
And diamond-pavèd lustrous long arcades,
Until he reached the great main cupola.
There standing fierce beneath, he stamped his foot,
And from the basement deep to the high towers
Jarred his own golden region; and before
The quavering thunder thereupon had ceased,
His voice leapt out, despite of god-like curb,
To this result: 'O dreams of day and night!
O monstrous forms! O effigies of pain!
O spectres busy in a cold, cold gloom!
O lank-eared Phantoms of black-weeded pools!
Why do I know ye? Why have I seen ye? Why
Is my eternal essence thus distraught
To see and to behold these horrors new?
Saturn is fallen, am I too to fall?
Am I to leave this haven of my rest,
This cradle of my glory, this soft clime,

This calm luxuriance of blissful light,
These crystalline pavilions, and pure fanes,
Of all my lucent empire? It is left
Deserted, void, nor any haunt of mine.
The blaze, the splendour, and the symmetry,
I cannot see—but darkness, death and darkness.
Even here, into my centre of repose,
The shady visions come to domineer,
Insult, and blind, and stifle up my pomp.—
Fall!—No, by Tellus and her briny robes!
Over the fiery frontier of my realms
I will advance a terrible right arm
Shall scare that infant thunderer, rebel Jove,
And bid old Saturn take his throne again.'—
He spake, and ceased, the while a heavier threat
Held struggle with his throat but came not forth;
For as in theatres of crowded men
Hubbub increases more they call out 'Hush!',
So at Hyperion's words the Phantoms pale
Bestirred themselves, thrice horrible and cold;
And from the mirrored level where he stood
A mist arose, as from a scummy marsh.
At this, through all his bulk an agony
Crept gradual, from the feet unto the crown,
Like a lithe serpent vast and muscular
Making slow way, with head and neck convulsed
From over-strainèd might. Released, he fled
To the eastern gates, and full six dewy hours
Before the dawn in season due should blush,
He breathed fierce breath against the sleepy portals,
Cleared them of heavy vapours, burst them wide
Suddenly on the ocean's chilly streams.
The planet orb of fire, whereon he rode
Each day from east to west the heavens through,
Spun round in sable curtaining of clouds;
Not therefore veilèd quite, blindfold, and hid,
But ever and anon the glancing spheres,
Circles, and arcs, and broad-belting colure,
Glowed through, and wrought upon the muffling dark
Sweet-shapèd lightnings from the nadir deep
Up to the zenith—hieroglyphics old
Which sages and keen-eyed astrologers
Then living on the earth, with labouring thought
Won from the gaze of many centuries—
Now lost, save what we find on remnants huge

Of stone, or marble swart, their import gone,
Their wisdom long since fled. Two wings this orb
Possessed for glory, two fair argent wings,
Ever exalted at the God's approach:
And now, from forth the gloom their plumes immense
Rose, one by one, till all outspreaded were;
While still the dazzling globe maintained eclipse,
Awaiting for Hyperion's command.
Fain would he have commanded, fain took throne
And bid the day begin, if but for change.
He might not.—No, though a primeval God:
The sacred seasons might not be disturbed.
Therefore the operations of the dawn
Stayed in their birth, even as here 'tis told.
Those silver wings expanded sisterly,
Eager to sail their orb; the porches wide
Opened upon the dusk demesnes of night;
And the bright Titan, frenzied with new woes,
Unused to bend, by hard compulsion bent
His spirit to the sorrow of the time;
And all along a dismal rack of clouds,
Upon the boundaries of day and night,
He stretched himself in grief and radiance faint.
There as he lay, the Heaven with its stars
Looked down on him with pity, and the voice
Of Coelus, from the universal space,
Thus whispered low and solemn in his ear:
'O brightest of my children dear, earth-born
And sky-engendered, Son of Mysteries
All unrevealèd even to the powers
Which met at thy creating; at whose joys
And palpitations sweet, and pleasures soft,
Coelus, wonder how they came and whence;
And at the fruits thereof what shapes they be,
Distinct, and visible—symbols divine,
Manifestations of that beauteous life
Diffused unseen throughout eternal space:
Of these new-formed art thou, O brightest child!
Of these, thy brethren and the Goddesses!
There is sad feud among ye, and rebellion
Of son against his sire. I saw him fall,
I saw my first-born tumbled from his throne!
To me his arms were spread, to me his voice
Found way from forth the thunders round his head!
Pale wox I, and in vapours hid my face.

Art thou, too, near such doom? Vague fear there is:
For I have seen my sons most unlike Gods.
Divine ye were created, and divine
In sad demeanour, solemn, undisturbed,
Unrufflèd, like high Gods, ye lived and ruled:
Now I behold in you fear," hope, and wrath;
Actions of rage and passion—even as
I see them, on the mortal world beneath,
In men who die. This is the grief, O Son!
Sad sign of ruin, sudden dismay, and fall!
Yet do thou strive; as thou art capable,
As thou canst move about, an evident God;
And canst oppose to each malignant hour
Ethereal presence. I am but a voice;
My life is but the life of winds and tides,
No more than winds and tides can I avail.—
But thou canst.—Be thou therefore in the van
Of circumstance; yea, seize the arrow's barb
Before the tense string murmur.—To the earth!
For there thou wilt find Saturn, and his woes.
Meantime I will keep watch on thy bright sun,
And of thy seasons be a careful nurse.'—
Ere half this region-whisper had come down,
Hyperion arose, and on the stars
Lifted his curvèd lids, and kept them wide
Until it ceased; and still he kept them wide;
And still they were the same bright, patient stars.
Then with a slow incline of his broad breast,
Like to a diver in the pearly seas,
Forward he stooped over the airy shore,
And plunged all noiseless into the deep night.

BOOK II

Just at the self-same beat of Time's wide wings,
Hyperion slid into the rustled air
And Saturn gained with Thea that sad place
Where Cybele and the bruised Titans mourned.
It was a den where no insulting light
Could glimmer on their tears; where their own groans
They felt, but heard not, for the solid roar
Of thunderous waterfalls and torrents hoarse,
Pouring a constant bulk, uncertain where,
Crag jutting forth to crag, and rocks that seemed
Ever as if just rising from a sleep,

Forehead to forehead held their monstrous horns;
And thus in thousand hugest fantasies
Made a fit roofing to this nest of woe.
Instead of thrones, hard flint they sat upon,
Couches of rugged stone, and slaty ridge
Stubborned with iron. All were not assembled:
Some chained in torture, and some wandering.
Coeus, and Gyges, and Briareiis,
Typhon, and Dolor, and Porphyrion,
With many more, the brawniest in assault,
Were pent in regions of laborious breath;
Dungeoned in opaque element, to keep
Their clenchèd teeth still clenched, and all their limbs
Locked up like veins of metal, cramped and screwed;
Without a motion, save of their big hearts
Heaving in pain, and horribly convulsed
With sanguine fev'rous boiling gurge of pulse.
Mnemosyne was straying in the world;
Far from her moon had Phoebe wanderèd;
And many else were free to roam abroad,
But for the main, here found they covert drear.
Scarce images of life, one here, one there,
Lay vast and edgeways; like a dismal cirque
Of Druid stones, upon a forlorn moor,
When the chill rain begins at shut of eve,
In dull November, and their chancel vault,
The Heaven itself, is blinded throughout night.
Each one kept shroud, nor to his neighbour gave
Or word, or look, or action of despair.
Creüs was one; his ponderous iron mace
Lay by him, and a shattered rib of rock
Told of his rage, ere he thus sank and pined.
Iäpetus another; in his grasp,
A serpent's plashy neck; its barbèd tongue
Squeezed from the gorge, and all its uncurled length
Dead—and because the creature could not spit
Its poison in the eyes of conquering Jove.
Next Cottus; prone he lay, chin uppermost,
As though in pain, for still upon the flint
He ground severe his skull, with open mouth
And eyes at horrid working. Nearest him
Asia, born of most enormous Caf,
Who cost her mother Tellus keener pangs,
Though feminine, than any of her sons:
More thought than woe was in her dusky face,

For she was prophesying of her glory;
And in her wide imagination stood
Palm-shaded temples, and high rival fanes,
By Oxus or in Ganges' sacred isles.
Even as Hope upon her anchor leans,
So leant she, not so fair, upon a tusk
Shed from the broadest of her elephants.
Above her, on a crag's uneasy shelve,
Upon his elbow raised, all prostrate else,
Shadowed Enceladus—once tame and mild
As grazing ox unworried in the meads;
Now tiger-passioned, lion-thoughted, wroth,
He meditated, plotted, and even now
Was hurling mountains in that second war,
Not long delayed, that scared the younger Gods
To hide themselves in forms of beast and bird.
Not far hence Atlas; and beside him prone
Phorcus, the sire of Gorgons. Neighboured close
Oceanus, and Tethys, in whose lap
Sobbed Clymene among her tangled hair.
In midst of all lay Themis, at the feet
Of Ops the queen all clouded round from sight;
No shape distinguishable, more than when
Thick night confounds the pine-tops with the clouds—
And many else whose names may not be told.
For when the Muse's wings are air-ward spread,
Who shall delay her flight? And she must chant
Of Saturn, and his guide, who now had climbed
With damp and slippery footing from a depth
More horrid still. Above a sombre cliff
Their heads appeared, and up their stature grew
Till on the level height their steps found ease:
Then Thea spread abroad her trembling arms
Upon the precincts of this nest of pain,
And sidelong fixed her eye on Saturn's face.
There saw she direst strife—the supreme God
At war with all the frailty of grief,
Of rage, of fear, anxiety, revenge,
Remorse, spleen, hope, but most of all despair.
Against these plagues he strove in vain; for Fate
Had poured a mortal oil upon his head,
A disanointing poison, so that Thea,
Affrighted, kept her still, and let him pass
First onwards in, among the fallen tribe.

As with us mortal men, the laden heart
Is persecuted more, and fevered more,
When it is nighing to the mournful house
Where other hearts are sick of the same bruise;
So Saturn, as he walked into the midst,
Felt faint, and would have sunk among the rest,
But that he met Enceladus's eye,
Whose mightiness, and awe of him, at once
Came like an inspiration; and he shouted,
'Titans, behold your God!' At which some groaned;
Some started on their feet; some also shouted;
Some wept, some wailed, all bowed with reverence;
And Ops, uplifting her black folded veil,
Showed her pale cheeks, and all her forehead wan,
Her eye-brows thin and jet, and hollow eyes.
There is a roaring in the bleak-grown pines
When Winter lifts his voice; there is a noise
Among immortals when a God gives sign,
With hushing finger, how he means to load
His tongue with the full weight of utterless thought,
With thunder, and with music, and with pomp:
Such noise is like the roar of bleak-grown pines,
Which, when it ceases in this mountained world,
No other sound succeeds; but ceasing here,
Among these fallen, Saturn's voice therefrom
Grew up like organ, that begins anew
Its strain, when other harmonies, stopped short,
Leave the dinned air vibrating silverly.
Thus grew it up: 'Not in my own sad breast,
Which is its own great judge and searcher-out,
Can I find reason why ye should be thus:
Not in the legends of the first of days,
Studied from that old spirit-leaved book
Which starry Uranus with finger bright
Saved from the shores of darkness, when the waves
Low-ebbed still hid it up in shallow gloom—
And the which book ye know I ever kept
For my firm-basèd footstool—Ah, infirm!
Not there, nor in sign, symbol, or portent
Of element, earth, water, air, and fire—
At war, at peace, or inter-quarrelling
One against one, or two, or three, or all
Each several one against the other three,
As fire with air loud warring when rain-floods
Drown both, and press them both against earth's face,

Where, finding sulphur, a quadruple wrath
Unhinges the poor world—not in that strife,
Wherefrom I take strange lore, and read it deep,
Can I find reason why ye should be thus—
No, nowhere can unriddle, though I search,
And pore on Nature's universal scroll
Even to swooning, why ye, Divinities,
The first-born of all shaped and palpable Gods,
Should cower beneath what, in comparison,
Is untremendous might. Yet ye are here,
O'erwhelmed, and spurned, and battered, ye are here I
O Titans, shall I say, "Arise!"?—Ye groan:
Shall I say "Crouch!"?—Ye groan. What can I then?
O Heaven wide! O unseen parent dear!
What can I? Tell me, all ye brethren Gods,
How we can war, how engine our great wrath!
O speak your counsel now, for Saturn's ear
Is all a-hungered. Thou, Oceanus,
Ponderest high and deep, and in thy face
I see, astonied, that severe content
Which comes of thought and musing. Give us help!'

So ended Saturn; and the God of the Sea,
Sophist and sage from no Athenian grove,
But cogitation in his watery shades,
Arose, with locks not oozy, and began,
In murmurs which his first-endeavouring tongue
Caught infant-like from the far-foamèd sands.
'O ye, whom wrath consumes! who, passion-stung,
Writhe at defeat, and nurse your agonies!
Shut up your senses, stifle up your ears,
My voice is not a bellows unto ire.
Yet listen, ye who will, whilst I bring proof
How ye, perforce, must be content to stoop;
And in the proof much comfort will I give,
If ye will take that comfort in its truth.
We fall by course of Nature's law, not force
Of thunder, or of Jove. Great Saturn, thou
Hast sifted well the atom-universe;
But for this reason, that thou art the King,
And only blind from sheer supremacy,
One avenue was shaded from thine eyes,
Through which I wandered to eternal truth.
And first, as thou wast not the first of powers,
So art thou not the last; it cannot be:

Thou art not the beginning nor the end.
From Chaos and parental Darkness came
Light, the first fruits of that intestine broil,
That sullen ferment, which for wondrous ends
Was ripening in itself. The ripe hour came,
And with it Light, and Light, engendering
Upon its own producer, forthwith touched
The whole enormous matter into life.
Upon that very hour, our parentage,
The Heavens, and the Earth, were manifest:
Then thou first born, and we the giant race,
Found ourselves ruling new and beauteous realms.
Now comes the pain of truth, to whom 'tis pain—
O folly! for to bear all naked truths,
And to envisage circumstance, all calm,
That is the top of sovereignty. Mark well!
As Heaven and Earth are fairer, fairer far
Than Chaos and blank Darkness, though once chiefs;
And as we show beyond that Heaven and Earth
In form and shape compact and beautiful,
In will, in action free, companionship,
And thousand other signs of purer life;
So on our heels a fresh perfection treads,
A power more strong in beauty, born of us
And fated to excel us, as we pass
In glory that old Darkness: nor are we
Thereby more conquered, than by us the rule
Of shapeless Chaos. Say, doth the dull soil
Quarrel with the proud forests it hath fed,
And feedeth still, more comely than itself?
Can it deny the chiefdom of green groves?
Or shall the tree be envious of the dove
Because it cooeth, and hath snowy wings
To wander wherewithal and find its joys?
We are such forest-trees, and our fair boughs
Have bred forth, not pale solitary doves,
But eagles golden-feathered, who do tower
Above us in their beauty, and must reign
In right thereof. For 'tis the eternal law
That first in beauty should be first in might.
Yea, by that law, another race may drive
Our conquerors to mourn as we do now.
Have ye beheld the young God of the Seas,
My dispossessor? Have ye seen his face?
Have ye beheld his chariot, foamed along

By noble wingèd creatures he hath made?
I saw him on the calmèd waters scud,
With such a glow of beauty in his eyes,
That it enforced me to bid sad farewell
To all my empire: farewell sad I took,
And hither came, to see how dolorous fate
Had wrought upon ye; and how I might best
Give consolation in this woe extreme.
Receive the truth, and let it be your balm.'

Whether through posed conviction, or disdain,
They guarded silence, when Oceanus
Left murmuring, what deepest thought can tell?
But so it was; none answered for a space,
Save one whom none regarded, Clymene;
And yet she answered not, only complained,
With hectic lips, and eyes up-looking mild,
Thus wording timidly among the fierce:
'O Father, I am here the simplest voice,
And all my knowledge is that joy is gone,
And this thing woe crept in among our hearts,
There to remain for ever, as I fear.
I would not bode of evil, if I thought
So weak a creature could turn off the help
Which by just right should come of mighty Gods;
Yet let me tell my sorrow, let me tell
Of what I heard, and how it made me weep,
And know that we had parted from all hope.
I stood upon a shore, a pleasant shore,
Where a sweet clime was breathed from a land
Of fragrance, quietness, and trees, and flowers.
Full of calm joy it was, as I of grief;
Too full of joy and soft delicious warmth;
So that I felt a movement in my heart
To chide, and to reproach that solitude
With songs of misery, music of our woes;
And sat me down, and took a mouthèd shell
And murmured into it, and made melody—
O melody no more! for while I sang,
And with poor skill let pass into the breeze
The dull shell's echo, from a bowery strand
Just opposite, an island of the sea,
There came enchantment with the shifting wind,
That did both drown and keep alive my ears.
I threw my shell away upon the sand,

And a wave filled it, as my sense was filled
With that new blissful golden melody.
A living death was in each gush of sounds,
Each family of rapturous hurried notes,
That fell, one after one, yet all at once,
Like pearl beads dropping sudden from their string;
And then another, then another strain,
Each like a dove leaving its olive perch,
With music winged instead of silent plumes,
To hover round my head, and make me sick
Of joy and grief at once. Grief overcame,
And I was stopping up my frantic ears,
When, past all hindrance of my trembling hands,
A voice came sweeter, sweeter than all tune,
And still it cried, "Apollo! young Apollo!
The morning-bright Apollo! young Apollo! "
I fled, it followed me, and cried "Apollo!"
O Father, and O Brethren, had ye felt
Those pains of mine—O Saturn, hadst thou felt,
Ye would not call this too indulgèd tongue
Presumptuous, in thus venturing to be heard.'

So far her voice flowed on, like timorous brook
That, lingering along a pebbled coast,
Doth fear to meet the sea: but sea it met,
And shuddered; for the overwhelming voice
Of huge Enceladus swallowed it in wrath:
The ponderous syllables, like sullen waves
In the half-glutted hollows of reef-rocks,
Came booming thus, while still upon his arm
He leaned—not rising, from supreme contempt:
'Or shall we listen to the over-wise,
Or to the over-foolish, Giant-Gods?
Not thunderbolt on thunderbolt, till all
That rebel Jove's whole armoury were spent,
Not world on world upon these shoulders piled
Could agonize me more than baby-words
In midst of this dethronement horrible.
Speak! Roar! Shout! Yell! ye sleepy Titans all.
Do ye forget the blows, the buffets vile?
Are ye not smitten by a youngling arm?
Dost thou forget, sham Monarch of the Waves,
Thy scalding in the seas? What, have I roused
Your spleens with so few simple words as these?
O joy! for now I see ye are not lost:

O joy! for now I see a thousand eyes
Wide-glaring for revenge!'—As this he said,
He lifted up his stature vast, and stood,
Still without intermission speaking thus:
'Now ye are flames, I'll tell you how to burn,
And purge the ether of our enemies;
How to feed fierce the crooked stings of fire,
And singe away the swollen clouds of Jove,
Stifling that puny essence in its tent.
O let him feel the evil he hath done;
For though I scorn Oceanus's lore,
Much pain have I for more than loss of realms:
The days of peace and slumbrous calm are fled;
Those days, all innocent of scathing war,
When all the fair Existences of heaven
Came open-eyed to guess what we would speak—
That was before our brows were taught to frown,
Before our lips knew else but solemn sounds;
That was before we knew the winged thing,
Victory, might be lost, or might be won.
And be ye mindful that Hyperion,
Our brightest brother, still is undisgraced—
Hyperion, lo! his radiance is here!'

All eyes were on Enceladus's face,
And they beheld, while still Hyperion's name
Flew from his lips up to the vaulted rocks,
A pallid gleam across his features stern—
Not savage, for he saw full many a God
Wroth as himself. He looked upon them all,
And in each face he saw a gleam of light,
But splendider in Saturn's, whose hoar locks
Shone like the bubbling foam about a keel
When the prow sweeps into a midnight cove.
In pale and silver silence they remained,
Till suddenly a splendour, like the morn,
Pervaded all the beetling gloomy steeps,
All the sad spaces of oblivion,
And every gulf, and every chasm old,
And every height, and every sullen depth,
Voiceless, or hoarse with loud tormented streams;
And all the everlasting cataracts,
And all the headlong torrents far and near,
Mantled before in darkness and huge shade,
Now saw the light and made it terrible.

It was Hyperion: a granite peak
His bright feet touched, and there he stayed to view
The misery his brilliance had betrayed
To the most hateful seeing of itself.
Golden his hair of short Numidian curl,
Regal his shape majestic, a vast shade
In midst of his own brightness, like the bulk
Of Memnon's image at the set of sun
To one who travels from the dusking East:
Sighs, too, as mournful as that Memnon's harp,
He uttered, while his hands contemplative
He pressed together, and in silence stood.
Despondence seized again the fallen Gods
At sight of the dejected King of Day,
And many hid their faces from the light:
But fierce Enceladus sent forth his eyes
Among the brotherhood; and, at their glare,
Uprose Iäpetus, and Creüs too,
And Phorcus, sea-born, and together strode
To where he towered on his eminence.
There those four shouted forth old Saturn's name;
Hyperion from the peak loud answered, 'Saturn!'
Saturn sat near the Mother of the Gods,
In whose face was no joy, though all the Gods
Gave from their hollow throats the name of 'Saturn!'

BOOK III

Thus in alternate uproar and sad peace,
Amazèd were those Titans utterly.
O leave them, Muse! O leave them to their woes;
For thou art weak to sing such tumults dire:
A solitary sorrow best befits
Thy lips, and antheming a lonely grief.
Leave them, O Muse! for thou anon wilt find
Many a fallen old Divinity
Wandering in vain about bewildered shores.
Meantime touch piously the Delphic harp,
And not a wind of heaven but will breathe
In aid soft warble from the Dorian flute;
For lo! 'tis for the Father of all verse.
Flush every thing that hath a vermeil hue,
Let the rose glow intense and warm the air,
And let the clouds of even and of morn
Float in voluptuous fleeces o'er the hills;

Let the red wine within the goblet boil,
Cold as a bubbling well; let faint-lipped shells,
On sands, or in great deeps, vermilion turn
Through all their labyrinths; and let the maid
Blush keenly, as with some warm kiss surprised.
Chief isle of the embowered Cyclades,
Rejoice, O Delos, with thine olives green,
And poplars, and lawn-shading palms, and beech,
In which the Zephyr breathes the loudest song,
And hazels thick, dark-stemmed beneath the shade:
Apollo is once more the golden theme!
Where was he, when the Giant of the Sun
Stood bright, amid the sorrow of his peers?
Together had he left his mother fair
And his twin-sister sleeping in their bower,
And in the morning twilight wandered forth
Beside the osiers of a rivulet,
Full ankle-deep in lilies of the vale.
The nightingale had ceased, and a few stars
Were lingering in the heavens, while the thrush
Began calm-throated. Throughout all the isle
There was no covert, no retirèd cave
Unhaunted by the murmurous noise of waves,
Though scarcely heard in many a green recess.
He listened, and he wept, and his bright tears
Went trickling down the golden bow he held.
Thus with half-shut suffusèd eyes he stood,
While from beneath some cumbrous boughs hard by
With solemn step an awful Goddess came,
And there was purport in her looks for him,
Which he with eager guess began to read
Perplexed, the while melodiously he said:
'How cam'st thou over the unfooted sea?
Or hath that antique mien and robed form
Moved in these vales invisible till now?
Sure I have heard those vestments sweeping o'er
The fallen leaves, when I have sat alone
In cool mid-forest. Surely I have traced
The rustle of those ample skirts about
These grassy solitudes, and seen the flowers
Lift up their heads, as still the whisper passed.
Goddess! I have beheld those eyes before,
And their eternal calm, and all that face,
Or I have dreamed.'—'Yes,' said the supreme shape,
Thou hast dreamed of me; and awaking up

Didst find a lyre all golden by thy side,
Whose strings touched by thy fingers, all the vast
Unwearied ear of the whole universe
Listened in pain and pleasure at the birth
Of such new tuneful wonder. Is't not strange
That thou shouldst weep, so gifted? Tell me, youth,
What sorrow thou canst feel; for I am sad
When thou dost shed a tear. Explain thy griefs
To one who in this lonely isle hath been
The watcher of thy sleep and hours of life,
From the young day when first thy infant hand
Plucked witless the weak flowers, till thine arm
Could bend that bow heroic to all times.
Show thy heart's secret to an ancient Power
Who hath forsaken old and sacred thrones
For prophecies of thee, and for the sake
Of loveliness new born.'—Apollo then,
With sudden scrutiny and gloomless eyes,
Thus answered, while his white melodious throat
Throbbed with the syllables: 'Mnemosyne!
Thy name is on my tongue, I know not how;
Why should I tell thee what thou so well seest?
Why should I strive to show what from thy lips
Would come no mystery? For me, dark, dark,
And painful vile oblivion seals my eyes:
I strive to search wherefore I am so sad,
Until a melancholy numbs my limbs;
And then upon the grass I sit, and moan,
Like one who once had wings. O why should I
Feel cursed and thwarted, when the liegeless air
Yields to my step aspirant? Why should I
Spurn the green turf as hateful to my feet?
Goddess benign, point forth some unknown thing:
Are there not other regions than this isle?
What are the stars? There is the sun, the sun!
And the most patient brilliance of the moon!
And stars by thousands! Point me out the way
To any one particular beauteous star,
And I will flit into it with my lyre,
And make its silvery splendour pant with bliss.
I have heard the cloudy thunder. Where is power?
Whose hand, whose essence, what Divinity
Makes this alarum in the elements,
While I here idle listen on the shores
In fearless yet in aching ignorance?

O tell me, lonely Goddess, by thy harp,
That waileth every morn and eventide,
Tell me why thus I rave, about these groves!
Mute thou remainest—mute! yet I can read
A wondrous lesson in thy silent face:
Knowledge enormous makes a God of me.
Names, deeds, grey legends, dire events, rebellions,
Majesties, sovran voices, agonies,
Creations and destroyings, all at once
Pour into the wide hollows of my brain,
And deify me, as if some blithe wine
Or bright elixir peerless I had drunk,
And so become immortal.'—Thus the God,
While his enkindlèd eyes, with level glance
Beneath his white soft temples, steadfast kept
Trembling with light upon Mnemosyne.
Soon wild commotions shook him, and made flush
All the immortal fairness of his limbs—
Most like the struggle at the gate of death;
Or liker still to one who should take leave
Of pale immortal death, and with a pang
As hot as death's is chill, with fierce convulse
Die into life: so young Apollo anguished.
His very hair, his golden tresses famed
Kept undulation round his eager neck.
During the pain Mnemosyne upheld
Her arms as one who prophesied.—At length
Apollo shrieked—and lo! from all his limbs
Celestial…

Fancy

Ever let the Fancy roam,
Pleasure never is at home:
At a touch sweet Pleasure melteth,
Like to bubbles when rain pelteth.
Then let winged Fancy wander
Through the thought still spread beyond her:
Open wide the mind's cage-door,
She'll dart forth, and cloudward soar.
O sweet Fancy! let her loose—
Summer's joys are spoilt by use,
And the enjoying of the Spring
Fades as does its blossoming;
Autumn's red-lipped fruitage too,

Blushing through the mist and dew,
Cloys with tasting. What do then?
Sit thee by the ingle, when
The sere faggot blazes bright,
Spirit of a winter's night;
When the soundless earth is muffled,
And the cakèd snow is shuffled
From the ploughboy's heavy shoon;
When the Night doth meet the Noon
In a dark conspiracy
To banish Even from her sky.
Sit thee there, and send abroad,
With a mind self-overawed,
Fancy, high-commissioned—send her!
She has vassals to attend her:
She will bring, in spite of frost,
Beauties that the earth hath lost;
She will bring thee, all together,
All delights of summer weather;
All the buds and bells of May,
From dewy sward or thorny spray;
All the heapèd Autumn's wealth,
With a still, mysterious stealth:
She will mix these pleasures up
Like three fit wines in a cup,
And thou shalt quaff it—thou shalt hear
Distant harvest-carols clear;
Rustle of the reaped corn;
Sweet birds antheming the morn:
And, in the same moment—hark!
'Tis the early April lark,
Or the rooks, with busy caw,
Foraging for sticks and straw.
Thou shalt, at one glance, behold
The daisy and the marigold;
White-plumed lilies, and the first
Hedge-grown primrose that hath burst;
Shaded hyacinth, alway
Sapphire queen of the mid-May;
And every leaf, and every flower
Pearlèd with the self-same shower.
Thou shalt see the field-mouse peep
Meagre from its cellèd sleep;
And the snake all winter-thin
Cast on sunny bank its skin;

Freckled nest-eggs thou shalt see
Hatching in the hawthorn-tree,
When the hen-bird's wing doth rest
Quiet on her mossy nest;
Then the hurry and alarm
When the bee-hive casts its swarm;
Acorns ripe down-pattering,
While the autumn breezes sing.

O, sweet Fancy! let her loose;
Every thing is spoilt by use:
Where's the cheek that doth not fade,
Too much gazed at? Where's the maid
Whose lip mature is ever new?
Where's the eye, however blue,
Doth not weary? Where's the face
One would meet in every place?
Where's the voice, however soft,
One would hear so very oft?
At a touch sweet Pleasure melteth
Like to bubbles when rain pelteth.
Let, then, wingèd Fancy find
Thee a mistress to thy mind:
Dulcet-eyed as Ceres' daughter,
Ere the God of Torment taught her
How to frown and how to chide;
With a waist and with a side
White as Hebe's, when her zone
Slipped its golden clasp, and down
Fell her kirtle to her feet,
While she held the goblet sweet,
And Jove grew languid.—Break the mesh
Of the Fancy's silken leash;
Quickly break her prison-string
And such joys as these she'll bring.
Let the wingèd Fancy roam,
Pleasure never is at home.

Ode

Bards of Passion and of Mirth,
Ye have left your souls on earth!
Have ye souls in heaven too,
Double-lived in regions new?
Yes, and those of heaven commune

With the spheres of sun and moon;
With the noise of fountains wondrous,
And the parle of voices thund'rous;
With the whisper of heaven's trees
And one another, in soft ease
Seated on Elysian lawns
Browsed by none but Dian's fawns;
Underneath large blue-bells tented,
Where the daisies are rose-scented,
And the rose herself has got
Perfume which on earth is not;
Where the nightingale doth sing
Not a senseless, trancèd thing,
But divine melodious truth;
Philosophic numbers smooth;
Tales and golden histories
Of heaven and its mysteries.

Thus ye live on high, and then
On the earth ye live again;
And the souls ye left behind you
Teach us, here, the way to find you,
Where your other souls are joying,
Never slumbered, never cloying.
Here, your earth-born souls still speak
To mortals, of their little week;
Of their sorrows and delights;
Of their passions and their spites;
Of their glory and their shame;
What doth strengthen and what maim.
Thus ye teach us, every day,
Wisdom, though fled far away.

Bards of Passion and of Mirth,
Ye have left your souls on earth!
Ye have souls in heaven too,
Double-lived in regions new!

Song

I had a dove and the sweet dove died;
And I have thought it died of grieving.
O, what could it grieve for? Its feet were tied,
With a silken thread of my own hand's weaving.
Sweet little red feet! why would you die—

Why would you leave me, sweet bird! why?
You lived alone on the forest-tree,
Why, pretty thing, could you not live with me?
I kissed you oft and gave you white peas;
Why not live sweetly, as in the green trees?

Song

I

Hush, hush! tread softly! hush, hush my dear!
  All the house is asleep, but we know very well
That the jealous, the jealous old bald-pate may hear,
  Though you've padded his night-cap—O sweet Isabel!
    Though your feet are more light than a faery's feet,
    Who dances on bubbles where brooklets meet—
Hush, hush! tread softly! hush, hush my dear!
For less than a nothing the jealous can hear.

II

No leaf doth tremble, no ripple is there
  On the river—all's still, and the night's sleepy eye
Closes up, and forgets all its Lethean care,
  Charmed to death by the drone of the humming mayfly;
    And the moon, whether prudish or complaisant,
    Hath fled to her bower, well knowing I want
No light in the darkness, no torch in the gloom,
But my Isabel's eyes, and her lips pulped with bloom.

III

Lift the latch! ah gently! ah tenderly—sweet!
  We are dead if that latchet gives one little clink!
Well done—now those lips, and a flowery seat—
  The old man may dream, and the planets may wink;
    The shut rose may dream of our loves, and awake
    Full-blown, and such warmth for the morning take,
The stock-dove shall hatch her soft brace and shall coo,
While I kiss to the melody, aching all through!

The Eve of St Agnes

I

St Agnes' Eve—Ah, bitter chill it was!
The owl, for all his feathers, was a-cold;
The hare limped trembling through the frozen grass,
And silent was the flock in woolly fold:
Numb were the Beadsman's fingers, while he told
His rosary, and while his frosted breath,
Like pious incense from a censer old,
Seemed taking flight for heaven, without a death,
Past the sweet Virgin's picture, while his prayer he saith.

II

His prayer he saith, this patient, holy man;
Then takes his lamp, and riseth from his knees,
And back returneth, meagre, barefoot, wan,
Along the chapel aisle by slow degrees:
The sculptured dead, on each side, seem to freeze,
Emprisoned in black, purgatorial rails;
Knights, ladies, praying in dumb orat'ries,
He passeth by; and his weak spirit fails
To think how they may ache in icy hoods and mails.

III

Northward he turneth through a little door,
And scarce three steps, ere Music's golden tongue
Flattered to tears this agèd man and poor;
But no—already had his deathbell rung:
The joys of all his life were said and sung:
His was harsh penance on St Agnes' Eve.
Another way he went, and soon among
Rough ashes sat he for his soul's reprieve,
And all night kept awake, for sinners' sake to grieve.

IV

That ancient Beadsman heard the prelude soft;
And so it chanced, for many a door was wide,
From hurry to and fro. Soon, up aloft,
The silver, snarling trumpets 'gan to chide:

The level chambers, ready with their pride,
Were glowing to receive a thousand guests:
The carvèd angels, ever eager-eyed,
Stared, where upon their heads the cornice rests,
With hair blown back, and wings put cross-wise on their breasts.

V

At length burst in the argent revelry,
With plume, tiara, and all rich array,
Numerous as shadows haunting faerily
The brain, new-stuffed, in youth, with triumphs gay
Of old romance. These let us wish away,
And turn, sole-thoughted, to one Lady there,
Whose heart had brooded, all that wintry day,
On love, and winged St Agnes' saintly care,
As she had heard old dames full many times declare.

VI

They told her how, upon St Agnes' Eve,
Young virgins might have visions of delight,
And soft adorings from their loves receive
Upon the honeyed middle of the night,
If ceremonies due they did aright;
As, supperless to bed they must retire,
And couch supine their beauties, lily white;
Nor look behind, nor sideways, but require
Of Heaven with upward eyes for all that they desire.

VII

Full of this whim was thoughtful Madeline:
The music, yearning like a God in pain,
She scarcely heard: her maiden eyes divine,
Fixed on the floor, saw many a sweeping train
Pass by—she heeded not at all: in vain
Came many a tip-toe, amorous cavalier,
And back retired—not cooled by high disdain,
But she saw not: her heart was otherwhere.
She sighed for Agnes' dreams, the sweetest of the year.

VIII

She danced along with vague, regardless eyes,
Anxious her lips, her breathing quick and short:
The hallowed hour was near at hand: she sighs
Amid the timbrels, and the thronged resort
Of whisperers in anger, or in sport;
'Mid looks of love, defiance, hate, and scorn,
Hoodwinked with faery fancy—all amort,
Save to St Agnes and her lambs unshorn,
And all the bliss to be before to-morrow morn.

IX

So, purposing each moment to retire,
She lingered still. Meantime, across the moors,
Had come young Porphyro, with heart on fire
For Madeline. Beside the portal doors,
Buttressed from moonlight, stands he, and implores
All saints to give him sight of Madeline
But for one moment in the tedious hours,
That he might gaze and worship all unseen;
Perchance speak, kneel, touch, kiss—in sooth such things have been.

X

He ventures in—let no buzzed whisper tell,
All eyes be muffled, or a hundred swords
Will storm his heart, Love's fev'rous citadel:
For him, those chambers held barbarian hordes,
Hyena foemen, and hot-blooded lords,
Whose very dogs would execrations howl
Against his lineage: not one breast affords
Him any mercy, in that mansion foul,
Save one old beldame, weak in body and in soul.

XI

Ah, happy chance! the agèd creature came,
Shuffling along with ivory-headed wand,
To where he stood, hid from the torch's flame,
Behind a broad hall-pillar, far beyond
The sound of merriment and chorus bland:

He startled her; but soon she knew his face,
And grasped his fingers in her palsied hand,
Saying, 'Mercy, Porphyro! hie thee from this place:
They are all here to-night, the whole blood-thirsty race!

XII

'Get hence! get hence! there's dwarfish Hildebrand—
He had a fever late, and in the fit
He cursed thee and thine, both house and land:
Then there's that old Lord Maurice, not a whit
More tame for his grey hairs—Alas me! flit!
Flit like a ghost away.' 'Ah, gossip dear,
We're safe enough; here in this arm-chair sit,
And tell me how—' 'Good Saints! not here, not here;
Follow me, child, or else these stones will be thy bier.'

XIII

He followed through a lowly archèd way,
Brushing the cobwebs with his lofty plume,
And as she muttered, 'Well-a—well-a-day!'
He found him in a little moonlight room,
Pale, latticed, chill, and silent as a tomb.
'Now tell me where is Madeline,' said he,
'O tell me, Angela, by the holy loom
Which none but secret sisterhood may see,
When they St Agnes' wool are weaving piously.'

XIV

'St Agnes? Ah! it is St Agnes' Eve—
Yet men will murder upon holy days:
Thou must hold water in a witch's sieve,
And be liege-lord of all the Elves and Fays,
To venture so: it fills me with amaze
To see thee, Porphyro!—St Agnes' Eve!
God's help! my lady fair the conjuror plays
This very night. Good angels her deceive!
But let me laugh awhile, I've mickle time to grieve.'

XV

Feebly she laugheth in the languid moon,
While Porphyro upon her face doth look,
Like puzzled urchin on an agèd crone
Who keepeth closed a wondrous riddle-book,
As spectacled she sits in chimney nook.
But soon his eyes grew brilliant, when she told
His lady's purpose; and he scarce could brook
Tears, at the thought of those enchantments cold,
And Madeline asleep in lap of legends old.

XVI

Sudden a thought came like a full-blown rose,
Flushing his brow, and in his painèd heart
Made purple riot; then doth he propose
A stratagem, that makes the beldame start:
'A cruel man and impious thou art:
Sweet lady, let her pray, and sleep, and dream
Alone with her good angels, far apart
From wicked men like thee. Go, go!—I deem
Thou canst not surely be the same that thou didst seem.'

XVII

'I will not harm her, by all saints I swear,'
Quoth Porphyro: 'O may I ne'er find grace
When my weak voice shall whisper its last prayer,
If one of her soft ringlets I displace,
Or look with ruffian passion in her face:
Good Angela, believe me by these tears,
Or I will, even in a moment's space,
Awake, with horrid shout, my foeman's ears,
And beard them, though they be more fanged than wolves and bears.'

XVIII

'Ah! why wilt thou affright a feeble soul?
A poor, weak, palsy-stricken, churchyard thing,
Whose passing-bell may ere the midnight toll;
Whose prayers for thee, each mom and evening,
Were never missed.'—Thus plaining, doth she bring

A gentler speech from burning Porphyro,
So woeful, and of such deep sorrowing,
That Angela gives promise she will do
Whatever he shall wish, betide her weal or woe.

XIX

Which was, to lead him, in close secrecy,
Even to Madeline's chamber, and there hide
Him in a closet, of such privacy
That he might see her beauty unespied,
And win perhaps that night a peerless bride,
While legioned faeries paced the coverlet,
And pale enchantment held her sleepy-eyed.
Never on such a night have lovers met,
Since Merlin paid his Demon all the monstrous debt.

XX

'It shall be as thou wishest,' said the Dame:
'All cates and dainties shall be storèd there
Quickly on this feast-night; by the tambour frame
Her own lute thou wilt see. No time to spare,
For I am slow and feeble, and scarce dare
On such a catering trust my dizzy head.
Wait here, my child, with patience; kneel in prayer
The while. Ah! thou must needs the lady wed,
Or may I never leave my grave among the dead.'

XXI

So saying, she hobbled off with busy fear.
The lover's endless minutes slowly passed;
The dame returned, and whispered in his ear
To follow her; with agèd eyes aghast
From fright of dim espial. Safe at last,
Through many a dusky gallery, they gain
The maiden's chamber, silken, hushed, and chaste;
Where Porphyro took covert, pleased amain.
His poor guide hurried back with agues in her brain.

XXII

Her faltering hand upon the balustrade,
Old Angela was feeling for the stair,
When Madeline, St Agnes' charmèd maid,
Rose, like a missioned spirit, unaware:
With silver taper's light, and pious care,
She turned, and down the agèd gossip led
To a safe level matting. Now prepare,
Young Porphyro, for gazing on that bed—
She comes, she comes again, like ring-dove frayed and fled.

XXIII

Out went the taper as she hurried in;
Its little smoke, in pallid moonshine, died:
She closed the door, she panted, all akin
To spirits of the air, and visions wide—
No uttered syllable, or, woe betide!
But to her heart, her heart was voluble,
Paining with eloquence her balmy side;
As though a tongueless nightingale should swell
Her throat in vain, and die, heart-stiflèd, in her dell.

XXIV

A casement high and triple-arched there was,
All garlanded with carven imag'ries
Of fruits, and flowers, and bunches of knot-grass,
And diamonded with panes of quaint device,
Innumerable of stains and splendid dyes,
As are the tiger-moth's deep-damasked wings;
And in the midst, 'mong thousand heraldries,
And twilight saints, and dim emblazonings,
A shielded scutcheon blushed with blood of queens and kings.

XXV

Full on this casement shone the wintry moon,
And threw warm gules on Madeline's fair breast,
As down she knelt for heaven's grace and boon;
Rose-bloom fell on her hands, together pressed,
And on her silver cross soft amethyst,
And on her hair a glory, like a saint:

She seemed a splendid angel, newly dressed,
Save wings, for Heaven—Porphyro grew faint;
She knelt, so pure a thing, so free from mortal taint.

XXVI

Anon his heart revives; her vespers done,
Of all its wreathèd pearls her hair she frees;
Unclasps her warmèd jewels one by one;
Loosens her fragrant bodice; by degrees
Her rich attire creeps rustling to her knees:
Half-hidden, like a mermaid in sea-weed,
Pensive awhile she dreams awake, and sees,
In fancy, fair St Agnes in her bed,
But dares not look behind, or all the charm is fled.

XXVII

Soon, trembling in her soft and chilly nest,
In sort of wakeful swoon, perplexed she lay,
Until the poppied warmth of sleep oppressed
Her soothèd limbs, and soul fatigued away—
Flown, like a thought, until the morrow-day;
Blissfully havened both from joy and pain;
Clasped like a missal where swart Paynims pray;
Blinded alike from sunshine and from rain,
As though a rose should shut, and be a bud again.

XXVIII

Stolen to this paradise, and so entranced,
Porphyro gazed upon her empty dress,
And listened to her breathing, if it chanced
To wake into a slumbrous tenderness;
Which when he heard, that minute did he bless,
And breathed himself: then from the closet crept,
Noiseless as fear in a wide wilderness,
And over the hushed carpet, silent, stepped,
And 'tween the curtains peeped, where, lo!—how fast she slept.

XXIX

Then by the bed-side, where the faded moon
Made a dim, silver twilight, soft he set
A table, and, half anguished, threw thereon
A cloth of woven crimson, gold, and jet—
O for some drowsy Morphean amulet!
The boisterous, midnight, festive clarion,
The kettle-drum, and far-heard clarinet,
Affray his ears, though but in dying tone;
The hall door shuts again, and all the noise is gone.

XXX

And still she slept an azure-lidded sleep,
In blanchèd linen, smooth, and lavendered,
While he from forth the closet brought a heap
Of candied apple, quince, and plum, and gourd,
With jellies soother than the creamy curd,
And lucent syrups, tinct with cinnamon;
Manna and dates, in argosy transferred
From Fez; and spicèd dainties, every one,
From silken Samarkand to cedared Lebanon.

XXXI

These delicates he heaped with glowing hand
On golden dishes and in baskets bright
Of wreathèd silver; sumptuous they stand
In the retirèd quiet of the night,
Filling the chilly room with perfume light.
'And now, my love, my seraph fair, awake!
Thou art my heaven, and I thine eremite:
Open thine eyes, for meek St Agnes' sake,
Or I shall drowse beside thee, so my soul doth ache.'

XXXII

Thus whispering, his warm, unnervèd arm
Sank in her pillow. Shaded was her dream
By the dusk curtains—'twas a midnight charm
Impossible to melt as icèd stream:
The lustrous salvers in the moonlight gleam;
Broad golden fringe upon the carpet lies.

It seemed he never, never could redeem
From such a steadfast spell his lady's eyes;
So mused awhile, entoiled in woofèd fantasies.

XXXIII

Awakening up, he took her hollow lute,
Tumultuous, and, in chords that tenderest be,
He played an ancient ditty, long since mute,
In Provence called, 'La belle dame sans mercy',
Close to her ear touching the melody—
Wherewith disturbed, she uttered a soft moan:
He ceased—she panted quick—and suddenly
Her blue affrayèd eyes wide open shone.
Upon his knees he sank, pale as smooth-sculptured stone.

XXXIV

Her eyes were open, but she still beheld,
Now wide awake, the vision of her sleep—
There was a painful change, that nigh expelled
The blisses of her dream so pure and deep.
At which fair Madeline began to weep,
And moan forth witless words with many a sigh,
While still her gaze on Porphyro would keep;
Who knelt, with joinèd hands and piteous eye,
Fearing to move or speak, she looked so dreamingly.

XXXV

'Ah, Porphyro!' said she, 'but even now
Thy voice was at sweet tremble in mine ear,
Made tuneable with every sweetest vow,
And those sad eyes were spiritual and clear:
How changed thou art! How pallid, chill, and drear!
Give me that voice again, my Porphyro,
Those looks immortal, those complainings dear!
O leave me not in this eternal woe,
For if thou diest, my Love, I know not where to go.'

XXXVI

Beyond a mortal man impassioned far
At these voluptuous accents, he arose,
Ethereal, flushed, and like a throbbing star
Seen mid the sapphire heaven's deep repose;
Into her dream he melted, as the rose
Blendeth its odour with the violet—
Solution sweet. Meantime the frost-wind blows
Like Love's alarum pattering the sharp sleet
Against the window-panes; St Agnes' moon hath set.

XXXVII

'Tis dark: quick pattereth the flaw-blown sleet.
'This is no dream, my bride, my Madeline!'
'Tis dark: the icèd gusts still rave and beat.
'No dream, alas! alas! and woe is mine!
Porphyro will leave me here to fade and pine.—
Cruel! what traitor could thee hither bring?
I curse not, for my heart is lost in thine,
Though thou forsakest a deceivèd thing—
A dove forlorn and lost with sick unprunèd wing.'

XXXVIII

'My Madeline! sweet dreamer! lovely bride!
Say, may I be for aye thy vassal blessed?
Thy beauty's shield, heart-shaped and vermeil dyed?
Ah, silver shrine, here will I take my rest
After so many hours of toil and quest,
A famished pilgrim—saved by miracle.
Though I have found, I will not rob thy nest
Saving of thy sweet self; if thou think'st well
To trust, fair Madeline, to no rude infidel.

XXXIX

'Hark! 'tis an elfin-storm from faery land,
Of haggard seeming, but a boon indeed:
Arise—arise! the morning is at hand.
The bloated wassaillers will never heed—
Let us away, my love, with happy speed—
There are no ears to hear, or eyes to see,

Drowned all in Rhenish and the sleepy mead;
Awake! arise! my love, and fearless be,
For o'er the southern moors I have a home for thee.'

XL

She hurried at his words, beset with fears,
For there were sleeping dragons all around,
At glaring watch, perhaps, with ready spears—
Down the wide stairs a darkling way they found.
In all the house was heard no human sound.
A chain-drooped lamp was flickering by each door;
The arras, rich with horseman, hawk, and hound,
Fluttered in the besieging wind's uproar;
And the long carpets rose along the gusty floor.

XLI

They glide, like phantoms, into the wide hall;
Like phantoms, to the iron porch, they glide;
Where lay the Porter, in uneasy sprawl,
With a huge empty flaggon by his side:
The wakeful bloodhound rose, and shook his hide,
But his sagacious eye an inmate owns.
By one, and one, the bolts full easy slide—
The chains lie silent on the footworn stones—
The key turns, and the door upon its hinges groans.

XLII

And they are gone—ay, ages long ago
These lovers fled away into the storm.
That night the Baron dreamt of many a woe,
And all his warrior-guests, with shade and form
Of witch, and demon, and large coffin-worm,
Were long be-nightmared. Angela the old
Died palsy-twitched, with meagre face deform;
The Beadsman, after thousand aves told,
For aye unsought for slept among his ashes cold.

The Eve of St Mark

Upon a Sabbath-day it fell;
Twice holy was the Sabbath bell,
That called the folk to evening prayer;
The city streets were clean and fair
From wholesome drench of April rains;
And, on the western window panes,
The chilly sunset faintly told
Of unmatured green valleys cold,
Of the green thorny bloomless hedge,
Of rivers new with spring-tide sedge,
Of primroses by sheltered rills,
And daisies on the aguish hills.
Twice holy was the Sabbath bell:
The silent streets were crowded well
With staid and pious companies,
Warm from their fireside orat'ries,
And moving, with demurest air,
To even-song, and vesper prayer.
Each archèd porch, and entry low,
Was filled with patient folk and slow,
With whispers hush, and shuffling feet,
While played the organs loud and sweet.

The bells had ceased, the prayers begun,
And Bertha had not yet half done
A curious volume, patched and torn,
That all day long, from earliest morn,
Had taken captive her two eyes,
Among its golden broideries;
Perplexed her with a thousand things—
The stars of Heaven, and angels' wings,
Martyrs in a fiery blaze,
Azure saints 'mid silver rays,
Aaron's breastplate, and the seven
Candlesticks John saw in Heaven,
The wingèd Lion of Saint Mark,
And the Covenantal Ark,
With its many mysteries,
Cherubim and golden mice.

Bertha was a maiden fair,
Dwelling in the old Minster Square;
From her fireside she could see,
Sidelong, its rich antiquity,
Far as the Bishop's garden wall,
Where sycamores and elm trees tall,
Full-leaved, the forest had outstripped,
By no sharp north-wind ever nipped,
So sheltered by the mighty pile.
Bertha arose, and read awhile,
With forehead 'gainst the window-pane.
Again she tried, and then again,
Until the dusk eve left her dark
Upon the legend of St Mark.
From pleated lawn-frill, fine and thin,
She lifted up her soft warm chin,
With aching neck and swimming eyes,
And dazed with saintly imageries.

All was gloom, and silent all,
Save now and then the still foot-fall
Of one returning townwards late,
Past the echoing Minster gate.

The clamorous daws, that all the day
Above tree-tops and towers play,
Pair by pair had gone to rest,
Each in its ancient belfry-nest,
Where asleep they fall betimes,
To music of the drowsy chimes.
All was silent, all was gloom,
Abroad and in the homely room:
Down she sat, poor cheated soul!
And struck a lamp from the dismal coal,
Leaned forward, with bright drooping hair,
And slant book full against the glare.
Her shadow, in uneasy guise,
Hovered about, a giant size,
On ceiling beam and old oak chair,
The parrot's cage, and panel square;
And the warm angled winter screen,
On which were many monsters seen,
Called doves of Siam, Lima mice,
And legless birds of Paradise,

Macaw, and tender Av'davat,
And silken-furred Angora cat.
Untired she read, her shadow still
Glowered about, as it would fill
The room with wildest forms and shades,
As though some ghostly Queen of Spades
Had come to mock behind her back,
And dance, and ruffle her garments black.
Untired she read the legend page,
Of holy Mark, from youth to age,
On land, on sea, in pagan chains,
Rejoicing for his many pains.
Sometimes the learned eremite,
With golden star, or dagger bright,
Referred to pious poesies
Written in smallest crow-quill size
Beneath the text; and thus the rhyme
Was parcelled out from time to time:
'—Als writith he of swevenis
Men han beforne they wake in bliss,
Whanne that hir friendes thinke hem bound
In crimpid shroude farre under grounde;
And how a litling child mote be
A saint er its nativitie,
Gif that the modre (God her blesse!)
Kepen in solitarinesse,
And kissen devoute the holy croce.
Of Goddis love, and Sathan's force,
He writith; and thinges many mo:
Of swichè thinges I may not show.
Bot I must tellen verilie
Somdel of Saintè Cicilie,
And chieflie what he auctorith
Of Saintè Markis life and death.'

At length her constant eyelids come
Upon the fervent martyrdom;
Then lastly to his holy shrine,
Exalt amid the tapers' shine
At Venice....

'Gifye wol stonden hardie wight'

Gif ye wol stonden hardie wight—
Amiddès of the blackè night—
Righte in the churchè porch, pardie,
Ye wol behold a companie
Approchen thee full dolourouse.
For sooth to sain, from everich house,
Be it in city or village,
Wol come the phantom and image
Of ilka gent and ilka carle,
Whom coldè Deathè hath in parle
And wol some day that very year,
Touchen with foulè venìme spear
And sadly do them all to die:
Hem all shalt thou see verilie.
And everichon shall by thee pass,
All who must die that year, alas…

'Why did I laugh tonight ...'

Why did I laugh tonight? No voice will tell:
  No God, no Demon of severe response,
Deigns to reply from Heaven or from Hell.
  Then to my human heart I turn at once—
Heart! thou and I are here sad and alone;
  Say, wherefore did I laugh! O mortal pain!
O Darkness! Darkness! ever must I moan,
  To question Heaven and Hell and Heart in vain.
Why did I laugh? I know this being's lease—
  My fancy to its utmost blisses spreads;
Yet could I on this very midnight cease,
  And the world's gaudy ensigns see in shreds.
Verse, Fame, and Beauty are intense indeed,
  But Death intenser—Death is Life's high meed.

Faery Bird's Song

Shed no tear—O, shed no tear!
The flower will bloom another year.
Weep no more! O! weep no more!
Young buds sleep in the root's white core.
Dry your eyes! O! dry your eyes,
For I was taught in Paradise

To ease my breast of melodies—
Shed no tear.

Overhead! look overhead!
'Mong the blossoms white and red—
Look up, look up. I flutter now
On this flush pomegranate bough.
See me! 'tis this silvery bill
Ever cures the good man's ill.
Shed no tear! O shed no tear!
The flower will bloom another year.
Adieu, adieu—I fly, adieu,
I vanish in the heaven's blue—
Adieu, adieu!

Faery Song

Ah! woe is me! poor silver-wing!
That I must chant thy lady's dirge,
And death to this fair haunt of spring,
Of melody, and streams of flowery verge—
Poor silver-wing! ah! woe is me!
That I must see
These blossoms snow upon thy lady's pall!
Go, pretty page! and in her ear
Whisper that the hour is near!
Softly tell her not to fear
Such calm Favonian burial!
Go, pretty page! and soothly tell—
The blossoms hang by a melting spell,
And fall they must, ere a star wink thrice
Upon her closèd eyes,
That now in vain are weeping their last tears,
At sweet life leaving, and these arbours green—
Rich dowry from the Spirit of the Spheres.
Alas! poor Queen!

'*When they were come unto the Faery's Court*'

When they were come unto the Faery's Court
They rang—no one at home; all gone to sport
And dance and kiss and love as faeries do,
For faeries be, as humans, lovers true.
Amid the woods they were, so lone and wild,
Where even the robin feels himself exiled,

And where the very brooks as if afraid
Hurry along to some less magic shade.
'No one at home!' the fretful princess cried,
'And all for nothing such a dreary ride,
And all for nothing my new diamond cross,
No one to see my Persian feathers toss,
No one to see my Ape, my Dwarf, my Fool,
Or how I pace my Otaheitan mule.
Ape, Dwarf and Fool, why stand you gaping there?
Burst the door open, quick—or I declare
I'll switch you soundly and in pieces tear.'
The Dwarf began to tremble and the Ape
Stared at the Fool, the Fool was all agape.
The Princess grasped her switch, but just in time
The Dwarf with piteous face began to rhyme.
'O mighty Princess, did you ne'er hear tell
What your poor servants know but too, too well?
Know you the three 'great crimes' in faery land?
The first—alas! poor Dwarf—I understand:
I made a whipstock of a faery's wand.
The next is snoring in their company.
The next, the last, the direst of the three,
Is making free when they are not at home.
I was a Prince, a baby prince—my doom
You see—I made a whipstock of a wand.
My top has henceforth slept in faery land.
He was a Prince, the Fool, a grown-up Prince,
But he has never been a King's son since
He fell a-snoring at a faery Ball.
Your poor Ape was a Prince, and he, poor thing,
Picklocked a faery's boudoir—now no king,
But ape—so pray your highness stay awhile;
'Tis sooth indeed, we know it to our sorrow—
Persist and *you* may be an ape tomorrow.'
While the Dwarf spake the Princess all for spite
Peeled the brown hazel twig to lily white,
Clenched her small teeth, and held her lips apart,
Tried to look unconcerned with beating heart.
They saw her Highness had made up her mind,
A-quavering like three reeds before the wind—
And they had had it, but—O happy chance!—
The Ape for very fear began to dance
And grinned as all his ugliness did ache—
She stayed her vixen fingers for his sake,
He was so very ugly: then she took

Her pocket mirror and began to look
First at herself and then at him and then
She smiled at her own beauteous face again.
Yet for all this—for all her pretty face—
She took it in her head to see the place.
Women gain little from experience
Either in lovers, husbands or expense.
'The more the beauty, the more fortune too:
Beauty before the wide world never knew—'
So each Fair reasons, though it oft miscarries.
She thought *her* pretty face would please the faeries.
'My darling Ape, I won't whip you today—
Give me the picklock, sirrah, and go play.'
They all three wept—but counsel was as vain
As crying 'C'up, biddy' to drops of rain.
Yet lingeringly did the sad Ape forth draw
The picklock from the pocket in his jaw.
The Princess took it and, dismounting straight,
Tripped in blue silvered slippers to the gate
And touched the wards; the door full courteously
Opened—she entered with her servants three.
Again it closed, and there was nothing seen
But the Mule grazing on the herbage green.
End of Canto xii

Canto the xiii
The Mule no sooner saw himself alone
Than he pricked up his ears—and said, 'Well done!
At least, unhappy Prince, I may be free—
No more a Princess shall side-saddle me.
O King of Otahietè—though as Mule,
"Ay, every inch a King", though "Fortune's fool"—
Well done—for by what Mr Dwarfy said
I would not give a sixpence for her head.'
Even as he spake he trotted in high glee
To the knotty side of an old pollard tree
And rubbed his sides against the mossed bark
Till his girths burst and left him naked stark
Except his bridle—how get rid of that,
Buckled and tied with many a twist and plait?
At last it struck him to pretend to sleep
And then the thievish Monkeys down would creep
And filch the unpleasant trammels quite away.
No sooner thought of than adown he lay,
Shammed a good snore—the Monkey-men descended

And whom they thought to injure, they befriended.
They hung his bridle on a topmost bough,
And off he went, run, trot, or anyhow....

'The House of Mourning written by Mr Scott'

The House of Mourning written by Mr Scott,
  A sermon at the Magdalen, a tear
  Dropped on a greasy novel, want of cheer
After a walk uphill to a friend's cot,
Tea with a maiden lady, a cursed lot
  Of worthy poems with the author near,
  A patron lord, a drunkenness from beer,
Haydon's great picture, a cold coffee pot
At midnight when the Muse is ripe for labour,
  The voice of Mr Coleridge, a French bonnet
Before you in the pit, a pipe and tabour,
A damned inseparable flute and neighbour—
  All these are vile, but viler Wordsworth's sonnet
On Dover. Dover!—who *could* write upon it?

Character of Charles Brown

I

  He is to weet a melancholy carle:
  Thin in the waist, with bushy head of hair,
  As hath the seeded thistle when in parle
  It holds the Zephyr, ere it sendeth fair
  Its light balloons into the summer air;
  Thereto his beard had not begun to bloom,
  No brush had touched his chin or razor sheer;
  No care had touched his cheek with mortal doom,
But new he was and bright as scarf from Persian loom.

II

  Ne cared he for wine, or half-and-half,
  Ne cared he for fish or flesh or fowl,
  And sauces held he worthless as the chaff;
  He 'sdained the swine-herd at the wassail-bowl,
  Ne with lewd ribbalds sat he cheek by jowl,
  Ne with sly Lemans in the scorner's chair,
  But after water-brooks this Pilgrim's soul
  Panted, and all his food was woodland air

Though he would oft-times feast on gillyflowers rare.

III

The slang of cities in no wise he knew,
Tipping the wink to him was heathen Greek.
He sipped no olden Tom or ruin blue,
Or Nantz or cheery-brandy drank full meek
By many a damsel hoarse and rouge of cheek.
Nor did he know each agèd watchman's beat,
Nor in obscurèd purlieus would he seek
For curlèd Jewesses, with ankles neat,
Who as they walk abroad make tinkling with their feet.

A Dream, after reading Dante's Episode of Paolo and Francesca

As Hermes once took to his feathers light,
When lulled Argus, baffled, swooned and slept,
So on a Delphic reed, my idle spright
So played, so charmed, so conquered, so bereft
The dragon-world of all its hundred eyes;
And, seeing it asleep, so fled away—
Not to pure Ida with its snow-cold skies,
Nor unto Tempe where Jove grieved that day;
But to that second circle of sad hell,
Where in the gust, the whirlwind, and the flaw
Of rain and hail-stones, lovers need not tell
Their sorrows. Pale were the sweet lips I saw,
Pale were the lips I kissed, and fair the form
I floated with, about that melancholy storm.

La Belle Dame sans Merci. A Ballad

I

O what can ail thee, knight-at-arms,
Alone and palely loitering?
The sedge has withered from the lake,
And no birds sing.

II

O what can ail thee, knight-at-arms,
So haggard and so woe-begone?
The squirrel's granary is full,
And the harvest's done.

III

I see a lily on thy brow,
With anguish moist and fever-dew,
And on thy cheeks a fading rose
Fast withereth too.

IV

I met a lady in the meads,
Full beautiful—a faery's child,
Her hair was long, her foot was light,
And her eyes were wild.

V

I made a garland for her head,
And bracelets too, and fragrant zone;
She looked at me as she did love,
And made sweet moan.

VI

I set her on my pacing steed,
And nothing else saw all day long,
For sidelong would she bend, and sing
A faery's song.

VII

She found me roots of relish sweet,
And honey wild, and manna-dew,
And sure in language strange she said—
'I love thee true'.

VIII

She took me to her elfin grot,
And there she wept and sighed full sore,
And there I shut her wild wild eyes
With kisses four.

IX

And there she lullèd me asleep
And there I dreamed—Ah! woe betide!—
The latest dream I ever dreamt
On the cold hill side.

X

I saw pale kings and princes too,
Pale warriors, death-pale were they all;
They cried—'La Belle Dame sans Merci
Thee hath in thrall!'

XI

I saw their starved lips in the gloam,
With horrid warning gapèd wide,
And I awoke and found me here,
On the cold hill's side.

XII

And this is why I sojourn here
Alone and palely loitering,
Though the sedge is withered from the lake,
And no birds sing.

Song of Four Faeries
Fire, Air, Earth and Water

SALAMANDER, ZEPHYR, DUSKETHA, AND BREAMA

SALAMANDER
Happy, happy glowing fire!

ZEPHYR
Fragrant air! delicious light!

DUSKETHA
Let me to my glooms retire!

BREAMA
I to green-weed rivers bright!

SALAMANDER
Happy, happy glowing fire!
Dazzling bowers of soft retire,
Ever let my nourished wing,
Like a bat's, still wandering,
Nimbly fan your fiery spaces,
Spirit sole in deadly places.
In unhaunted roar and blaze,
Open eyes that never daze,
Let me see the myriad shapes
Of men and beasts, and fish, and apes,
Portrayed in many a fiery den,
And wrought by spumy bitumen
On the deep intenser roof,
Archèd every way aloof.
Let me breathe upon their skies,
And anger their live tapestries;
Free from cold, and every care,
Of chilly rain, and shivering air.

ZEPHYR
Spirit of Fire! away! away!
Or your very roundelay
Will sear my plumage newly budded
From its quillèd sheath, and studded
With the self-same dews that fell
On the May-grown asphodel.
Spirit of Fire! away! away!

BREAMA
Spirit of Fire! away! away!
Zephyr, blue-eyed, Faery, turn,
And see my cool sedge-buried urn,
Where it rests its mossy brim
'Mid water-mint and cresses dim;

And the flowers, in sweet troubles,
Lift their eyes above the bubbles,
Like our Queen, when she would please
To sleep, and Oberon *will* tease,
Love me, blue-eyed Faery true,
Soothly I am sick for you.

ZEPHYR

Gentle Breama! by the first
Violet young nature nursed,
I will bathe myself with thee,
So you sometime follow me
To my home, far, far, in west,
Beyond the nimble-wheelèd quest
Of the golden-presenced sun;
Come with me, o'er tops of trees,
To my fragrant palaces,
Where they ever floating are
Beneath the cherish of a star
Called Vesper, who with silver veil
Ever hides his brilliance pale,
Ever gently-drowsed doth keep
Twilight for the Fays to sleep.
Fear not that your watery hair
Will thirst in drouthy ringlets there;
Clouds of storèd summer rains
Thou shalt taste, before the stains
From the mountain soil they take,
And too unlucent for thee make.
I love thee, crystal Faery, true!
Sooth I am as sick for you!

SALAMANDER

Out, ye aguish Faeries, out!
Chilly lovers, what a rout
Keep ye with your frozen breath,
Colder than the mortal death.
Adder-eyed Dusketha, speak,
Shall we leave these, and go seek
In the earth's wide entrails old
Couches warm as theirs is cold?
O for a fiery gloom and thee,
Dusketha, so enchantingly
Freckle-winged and lizard-sided!

DUSKETHA
By thee, Sprite, will I be guided!
I care not for cold or heat;
Frost or flame, or sparks, or sleet,
To my essence are the same—
But I honour more the flame.
Sprite of Fire, I follow thee
Wheresoever it may be,
To the torrid spouts and fountains,
Underneath earth-quakèd mountains;
Or, at thy supreme desire,
Touch the very pulse of fire
With my bare unlidded eyes.

SALAMANDER
Sweet Dusketha! Paradise!
Off, ye icy Spirits, fly!
Frosty creatures of the sky!

DUSKETHA
Breathe upon them, fiery Sprite!

ZEPHYR AND BREAMA
Away! away to our delight!

SALAMANDER
Go, feed on icicles, while we
Bedded in tongued flames will be.

DUSKETHA
Lead me to those feverous glooms,
Sprite of Fire!

BREAMA
Me to the blooms,
Blue-eyed Zephyr, of those flowers
Far in the west where the May-cloud lowers;
And the beams of still Vesper, when winds are all whist,
Are shed through the rain and the milder mist,
And twilight your floating bowers.

To Sleep

O soft embalmer of the still midnight,
  Shutting, with careful fingers and benign,
Our gloom-pleased eyes, embowered from the light,
  Enshaded in forgetfulness divine:
O soothest Sleep! if so it please thee, close
  In midst of this thine hymn, my willing eyes,
Or wait the 'Amen', ere thy poppy throws
  Around my bed its lulling charities.
Then save me, or the passèd day will shine
Upon my pillow, breeding many woes;
  Save me from curious conscience, that still hoards
Its strength for darkness, burrowing like the mole;
  Turn the key deftly in the oilèd wards,
And seal the hushèd casket of my soul.

'If by dull rhymes our English must be chained'

If by dull rhymes our English must be chained,
And, like Andromeda, the Sonnet sweet
Fettered, in spite of painèd loveliness,
Let us find out, if we must be constrained,
Sandals more interwoven and complete
To fit the naked foot of Poesy:
Let us inspect the lyre, and weigh the stress
Of every chord, and see what may be gained
By ear industrious, and attention meet;
Misers of sound and syllable, no less
Than Midas of his coinage, let us be
Jealous of dead leaves in the bay wreath crown;
So, if we may not let the Muse be free,
She will be bound with garlands of her own.

Ode to Psyche

O Goddess! hear these tuneless numbers, wrung
  By sweet enforcement and remembrance dear,
And pardon that thy secrets should be sung
  Even into thine own soft-conchèd ear:
Surely I dreamt to-day, or did I see
  The wingèd Psyche with awakened eyes?
I wandered in a forest thoughtlessly,
  And, on the sudden, fainting with surprise,

Saw two fair creatures, couchèd side by side
In deepest grass, beneath the whispering roof
Of leaves and tremblèd blossoms, where there ran
A brooklet, scarce espied:
'Mid hushed, cool-rooted flowers, fragrant-eyed,
Blue, silver-white, and budded Tyrian,
They lay calm-breathing on the bedded grass;
Their arms embraced, and their pinions too;
Their lips touched not, but had not bade adieu,
As if disjoined by soft-handed slumber,
And ready still past kisses to outnumber
At tender eye-dawn of aurorean love:
The wingèd boy I knew;
But who wast thou, O happy, happy dove?
His Psyche true!

O latest born and loveliest vision far
Of all Olympus' faded hierarchy!
Fairer than Phoebe's sapphire-regioned star,
Or Vesper, amorous glow-worm of the sky;
Fairer than these, though temple thou hast none,
Nor altar heaped with flowers;
Nor virgin-choir to make delicious moan
Upon the midnight hours;
No voice, no lute, no pipe, no incense sweet
From chain-swung censer teeming;
No shrine, no grove, no oracle, no heat
Of pale-mouthed prophet dreaming.

O brightest! though too late for antique vows,
Too, too late for the fond believing lyre,
When holy were the haunted forest boughs,
Holy the air, the water, and the fire;
Yet even in these days so far retired
From happy pieties, thy lucent fans,
Fluttering among the faint Olympians,
I see, and sing, by my own eyes inspired.
So let me be thy choir, and make a moan
Upon the midnight hours;
Thy voice, thy lute, thy pipe, thy incense sweet
From swingèd censer teeming—
Thy shrine, thy grove, thy oracle, thy heat
Of pale-mouthed prophet dreaming.

Yes, I will be thy priest, and build a fane
  In some untrodden region of my mind,
Where branchèd thoughts, new grown with pleasant pain,
  Instead of pines shall murmur in the wind:
Far, far around shall those dark-clustered trees
  Fledge the wild-ridgèd mountains steep by steep;
And there by zephyrs, streams, and birds, and bees,
  The moss-lain Dryads shall be lulled to sleep;
And in the midst of this wide quietness
  A rosy sanctuary will I dress
With the wreathed trellis of a working brain,
  With buds, and bells, and stars without a name,
With all the gardener Fancy e'er could feign,
  Who breeding flowers, will never breed the same:
And there shall be for thee all soft delight
  That shadowy thought can win,
A bright torch, and a casement ope at night,
  To let the warm Love in!

On Fame (I)

Fame, like a wayward girl, will still be coy
  To those who woo her with too slavish knees,
But makes surrender to some thoughtless boy,
  And dotes the more upon a heart at ease;
She is gipsy, will not speak to those
  Who have not learnt to be content without her;
A jilt, whose ear was never whispered close,
  Who thinks they scandal her who talk about her—
A very gipsy is she, Nilus-born,
  Sister-in-law to jealous Potiphar.
Ye love-sick bards! repay her scorn for scorn;
  Ye artists lovelorn! madmen that ye are,
Make your best bow to her and bid adieu—
Then, if she likes it, she will follow you.

On Fame (II)

'*You cannot eat your cake and have it too.*'
Proverb

How fevered is the man who cannot look
  Upon his mortal days with temperate blood,
Who vexes all the leaves of his life's book,

And robs his fair name of its maidenhood;
It is as if the rose should pluck herself,
Or the ripe plum finger its misty bloom,
As if a Naiad, like a meddling elf,
Should darken her pure grot with muddy gloom:
But the rose leaves herself upon the briar,
For winds to kiss and grateful bees to feed,
And the ripe plum still wears its dim attire,
The undisturbed lake has crystal space;
Why then should man, teasing the world for grace,
Spoil his salvation for a fierce mi screed?

'*Two or three posies*'

Two or three posies
With two or three simples—
Two or three noses
With two or three pimples—
Two or three wise men
And two or three ninnies—
Two or three purses
And two or three guineas—
Two or three raps
At two or three doors—
Two or three naps
Of two or three hours—
Two or three cats
And two or three mice—
Two or three sprats
At a very great price—
Two or three sandies
And two or three tabbies—
Two or three dandies
And two Mrs —— mum!
Two or three smiles
And two or three frowns—
Two or three miles
To two or three towns—
Two or three pegs
For two or three bonnets—
Two or three dove's eggs
To hatch into sonnets.

Ode on a Grecian Urn

I

Thou still unravished bride of quietness,
Thou foster-child of silence and slow time,
Sylvan historian, who canst thus express
A flowery tale more sweetly than our rhyme:
What leaf-fringed legend haunts about thy shape
Of deities or mortals, or of both,
In Tempe or the dales of Arcady?
What men or gods are these? What maidens loth?
What mad pursuit? What struggle to escape?
What pipes and timbrels? What wild ecstasy?

II

Heard melodies are sweet, but those unheard
Are sweeter; therefore, ye soft pipes, play on;
Not to the sensual ear, but, more endeared,
Pipe to the spirit ditties of no tone:
Fair youth, beneath the trees, thou canst not leave
Thy song, nor ever can those trees be bare;
Bold Lover, never, never canst thou kiss,
Though winning near the goal—yet, do not grieve:
She cannot fade, though thou hast not thy bliss,
For ever wilt thou love, and she be fair!

III

Ah, happy, happy boughs! that cannot shed
Your leaves, nor ever bid the Spring adieu;
And, happy melodist, unwearièd,
For ever piping songs for ever new;
More happy love! more happy, happy love!
For ever warm and still to be enjoyed,
For ever panting, and for ever young—
All breathing human passion far above,
That leaves a heart high-sorrowful and cloyed,
A burning forehead, and a parching tongue.

IV

Who are these coming to the sacrifice?
To what green altar, O mysterious priest,
Lead'st thou that heifer lowing at the skies,
And all her silken flanks with garlands dressed?
What little town by river or sea shore,
Or mountain-built with peaceful citadel,
Is emptied of this folk, this pious morn?
And, little town, thy streets for evermore
Will silent be; and not a soul to tell
Why thou art desolate, can e'er return.

V

O Attic shape! Fair attitude! with brede
Of marble men and maidens overwrought,
With forest branches and the trodden weed;
Thou, silent form, dost tease us out of thought
As doth eternity: Cold Pastoral!
When old age shall this generation waste,
Thou shalt remain, in midst of other woe
Than ours, a friend to man, to whom thou say'st,
'Beauty is truth, truth beauty,—that is all
Ye know on earth, and all ye need to know.'

Ode to a Nightingale

I

My heart aches, and a drowsy numbness pains
My sense, as though of hemlock I had drunk,
Or emptied some dull opiate to the drains
One minute past, and Lethe-wards had sunk:
'Tis not through envy of thy happy lot,
But being too happy in thine happiness—
That thou, light-wingèd Dryad of the trees,
In some melodious plot
Of beechen green, and shadows numberless,
Singest of summer in full-throated ease.

II

O, for a draught of vintage! that hath been
Cooled a long age in the deep-delvèd earth,
Tasting of Flora and the country green,
Dance, and Provençal song, and sunburnt mirth!
O for a beaker full of the warm South,
Full of the true, the blushful Hippocrene,
With beaded bubbles winking at the brim,
And purple-stainèd mouth,
That I might drink, and leave the world unseen,
And with thee fade away into the forest dim—

III

Fade far away, dissolve, and quite forget
What thou among the leaves hast never known,
The weariness, the fever, and the fret
Here, where men sit and hear each other groan;
Where palsy shakes a few, sad, last grey hairs,
Where youth grows pale, and spectre-thin, and dies;
Where but to think is to be full of sorrow
And leaden-eyed despairs;
Where Beauty cannot keep her lustrous eyes,
Or new Love pine at them beyond to-morrow.

IV

Away! away! for I will fly to thee,
Not charioted by Bacchus and his pards,
But on the viewless wings of Poesy,
Though the dull brain perplexes and retards.
Already with thee! tender is the night,
And haply the Queen-Moon is on her throne,
Clustered around by all her starry Fays;
But here there is no light,
Save what from heaven is with the breezes blown
Through verdurous glooms and winding mossy ways.

V

I cannot see what flowers are at my feet,
Nor what soft incense hangs upon the boughs,
But, in embalmèd darkness, guess each sweet
Wherewith the seasonable month endows
The grass, the thicket, and the fruit-tree wild—
White hawthorn, and the pastoral eglantine;
Fast fading violets covered up in leaves;
And mid-May's eldest child,
The coming musk-rose, full of dewy wine,
The murmurous haunt of flies on summer eves.

VI

Darkling I listen; and, for many a time
I have been half in love with easeful Death,
Called him soft names in many a musèd rhyme,
To take into the air my quiet breath;
Now more than ever seems it rich to die,
To cease upon the midnight with no pain,
While thou art pouring forth thy soul abroad
In such an ecstasy!
Still wouldst thou sing, and I have ears in vain—
To thy high requiem become a sod.

VII

Thou wast not born for death, immortal Bird I
No hungry generations tread thee down;
The voice I hear this passing night was heard
In ancient days by emperor and clown:
Perhaps the self-same song that found a path
Through the sad heart of Ruth, when, sick for home,
She stood in tears amid the alien com;
The same that oft-times hath
Charmed magic casements, opening on the foam
Of perilous seas, in faery lands forlorn.

VIII

Forlorn! the very word is like a bell
  To toll me back from thee to my sole self I
Adieu! the fancy cannot cheat so well
  As she is famed to do, deceiving elf.
Adieu! adieu! thy plaintive anthem fades
  Past the near meadows, over the still stream,
    Up the hill-side; and now 'tis buried deep
      In the next valley-glades:
  Was it a vision, or a waking dream?
    Fled is that music—Do I wake or sleep?

Ode on Melancholy

I

No, no, go not to Lethe, neither twist
  Wolf's-bane, tight-rooted, for its poisonous wine:
Nor suffer thy pale forehead to be kissed
  By nightshade, ruby grape of Proserpine;
Make not your rosary of yew-berries,
  Nor let the beetle, nor the death-moth be
    Your mournful Psyche, nor the downy owl
A partner in your sorrow's mysteries;
  For shade to shade will come too drowsily,
    And drown the wakeful anguish of the soul.

II

But when the melancholy fit shall fall
  Sudden from heaven like a weeping cloud,
That fosters the droop-headed flowers all,
  And hides the green hill in an April shroud;
Then glut thy sorrow on a morning rose,
  Or on the rainbow of the salt sand-wave,
    Or on the wealth of globèd peonies;
Or if thy mistress some rich anger shows,
  Emprison her soft hand, and let her rave,
    And feed deep, deep upon her peerless eyes.

III

She dwells with Beauty—Beauty that must die;
And Joy, whose hand is ever at his lips
Bidding adieu; and aching Pleasure nigh,
Turning to poison while the bee-mouth sips:
Ay, in the very temple of Delight
Veiled Melancholy has her sovran shrine,
Though seen of none save him whose strenuous tongue
Can burst Joy's grape against his palate fine;
His soul shall taste the sadness of her might,
And be among her cloudy trophies hung.

Ode on Indolence

'They toil not, neither do they spin.'

I

One mom before me were three figures seen,
With bowèd necks, and joinèd hands, side-faced;
And one behind the other stepped serene,
In placid sandals, and in white robes graced;
They passed, like figures on a marble urn,
When shifted round to see the other side;
They came again; as when the um once more
Is shifted round, the first seen shades return;
And they were strange to me, as may betide
With vases, to one deep in Phidian lore.

II

How is it, Shadows! that I knew ye not?
How came ye muffled in so hush a masque?
Was it a silent deep-disguisèd plot
To steal away, and leave without a task
My idle days? Ripe was the drowsy hour;
The blissful cloud of summer-indolence
Benumbed my eyes; my pulse grew less and less
Pain had no sting, and pleasure's wreath no flower:
O, why did ye not melt, and leave my sense
Unhaunted quite of all but—nothingness?

III

A third time passed they by, and, passing, turned
  Each one the face a moment whiles to me;
Then faded, and to follow them I burned
  And ached for wings because I knew the three;
The first was a fair Maid, and Love her name;
  The second was Ambition, pale of cheek,
    And ever watchful with fatiguèd eye;
The last, whom I love more, the more of blame
  Is heaped upon her, maiden most unmeek—
    I knew to be my demon Poesy.

IV

They faded, and, forsooth! I wanted wings.
  O folly! What is love! and where is it?
And, for that poor Ambition—it springs
  From a man's little heart's short fever-fit.
For Poesy!—no, she has not a joy—
  At least for me—so sweet as drowsy noons,
    And evenings steeped in honeyed indolence.
O, for an age so sheltered from annoy,
  That I may never know how change the moons,
    Or hear the voice of busy common-sense!

V

A third time came they by—alas! wherefore?
  My sleep had been embroidered with dim dreams;
My soul had been a lawn besprinkled o'er
  With flowers, and stirring shades, and baffled beams:
The mom was clouded, but no shower fell,
  Though in her lids hung the sweet tears of May;
    The open casement pressed a new-leaved vine,
  Let in the budding warmth and throstle's lay;
O Shadows! 'twas a time to bid farewell!
    Upon your skirts had fallen no tears of mine.

VI

So, ye three Ghosts, adieu! Ye cannot raise
  My head cool-bedded in the flowery grass;
For I would not be dieted with praise,
  A pet-lamb in a sentimental farce!
Fade softly from my eyes, and be once more
  In masque-like figures on the dreamy urn.
    Farewell! I yet have visions for the night,
And for the day faint visions there is store.
    Vanish, ye Phantoms! from my idle sprite,
  Into the clouds, and never more return!

Otho the Great. A Tragedy in Five Acts

Dramatis Personae

OTHO, the great Emperor of Germany
LUDOLPH, his son
CONRAD, Duke of Franconia
ALBERT, a Knight, favoured by Otho
SIGIFRED, an Officer friend of Ludolph
THEODORE, Officer
GONFRID, Officer
ETHELBERT, an Abbot
GERSA Prince of Hungary
An Hungarian Captain
Physician
Page
Nobles, Knights, Attendants, and Soldiers

ERMINIA, Niece of Otho
AURANTHE, Conrad's Sister
Ladies and Attendants

Scene: the Castle of Friedburg, its vicinity, and the Hungarian Camp

Time: one day

ACT I

SCENE I. *An Apartment in the Castle. Enter* CONRAD.

CONRAD. So, I am safe emergèd from these broils!
Amid the wreck of thousands I am whole;
For every crime I have a laurel-wreath,
For every lie a lordship. Nor yet hash
My ship of fortune furled her silken sails—
Let her glide on! This dangered neck is saved,
By dexterous policy, from the rebel's axe;
And of my ducal palace not one stone
Is bruised by the Hungarian petards.
Toil hard, ye slaves, and from the miser-earth
Bring forth once more my bullion, treasured deep,
With all my jewelled salvers, silver and gold,
And precious goblets that make rich the wine.
But why do I stand babbling to myself?
Where is Auranthe? I have news for her
Shall—

[*Enter* AURANTHE.]

AURANTHE. Conrad! what tidings? Good, if I may guess
From your alert eyes and high-lifted brows.
What tidings of the battle? Albert? Ludolph?
Otho?
CONRAD. You guess aright. And, sister, slurring o'er
Our by-gone quarrels, I confess my heart
Is beating with a child's anxiety,
To make our golden fortune known to you.
AURANTHE. So serious?
CONRAD. Yes, so serious, that before
I utter even the shadow of a hint
Concerning what will make that sin-worn cheek
Blush joyous blood through every lineament,
You must make here a solemn vow to me.
AURANTHE. I prithee, Conrad, do not overact
The hypocrite. What vow would you impose?
CONRAD. Trust me for once. That you may be assured
'Tis not confiding in a broken reed,
A poor court-bankrupt, outwitted and lost,
Revolve these facts in your acutest mood,
In such a mood as now you listen to me.

A few days since, I was an open rebel—
Against the Emperor, had suborned his son—
Drawn off his nobles to revolt, and shown
Contented fools causes for discontent,
Fresh hatched in my ambition's eagle nest.
So thrived I as a rebel, and, behold—
Now I am Otho's favourite, his dear friend,
His right hand, his brave Conrad!
AURANTHE. I confess
You have intrigued with these unsteady times
To admiration. But to be a favourite—
CONRAD. I saw my moment. The Hungarians,
Collected silently in holes and comers,
Appeared, a sudden host, in the open day.
I should have perished in our empire's wreck,
But, calling interest loyalty, swore faith
To most believing Otho; and so helped
His blood-stained ensigns to the victory
In yesterday's hard fight, that it has turned
The edge of his sharp wrath to eager kindness.
AURANTHE. So far yourself. But what is this to me
More than that I am glad? I gratulate you.
CONRAD. Yes, sister, but it does regard you greatly,
Nearly, momentously—ay, painfully!
Make me this vow—
AURANTHE. Concerning whom or what?
CONRAD. Albert!
AURANTHE. I would inquire somewhat of him:
You had a letter from me touching him?
No treason 'gainst his head in deed or word!
Surely you spared him at my earnest prayer?
Give me the letter—it should not exist!
CONRAD. At one pernicious charge of the enemy,
I, for a moment-whiles, was prisoner ta'en
And rifled—stuff! the horses' hoofs have minced it!
AURANTHE. He is alive?
CONRAD. He is! but here make oath
To alienate him from your scheming brain,
Divorce him from your solitary thoughts,
And cloud him in such utter banishment,
That when his person meets again your eye,
Your vision shall quite lose its memory,
And wander past him as through vacancy.
AURANTHE. I'll not be perjured.
CONRAD. No, nor great, nor mighty;

You would not wear a crown, or rule a kingdom.
To you it is indifferent.
AURANTHE. What means this?
CONRAD. You'll not be perjured! Go to Albert then,
That camp-mushroom—dishonour of our house.
Go, page his dusty heels upon a march,
Furbish his jingling baldric while he sleeps,
And share his mouldy ratio in a siege.
Yet stay—perhaps a charm may call you back,
And make the widening circlets of your eyes
Sparkle with healthy fevers. The Emperor
Hath given consent that you should marry Ludolph!
AURANTHE. Can it be, brother? For a golden crown
With a queen's awful lips I doubly thank you!
This is to wake in Paradise! Farewell
Thou clod of yesterday—'twas not myself!
Not till this moment did I ever feel
My spirit's faculties! I'll flatter you
For this, and be you ever proud of it;
Thou, Jove-like, struck'd'st thy forehead,
And from the teeming marrow of thy brain
I spring complete Minerva! But the prince—
His highness Ludolph—where is he?
CONRAD. I know not:
When, lackeying my counsel at a beck,
The rebel lords, on bended knees, received
The Emperor's pardon, Ludolph kept aloof,
Sole, in a stiff, fool-hardy, sulky pride;
Yet, for all this, I never saw a father
In such a sickly longing for his son.
We shall soon see him, for the Emperor
He will be here this morning.
AURANTHE. That I heard
Among the midnight rumours from the camp.
CONRAD. You give up Albert to me?
AURANTHE. Harm him not!
E'en for his highness Ludolph's sceptry hand,
I would not Albert suffer any wrong.
CONRAD. Have I not laboured, plotted—?
AURANTHE. See you spare him
Nor be pathetic, my kind benefactor,
On all the many bounties of your hand—
'Twas for yourself you laboured—not for me!
Do you not count, when I am queen, to take
Advantage of your chance discoveries

Of my poor secrets, and so hold a rod
Over my life? Conrad. Let not this slave—this villain—
Be cause of feud between us. See! he comes!
Look, woman, look, your Albert is quite safe!
In haste it seems. Now shall I be in the way,
And wish'd with silent curses in my grave,
Or side by side with 'whelmèd mariners.

[*Enter* ALBERT.]

ALBERT. Fair on your graces fall this early morrow!
So it is like to do, without my prayers,
For your right noble names, like favourite tunes,
Have fall'n full frequent from our Emperor's lips,
High commented with smiles.
AURANTHE. Noble Albert!
CONRAD. [*aside.*] Noble!
AURANTHE. Such salutation argues a glad heart
In our prosperity. We thank you, sir.
ALBERT. Lady! O, would to Heaven your poor servant
Could do you better service than mere words!
But I have other greeting than mine own,
From no less man than Otho, who has sent
This ring as pledge of dearest amity;
'Tis chosen I hear from Hymen's jewel'ry,
And you will prize it, lady, I doubt not,
Beyond all pleasures past, and all to come.
To you great duke—
CONRAD. To me! What of me, ha?
ALBERT. What pleased your grace to say?
CONRAD. Your message, sir!
ALBERT. You mean not this to me?
CONRAD. Sister, this way;
For there shall be no 'gentle Alberts' now,
No 'sweet Auranthes!' [*aside.*]

[*Exeunt* CONRAD *and* AURANTHE.]

ALBERT. [*solus.*] The duke is out of temper; if he knows
More than a brother of a sister ought,
I should not quarrel with his peevishness.
Auranthe—Heaven preserve her always fair!—
Is in the heady, proud, ambitious vein;
I bicker not with her—bid her farewell!
She has taken flight from me, then let her soar—

He is a fool who stands at pining gaze!
But for poor Ludolph, he is food for sorrow:
No levelling bluster of my licensed thoughts,
No military swagger of my mind,
Can smother from myself the wrong I've done him—
Without design, indeed—yet it is so—
And opiate for the conscience have I none! [*Exit.*]

SCENE 2. *The Court-yard of the Castle.*

[*Martial Music. Enter, from the outer gate,* OTHO, *Nobles, Knights, and Attendants. The Soldiers halt at the gate, with banners in sight.*]

OTHO. Where is my noble herald?

[*Enter* CONRAD, *from the Castle, attended by two Knights and Servants, Albert following.*]

Well, hast told
Auranthe our intent imperial?
Lest our rent banners, too o' the sudden shown,
Should fright her silken casements, and dismay
Her household to our lack of entertainment.
A victory!
CONRAD. God save illustrious Otho!
OTHO. Ay, Conrad, it will pluck out all grey hairs;
It is the best physician for the spleen;
The courtliest inviter to a feast;
The subtlest excuser of small faults;
And a nice judge in the age and smack of wine.

[*Enter, from the Castle,* AURANTHE, *followed by Pages holding up her robes, and a train of Women. She kneels.*]

Hail my sweet hostess! I do thank the stars,
Or my good soldiers, or their ladies' eyes,
That, after such a merry battle fought,
I can, all safe in body and in soul,
Kiss your fair hand and Lady Fortune's too.
My ring! now, on my life, it doth rejoice
These lips to feel't on this soft ivory!
Keep it, my brightest daughter; it may prove
The little prologue to a line of kings.
I strove against thee and my hot-blood son,

Dull blockhead that I was to be so blind,
But now my sight is clear; forgive me, lady.
AURANTHE. My lord, I was a vassal to your frown,
And now your favour makes me but more humble;
In wintry winds the simple snow is safe,
But fadeth at the greeting of the sun:
Unto thine anger I might well have spoken,
Taking on me a woman's privilege,
But this so sudden kindness makes me dumb.
OTHO. What need of this? Enough, if you will be
A potent tutoress to my wayward boy,
And teach him, what it seems his nurse could not,
To say, for once, I thank you, Sigifred!
ALBERT. He has not yet returned, my gracious liege.
OTHO. What then! No tidings of my friendly Arab?
CONRAD. None, mighty Otho.

[*To one of his Knights, who goes out.*]

Send forth instantly
An hundred horsemen from my honoured gates,
To scour the plains and search the cottages.
Cry a reward, to him who shall first bring
News of that vanished Arabian,
A full-heaped helmet of the purest gold.
OTHO. More thanks, good Conrad; for, except my son's,
There is no face I rather would behold
Than that same quick-eyed pagan's. By the saints,
This coming night of banquets must not light
Her dazzling torches; nor the music breathe
Smooth, without clashing cymbal, tones of peace
And in-door melodies; nor the ruddy wine
Ebb spouting to the lees; if I pledge not,
In my first cup, that Arab!
ALBERT. Mighty Monarch,
I wonder not this stranger's victor-deeds
So hang upon your spirit. Twice in the fight
It was my chance to meet his olive brow,
Triumphant in the enemy's shattered rhomb;
And, to say truth, in any Christian arm
I never saw such prowess.
OTHO. Did you ever?
O, 'tis a noble boy!—tut!—what do I say?
I mean a triple Saladin, whose eyes,
When in the glorious scuffle they met mine,

Seemed to say—'Sleep, old man, in safety sleep;
I am the victory!'
CONRAD. Pity he's not here.
OTHO. And my son too, pity he is not here.
Lady Auranthe, I would not make you blush,
But can you give a guess where Ludolph is?
Know you not of him?
AURANTHE. Indeed, my liege, no secret—
OTHO. Nay, nay, without more words, dost know of him?
AURANTHE. I would I were so over-fortunate,
Both for his sake and mine, and to make glad
A father's ears with tidings of his son.
OTHO. I see 'tis like to be a tedious day.
Were Theodore and Gonfrid and the rest
Sent forth with my commands?
ALBERT. Ay, my lord.
OTHO. And no news! No news! 'Faith! 'tis very strange
He thus avoids us. Lady, is't not strange?
Will he be truant to you too? It is a shame.
CONRAD. Will't please your highness enter, and accept
The unworthy welcome of your servant's house?
Leaving your cares to one whose diligence
May in few hours make pleasures of them all.
OTHO. Not so tedious, Conrad. No, no, no, no—
I must see Ludolph or the—What's that shout!
VOICES. Without. Huzza! huzza! Long live the Emperor!
OTHER VOICES. Fall back! Away there!
OTHO. Say, what noise is that?

[ALBERT *advancing from the back of the stage, whither he had hastened on hearing the cheers of the soldiery.*]

ALBERT. It is young Gersa, the Hungarian prince,
Picked like a red stag from the fallow herd
Of prisoners. Poor prince, forlorn he steps,
Slow, and demure, and proud in his despair.
If I may judge by his so tragic bearing.
His eye not downcast, and his folded arm,
He doth this moment wish himself asleep
Among his fallen captains on yon plains.

[*Enter* GERSA, *in chains, and guarded.*]

OTHO. Well said, Sir Albert.
GERSA. Not a word of greeting,

No welcome to a princely visitor,
Most mighty Otho? Will not my great host
Vouchsafe a syllable, before he bids
His gentlemen conduct me with all care
To some securest lodging?—cold perhaps!
OTHO. What mood is this? Hath fortune touched thy brain?
GERSA. O kings and princes of this feverous world,
What abject things, what mockeries must ye be,
What nerveless minions of safe palaces!
When here, a monarch, whose proud foot is used
To fallen princes' necks, as to his stirrup,
Must needs exclaim that I am mad forsooth,
Because I cannot flatter with bent knees
My conqueror!
OTHO. Gersa, I think you wrong me:
I think I have a better fame abroad.
GERSA. I prithee mock me not with gentle speech,
But, as a favour, bid me from thy presence;
Let me no longer be the wondering food
Of all these eyes; prithee command me hence!
OTHO. Do not mistake me, Gersa. That you may not,
Come, fair Auranthe, try if your soft hands
Can manage those hard rivets to set free
So brave a prince and soldier.
AURANTHE. [*sets him free.*] Welcome task!
GERSA. I am wound up in deep astonishment!
Thank you, fair lady. Otho! emperor!
You rob me of myself; my dignity
Is now your infant; I am a weak child.
OTHO. Give me your hand, and let this kindly grasp
Live in our memories.
GERSA. In mine it will.
I blush to think of my unchastened tongue;
But I was haunted by the monstrous ghost
Of all our slain battalions. Sire, reflect,
And pardon you will grant, that, at this hour,
The bruisèd remnants of our stricken camp
Are huddling undistinguished, my dear friends
With common thousands, into shallow graves.
OTHO. Enough, most noble Gersa. You are free
To cheer the brave remainder of your host
By your own healing presence, and that too,
Not as their leader merely, but their king;
For, as I hear, the wily enemy,
Who eased the crownet from your infant brows,

Bloody Taraxa, is among the dead.
GERSA. Then I retire, so generous Otho please,
Bearing with me a weight of benefits
Too heavy to be borne.
OTHO. It is not so;
Still understand me, King of Hungary,
Nor judge my open purposes awry.
Though I did hold you high in my esteem
For your self's sake, I do not personate
The stage-play emperor to entrap applause,
To set the silly sort o' the world agape,
And make the politic smile; no, I have heard
How in the Council you condemned this war,
Urging the perfidy of broken faith—
For that I am your friend.
GERSA. If ever, sire,
You are my enemy, I dare here swear
'Twill not be Gersa's fault. Otho, farewell!
OTHO. Will you return, Prince, to our banqueting?
GERSA. As to my father's board I will return.
OTHO. Conrad, with all due ceremony, give
The prince a regal escort to his camp;
Albert, go thou and bear him company.
Gersa, farewell!
GERSA. All happiness attend you!
OTHO. Return with what good speed you may; for soon
We must consult upon our terms of peace.

[*Exeunt* GERSA *and* ALBERT *with others.*]

And thus a marble column do I build
To prop my empire's dome. Conrad, in thee
I have another steadfast one, to uphold
The portals of my state; and, for my own
Pre-eminence and safety, I will strive
To keep thy strength upon its pedestal.
For, without thee, this day I might have been
A show-monster about the streets of Prague,
In chains, as just now stood that noble prince:
And then to me no mercy had been shown,
For when the conquered lion is once dungeoned,
Who lets him forth again? or dares to give
An old lion sugar-cates of mild reprieve?
Not to thine ear alone I make confession,
But to all here, as, by experience,

I know how the great basement of all power
Is frankness, and a true tongue to the world;
And how intriguing secrecy is proof
Of fear and weakness, and a hollow state.
Conrad, I owe thee much.
CONRAD. To kiss that hand,
My emperor, is ample recompense,
For a mere act of duty.
OTHO. Thou art wrong;
For what can any man on earth do more?
We will make trial of your house's welcome,
My bright Auranthe!
CONRAD. How is Friedburg honoured!

[*Enter* ETHELBERT *and six Monks.*]

ETHELBERT. The benison of heaven on your head,
Imperial Otho!
OTHO. Who stays me? Speak! Quick!
ETHELBERT. Pause but one moment, mighty conqueror,
Upon the threshold of this house of joy.
OTHO. Pray, do not prose, good Ethelbert, but speak
What is your purpose.
ETHELBERT. The restoration of some captive maids,
Devoted to Heaven's pious ministries,
Who, driven forth from their religious cells,
And kept in thraldom by our enemy,
When late this province was a lawless spoil,
Still weep amid the wild Hungarian camp,
Though hemmed around by thy victorious arms.
OTHO. Demand the holy sisterhood in our name
From Gersa's tents. Farewell, old Ethelbert.
ETHELBERT. The saints will bless you for this pious care.
OTHO. Daughter, your hand; Ludolph's would fit it best.
CONRAD. Ho! let the music sound!

[*Music*, Ethelbert *raises his hands, as in benediction of* OTHO. *Exeunt severally. The scene closes on them.*]

SCENE 3. *The Country, with the Castle in the distance.*

[*Enter* LUDOLPH *and* SIGIFRED.]

LUDOLPH. You have my secret; let it not be breath'd.
SIGIFRED. Still give me leave to wonder that the Prince
Ludolph and the swift Arab are the same;
Still to rejoice that 'twas a German arm
Death doing in a turbaned masquerade.
LUDOLPH. The Emperor must not know it, Sigifred.
SIGIFRED. I prithee, why? What happier hour of time
Could thy pleased star point down upon from heaven
With silver index, bidding thee make peace?
LUDOLPH. Still it must not be known, good Sigifred;
The star may point oblique.
SIGIFRED. If Otho knew
His son to be that unknown Mussulman
After whose spurring heels he sent me forth,
With one of his well-pleased Olympian oaths,
The charters of man's greatness, at this hour
He would be watching round the castle walls,
And, like an anxious warder, strain his sight
For the first glimpse of such a son returned—
Ludolph, that blast of the Hungarians,
That Saracenic meteor of the fight,
That silent fury, whose fell scimitar
Kept danger all aloof from Otho's head,
And left him space for wonder.
LUDOLPH. Say no more.
Not as a swordsman would I pardon claim,
But as a son. The bronzed centurion,
Long toiled in foreign wars, and whose high deeds
Are shaded in a forest of tall spears,
Known only to his troop, hath greater plea
Of favour with my sire than I can have.
SIGIFRED. My lord, forgive me that I cannot see
How this proud temper with clear reason squares.
What made you then, with such an anxious love,
Hover around that life, whose bitter days
You vexed with bad revolt? Was't opium,
Or the mad-fumèd wine? Nay, do not frown,
I rather would grieve with you than upbraid.
LUDOLPH. I do believe you. No, 'twas not to make
A father his son's debtor, or to heal

His deep heart-sickness for a rebel child.
'Twas done in memory of my boyish days,
Poor cancel for his kindness to my youth,
For all his calming of my childish griefs,
And all his smiles upon my merriment.
No, not a thousand foughten fields could sponge
Those days paternal from my memory,
Though now upon my head he heaps disgrace.
SIGIFRED. My Prince, you think too harshly—
LUDOLPH. Can I so?
Hath he not galled my spirit to the quick?
And with a sullen rigour obstinate
Poured out a phial of wrath upon my faults?
Hunted me as a Tartar does the boar,
Driven me to the very edge o' the world,
And almost put a price upon my head?
SIGIFRED. Remember how he spared the rebel lords.
LUDOLPH. Yes, yes, I know he hath a noble nature
That cannot trample on the fallen. But his
Is not the only proud heart in his realm.
He hath wronged me, and I have done him wrong;
He hath loved me, and I have shown him kindness;
We should be almost equal.
SIGIFRED. Yet, for all this,
I would you had appeared among those lords,
And taken his favour.
LUDOLPH. Ha! till now I thought
My friend had held poor Ludolph's honour dear.
What! would you have me sue before his throne
And kiss the courtier's missal, its silk steps?
Or hug the golden housings of his steed,
Amid a camp, whose steelèd swarms I dared
But yesterday? And, at the trumpet sound,
Bow like some unknown mercenary's flag,
And lick the soilèd grass? No, no, my friend,
I would not, I, be pardoned in the heap,
And bless indemnity with all that scum—
Those men I mean, who on my shoulders propped
Their weak rebellion, winning me with lies,
And pitying forsooth my many wrongs;
Poor self-deceived wretches, who must think
Each one himself a king in embryo,
Because some dozen vassals cried—'My Lord!'
Cowards, who never knew their little hearts,
Till flurried danger held the mirror up,

And then they owned themselves without a blush,
Curling, like spaniels, round my father's feet.
Such things deserted me and are forgiven,
While I, least guilty, am an outcast still,
And will be, for I love such fair disgrace.
SIGIFRED. I know the clear truth; so would Otho see,
For he is just and noble. Fain would I
Be pleader for you—
LUDOLPH. He'll hear none of it;
You know his temper, hot, proud, obstinate;
Endanger not yourself so uselessly.
I will encounter his thwart spleen myself,
To-day, at the Duke Conrad's, where he keeps
His crowded state after the victory,
There will I be, a most unwelcome guest,
And parley with him, as a son should do,
Who doubly loathes a father's tyranny;
Tell him how feeble is that tyranny;
How the relationship of father and son
Is no more valid than a silken leash
Where lions tug adverse, if love grow not
From interchangèd love through many years.
Ay, and those turreted Franconian walls,
Like to a jealous casket, hold my pearl—
My fair Auranthe! Yes, I will be there.
SIGIFRED. Be not so rash; wait till his wrath shall pass,
Until his royal spirit softly ebbs
Self-influenced; then, in his morning dreams
He will forgive thee, and awake in grief
To have not thy good morrow.
LUDOLPH. Yes, today
I must be there, while her young pulses beat
Among the new-plumed minions of the war.
Have you seen her of late? No? Auranthe,
Franconia's fair sister, 'tis I mean.
She should be paler for my troublous days—
And there it is—my father's iron lips
Have sworn divorcement 'twixt me and my right.
SIGIFRED. [*aside.*] Auranthe! I had hoped this whim had passed.
LUDOLPH. And, Sigifred, with all his love of justice,
When will he take that grandchild in his arms,
That, by my love I swear, shall soon be his?
This reconcilement is impossible,
For see—but who are these?
SIGIFRED. They are messengers

From our great emperor; to you, I doubt not,
For couriers are abroad to seek you out.

[*Enter* THEODORE and GONFRID.]

THEODORE. Seeing so many vigilant eyes explore
The province to invite your highness back
To your high dignities, we are too happy.
GONFRID. We have no eloquence to colour justly
The emperor's anxious wishes.
LUDOLPH. Go. I follow you.

[*Exeunt* THEODORE *and* GONFRID.]

I play the prude: it is but venturing—
Why should he be so earnest? Come, my friend,
Let us to Friedburg castle.

ACT II

SCENE 1. *An Antechamber in the Castle.*

[*Enter* LUDOLPH *and* SIGIFRED.]

LUDOLPH. No more advices, no more cautioning:
I leave it all to fate—to any thing!
I cannot square my conduct to time, place,
Or circumstance; to me 'tis all a mist!
SIGIFRED. I say no more.
LUDOLPH. It seems I am to wait
Here in the anteroom—that may be a trifle.
You see now how I dance attendance here,
Without that tyrant temper, you so blame,
Snapping the rein. You have medicined me
With good advices; and I here remain,
In this most honourable anteroom,
Your patient scholar.
SIGIFRED. Do not wrong me, Prince.
By Heavens, I'd rather kiss Duke Conrad's slipper,
When in the morning he doth yawn with pride,
Than see you humbled but a half-degree!
Truth is, the Emperor would fain dismiss
The nobles ere he sees you.

[*Enter* GONFRID, *from the Council-room.*]

LUDOLPH. Well, sir! what?
GONFRID. Great honour to the Prince! The Emperor,
Hearing that his brave son had re-appeared,
Instant dismissed the Council from his sight,
As Jove fans off the clouds. Even now they pass.

[*Enter the Nobles from the Council-room. They cross the stage, bowing with respect to* LUDOLPH, *he frowning on them,* CONRAD *follows. Exeunt Nobles.*]

LUDOLPH. Not the discoloured poisons of a fen,
Which he who breathes feels warning of his death,
Could taste so nauseous to the bodily sense
As these prodigious sycophants disgust
The soul's fine palate.
CONRAD. Princely Ludolph, hail!
Welcome, thou younger sceptre to the realm!
Strength to thy virgin crownet's golden buds,
That they, against the winter of thy sire,
May burst, and swell, and flourish round thy brows,
Maturing to a weighty diadem!
Yet be that hour far off; and may he live,
Who waits for thee, as the chapped earth for rain.
Set my life's star! I have lived long enough,
Since under my glad roof, propitiously,
Father and son each other re-possess.
LUDOLPH. Fine wording, Duke! but words could never yet
Forestall the fates; have you not learnt that yet?
Let me look well—your features are the same;
Your gait the same; your hair of the same shade;
As one I knew some passèd weeks ago,
Who sung far different notes into mine ears.
I have mine own particular comments on't;
You have your own, perhaps.
CONRAD. My gracious Prince,
All men may err. In truth I was deceived
In your great father's nature, as you were.
Had I known that of him I have since known,
And what you soon will learn, I would have turned
My sword to my own throat, rather than held
Its threatening edge against a good King's quiet:
Or with one word fevered you, gentle Prince,
Who seemed to me, as rugged times then went,
Indeed too much oppressed. May I be bold

To tell the Emperor you will haste to him?
LUDOLPH. Your Dukedom's privilege will grant so much.

[*Exit* CONRAD.]

He's very close to Otho, a tight leech!
Your hand—I go. Ha! here the thunder comes
Sullen against the wind! If in two angry brows
My safety lies, then Sigifred, I'm safe.

[*Enter* OTHO *and* CONRAD.]

OTHO. Will you make Titan play the lackey-page
To chattering pigmies? I would have you know
That such neglect of our high Majesty
Annuls all feel of kindred. What is son—
Or friend, or brother, or all ties of blood—
When the whole kingdom, centred in ourself,
Is rudely slighted? Who am I to wait?
By Peter's chair! I have upon my tongue
A word to fright the proudest spirit here!—
Death!—and slow tortures to the hardy fool,
Who dares take such large charter from our smiles!
Conrad, we would be private. Sigifred!
Off! And none pass this way on pain of death!

[*Exeunt* CONRAD *and* SIGIFRED.]

LUDOLPH. This was but half expected, my good sire,
Yet I am grieved at it, to the full height,
As though my hopes of favour had been whole.
OTHO. How you indulge yourself! What can you hope for?
LUDOLPH. Nothing, my liege; I have to hope for nothing.
I come to greet you as a loving son,
And then depart, if I may be so free,
Seeing that blood of yours in my warm veins
Has not yet mitigated into milk.
OTHO. What would you, sir?
LUDOLPH. A lenient banishment;
So please you let me unmolested pass
This Conrad's gates, to the wide air again.
I want no more. A rebel wants no more.
OTHO. And shall I let a rebel loose again
To muster kites and eagles 'gainst my head?
No, obstinate boy, you shall be kept caged up,

Served with harsh food, with scum for Sunday-drink.
LUDOLPH. Indeed!
OTHO. And chains too heavy for your life:
I'll choose a gaoler, whose swart monstrous face
Shall be a hell to look upon, and she—
LUDOLPH. Ha!
OTHO. Shall be your fair Auranthe.
LUDOLPH. Amaze! Amaze!
OTHO. Today you marry her.
LUDOLPH. This is a sharp jest!
OTHO. No. None at all. When have I said a lie?
LUDOLPH. If I sleep not, I am a waking wretch.
OTHO. Not a word more. Let me embrace my child.
LUDOLPH. I dare not. 'Twould pollute so good a father!
O heavy crime! that your son's blinded eyes
Could not see all his parent's love aright,
As now I see it. Be not kind to me—
Punish me not with favour.
OTHO. Are you sure,
Ludolph, you have no saving plea in store?
LUDOLPH. My father, none!
OTHO. Then you astonish me.
LUDOLPH. No, I have no plea. Disobedience,
Rebellion, obstinacy, blasphemy,
Are all my counsellors. If they can make
My crooked deeds show good and plausible,
Then grant me loving pardon, but not else,
Good Gods! not else, in any way, my liege!
OTHO. You are a most perplexing, noble boy.
LUDOLPH. You not less a perplexing noble father.
OTHO. Well, you shall have free passport through the gates.
Farewell!
LUDOLPH. Farewell! and by these tears believe,
And still remember, I repent in pain
All my misdeeds!
OTHO. Ludolph, I will! I will!
But, Ludolph, ere you go, I would inquire
If you, in all your wandering, ever met
A certain Arab haunting in these parts.
LUDOLPH. No, my good lord, I cannot say I did.
OTHO. Make not your father blind before his time;
Nor let these arms paternal hunger more
For an embrace, to dull the appetite
Of my great love for thee, my supreme child!
Come close, and let me breathe into thine ear.

I knew you through disguise. You are the Arab!
You can't deny it. [*Embracing him.*]
LUDOLPH. Happiest of days!
OTHO. We'll make it so.
LUDOLPH. 'Stead of one fatted calf
Ten hecatombs shall bellow out their last,
Smote 'twixt the horns by the death-stunning mace
Of Mars, and all the soldiery shall feast
Nobly as Nimrod's masons, when the towers
Of Nineveh new kissed the parted clouds!
OTHO. Large as a God speak out, where all is thine.
LUDOLPH. Ay, father, but the fire in my sad breast
Is quenched with inward tears! I must rejoice
For you, whose wings so shadow over me
In tender victory, but for myself
I still must mourn. The fair Auranthe mine!
Too great a boon! I prithee let me ask
What more than I know of could so have changed
Your purpose touching her?
OTHO. At a word, this:
In no deed did you give me more offence
Than your rejection of Erminia.
To my appalling, I saw too good proof
Of your keen-eyed suspicion—she is naught!
LUDOLPH. You are convinced?
OTHO. Ay, spite of her sweet looks.
O, that my brother's daughter should so fall!
Her fame has passed into the grosser lips
Of soldiers in their cups.
LUDOLPH. 'Tis very sad.
OTHO. No more of her, Auranthe—Ludolph, come!
This marriage be the bond of endless peace! [*Exeunt.*]

SCENE 2 *The Entrance of* GERSA'S *Tent in the Hungarian Camp.*

[*Enter* ERMINIA.]

ERMINIA. Where! where! where shall I find a messenger?
A trusty soul? a good man in the camp?
Shall I go myself? Monstrous wickedness!
O cursed Conrad! devilish Auranthe!
Here is proof palpable as the bright sun!
O for a voice to reach the Emperor's ears!

[*Shouts in the Camp.*]

[*Enter an Hungarian Captain.*]

CAPTAIN. Fair prisoner, you hear those joyous shouts?
The king—ay, now our king—but still your slave,
Young Gersa, from a short captivity
Has just returned. He bids me say, bright Dame,
That even the homage of his rangèd chiefs
Cures not his keen impatience to behold
Such beauty once again. What ails you, lady?
ERMINIA. Say, is not that a German, yonder? There!
CAPTAIN. Methinks by his stout bearing he should be—
Yes—it is Albert; a brave German knight,
And much in the Emperor's favour.
ERMINIA. I would fain
Inquire of friends and kinsfolk, how they fared
In these rough times. Brave soldier, as you pass
To royal Gersa with my humble thanks,
Will you send yonder knight to me?
CAPTAIN. I will. [*Exit.*]
ERMINIA. Yes, he was ever known to be a man
Frank, open, generous; Albert I may trust.
O proof! proof! proof! Albert's an honest man;
Not Ethelbert the monk, if he were here,
Would I hold more trustworthy. Now!

[*Enter* ALBERT.]

ALBERT. Good Gods!
Lady Erminia! are you prisoner
In this beleaguered camp? Or are you here
Of your own will? You pleased to send for me.
By Venus, 'tis a pity I knew not
Your plight before and, by her son, I swear
To do you every service you can ask.
What would the fairest—?
ERMINIA. Albert, will you swear?
ALBERT. I have. Well?
ERMINIA. Albert, you have fame to lose.
If men, in court and camp, lie not outright,
You should be, from a thousand, chosen forth
To do an honest deed. Shall I confide—?
ALBERT. Ay, anything to me, fair creature. Do;
Dictate my task. Sweet woman—
ERMINIA. Truce with that.

You understand me not; and, in your speech,
I see how far the slander is abroad.
Without proof could you think me innocent?
ALBERT. Lady, I should rejoice to know you so.
ERMINIA. If you have any pity for a maid,
Suffering a daily death from evil tongues;
Any compassion for that Emperor's niece,
Who, for your bright sword and clear honesty,
Lifted you from the crowd of common men
Into the lap of honour—save me, knight!
ALBERT. How? Make it clear; if it be possible,
I by the banner of Saint Maurice, swear
To right you.
ERMINIA. Possible!—Easy. O my heart!
This letter's not so soiled but you may read it—
Possible! There—that letter! Read—read it.

[*Gives him a letter.*]

ALBERT. [*reads it.*] 'To the Duke Conrad.—Forget the threat you made at parting, and I will forget to send the Emperor letters and papers of yours I have become possessed of. His life is no trifle to me; his death you shall find none to yourself.' [*Speaks to himself.*] 'Tis me —my life that's pleaded for! [*Reads.*] 'He, for his own sake, will be dumb as the grave. Erminia has my shame fixed upon her, sure as a wen. We are safe. *Auranthe.*'
A she-devil! A dragon! I her imp!
Fire of Hell! Auranthe—lewd demon!
Where got you this? Where? When?
ERMINIA. I found it in the tent, among some spoils
Which, being noble, fell to Gersa's lot.
Come in, and see. [*They go in and return.*]
Albert Villainy! Villainy!
Conrad's sword, his corselet, and his helm,
And his letter. Caitiff, he shall feel—
ERMINIA. I see you are thunderstruck. Haste, haste away!
ALBERT. O I am tortured by this villainy.
ERMINIA. You needs must be. Carry it swift to Otho;
Tell him, moreover, I am prisoner
Here in this camp, where all the sisterhood,
Forced from their quiet cells, are parcelled out
For slaves among these Huns. Away! Away!
ALBERT. I am gone.
ERMINIA. Swift be your steed! Within this hour

The Emperor will see it.
ALBERT. Ere I sleep:
That I can swear. [*Hurries out.*]
GERSA. [*without.*] Brave captains! thanks. Enough
Of loyal homage now!

[*Enter* GERSA.]

ERMINIA. Hail, royal Hun!
GERSA. What means this, fair one? Why in such alarm?
Who was it hurried by me so distract?
It seemed you were in deep discourse together;
Your doctrine has not been so harsh to him
As to my poor deserts. Come, come, be plain.
I am no jealous fool to kill you both,
Or, for such trifles, rob the adorned world
Of such a beauteous vestal.
ERMINIA. I grieve, my Lord,
To hear you condescend to ribald phrase.
GERSA. This is too much! Hearken, my lady pure!
ERMINIA. Silence! and hear the magic of a name—
Erminia! I am she—the Emperor's niece!
Praised be the Heavens, I now dare own myself!
GERSA. Erminia! Indeed! I've heard of her.
Prithee, fair lady, what chance brought you here?
ERMINIA. Ask your own soldiers.
GERSA. And you dare own your name.
For loveliness you may—and for the rest
My vein is not censorious.
ERMINIA. Alas! poor me!
'Tis false indeed.
GERSA. Indeed you are too fair:
The swan, soft leaning on her fledgy breast,
When to the stream she launches, looks not back
With such a tender grace; nor are her wings
So white as your soul is, if that but be
Twin-picture to your face. Erminia!
Today, for the first day, I am a king,
Yet would I give my unworn crown away
To know you spotless.
ERMINIA. Trust me one day more,
Generously, without more certain guarantee,
Than this poor face you deign to praise so much;
After that, say and do whate'er you please.
If I have any knowledge of you, sir,

I think, nay I am sure, you will grieve much
To hear my story. O be gentle to me,
For I am sick and faint with many wrongs,
Tired out, and weary-worn with contumelies.
GERSA. Poor lady!

[*Enter* ETHELBERT.]

ERMINIA. Gentle Prince, 'tis false indeed.
Good morrow, holy father! I have had
Your prayers, though I looked for you in vain.
ETHELBERT. Blessings upon you, daughter! Sure you look
Too cheerful for these foul pernicious days.
Young man, you heard this virgin say 'twas false—
'Tis false, I say. What! can you not employ
Your temper elsewhere, 'mong these burly tents,
But you must taunt this dove, for she hath lost
The Eagle Otho to beat off assault?
Fie! fie! But I will be her guard myself;
In the Emperor's name, I here demand of you
Herself, and all her sisterhood. She false!
GERSA. Peace! peace, old man! I cannot think she is.
ETHELBERT. Whom I have known from her first infancy,
Baptized her in the bosom of the Church,
Watched her, as anxious husbandmen the grain,
From the first shoot till the unripe mid-May,
Then to the tender ear of her June days,
Which, lifting sweet abroad its timid green,
Is blighted by the touch of calumny;
You cannot credit such a monstrous tale.
GERSA. I cannot. Take her. Fair Erminia,
I follow you to Friedburg—is't not so?
ERMINIA. Ay, so we purpose.
ETHELBERT. Daughter, do you so?
How's this? I marvel! Yet you look not mad.
ERMINIA. I have good news to tell you, Ethelbert.
GERSA. Ho! ho, there! Guards!
Your blessing, father! Sweet Erminia,
Believe me, I am well nigh sure—
ERMINIA. Farewell!
Short time will show.

[*Enter Chiefs.*]

Yes, father Ethelbert,
I have news precious as we pass along.
ETHELBERT. Dear daughter, you shall guide me.
ERMINIA. To no ill.
GERSA. Command an escort to the Friedburg lines.

[*Exeunt Chiefs.*]

Pray let me lead. Fair lady, forget not
Gersa, how he believed you innocent.
I follow you to Friedburg with all speed. [*Exeunt.*]

ACT III

SCENE I. *The Country.*

[*Enter* ALBERT.]

ALBERT. O that the earth were empty, as when Cain
Had no perplexity to hide his head!
Or that the sword of some brave enemy
Had put a sudden stop to my hot breath,
And hurled me down the illimitable gulf
Of times past, unremembered! Better so
Than thus fast-limèd in a cursèd snare,
The limbo of a wanton. This the end
Of an aspiring life! My boyhood passed
In feud with wolves and bears, when no eye saw
The solitary warfare, fought for love
Of honour 'mid the growling wilderness.
My sturdier youth, maturing to the sword,
Won by the siren-trumpets, and the ring
Of shields upon the pavement, when bright-mailed
Henry the Fowler passed the streets of Prague.
Was't to this end I louted and became
The menial of Mars, and held a spear
Swayed by command, as corn is by the wind?
Is it for this, I now am lifted up
By Europe's thronèd Emperor, to see
My honour be my executioner—
My love of fame, my prided honesty
Put to the torture for confessional?
Then the damned crime of blurting to the world
A woman's secret!—though a fiend she be,

Too tender of my ignominious life—
But then to wrong the generous Emperor
In such a searching point, were to give up
My soul for football at Hell's holiday!
I must confess—and cut my throat—today?
Tomorrow? Ho! some wine!

[*Enter* SIGIFRED.]

SIGIFRED. A fine humour—
ALBERT. Who goes there? Count Sigifred? Ha! Ha! Ha!
SIGIFRED. What, man, do you mistake the hollow sky
For a thronged tavern—and these stubbèd trees
For old serge hangings—me, your humble friend,
For a poor waiter? Why, man, how you stare!
What gipsies have you been carousing with?
No, no more wine; methinks you've had enough.
ALBERT. You well may laugh and banter. What a fool
An injury may make of a staid man!
You shall know all anon.
SIGIFRED. Some tavern brawl?
ALBERT. 'Twas with some people out of common reach;
Revenge is difficult.
SIGIFRED. I am your friend;
We meet again today, and can confer
Upon it. For the present I'm in haste.
ALBERT. Whither?
SIGIFRED. To fetch King Gersa to the feast.
The Emperor on this marriage is so hot,
Pray Heaven it end not in apoplexy!
The very porters, as I passed the doors,
Heard his loud laugh, and answered in full choir.
I marvel, Albert, you delay so long
From these bright revelries; go, show yourself,
You may be made a duke.
ALBERT. Ay, very like:
Pray, what day has his Highness fixed upon?
SIGIFRED. For what?
ALBERT. The marriage. What else can I mean?
SIGIFRED. Today! O, I forgot, you could not know;
The news is scarce a minute old with me.
ALBERT. Married today! Today! You did not say so?
SIGIFRED. Now, while I speak to you, their comely heads
Are bowed before the mitre.
ALBERT. O! monstrous!

SIGIFRED. What is this?
ALBERT. Nothing, Sigifred. Farewell!
We'll meet upon our subject. Farewell, count! [*Exit.*]
SIGIFRED. Is this clear-headed Albert? He brain-turned!
'Tis as portentous as a meteor. [*Exit.*]

SCENE 2. *An Apartment in the Castle.*

[*Enter, as from the Marriage,* OTHO, LUDOLPH, AURANTHE, CONRAD, *Nobles, Knights, Ladies, etc. Music.*]

OTHO. Now, Ludolph! Now, Auranthe! Daughter fair!
What can I find to grace your nuptial day
More than my love, and these wide realms in fee?
LUDOLPH. I have too much.
AURANTHE. And I, my liege, by far.
LUDOLPH. Auranthe! I have! O, my bride, my love!
Not all the gaze upon us can restrain
My eyes, too long poor exiles from thy face,
From adoration, and my foolish tongue
From uttering soft responses to the love
I see in thy mute beauty beaming forth!
Fair creature, bless me with a single word!
All mine!
AURANTHE. Spare, spare me, my Lord; I swoon else.
LUDOLPH. Soft beauty! by tomorrow I should die,
Wert thou not mine. [*They talk apart.*]
FIRST LADY. How deep she has bewitched him!
FIRST KNIGHT. Ask you for her receipt for love philtres.
SECOND LADY. They hold the Emperor in admiration.
OTHO. If ever king was happy, that am I!
What are the cities 'yond the Alps to me,
The provinces about the Danube's mouth,
The promise of fair sail beyond the Rhone;
Or routing out of Hyperborean hordes,
To these fair children, stars of a new age?
Unless perchance I might rejoice to win
This little ball of earth, and chuck it them
To play with!
AURANTHE. Nay, my Lord, I do not know.
LUDOLPH. Let me not famish.
OTHO. [*to Conrad.*] Good Franconia,
You heard what oath I sware, as the sun rose,
That unless Heaven would send me back my son,
My Arab, no soft music should enrich

The cool wine, kissed off with a soldier's smack;
Now all my empire, bartered for one feast,
Seems poverty.
CONRAD. Upon the neighbour-plain
The heralds have prepared a royal lists;
Your knights, found war-proof in the bloody field,
Speed to the game.
OTHO. Well, Ludolph, what say you?
LUDOLPH. My lord!
OTHO. A tourney?
CONRAD. Or, if't please you best—
LUDOLPH. I want no more!
FIRST LADY. He soars!
SECOND LADY. Past all reason.
LUDOLPH. Though heaven's choir
Should in a vast circumference descend
And sing for my delight, I'd stop my ears!
Though bright Apollo's car stood burning here,
And he put out an arm to bid me mount,
His touch an immortality, not I!
This earth, this palace, this room, Auranthe!
OTHO. This is a little painful; just too much.
Conrad, if he flames longer in this wise,
I shall believe in wizard-woven loves
And old romances; but I'll break the spell.
Ludolph!
CONRAD. He'll be calm, anon.
LUDOLPH. You called?
Yes, yes, yes, I offend. You must forgive me;
Not being quite recovered from the stun
Of your large bounties. A tourney, is it not?

[*A sennet heard faintly.*]

CONRAD. The trumpets reach us.
ETHELBERT. [*without.*] On your peril, sirs,
Detain us!
FIRST VOICE. [*without.*] Let not the Abbot pass.
SECOND VOICE. [*without.*] No,
On your lives!
FIRST VOICE. [*without.*] Holy father, you must not.
ETHELBERT. [*without.*] Otho!
OTHO. Who calls on Otho?
ETHELBERT. [*without.*] Ethelbert!
OTHO. Let him come in.

[*Enter* ETHELBERT *leading in* ERMINIA.]

Thou cursèd Abbot, why
Hast brought pollution to our holy rites?
Hast thou no fear of hangmen, or the faggot?
LUDOLPH. What portent—what strange prodigy is this?
CONRAD. Away!
ETHELBERT. You, Duke?
ERMINIA. Albert has surely failed me!
Looked at the Emperor's brow upon me bent!
ETHELBERT. A sad delay!
CONRAD. Away, thou guilty thing!
ETHELBERT. You again, Duke? Justice, most noble Otho!
You—go to your sister there and plot again,
A quick plot, swift as thought to save your heads;
For lo! the toils are spread around your den,
The world is all agape to see dragged forth
Two ugly monsters.
LUDOLPH. What means he, my lord?
CONRAD. I cannot guess.
ETHELBERT. Best ask your lady sister,
Whether the riddle puzzles her beyond
The power of utterance.
CONRAD. Foul barbarian, cease:
The Princess faints!
LUDOLPH. Stab him! O, sweetest wife!

[*Attendants bear off* AURANTHE.]

ERMINIA. Alas!
ETHELBERT. Your wife?
LUDOLPH. Ay, Satan! does that yerk ye?
ETHELBERT. Wife! so soon!
LUDOLPH. Ay, wife! O, impudence!
Thou bitter mischief! Venomous bad priest!
How darest thou lift those beetle brows at me?
Me—the prince Ludolph, in this presence here,
Upon my marriage-day, and scandalize
My joys with such opprobrious surprise?
Wife! Why dost linger on that syllable,
As if it were some demon's name pronounced
To summon harmful lightning, and make yawn
The sleepy thunder? Hast no sense of fear?
No ounce of man in thy mortality?

Tremble! for, at my nod, the sharpened axe
Will make thy bold tongue quiver to the roots,
Those grey lids wink, and thou not know it, monk!
ETHELBERT. O, poor deceived Prince! I pity thee!
Great Otho! I claim justice—
LUDOLPH. Thou shalt have't!
Thine arms from forth a pulpit of hot fire
Shall sprawl distracted! O that that dull cowl
Were some most sensitive portion of thy life,
That I might give it to my hounds to tear!
Thy girdle some fine zealous-painèd nerve
To girth my saddle! And those devil's beads
Each one a life, that I might, every day,
Crush one with Vulcan's hammer!
OTHO. Peace, my son;
You far outstrip my spleen in this affair.
Let us be calm, and hear the abbot's plea
For this intrusion.
LUDOLPH. I am silent, sire.
OTHO. Conrad, see all depart not wanted here.

[*Exeunt Knights, Ladies, etc.*]

Ludolph, be calm. Ethelbert, peace awhile.
This mystery demands an audience
Of a just judge, and that will Otho be.
LUDOLPH. Why has he time to breathe another word?
OTHO. Ludolph, old Ethelbert, be sure, comes not
To beard us for no cause; he's not the man
To cry himself up an ambassador
Without credentials,
LUDOLPH. I'll chain up myself.
OTHO. Old Abbot, stand here forth. Lady Erminia,
Sit. And now, Abbot! what have you to say?
Our ear is open. First we here denounce
Hard penalties against thee, if't be found
The cause for which you have disturbed us here,
Making our bright hours muddy, be a thing
Of little moment.
ETHELBERT. See this innocent!
Otho! thou father of the people called,
Is her life nothing? Her fair honour nothing?
Her tears from matins until even-song
Nothing? Her burst heart nothing? Emperor!
Is this your gentle niece—the simplest flower

Of the world's herbal—this fair lily blanched
Still with the dews of piety, this meek lady
Here sitting like an angel newly-shent,
Who veils its snowy wings and grows all pale—
Is she nothing?
OTHO. What more to the purpose, Abbot?
LUDOLPH. Whither is he winding?
CONRAD. No clue yet!
ETHELBERT. You have heard, my liege, and so, no doubt, all here,
Foul, poisonous, malignant whisperings;
Nay open speech, rude mockery grown common,
Against the spotless nature and clear fame
Of the Princess Erminia, your niece.
I have intruded here thus suddenly,
Because I hold those base weeds, with tight hand,
Which now disfigure her fair growing stem,
Waiting but for your sign to pull them up
By the dark roots, and leave her palpable,
To all men's sight, a lady, innocent.
The ignominy of that whispered tale
About a midnight gallant, seen to climb
A window to her chamber neighboured near,
I will from her turn off, and put the load
On the right shoulders; on that wretch's head,
Who, by close stratagems, did save herself,
Chiefly by shifting to this lady's room
A rope-ladder for false witness.
LUDOLPH. Most atrocious!
OTHO. Ethelbert, proceed.
ETHELBERT. With sad lips I shall:
For, in the healing of one wound, I fear
To make a greater. His young highness here
Today was married.
LUDOLPH. Good.
ETHELBERT. Would it were good!
Yet why do I delay to spread abroad
The names of those two vipers, from whose jaws
A deadly breath went forth to taint and blast
This guileless lady?
OTHO. Abbot, speak their names.
ETHELBERT. A minute first. It cannot be—but may
I ask, great judge, if you today have put
A letter by unread?
OTHO. Does't end in this?

CONRAD. Out with their names!
ETHELBERT. Bold sinner, say you so?
LUDOLPH. Out, tedious monk!
OTHO. Confess, or by the wheel—
ETHELBERT. My evidence cannot be far away;
And, though it never come, be on my head
The crime of passing an attaint upon
The slanderers of this virgin.
LUDOLPH. Speak aloud!
ETHELBERT. Auranthe, and her brother there.
CONRAD. Amaze!
LUDOLPH. Throw them from the windows!
OTHO. Do what you will!
LUDOLPH. What shall I do with them?
Something of quick dispatch, for should she hear,
My soft Auranthe, her sweet mercy would
Prevail against my fury. Damnèd priest!
What swift death wilt thou die? As to the lady
I touch her not.
ETHELBERT. Illustrious Otho, stay!
An ample store of misery thou hast,
Choke not the granary of thy noble mind
With more bad bitter grain, too difficult
A cud for the repentance of a man
Grey-growing. To thee only I appeal,
Not to thy noble son, whose yeasting youth
Will clear itself, and crystal turn again.
A young man's heart, by Heaven's blessing, is
A wide world, where a thousand new-born hopes
Empurple fresh the melancholy blood:
But an old man's is narrow, tenantless
Of hopes, and stuffed with many memories,
Which, being pleasant, ease the heavy pulse—
Painful, clog up and stagnate. Weight this matter
Even as a miser balances his coin;
And, in the name of mercy, give command
That your knight Albert be brought here before you.
He will expound this riddle; he will show
A noon-day proof of bad Auranthe's guilt.
OTHO. Let Albert straight be summoned.

[*Exit one of the Nobles.*]

LUDOLPH. Impossible!
I cannot doubt—I will not—no—to doubt

Is to be ashes!—withered up to death!
OTHO. My gentle Ludolph, harbour not a fear;
You do yourself much wrong.
LUDOLPH. O, wretched dolt!
Now, when my foot is almost on thy neck,
Wilt thou infuriate me? Proof! Thou fool!
Why wilt thou tease impossibility
With such a thick-skulled persevering suit?
Fanatic obstinacy! Prodigy!
Monster of folly! Ghost of a turned brain!
You puzzle me—you haunt me—when I dream
Of you my brain will split! Bald sorcerer!
Juggler! May I come near you? On my soul
I know not whether to pity, curse, or laugh.

[*Enter* ALBERT, *and the Nobleman.*]

Here, Albert, this old phantom wants a proof!
Give him his proof! A camel's load of proofs!
OTHO. Albert, I speak to you as to a man
Whose words once uttered pass like current gold;
And therefore fit to calmly put a close
To this brief tempest. Do you stand possessed
Of any proof against the honourableness
Of Lady Auranthe, our new-spoused daughter?
ALBERT. You chill me with astonishment. How's this?
My Liege, what proof should I have 'gainst a fame
Impossible of slur? [OTHO *rises.*]
ERMINIA. O wickedness!
ETHELBERT. Deluded monarch, 'tis a cruel lie.
OTHO. Peace, rebel-priest!
CONRAD. Insult beyond credence!
ERMINIA. Almost a dream!
LUDOLPH. We have awaked from
A foolish dream that from my brow hath wrung
A wrathful dew. O folly! why did I
So act the lion with this silly gnat?
Let them depart. Lady Erminia!
I ever grieved for you, as who did not?
But now you have, with such a brazen front,
So most maliciously, so madly striven
To dazzle the soft moon, when tenderest clouds
Should be unlooped around to curtain her;
I leave you to the desert of the world
Almost with pleasure. Let them be set free

For me! I take no personal revenge
More than against a nightmare, which a man
Forgets in the new dawn. [*Exit* LUDOLPH.]
OTHO. Still in extremes! No, they must not be loose.
ETHELBERT. Albert, I must suspect thee of a crime
So fiendish—
OTHO. Fear'st thou not my fury, monk?
Conrad, be they in your safe custody
Till we determine some fit punishment.
It is so mad a deed, I must reflect
And question them in private; for perhaps,
By patient scrutiny, we may discover
Whether they merit death, or should be placed
In care of the physicians.

[*Exeunt* OTHO *and Nobles*, ALBERT *following.*]

CONRAD. My guards, ho!
ERMINIA. Albert, wilt thou follow there?
Wilt thou creep dastardly behind his back,
And shrink away from a weak woman's eye?
Turn, thou court-Janus! thou forget'st thyself;
Here is the Duke, waiting with open arms,

[*Enter Guards.*]

To thank thee; here congratulate each other;
Wring hands; embracc; and swear how lucky 'twas
That I, by happy chance, hit the right man
Of all the world to trust in.
ALBERT. Trust! to me!
CONRAD. [*aside.*] He is the sole one in this mystery.
ERMINIA. Well, I give up, and save my prayers for Heaven!
You, who could do this deed, would ne'er relent,
Though, at my words, the hollow prison-vaults
Would groan for pity.
CONRAD. Manacle them both!
ETHELBERT. I know it—it must be—I see it all!
Albert, thou art the minion!
ERMINIA. Ah! too plain—
CONRAD. Silence! Gag up their mouths! I cannot bear
More of this brawling. That the Emperor
Had placed you in some other custody!
Bring them away. [*Exeunt all but* ALBERT.]
ALBERT. Though my name perish from the book of honour,

Almost before the recent ink is dry,
And be no more remembered after death,
Than any drummer's in the muster-roll;
Yet shall I season high my sudden fall
With triumph o'er that evil-witted duke!
He shall feel what it is to have the hand
Of a man drowning, on his hateful throat.

[*Enter* GERSA *and* SIGIFRED.]

GERSA. What discord is at ferment in this house?
SIGIFRED. We are without conjecture; not a soul
We met could answer any certainty.
GERSA. Young Ludolph, like a fiery arrow, shot
By us.
SIGIFRED. The Emperor, with crossed arms, in thought.
GERSA. In one room music, in another sadness,
Perplexity everywhere!
ALBERT. A trifle mere!
Follow; your presences will much avail
To tune our jarrèd spirits. I'll explain. [*Exeunt.*]

ACT IV

SCENE 1. AURANTHE'S *Apartment.*

[AURANTHE *and* CONRAD *discovered.*]

CONRAD. Well, well, I know what ugly jeopardy
We are caged in; you need not pester that
Into my ears. Prithee, let me be spared
A foolish tongue, that I may bethink me
Of remedies with some deliberation.
You cannot doubt but 'tis in Albert's power
To crush or save us?
AURANTHE. No, I cannot doubt.
He has, assure yourself, by some strange means,
My secret; which I ever hid from him,
Knowing his mawkish honesty.
CONRAD. Cursed slave!
AURANTHE. Ay, I could almost curse him now myself.
Wretched impediment! Evil genius!
A glue upon my wings, that cannot spread,
When they should span the provinces! A snake,
A scorpion, sprawling on the first gold step,

Conducting to the throne, high canopied.
CONRAD. You would not hear my counsel, when his life
Might have been trodden out, all sure and hushed;
Now the dull animal forsooth must be
Entreated, managed! When can you contrive
The interview he demands?
AURANTHE. As speedily
It must be done as my bribed woman can
Unseen conduct him to me; but I fear
'Twill be impossible, while the broad day
Comes through the panes with persecuting glare.
Methinks, if't now were night I could intrigue
With darkness, bring the stars to second me,
And settle all this trouble.
CONRAD. Nonsense! Child!
See him immediately; why not now?
AURANTHE. Do you forget that even the senseless doorposts
Are on the watch and gape through all the house?
How many whisperers there are about,
Hungry for evidence to ruin me;
Men I have spurned, and women I have taunted?
Besides, the foolish prince sends, minute whiles,
His pages—so they tell me—to inquire
After my health, entreating, if I please,
To see me.
CONRAD. Well, suppose this Albert here;
What is your power with him?
AURANTHE. He should be
My echo, my taught parrot! but I fear
He will be cur enough to bark at me;
Have his own say; read me some silly creed
'Bout shame and pity.
CONRAD. What will you do then?
AURANTHE. What I shall do, I know not: what I would
Cannot be done; for see, this chamber-floor
Will not yield to the pick-axe and the spade—
Here is no quiet depth of hollow ground.
CONRAD. Sister, you have grown sensible and wise,
Seconding, ere I speak it, what is now,
I hope, resolved between us.
AURANTHE. Say, what is't?
CONRAD. You need not be his sexton too: a man
May carry that with him shall make him die
Elsewhere—give that to him; pretend the while
You will tomorrow succumb to his wishes,

Be what they may, and send him from the Castle
On some fool's errand; let his latest groan
Frighten the wolves!
AURANTHE. Alas! he must not die!
CONRAD. Would you were both hearsed up in stifling lead!
Detested—
AURANTHE. Conrad, hold! I would not bear
The little thunder of your fretful tongue,
Though I alone were taken in these toils,
And you could free me; but remember, sir,
You live alone in my security:
So keep your wits at work, for your own sake,
Not mine, and be more mannerly.
CONRAD. Thou wasp!
If my domains were emptied of these folk,
And I had thee to starve—
AURANTHE. O, marvellous!
But Conrad, now be gone; the host is looked for;
Cringe to the Emperor, entertain the lords.
And, do ye mind, above all things, proclaim
My sickness, with a brother's saddened eye,
Condoling with Prince Ludolph. In fit time
Return to me.
CONRAD. I leave you to your thoughts. [*Exit.*]
AURANTHE. [*sola.*] Down, down, proud temper! down, Auranthe's pride!
Why do I anger him when I should kneel?
Conrad! Albert! help! help! What can I do?
O wretched woman! Lost, wrecked, swallowed up,
Accursèd, blasted! O, thou golden crown,
Orbing along the serene firmament
Of a wide empire, like a glowing moon;
And thou, bright sceptre! lustrous in my eyes—
There—as the fabled fair Hesperian tree,
Bearing a fruit more precious! Graceful thing,
Delicate, godlike, magic! must I leave
Thee to melt in the visionary air,
Ere, by one grasp this common hand is made
Imperial? I do not know the time
When I have wept for sorrow; but methinks
I could now sit upon the ground, and shed
Tears, tears of misery. O, the heavy day!
How shall I bear my life till Albert comes?
Ludolph! Erminia! Proofs! O heavy day!
Bring me some mourning weeds, that I may 'tire

Myself, as fits one wailing her own death:
Cut off these curls, and brand this lily hand,
And throw these jewels from my loathing sight—
Fetch me a missal, and a string of beads—
A cup of bittered water, and a crust—
I will confess, O holy Abbot!—How!
What is this? Auranthe! thou fool, dolt,
Whimpering idiot! Up! Up! and quell!
I am safe! Coward! why am I in fear?
Albert! he cannot stickle, chew the cud
In such a fine extreme—impossible!
Who knocks?

[*Goes to the door, listens, and opens it.*]

[*Enter* ALBERT.]

Albert, I have been waiting for you here
With such an aching heart, such swooning throbs
On my poor brain, such cruel—cruel sorrow,
That I should claim your pity! Art not well?
ALBERT. Yes, lady, well.
AURANTHE. You look not so, alas!
But pale, as if you brought some heavy news.
ALBERT. You know full well what makes me look so pale.
AURANTHE. No! Do I? Surely I am still to learn
Some horror; all I know, this present, is
I am near hustled to a dangerous gulf,
Which you can save me from—and therefore safe,
So trusting in thy love; that should not make
Thee pale, my Albert.
ALBERT. It doth make me freeze.
AURANTHE. Why should it, love?
ALBERT. You should not ask me that,
But make your own heart monitor, and save
Me the great pain of telling. You must know.
AURANTHE. Something has vexed you, Albert. There are times
When simplest things put on a sombre cast;
A melancholy mood will haunt a man,
Until most easy matters take the shape
Of unachievable tasks; small rivulets
Then seem impassable.
ALBERT. Do not cheat yourself
With hope that gloss of words, or suppliant action,
Or tears, or ravings, or self-threatened death,

Can alter my resolve.
AURANTHE. You make me tremble;
Not so much at your threats, as at your voice,
Untuned, and harsh, and barren of all love.
ALBERT. You suffocate me! Stop this devil's parley,
And listen to me; know me once for all.
AURANTHE. I thought I did. Alas! I am deceived.
ALBERT. No, you are not deceived. You took me for
A man detesting all inhuman crime;
And therefore kept from me your demon's plot
Against Erminia. Silence? Be so still—
For ever! Speak no more; but hear my words,
Thy fate. Your safety I have bought today
By blazoning a lie, which in the dawn
I'll expiate with truth.
AURANTHE. O cruel traitor!
ALBERT. For I would not set eyes upon thy shame;
I would not see thee dragged to death by the hair,
Penanced, and taunted on a scaffolding!
Tonight, upon the skirts of the blind wood
That blackens northward of these horrid towers,
I wait for you with horses. Choose your fate.
Farewell.
AURANTHE. Albert, you jest; I'm sure you must.
You, an ambitious soldier! I, a Queen,
One who could say,—Here, rule these provinces!
Take tribute from those cities for thyself!
Empty these armouries, these treasuries,
Muster thy warlike thousands at a nod!
Go! conquer Italy!
ALBERT. Auranthe, you have made
The whole world chaff to me. Your doom is fixed.
AURANTHE. Out, villain! dastard!
ALBERT. Look there to the door!
Who is it?
AURANTHE. Conrad, traitor!
ALBERT. Let him in.

[*Enter* CONRAD.]

Do not affect amazement, hypocrite,
At seeing me in this chamber.
CONRAD. Auranthe?
ALBERT. Talk not with eyes, but speak your curses out
Against me, who would sooner crush and grind

A brace of toads, than league with them t'oppress
An innocent lady, gull an Emperor,
More generous to me than autumn sun
To ripening harvests.
AURANTHE. No more insult, sir!
ALBERT. Ay, clutch your scabbard; but, for prudence' sake,
Draw not the sword; 'twould make an uproar, Duke,
You would not hear the end of. At nightfall
Your lady sister, if I guess aright,
Will leave this busy castle. You had best
Take farewell too of worldly vanities.
CONRAD. Vassal!
ALBERT. Tomorrow, when the Emperor sends
For loving Conrad, see you fawn on him.
Good even!
AURANTHE. You'll be seen!
ALBERT. See the coast clear then.
AURANTHE. [*as he goes.*] Remorseless Albert! Cruel, cruel, wretch!

[*She lets him out.*]

CONRAD. So, we must lick the dust?
AURANTHE. I follow him.
CONRAD. How? Where? The plan of your escape?
AURANTHE. He waits
For me with horses by the forest-side,
Northward.
CONRAD. Good, good! he dies. You go, say you?
AURANTHE. Perforce.
CONRAD. Be speedy, darkness! Till that comes,
Fiends keep you company! [*Exit.*]
AURANTHE. And you! And you!
And all men! Vanish! Oh! Oh! Oh!

[*Retires to an inner apartment.*]

SCENE 2. *An Apartment in the Castle.*

[*Enter* LUDOLPH *and Page.*]

PAGE. Still very sick, my Lord; but now I went
[Knowing my duty to so good a Prince;]
And there her women in a mournful throng
Stood in the passage whispering: if any

Moved 'twas with careful steps and hushed as death;
They bade me stop.

LUDOLPH. Good fellow, once again
Make soft enquiry; prithee be not stayed
By any hindrance, but with gentlest force
Break through her weeping servants, till thou com'st
E'en to her chamber door, and there, fair boy—
If with thy mother's milk thou hast sucked in
Any diviner eloquence—woo her ears
With plaints for me, more tender than the voice
Of dying Echo, echoed.

PAGE. Kindest master!
To know thee sad thus, will unloose my tongue
In mournful syllables. Let but my words reach
Her ears and she shall take them coupled with
Moans from my heart and sighs not counterfeit.
May I speed better! [*Exit Page.*]

LUDOLPH. Auranthe! My Life!
Long have I loved thee, yet till now not loved:
Remembering, as I do, hard-hearted times
When I had heard even of thy death perhaps,
And thoughtless! suffered thee to pass alone
Into Elysium! Now I follow thee
A substance or a shadow, wheresoe'er
Thou leadest me—whether thy white feet press,
With pleasant weight, the amorous-aching earth
Or through the air thou pioneerest me,
A shade! Yet sadly I predestinate!
O unbenignest Love, why wilt thou let
Darkness steal out upon the sleepy world
So wearily, as if night's chariot wheels
Were clogged in some thick cloud. O, changeful Love,
Let not her steeds with drowsy-footed pace
Pass the high stars, before sweet embassage
Comes from the pillowed beauty of that fair
Completion of all delicate nature's wit.
Pout her faint lips anew with rubious health,
And with thine infant fingers lift the fringe
Of her sick eyelids; that those eyes may glow
With wooing light upon me, ere the morn
Peers with disrelish, grey, barren, and cold.

[*Enter* GERSA *and Courtiers.*]

Otho calls me his Lion—should I blush
To be so tamed? so—
GERSA. Do me the courtesy
Gentlemen to pass on.
COURTIER. We are your servants.

[*Exeunt Courtiers.*]

LUDOLPH. It seems then, Sir, you have found out the man
You would confer with—me?
GERSA. If I break not
Too much upon your thoughtful mood, I will
Claim a brief while your patience.
LUDOLPH. For what cause
Soe'er I shall be honoured.
GERSA. I not less.
LUDOLPH. What may it be? No trifle can take place
Of such deliberate prologue, serious 'haviour.
But be it what it may I cannot fail
To listen with no common interest—
For though so new your presence is to me,
I have a soldier's friendship for your fame—
Please you explain.
GERSA. As thus—for, pardon me,
I cannot in plain terms grossly assault
A noble nature; and would faintly sketch
What your quick apprehension will fill up,
So finely I esteem you.
LUDOLPH. I attend.
GERSA. Your generous father, most illustrious Otho,
Sits in the banquet-room among his chiefs:
His wine is bitter, for you are not there,
His eyes are fixed still on the open doors,
And every passer in he frowns upon,
Seeing no Ludolph comes.
LUDOLPH. I do neglect—
GERSA. And for your absence, may I guess the cause?
LUDOLPH. Stay there! No! Guess? More princely you must be
Than to make guesses at me. 'Tis enough.
I'm sorry I can hear no more.
GERSA. And I
As grieved to force it on you so abrupt;
Yet, one day, you must know a grief whose sting
Will sharpen more the longer 'tis concealed.

LUDOLPH. Say it at once, sir! Dead—dead—is she dead?
GERSA. Mine is a cruel task: she is not dead—
And would, for your sake, she were innocent.
LUDOLPH. Hungarian! thou amazest me beyond
All scope of thought; convulsest my heart's blood
To deadly churning!—Gersa, you are young
As I am; let me observe you face to face:
Not grey-browed like the poisonous Ethelbert,
No rheumèd eyes, no furrowing of age,
No wrinkles where all vices nestle in
Like crannied vermin—no! but fresh and young
And hopeful featured. Ha! by Heaven you weep
Tears, human tears! Do you repent you then
Of a cursed torturer's office! Why shouldst join—
Tell me—the league of Devils? Confess—confess
The lie!
GERSA. Lie!—but begone all ceremonious points
Of honour battailous! I could not turn
My wrath against thee for the orbèd world.
LUDOLPH. Your wrath, weak boy? Tremble at mine unless
Retraction follow close upon the heels
Of that late stounding insult. Why has my sword
Not done already a sheer judgement on thee?
Despair, or eat thy words! Why, thou wast nigh
Whimpering away my reason! Harkee, Sir,
It is no secret that Erminia,
Erminia, Sir, was hidden in your tent—
O blessed asylum! Comfortable home!
Begone! I pity thee; thou art a gull—
Erminia's fresh puppet—
GERSA. Furious fire!
Thou mak'st me boil as hot as thou canst flame!
And in thy teeth I give thee back the lie!
Thou liest! Thou, Auranthe's fool! A wittol!
LUDOLPH. Look! look at this bright sword;
There is no part of it to the very hilt
But shall indulge itself about thine heart!
Draw! but remember thou must cower thy plumes,
As yesterday the Arab made thee stoop.
GERSA. Patience! Not here, I would not spill thy blood
Here underneath this roof where Otho breathes,
Thy father—almost mine—
Ludolph O faltering coward!

[*Re-enter Page.*]

Stay, stay; here is one I have half a word with—
Well? What ails thee, child?
PAGE. My lord …
LUDOLPH. What wouldst say?
PAGE. They are fled!
LUDOLPH.They! Who?
PAGE. When anxiously
I hastened back, your grieving messenger,
I found the stairs all dark, the lamps extinct,
And not a foot or whisper to be heard.
I thought her dead, and on the lowest step
Sat listening; when presently came by
Two muffled up—one sighing heavily,
The other cursing low, whose voice I knew
For the Duke Conrad's. Close I followed them
Through the dark ways they chose to the open air;
And, as I followed, heard my lady speak.
LUDOLPH. Thy life answer the truth!
PAGE. The chamber's empty!
LUDOLPH. As I will be of mercy! So, at last,
This nail is in my temples!
GERSA. Be calm in this.
LUDOLPH. I am.
GERSA. And Albert too has disappeared;
Ere I met you, I sought him everywhere;
You would not hearken.
LUDOLPH. Which way went they, boy?
GERSA. I'll hunt with you.
LUDOLPH. No, no, no. My senses are
Still whole. I have survived. My arm is strong,
My appetite sharp—for revenge! I'll no sharer
In my feast; my injury is all my own,
And so is my revenge, my lawful chattels!
Terrier, ferret them out! Burn—burn the witch!
Trace me their footsteps! Away! [*Exeunt.*]

ACT V

SCENE 1. *A Part of the Forest.*

[*Enter* CONRAD *and* AURANTHE.]

AURANTHE. Go no further; not a step more. Thou art
A master-plague in the midst of miseries.
Go—I fear thee! I tremble every limb,
Who never shook before. There's moody death
In thy resolvèd looks! Yes, I could kneel
To pray thee far away. Conrad, go! go!—
There! yonder underneath the boughs I see
Our horses!
CONRAD. Aye, and the man.
AURANTHE. Yes, he is there!
Go, go—no blood! no blood! Go, gentle Conrad!
CONRAD. Farewell!
AURANTHE. Farewell, for this Heaven pardon you.

[*Exit* AURANTHE.]

CONRAD. If he survive one hour, then may I die
In unimagined tortures—or breathe through
A long life in the foulest sink O' the world!
He dies. 'Tis well she do not advertize
The caitiff of the cold steel at his back. [*Exit* CONRAD.]

[*Enter* LUDOLPH *and Page.*]

LUDOLPH. Missed the way, boy? Say not that on your peril!
PAGE. Indeed, indeed I cannot trace them further.
LUDOLPH. Must I stop here? Here solitary die?
Stifled beneath the thick oppressive shade
Of these dull boughs—this oven of dark thickets—
Silent—without revenge? Pshaw!—bitter end—
A bitter death—a suffocating death—
A gnawing—silent—deadly, quiet death!
Escaped?—Fled?—Vanished? Melted into air?
She's gone! I cannot clutch her! No revenge!
A muffled death, ensnared in horrid silence!
Sucked to my grave amid a dreary calm!
O, where is that illustrious noise of war,
To smother up this sound of labouring breath,

This rustle of the trees!

[AURANTHE *shrieks at a distance.*]

PAGE. My Lord, a noise!
This way—hark!
LUDOLPH. Yes, yes! A hope! A music!
A glorious clamour! Now I live again! [*Exeunt.*]

SCENE 2. *Another Part of the Forest.*

[*Enter* ALBERT (*wounded*).]

ALBERT. O for enough life to support me on
To Otho's feet!

[*Enter* LUDOLPH.]

LUDOLPH. Thrice villainous, stay there!
Tell me where that detested woman is,
Or this is through thee!
ALBERT. My good Prince, with me
The sword has done its worst; not without worst
Done to another—Conrad has it home!
I see you know it all!
LUDOLPH. Where is his sister?

[AURANTHE *rushes in.*]

AURANTHE. Albert!
LUDOLPH. Ha! There! there!—He is the paramour!—
There—hug him—dying! O, thou innocence,
Shrive him and comfort him at his last gasp,
Kiss down his eyelids! Was he not thy love?
Wilt thou forsake him at his latest hour?
Keep fearful and aloof from his last gaze,
His most uneasy moments, when cold death
Stands with the door ajar to let him in?
ALBERT. O, that that door with hollow slam would close
Upon me sudden, for I cannot meet,
In all the unknown chambers of the dead,
Such horrors!
LUDOLPH. Auranthe! what can he mean?
What horrors? Is it not a joyous time?
Am I not married to a paragon

'Of personal beauty and untainted soul?'
A blushing fair-eyed purity! A sylph,
Whose snowy timid hand has never sinned
Beyond a flower plucked, white as itself?
Albert, you do insult my bride—your mistress—
To talk of horrors on our wedding night.
ALBERT. Alas! poor Prince, I would you knew my heart!
'Tis not so guilty—
LUDOLPH. Hear, he pleads not guilty!
You are not? or, if so, what matters it?
You have escaped me, free as the dusk air,
Hid in the forest—safe from my revenge.
I cannot catch you! You should laugh at me,
Poor cheated Ludolph! Make the forest hiss
With jeers at me! You tremble—faint at once,
You will come to again. O cockatrice,
I have you! Whither wander those fair eyes
To entice the Devil to your help, that he
May change you to a spider, so to crawl
Into some cranny to escape my wrath?
ALBERT. Sometimes the counsel of a dying man
Doth operate quietly when his breath is gone:
Disjoin those hands—part—part, do not destroy
Each other—forget her! Our miseries
Are equal shared, and mercy is—
LUDOLPH. A boon
When one can compass it. Auranthe, try
Your oratory; your breath is not so hitched—
Ay, stare for help—

[ALBERT *dies.*]

There goes a spotted soul
Howling in vain along the hollow night!
Hear him! He calls you—sweet Auranthe, come!
AURANTHE. Kill me!
LUDOLPH. No! What? Upon our marriage-night?
The earth would shudder at so foul a deed—
A fair bride! A sweet bride! An innocent bride!
No, we must revel it, as 'tis in use
In times of delicate brilliant ceremony:
Come, let me lead you to our halls again!
Nay, linger not—make no resistance, sweet—
Will you?—Ah wretch, thou canst not, for I have
The strength of twenty lions 'gainst a lamb!

Now—one adieu for Albert!—Come away! [*Exeunt.*]

SCENE 3. *An inner Court of the Castle.*

[*Enter* SIGIFRED, GONFRID, *and* THEODORE *meeting.*]

THEODORE. Was ever such a night?
SIGIFRED. What horrors more?
Things unbelieved one hour, so strange they are,
The next hour stamps with credit.
THEODORE. Your last news?
GONFRID. After the page's story of the death
Of Albert and Duke Conrad?
SIGIFRED. And the return
Of Ludolph with the Princess.
GONFRID. No more, save
Prince Gersa's freeing Abbot Ethelbert,
And the sweet lady, fair Erminia,
From prison.
THEODORE. Where are they now? Hast yet heard?
GONFRID. With the sad Emperor they are closeted;
I saw the three pass slowly up the stairs,
The lady weeping, the old Abbot cowled.
SIGIFRED. What next?
THEODORE. I ache to think on't.
GONFRID. 'Tis with fate.
THEODORE. One while these proud towers are hushed as death.
GONFRID. The next our poor Prince fills the arched rooms
With ghastly ravings.
SIGIFRED. I do fear his brain.
GONFRID. I will see more. Bear you so stout a heart?

[*Exeunt into the Castle.*]

SCENE 4. *A Cabinet, opening towards a Terrace.*

[OTHO, ERMINIA, ETHELBERT, *and a Physician, discovered*]

OTHO. O, my poor boy! My son! My son! My Ludolph!
Have ye no comfort for me, ye physicians
Of the weak body and soul?
ETHELBERT. 'Tis not in medicine
Either of heaven or earth can cure, unless
Fit time be chosen to administer.
OTHO. A kind forbearance, holy Abbot—come

Erminia; here, sit by me, gentle girl;
Give me thy hand—hast thou forgiven me?
ERMINIA. Would I were with the saints to pray for you!
OTHO. Why will ye keep me from my darling child?
PHYSICIAN. Forgive me, but he must not see thy face.
OTHO. Is then a father's countenance a Gorgon?
Hath it not comfort in it? Would it not
Console my poor boy, cheer him, heal his spirits?
Let me embrace him, let me speak to him;
I will! Who hinders me? Who's Emperor?
PHYSICIAN. You may not, Sire; 'twould overwhelm him quite,
He is so full of grief and passionate wrath;
Too heavy a sigh would kill him, or do worse.
He must be saved by fine contrivances,
And most especially we must keep clear
Out of his sight a father whom he loves;
His heart is full, it can contain no more,
And do its ruddy office.
ETHELBERT. Sage advice;
We must endeavour how to ease and slacken
The tight-wound energies of his despair,
Not make them tenser.
OTHO. Enough! I hear, I hear.
Yet you were about to advise more—I listen.
ETHELBERT. This learned doctor will agree with me,
That not in the smallest point should he be thwarted,
Or gainsaid by one word; his very motions,
Nods, becks and hints, should be obeyed with care,
Even on the moment: so his troubled mind
May cure itself.
PHYSICIAN. There are no other means.
OTHO. Open the door: let's hear if all is quiet.
PHYSICIAN. Beseech you, Sire, forbear.
ERMINIA. Do, do.
OTHO. I command!
Open it straight—hush!—quiet!—my lost boy!
My miserable child!
LUDOLPH. [*indistinctly without.*] Fill fill my goblet—
here's a health!
ERMINIA. O, close the door!
OTHO. Let, let me hear his voice; this cannot last—
And fain would I catch up his dying words
Though my own knell they be—this cannot last—
O let me catch his voice—for lo! I hear
A whisper in this silence that he's dead!

It is so! Gersa?

[*Enter* GERSA.]

PHYSICIAN. Say, how fares the prince?
GERSA. More calm—his features are less wild and flushed;
Once he complained of weariness.
PHYSICIAN. Indeed!
'Tis good—'tis good; let him but fall asleep,
That saves him.
OTHO. Gersa, watch him like a child;
Ward him from harm—and bring me better news!
PHYSICIAN. Humour him to the height. I fear to go;
For should he catch a glimpse of my dull garb,
It might affright him, fill him with suspicion
That we believe him sick, which must not be.
GERSA. I will invent what soothing means I can.

[*Exit* GERSA.]

PHYSICIAN. This should cheer up your Highness; the weariness
Is a good symptom, and most favourable;
It gives me pleasant hopes. Please you, walk forth
Upon the terrace; the refreshing air
Will blow one half of your sad doubts away. [*Exeunt.*]

SCENE 5. *A Banqueting Hall, brilliantly illuminated, and set forth with all costly magnificence, with supper-tables, laden with services of gold and silver. A door in the back scene, guarded by two Soldiers. Lords, Ladies, Knights, Gentlemen, etc., whispering sadly, and ranging themselves; part entering and part discovered.*

FIRST KNIGHT. Grievously are we tantalized, one and all;
Swayed here and there, commanded to and fro
As though we were the shadows of a sleep,
And linked to a dreaming fancy. What do we here?
GONFRID. I am no seer; you know we must obey
The Prince from A to Z, though it should be
To set the place in flames. I pray hast heard
Where the most wicked Princess is?
FIRST KNIGHT. There, sir,
In the next room. Have you remarked those two
Stout soldiers posted at the door?
GONFRID. For what? [*They whisper.*]
FIRST LADY. How ghast a train!

SECOND LADY. Sure this should be some splendid burial.
FIRST LADY. What fearful whispering! See, see—Gersa there!

[*Enter* GERSA.]

GERSA. Put on your brightest looks; smile if you can;
Behave as all were happy; keep your eyes
From the least watch upon him; if he speaks
To any one, answer collectedly,
Without surprise, his questions, howe'er strange.
Do this to the utmost—though, alas! with me
The remedy grows hopeless! Here he comes—
Observe what I have said—show no surprise.

[*Enter* LUDOLPH, *followed by* SIGIFRED *and Page.*]

LUDOLPH. A splendid company! rare beauties here!
I should have Orphean lips, and Plato's fancy,
Amphion's utterance, tonèd with his lyre,
Or the deep key of Jove's sonorous mouth,
To give fit salutation. Methought I heard,
As I came in, some whispers—what of that?
'Tis natural men should whisper; at the kiss
Of Psyche given by Love, there was a buzz
Among the gods!—and silence is as natural.
These draperies are fine, and, being a mortal,
I should desire no better; yet, in truth,
There must be some superior costliness,
Some wider-domèd high magnificence!
I would have, as a mortal I may not,
Hangings of heaven's clouds, purple and gold,
Slung from the spheres; gauzes of silver mist,
Looped up with cords of twisted wreathèd light,
And tasselled round with weeping meteors!
These pendent lamps and chandeliers are bright
As earthly fires from dull dross can be cleansed;
Yet could my eyes drink up intenser beams
Undazzled—this is darkness. When I close
These lids, I see far fiercer brilliances—
Skies full of splendid moons, and shooting stars,
And spouting exhalations, diamond fires,
And panting fountains quivering with deep glows!
Yes—this is dark—is it not dark?
SIGIFRED. My Lord,
'Tis late; the lights of festival are ever

Quenched in the morn.
LUDOLPH. 'Tis not tomorrow then?
SIGIFRED. 'Tis early dawn.
GERSA. Indeed full time we slept;
Say you so, Prince?
LUDOLPH. I say I quarrelled with you;
We did not tilt each other—that's a blessing,
Good gods! No innocent blood upon my head!
SIGIFRED. Retire, Gersa!
LUDOLPH. There should be three more here:
For two of them, they stay away perhaps,
Being gloomy-minded, haters of fair revels—
They know their own thoughts best. As for the third,
We'll have her presendy; ay, you shall see her,
And wonder at her, friends, she is so fair;
Deep blue eyes, semi-shaded in white lids,
Finished with lashes fine for more soft shade,
Completed by her twin-arched ebon brows;
White temples of exactest elegance,
Of even mould felicitous and smooth;
Cheeks fashioned tenderly on either side,
So perfect, so divine that our poor eyes
Are dazzled with the sweet proportioning,
And wonder that 'tis so—the magic chance!
Her nostrils, small, fragrant, faery-delicate;
Her lips—I swear no human bones e'er wore
So taking a disguise—you shall behold her!
She is the world's chief jewel, and by heaven
She's mine by right of marriage!—she is mine!
Patience, good people, in fit time I send
A summoner. She will obey my call,
Being a wife most mild and dutiful.
First I would hear what music is prepared
To herald and receive her—let me hear!
SIGIFRED. Bid the musicians soothe him tenderly.

[*A soft strain of music.*]

LUDOLPH. Ye have none better? No—I am content;
'Tis a rich sobbing melody, with reliefs
Full and majestic; it is well enough,
And will be sweeter, when ye see her pace
Sweeping into this presence, glistened o'er
With emptied caskets, and her train upheld
By ladies, habited in robes of lawn,

Sprinkled with golden crescents, others bright
In silks, with spangles showered, and bow'd to
By Duchesses and pearlèd Margravines!
Sad, that the fairest creature of the earth—
I pray you mind me not—'tis sad, I say,
That the extremest beauty of the world
Should so entrench herself away from me,
Behind a barrier of engendered guilt!
SECOND LADY. Ah! what a moan!
FIRST KNIGHT. Most piteous indeed!
LUDOLPH. She shall be brought before this company,
And then—then—
FIRST LADY. He muses.
GERSA. O, Fortune, where will this end?
SIGIFRED. I guess his purpose! Indeed he must not have
That pestilence brought in—that cannot be,
There we must stop him.
GERSA. I am lost! Hush, hush!
He is about to rave again.
LUDOLPH. A barrier of guilt! I was the fool,
She was the cheater! Who's the cheater now,
And who the fool? The entrapped, the caged fool,
The bird-limed raven? She shall croak to death
Secure! Methinks I have her in my fist,
To crush her with my heel! Wait, wait! I marvel
My father keeps away. Good friend—ah! Sigifred!
Do bring him to me—and Erminia
I fain would see before I sleep—and Ethelbert,
That he may bless me, as I know he will
Though I have cursed him.
SIGIFRED. Rather suffer me
To lead you to them.
LUDOLPH. No, excuse me, no!
The day is not quite done. Go bring them hither.

[*Exit* SIGIFRED.]

Certes, a father's smile should, like sunlight,
Slant on my sheavèd harvest of ripe bliss.
Besides, I thirst to pledge my lovely bride
In a deep goblet: let me see—what wine?
The strong Iberian juice, or mellow Greek?
Or pale Calabrian? Or the Tuscan grape?
Or of old Aetna's pulpy wine presses,
Black stained with the fat vintage, as it were

The purple slaughter-house, where Bacchus' self
Pricked his own swollen veins? Where is my Page?
PAGE. Here, here!
LUDOLPH. Be ready to obey me; anon thou shalt
Bear a soft message for me; for the hour
Draws near when I must make a winding up
Of bridal mysteries—a fine-spun vengeance!
Carve it on my tomb, that when I rest beneath,
Men shall confess—This Prince was gulled and cheated,
But from the ashes of disgrace he rose
More than a fiery dragon, and did burn
His ignominy up in purging fires!
Did I not send, sir, but a moment past,
For my father?
GERSA. You did.
LUDOLPH. Perhaps 'twould be
Much better he came not.
GERSA. He enters now!

[*Enter* OTHO, ERMINIA, ETHELBERT, SIGIFRED, *and Physician.*]

LUDOLPH. O thou good man, against whose sacred head
I was a mad conspirator, chiefly too
For the sake of my fair newly wedded wife,
Now to be punished—do not look so sad!
Those charitable eyes will thaw my heart,
Those tears will wash away a just resolve,
A verdict ten times sworn! Awake—awake—
Put on a judge's brow, and use a tongue
Made iron-stern by habit! Thou shalt see
A deed to be applauded, 'scribed in gold!
Join a loud voice to mine, and so denounce
What I alone will execute!
OTHO. Dear son,
What is it? By your father's love, I sue
That it be nothing merciless!
LUDOLPH. To that demon?
Not so! No! She is in temple-stall
Being garnished for the sacrifice, and I,
The Priest of Justice, will immolate her
Upon the altar of wrath! She stings me through!—
Even as the worm doth feed upon the nut,
So she, a scorpion, preys upon my brain!
I feel her gnawing here! Let her but vanish,

Then, father, I will lead your legions forth,
Compact in steelèd squares, and spearèd files
And bid our trumpets speak a fell rebuke
To nations drowsed in peace!
OTHO. Tomorrow, son,
Be your word law; forget today—
LUDOLPH. I will
When I have finished it! Now, now I'm pight,
Tight-footed for the deed!
ERMINIA. Alas! Alas!
LUDOLPH. What angel's voice is that? Erminia!
Ah! gentlest creature, whose sweet innocence
Was almost murdered; I am penitent,
Wilt thou forgive me? And thou, holy man,
Good Ethelbert, shall I die in peace with you?
ERMINIA. Die, my lord!
LUDOLPH. I feel it possible.
OTHO. Physician?
PHYSICIAN. I fear me he is past my skill.
OTHO. Not so!
LUDOLPH. I see it—I see it—I have been wandering!
Half-mad—not right here—I forget my purpose.
Bestir—bestir—Auranthe! Ha! ha! ha!
Youngster! Page! go bid them drag her to me!
Obey! This shall finish it! [*Draws a dagger.*]
OTHO. O my son! my son!
SIGIFRED. This must not be—stop there!
LUDOLPH. Am I obeyed?
A little talk with her—no harm—haste! haste!

[*Exit Page.*]

Set her before me—never fear I can strike.
SEVERAL VOICES. My Lord! My Lord!
GERSA. Good Prince!
LUDOLPH. Why do ye trouble me? Out—out away!
There she is! take that! and that! no, no—
That's not well done. Where is she?

[*The doors open. Enter Page. Several women are seen grouped about* AURANTHE *in the inner room.*]

PAGE. Alas! My Lord, my Lord! they cannot move her!
Her arms are stiff—her fingers clenched and cold!
LUDOLPH. She's dead! [*Staggers and falls into their arms.*]

ETHELBERT. Take away the dagger.
GERSA. Softly; so!
OTHO. Thank God for that!
SIGIFRED. It could not harm him now.
GERSA. No!—brief be his anguish!
LUDOLPH. She's gone—I am content—Nobles, good night!
Where is your hand, father?—what sultry air!
We are all weary—faint—set ope the doors—
I will to bed!—Tomorrow—[*Dies.*]

[*The curtain falls.*]

Lamia

PART I

Upon a time, before the faery broods
Drove Nymph and Satyr from the prosperous woods,
Before King Oberon's bright diadem,
Sceptre, and mantle, clasped with dewy gem,
Frighted away the Dryads and the Fauns
From rushes green, and brakes, and cowslipped lawns,
The ever-smitten Hermes empty left
His golden throne, bent warm on amorous theft:
From high Olympus had he stolen light,
On this side of Jove's clouds, to escape the sight
Of his great summoner, and made retreat
Into a forest on the shores of Crete.
For somewhere in that sacred island dwelt
A nymph, to whom all hoofèd Satyrs knelt,
At whose white feet the languid Tritons poured
Pearls, while on land they withered and adored.
Fast by the springs where she to bathe was wont,
And in those meads where sometime she might haunt,
Were strewn rich gifts, unknown to any Muse,
Though Fancy's casket were unlocked to choose.
Ah, what a world of love was at her feet!
So Hermes thought, and a celestial heat
Burnt from his wingèd heels to either ear,
That from a whiteness, as the lily clear,
Blushed into roses 'mid his golden hair,
Fallen in jealous curls about his shoulders bare.

From vale to vale, from wood to wood, he flew,
Breathing upon the flowers his passion new,
And wound with many a river to its head
To find where this sweet nymph prepared her secret bed.
In vain; the sweet nymph might nowhere be found,
And so he rested, on the lonely ground,
Pensive, and full of painful jealousies
Of the Wood-Gods, and even the very trees.
There as he stood, he heard a mournful voice,
Such as, once heard, in gentle heart destroys
All pain but pity; thus the lone voice spake:
'When from this wreathèd tomb shall I awake!
When move in a sweet body fit for life,
And love, and pleasure, and the ruddy strife
Of hearts and lips! Ah, miserable me!'
The God, dove-footed, glided silently
Round bush and tree, soft-brushing, in his speed,
The taller grasses and full-flowering weed,
Until he found a palpitating snake,
Bright, and cirque-couchant in a dusky brake.

She was a gordian shape of dazzling hue,
Vermilion-spotted, golden, green, and blue;
Striped like a zebra, freckled like a pard,
Eyed like a peacock, and all crimson barred;
And full of silver moons, that, as she breathed,
Dissolved, or brighter shone, or interwreathed
Their lustres with the gloomier tapestries—
So rainbow-sided, touched with miseries,
She seemed, at once, some penanced lady elf,
Some demon's mistress, or the demon's self.
Upon her crest she wore a wannish fire
Sprinkled with stars, like Ariadne's tiar;
Her head was serpent, but ah, bitter-sweet!
She had a woman's mouth with all its pearls complete;
And for her eyes—what could such eyes do there
But weep, and weep, that they were born so fair,
As Proserpine still weeps for her Sicilian air?
Her throat was serpent, but the words she spake
Came, as through bubbling honey, for Love's sake,
And thus—while Hermes on his pinions lay,
Like a stooped falcon ere he takes his prey—

'Fair Hermes, crowned with feathers, fluttering light,
I had a splendid dream of thee last night:
I saw thee sitting, on a throne of gold,
Among the Gods, upon Olympus old,
The only sad one; for thou didst not hear
The soft, lute-fingered Muses chanting clear,
Nor even Apollo when he sang alone,
Deaf to his throbbing throat's long, long melodious moan.
I dreamt I saw thee, robed in purple flakes,
Break amorous through the clouds, as morning breaks,
And, swiftly as a bright Phoebean dart,
Strike for the Cretan isle; and here thou art!
Too gentle Hermes, hast thou found the maid?'
Whereat the star of Lethe not delayed
His rosy eloquence, and thus inquired :
'Thou smooth-lipped serpent, surely high inspired!
Thou beauteous wreath, with melancholy eyes,
Possess whatever bliss thou canst devise,
Telling me only where my nymph is fled—
Where she doth breathe!' 'Bright planet, thou hast said,'
Returned the snake, 'but seal with oaths, fair God!'
'I swear,' said Hermes, 'by my serpent rod,
And by thine eyes, and by thy starry crown!'
Light flew his earnest words, among the blossoms blown.
Then thus again the brilliance feminine:
'Too frail of heart! for this lost nymph of thine,
Free as the air, invisibly, she strays
About these thornless wilds; her pleasant days
She tastes unseen; unseen her nimble feet
Leave traces in the grass and flowers sweet;
From weary tendrils, and bowed branches green,
She plucks the fruit unseen, she bathes unseen;
And by my power is her beauty veiled
To keep it unaffronted, unassailed
By the love-glances of unlovely eyes
Of Satyrs, Fauns, and bleared Silenus' sighs.
Pale grew her immortality, for woe
Of all these lovers, and she grieved so
I took compassion on her, bade her steep
Her hair in weird syrops, that would keep
Her loveliness invisible, yet free
To wander as she loves, in liberty,
Thou shalt behold her, Hermes, thou alone,
If thou wilt, as thou swearest, grant my boon!'

Then, once again, the charmed God began
An oath, and through the serpent's ears it ran
Warm, tremulous, devout, psalterian.
Ravished, she lifted her Circean head,
Blushed a live damask, and swift-lisping said,
'I was a woman, let me have once more
A woman's shape, and charming as before.
I love a youth of Corinth—O the bliss!
Give me my woman's form, and place me where he is.
Stoop, Hermes, let me breathe upon thy brow,
And thou shalt see thy sweet nymph even now.'
The God on half-shut feathers sank serene,
She breathed upon his eyes, and swift was seen
Of both the guarded nymph near-smiling on the green.
It was no dream; or say a dream it was,
Real are the dreams of Gods, and smoothly pass
Their pleasures in a long immortal dream.
One warm, flushed moment, hovering, it might seem
Dashed by the wood-nymph's beauty, so he burned;
Then, lighting on the printless verdure, turned
To the swooned serpent, and with languid arm,
Delicate, put to proof the lithe Caducean charm.
So done, upon the nymph his eyes he bent
Full of adoring tears and blandishment,
And towards her stepped: she, like a moon in wane,
Faded before him, cowered, nor could restrain
Her fearful sobs, self-folding like a flower
That faints into itself at evening hour:
But the God fostering her chilled hand,
She felt the warmth, her eyelids opened bland,
And, like new flowers at morning song of bees,
Bloomed, and gave up her honey to the lees.
Into the green-recessèd woods they flew;
Nor grew they pale, as mortal lovers do.

Left to herself, the serpent now began
To change; her elfin blood in madness ran,
Her mouth foamed, and the grass, therewith besprent,
Withered at dew so sweet and virulent;
Her eyes in torture fixed, and anguish drear,
Hot, glazed, and wide, with lid-lashes all sear,
Flashed phosphor and sharp sparks, without one cooling tear.
The colours all inflamed throughout her train,
She writhed about, convulsed with scarlet pain:
A deep volcanian yellow took the place

Of all her milder-moonèd body's grace;
And, as the lava ravishes the mead,
Spoilt all her silver mail, and golden brede;
Made gloom of all her frecklings, streaks and bars,
Eclipsed her crescents, and licked up her stars.
So that, in moments few, she was undressed
Of all her sapphires, greens, and amethyst,
And rubious-argent; of all these bereft,
Nothing but pain and ugliness were left.
Still shone her crown; that vanished, also she
Melted and disappeared as suddenly;
And in the air, her new Voice luting soft,
Cried, 'Lycius! gentle Lycius!'—Borne aloft
With the bright mists about the mountains hoar
These words dissolved: Crete's forests heard no more.

Whither fled Lamia, now a lady bright,
A full-born beauty new and exquisite?
She fled into that valley they pass o'er
Who go to Corinth from Cenchreas' shore;
And rested at the foot of those wild hills,
The rugged founts of the Peraean rills,
And of that other ridge whose barren back
Stretches, with all its mist and cloudy rack,
South-westward to Cleone. There she stood
About a young bird's flutter from a wood,
Fair, on a sloping green of mossy tread,
By a clear pool, wherein she passioned
To see herself escaped from so sore ills,
While her robes flaunted with the daffodils.

Ah, happy Lycius!—for she was a maid
More beautiful than ever twisted braid,
Or sighed, or blushed, or on spring-flowered lea
Spread a green kirtle to the minstrelsy:
A virgin purest lipped, yet in the lore
Of love deep learnèd to the red heart's core;
Not one hour old, yet of sciential brain
To unperplex bliss from its neighbour pain,
Define their pettish limits, and estrange
Their points of contact, and swift counterchange;
Intrigue with the specious chaos, and dispart
Its most ambiguous atoms with sure art;
As though in Cupid's college she had spent
Sweet days a lovely graduate, still unshent,

And kept his rosy terms in idle languishment.

Why this fair creature chose so fierily
By the wayside to linger, we shall see;
But first 'tis fit to tell how she could muse
And dream, when in the serpent prison-house,
Of all she list, strange or magnificent:
How, ever, where she willed, her spirit went;
Whether to faint Elysium, or where
Down through tress-lifting waves the Nereids fair
Wind into Thetis' bower by many a pearly stair;
Or where God Bacchus drains his cups divine,
Stretched out, at ease, beneath a glutinous pine;
Or where in Pluto's gardens palatine
Mulciber's columns gleam in far piazzian line.
And sometimes into cities she would send
Her dream, with feast and rioting to blend;
And once, while among mortals dreaming thus,
She saw the young Corinthian Lycius
Charioting foremost in the envious race,
Like a young Jove with calm uneager face,
And fell into a swooning love of him.
Now on the moth-time of that evening dim
He would return that way, as well she knew,
To Corinth from the shore; for freshly blew
The eastern soft wind, and his galley now
Grated the quaystones with her brazen prow
In port Cenchreas, from Egina isle
Fresh anchored; whither he had been awhile
To sacrifice to Jove, whose temple there
Waits with high marble doors for blood and incense rare.
Jove heard his vows, and bettered his desire;
For by some freakful chance he made retire
From his companions, and set forth to walk,
Perhaps grown wearied of their Corinth talk:
Over the solitary hills he fared,
Thoughtless at first, but ere eve's star appeared
His fantasy was lost, where reason fades,
In the calmed twilight of Platonic shades.
Lamia beheld him coming, near, more near—
Close to her passing, in indifference dread,
His silent sandals swept the mossy green;
So neighboured to him, and yet so unseen
She stood: he passed, shut up in mysteries,
His mind wrapped like his mantle, while her eyes

Followed his steps, and her neck regal white
Turned—syllabling thus, 'Ah, Lycius bright,
And will you leave me on the hills alone?
Lycius, look back! and be some pity shown.'
He did—not with cold wonder fearingly,
But Orpheus-like at an Eurydice—
For so delicious were the words she sung,
It seemed he had loved them a whole summer long.
And soon his eyes had drunk her beauty up,
Leaving no drop in the bewildering cup,
And still the cup was full—while he, afraid
Lest she should vanish ere his lip had paid
Due adoration, thus began to adore
(Her soft look growing coy, she saw his chain so sure):
'Leave thee alone! Look back! Ah, Goddess, see
Whether my eyes can ever turn from thee!
For pity do not this sad heart belie—
Even as thou vanisheth so I shall die.
Stay! though a Naiad of the rivers, stay!
To thy far wishes will thy streams obey.
Stay! though the greenest woods be thy domain,
Alone they can drink up the morning rain:
Though a descended Pleiad, will not one
Of thine harmonious sisters keep in tune
Thy spheres, and as thy silver proxy shine?
So sweetly to these ravished ears of mine
Came thy sweet greeting, that if thou shouldst fade
Thy memory will waste me to a shade—
For pity do not melt!'—'If I should stay,'
Said Lamia, 'here, upon this floor of clay,
And pain my steps upon these flowers too rough,
What canst thou say or do of charm enough
To dull the nice remembrance of my home?
Thou canst not ask me with thee here to roam
Over these hills and vales, where no joy is—
Empty of immortality and bliss!
Thou art a scholar, Lycius, and must know
That finer spirits cannot breathe below
In human climes, and live. Alas! poor youth,
What taste of purer air hast thou to soothe
My essence? What serener palaces,
Where I may all my many senses please,
And by mysterious sleights a hundred thirsts appease?
It cannot be—Adieu!' So said, she rose
Tip-toe with white arms spread. He, sick to lose

The amorous promise of her lone complain,
Swooned, murmuring of love, and pale with pain.
The cruel lady, without any show
Of sorrow for her tender favourite's woe,
But rather, if her eyes could brighter be,
With brighter eyes and slow amenity,
Put her new lips to his, and gave afresh
The life she had so tangled in her mesh;
And as he from one trance was wakening
Into another, she began to sing,
Happy in beauty, life, and love, and every thing,
A song of love, too sweet for earthly lyres,
While, like held breath, the stars drew in their panting fires.
And then she whispered in such trembling tone,
As those who, safe together met alone
For the first time through many anguished days,
Use other speech than looks; bidding him raise
His drooping head, and clear his soul of doubt,
For that she was a woman, and without
Any more subtle fluid in her veins
Than throbbing blood, and that the self-same pains
Inhabited her frail-strung heart as his.
And next she wondered how his eyes could miss
Her face so long in Corinth, where, she said,
She dwelt but half retired, and there had led
Days happy as the gold coin could invent
Without the aid of love; yet in content
Till she saw him, as once she passed him by,
Where 'gainst a column he leant thoughtfully
At Venus' temple porch, 'mid baskets heaped
Of amorous herbs and flowers, newly reaped
Late on that eve, as 'twas the night before
The Adonian feast; whereof she saw no more,
But wept alone those days, for why should she adore?
Lycius from death awoke into amaze,
To see her still, and singing so sweet lays;
Then from amaze into delight he fell
To hear her whisper woman's lore so well;
And every word she spake enticed him on
To unperplexed delight and pleasure known.
Let the mad poets say whate'er they please
Of the sweets of Faeries, Peris, Goddesses,
There is not such a treat among them all,
Haunters of cavern, lake, and waterfall,

As a real woman, lineal indeed
From Pyrrha's pebbles or old Adam's seed.
Thus gentle Lamia judged, and judged aright,
That Lycius could not love in half a fright,
So threw the goddess off, and won his heart
More pleasantly by playing woman's part,
With no more awe than what her beauty gave,
That, while it smote, still guaranteed to save.
Lycius to all made eloquent reply,
Marrying to every word a twinbom sigh;
And last, pointing to Corinth, asked her sweet,
If 'twas too far that night for her soft feet.
The way was short, for Lamia's eagerness
Made, by a spell, the triple league decrease
To a few paces; not at all surmised
By blinded Lycius, so in her comprised.
They passed the city gates, he knew not how,
So noiseless, and he never thought to know.

As men talk in a dream, so Corinth all,
Throughout her palaces imperial,
And all her populous streets and temples lewd,
Muttered, like tempest in the distance brewed,
To the wide-spreaded night above her towers.
Men, women, rich and poor, in the cool hours,
Shuffled their sandals o'er the pavement white,
Companioned or alone; while many a light
Flared, here and there, from wealthy festivals,
And threw their moving shadows on the walls,
Or found them clustered in the corniced shade
Of some arched temple door, or dusky colonnade.

Muffling his face, of greeting friends in fear,
Her fingers he pressed hard, as one came near
With curled grey beard, sharp eyes, and smooth bald crown,
Slow-stepped, and robed in philosophic gown:
Lycius shrank closer, as they met and passed,
Into his mantle, adding wings to haste,
While hurried Lamia trembled: 'Ah,' said he,
'Why do you shudder, love, so ruefully?
Why does your tender palm dissolve in dew?'—
'I'm wearied,' said fair Lamia, 'tell me who
Is that old man? I cannot bring to mind
His features—Lycius! wherefore did you blind
Yourself from his quick eyes?' Lycius replied,

‘’Tis Apollonius sage, my trusty guide
And good instructor; but tonight he seems
The ghost of folly haunting my sweet dreams.’

While yet he spake they had arrived before
A pillared porch, with lofty portal door,
Where hung a silver lamp, whose phosphor glow
Reflected in the slabbèd steps below,
Mild as a star in water; for so new,
And so unsullied was the marble hue,
So through the crystal polish, liquid fine,
Ran the dark veins, that none but feet divine
Could e’er have touched there. Sounds Aeolian
Breathed from the hinges, as the ample span
Of the wide doors disclosed a place unknown
Some time to any, but those two alone,
And a few Persian mutes, who that same year
Were seen about the markets: none knew where
They could inhabit; the most curious
Were foiled, who watched to trace them to their house.
And but the flitter-wingèd verse must tell,
For truth’s sake, what woe afterwards befell,
’Twould humour many a heart to leave them thus,
Shut from the busy world, of more incredulous.

PART II

Love in a hut, with water and a crust,
Is—Love, forgive us!—cinder, ashes, dust;
Love in a palace is perhaps at last
More grievous torment than a hermit’s fast.
That is a doubtful tale from faery land,
Hard for the non-elect to understand.
Had Lycius lived to hand his story down,
He might have given the moral a fresh frown,
Or clenched it quite: but too short was their bliss
To breed distrust and hate, that make the soft voice hiss.
Besides, there, nightly, with terrific glare,
Love, jealous grown of so complete a pair,
Hovered and buzzed his wings, with fearful roar,
Above the lintel of their chamber door,
And down the passage cast a glow upon the floor.

For all this came a ruin: side by side
They were enthronèd, in the eventide,

Upon a couch, near to a curtaining
Whose airy texture, from a golden string,
Floated into the room, and let appear
Unveiled the summer heaven, blue and clear,
Betwixt two marble shafts. There they reposed,
Where use had made it sweet, with eyelids closed,
Saving a tithe which love still open kept,
That they might see each other while they almost slept;
When from the slope side of a suburb hill,
Deafening the swallow's twitter, came a thrill
Of trumpets—Lycius started—the sounds fled,
But left a thought, a buzzing in his head.
For the first time, since first he harboured in
That purple-linèd palace of sweet sin,
His spirit passed beyond its golden bourne
Into the noisy world almost forsworn.
The lady, ever watchful, penetrant,
Saw this with pain, so arguing a want
Of something more, more than her empery
Of joys; and she began to moan and sigh
Because he mused beyond her, knowing well
That but a moment's thought is passion's passing-bell.
'Why do you sigh, fair creature?' whispered he:
'Why do you think?' returned she tenderly,
'You have deserted me—where am I now?
Not in your heart while care weighs on your brow:
No, no, you have dismissed me; and I go
From your breast houseless—ay, it must be so.'
He answered, bending to her open eyes,
Where he was mirrored small in paradise,
'My silver planet, both of eve and morn!
Why will you plead yourself so sad forlorn,
While I am striving how to fill my heart
With deeper crimson, and a double smart?
How to entangle, trammel up and snare
Your soul in mine, and labyrinth you there
Like the hid scent in an unbudded rose?
Ay, a sweet kiss—you see your mighty woes.
My thoughts! shall I unveil them? Listen then!
What mortal hath a prize, that other men
May be confounded and abashed withal,
But lets it sometimes pace abroad majestical,
And triumph, as in thee I should rejoice
Amid the hoarse alarm of Corinth's voice.
Let my foes choke, and my friends shout afar,

While through the throngèd streets your bridal car
Wheels round its dazzling spokes.'—The lady's cheek
Trembled; she nothing said, but, pale and meek,
Arose and knelt before him, wept a rain
Of sorrows at his words; at last with pain
Beseeching him, the while his hand she wrung,
To change his purpose. He thereat was stung,
Perverse, with stronger fancy to reclaim
Her wild and timid nature to his aim:
Besides, for all his love, in self-despite,
Against his better self, he took delight
Luxurious in her sorrows, soft and new.
His passion, cruel grown, took on a hue
Fierce and sanguineous as 'twas possible
In one whose brow had no dark veins to swell.
Fine was the mitigated fury, like
Apollo's presence when in act to strike
The serpent—Ha, the serpent! Certes, she
Was none. She burnt, she loved the tyranny,
And, all subdued, consented to the hour
When to the bridal he should lead his paramour.
Whispering in midnight silence, said the youth,
'Sure some sweet name thou hast, though, by my truth,
I have not asked it, ever thinking thee
Not mortal, but of heavenly progeny,
As still I do. Hast any mortal name,
Fit appellation for this dazzling frame?
Or friends or kinsfolk on the citied earth,
To share our marriage feast and nuptial mirth?'
'I have no friends,' said Lamia, 'no, not one;
My presence in wide Corinth hardly known:
My parents' bones are in their dusty urns
Sepulchred, where no kindled incense burns,
Seeing all their luckless race are dead, save me,
And I neglect the holy rite for thee.
Even as you list invite your many guests;
But if, as now it seems, your vision rests
With any pleasure on me, do not bid
Old Apollonius—from him keep me hid.'
Lycius, perplexed at words so blind and blank,
Made close inquiry; from whose touch she shrank,
Feigning a sleep; and he to the dull shade
Of deep sleep in a moment was betrayed.

It was the custom then to bring away
The bride from home at blushing shut of day,
Veiled, in a chariot, heralded along
By strewn flowers, torches, and a marriage song,
With other pageants: but this fair unknown
Had not a friend. So being left alone,
(Lycius was gone to summon all his kin)
And knowing surely she could never win
His foolish heart from its mad pompousness,
She set herself, high-thoughted, how to dress
The misery in fit magnificence.
She did so, but 'tis doubtful how and whence
Came, and who were her subtle servitors.
About the halls, and to and from the doors,
There was a noise of wings, till in short space
The glowing banquet-room shone with wide-arched grace.
A haunting music, sole perhaps and lone
Supportress of the faery-roof, made moan
Throughout, as fearful the whole charm might fade.
Fresh carvèd cedar, mimicking a glade
Of palm and plantain, met from either side,
High in the midst, in honour of the bride;
Two palms and then two plantains, and so on,
From either side their stems branched one to one
All down the aislèd place; and beneath all
There ran a stream of lamps straight on from wall to wall.
So canopied, lay an untasted feast
Teeming with odours. Lamia, regal dressed,
Silently paced about, and as she went,
In pale contented sort of discontent,
Missioned her viewless servants to enrich
The fretted splendour of each nook and niche.
Between the tree-stems, marbled plain at first,
Came jasper panels; then anon, there burst
Forth creeping imagery of slighter trees,
And with the larger wove in small intricacies.
Approving all, she faded at self-will,
And shut the chamber up, close, hushed and still,
Complete and ready for the revels rude,
When dreadful guests would come to spoil her solitude.

The day appeared, and all the gossip rout.
O senseless Lycius! Madman! wherefore flout
The silent-blessing fate, warm cloistered hours,

And show to common eyes these secret bowers?
The herd approached; each guest, with busy brain,
Arriving at the portal, gazed amain,
And entered marvelling—for they knew the street,
Remembered it from childhood all complete
Without a gap, yet ne'er before had seen
That royal porch, that high-built fair demesne.
So in they hurried all, mazed, curious and keen—
Save one, who looked thereon with eye severe,
And with calm-planted steps walked in austere.
'Twas Apollonius: something too he laughed,
As though some knotty problem, that had daffed
His patient thought, had now begun to thaw,
And solve and melt—'twas just as he foresaw.

He met within the murmurous vestibule
His young disciple. ''Tis no common rule,
Lycius,' said he, 'for uninvited guest
To force himself upon you, and infest
With an unbidden presence the bright throng
Of younger friends; yet must I do this wrong,
And you forgive me.' Lycius blushed, and led
The old man through the inner doors broad-spread;
With reconciling words and courteous mien
Turning into sweet milk the sophist's spleen.

Of wealthy lustre was the banquet-room,
Filled with pervading brilliance and perfume:
Before each lucid panel fuming stood
A censer fed with myrrh and spiced wood,
Each by a sacred tripod held aloft,
Whose slender feet wide-swerved upon the soft
Wool-woofèd carpets; fifty wreaths of smoke
From fifty censers their light voyage took
To the high roof, still mimicked as they rose
Along the mirrored walls by twin-clouds odorous.
Twelve spherèd tables, by silk seats ensphered,
High as the level of a man's breast reared
On libbard's paws, upheld the heavy gold
Of cups and goblets, and the store thrice told
Of Ceres' horn, and, in huge vessels, wine
Come from the gloomy tun with merry shine.
Thus loaded with a feast the tables stood,
Each shrining in the midst the image of a God.

When in an antechamber every guest
Had felt the cold full sponge to pleasure pressed,
By ministering slaves, upon his hands and feet,
And fragrant oils with ceremony meet
Poured on his hair, they all moved to the feast
In white robes, and themselves in order placed
Around the silken couches, wondering
Whence all this mighty cost and blaze of wealth could spring.

Soft went the music the soft air along,
While fluent Greek a vowelled undersong
Kept up among the guests, discoursing low
At first, for scarcely was the wine at flow;
But when the happy vintage touched their brains,
Louder they talk, and louder come the strains
Of powerful instruments. The gorgeous dyes,
The space, the splendour of the draperies,
The roof of awful richness, nectarous cheer,
Beautiful slaves, and Lamia's self, appear,
Now, when the wine has done its rosy deed,
And every soul from human trammels freed,
No more so strange; for merry wine, sweet wine,
Will make Elysian shades not too fair, too divine.

Soon was God Bacchus at meridian height;
Flushed were their cheeks, and bright eyes double bright:
Garlands of every green, and every scent
From vales deflowered, or forest-trees branch-rent,
In baskets of bright osiered gold were brought
High as the handles heaped, to suit the thought
Of every guest—that each, as he did please,
Might fancy-fit his brows, silk-pillowed at his ease.

What wreath for Lamia? What for Lycius?
What for the sage, old Apollonius?
Upon her aching forehead be there hung
The leaves of willow and of adder's tongue;
And for the youth, quick, let us strip for him
The thyrsus, that his watching eyes may swim
Into forgetfulness; and, for the sage,
Let spear-grass and the spiteful thistle wage
War on his temples. Do not all charms fly
At the mere touch of cold philosophy?
There was an awful rainbow once in heaven:

We know her woof, her texture; she is given
In the dull catalogue of common things.
Philosophy will clip an Angel's wings,
Conquer all mysteries by rule and line,
Empty the haunted air, and gnomèd mine—
Unweave a rainbow, as it erewhile made
The tender-personed Lamia melt into a shade.

By her glad Lycius sitting, in chief place,
Scarce saw in all the room another face,
Till, checking his love trance, a cup he took
Full brimmed, and opposite sent forth a look
'Cross the broad table, to beseech a glance
From his old teacher's wrinkled countenance,
And pledge him. The bald-head philosopher
Had fixed his eye, without a twinkle or stir
Full on the alarmed beauty of the bride,
Brow-beating her fair form, and troubling her sweet pride.
Lycius then pressed her hand, with devout touch,
As pale it lay upon the rosy couch:
'Twas icy, and the cold ran through his veins;
Then sudden it grew hot, and all the pains
Of an unnatural heat shot to his heart.
'Lamia, what means this? Wherefore dost thou start?
Know'st thou that man?' Poor Lamia answered not.
He gazed into her eyes, and not a jot
Owned they the lovelorn piteous appeal;
More, more he gazed; his human senses reel;
Some hungry spell that loveliness absorbs;
There was no recognition in those orbs.
'Lamia!' he cried—and no soft-toned reply.
The many heard, and the loud revelry
Grew hush; the stately music no more breathes;
The myrtle sickened in a thousand wreaths.
By faint degrees, voice, lute, and pleasure ceased;
A deadly silence step by step increased,
Until it seemed a horrid presence there,
And not a man but felt the terror in his hair.
'Lamia!' he shrieked; and nothing but the shriek
With its sad echo did the silence break.
'Begone, foul dream!' he cried, gazing again
In the bride's face, where now no azure vein
Wandered on fair-spaced temples; no soft bloom
Misted the cheek; no passion to illume
The deep-recessèd vision. All was blight;

Lamia, no longer fair, there sat a deadly white.
'Shut, shut those juggling eyes, thou ruthless man!
Turn them aside, wretch! or the righteous ban
Of all the Gods, whose dreadful images
Here represent their shadowy presences,
May pierce them on the sudden with the thorn
Of painful blindness; leaving thee forlorn,
In trembling dotage to the feeblest fright
Of conscience, for their long offended might,
For all thine impious proud-heart sophistries,
Unlawful magic, and enticing lies.
Corinthians! look upon that grey-beard wretch!
Mark how, possessed, his lashless eyelids stretch
Around his demon eyes! Corinthians, see!
My sweet bride withers at their potency.'
'Fool!' said the sophist, in an undertone
Gruff with contempt; which a death-nighing moan
From Lycius answered, as heart-struck and lost,
He sank supine beside the aching ghost.
'Fool! Fool!' repeated he, while his eyes still
Relented not, nor moved: 'From every ill
Of life have I preserved thee to this day,
And shall I see thee made a serpent's prey?'
Then Lamia breathed death-breath; the sophist's eye,
Like a sharp spear, went through her utterly,
Keen, cruel, perceant, stinging: she, as well
As her weak hand could any meaning tell,
Motioned him to be silent; vainly so,
He looked and looked again a level—*No*!
'A Serpent!' echoed he; no sooner said,
Than with a frightful scream she vanished:
And Lycius' arms were empty of delight,
As were his limbs of life, from that same night.
On the high couch he lay!—his friends came round—
Supported him—no pulse, or breath they found,
And, in its marriage robe, the heavy body wound.

'*Pensive they sit, and roll their languid eyes*'

Pensive they sit, and roll their languid eyes,
Nibble their toasts and cool their tea with sighs;
Or else forget the purpose of the night,
Forget their tea, forget their appetite.
See, with crossed arms they sit—Ah! hapless crew,
The fire is going out and no one rings

For coals, and therefore no coals Betty brings.
A fly is in the milk-pot—must he die
Circled by a Humane Society?
No, no; there, Mr Werter takes his spoon,
Inverts it, dips the handle, and lo! soon
The little struggler, saved from perils dark,
Across the teaboard draws a long wet mark.
Romeo! Arise! take snuffers by the handle,
There's a large cauliflower in each candle.
A winding-sheet—ah, me! I must away
To No. 7, just beyond the Circus gay.
'Alas, my friend, your coat sits very well;
Where may your tailor live?' 'I may not tell.
O pardon me—I'm absent now and then.
Where *might* my tailor live? I say again
I cannot tell. Let me no more be teased—
He lives in Wapping, *might* live where he pleased.'

To Autumn

I

Season of mists and mellow fruitfulness,
  Close bosom-friend of the maturing sun,
Conspiring with him how to load and bless
  With fruit the vines that round the thatch-eves run;
To bend with apples the mossed cottage-trees,
  And fill all fruit with ripeness to the core;
    To swell the gourd, and plump the hazel shells
  With a sweet kernel; to set budding more,
And still more, later flowers for the bees,
Until they think warm days will never cease,
    For Summer has o'er-brimmed their clammy cells.

II

Who hath not seen thee oft amid thy store?
  Sometimes whoever seeks abroad may find
Thee sitting careless on a granary floor,
  Thy hair soft-lifted by the winnowing wind;
Or on a half-reaped furrow sound asleep,
  Drowsed with the fume of poppies, while thy hook
    Spares the next swath and all its twinèd flowers;
And sometimes like a gleaner thou dost keep
  Steady thy laden head across a brook;

Or by a cider-press, with patient look,
 Thou watchest the last oozings hours by hours.

III

Where are the songs of Spring? Ay, where are they?
 Think not of them, thou hast thy music too—
While barrèd clouds bloom the soft-dying day,
 And touch the stubble-plains with rosy hue:
Then in a wailful choir the small gnats mourn
 Among the river sallows, borne aloft
 Or sinking as the light wind lives or dies;
And full-grown lambs loud bleat from hilly bourn;
 Hedge-crickets sing; and now with treble soft
 The red-breast whistles from a garden-croft;
 And gathering swallows twitter in the skies.

The Fall of Hyperion. A Dream

CANTO I

Fanatics have their dreams, wherewith they weave
A paradise for a sect; the savage too
From forth the loftiest fashion of his sleep
Guesses at Heaven: pity these have not
Traced upon vellum or wild Indian leaf
The shadows of melodious utterance.
But bare of laurel they live, dream, and die;
For Poesy alone can tell her dreams,
With the fine spell of words alone can save
Imagination from the sable charm
And dumb enchantment. Who alive can say,
'Thou art no Poet—mayst not tell thy dreams'?
Since every man whose soul is not a clod
Hath visions, and would speak, if he had loved,
And been well nurtured in his mother tongue.
Whether the dream now purposed to rehearse
Be Poet's or Fanatic's will be known
When this warm scribe my hand is in the grave.

 Methought I stood where trees of every clime,
Palm, myrtle, oak, and sycamore, and beech,
With plantain, and spice-blossoms, made a screen—
In neighbourhood of fountains, by the noise
Soft-showering in mine ears, and, by the touch

Of scent, not far from roses. Turning round,
I saw an arbour with a drooping roof
Of trellis vines, and bells, and larger blooms,
Like floral censers, swinging light in air;
Before its wreathèd doorway, on a mound
Of moss, was spread a feast of summer fruits,
Which, nearer seen, seemed refuse of a meal
By angel tasted, or our Mother Eve;
For empty shells were scattered on the grass,
And grape-stalks but half bare, and remnants more,
Sweet-smelling, whose pure kinds I could not know.
Still was more plenty than the fabled horn
Thrice emptied could pour forth at banqueting
For Proserpine returned to her own fields,
Where the white heifers low. And appetite
More yearning than on earth I ever felt
Growing within, I ate deliciously;
And, after not long, thirsted, for thereby
Stood a cool vessel of transparent juice,
Sipped by the wandered bee, the which I took,
And, pledging all the mortals of the world,
And all the dead whose names are in our lips,
Drank. That full draught is parent of my theme.
No Asian poppy, nor elixir fine
Of the soon-fading jealous Caliphat;
No poison gendered in close monkish cell,
To thin the scarlet conclave of old men,
Could so have rapt unwilling life away.
Among the fragrant husks and berries crushed,
Upon the grass I struggled hard against
The domineering potion; but in vain—
The cloudy swoon came on, and down I sunk,
Like a Silenus on an antique vase.
How long I slumbered 'tis a chance to guess.
When sense of life returned, I started up
As if with wings; but the fair trees were gone,
The mossy mound and arbour were no more.
I looked around upon the carvèd sides
Of an old sanctuary with roof august,
Builded so high, it seemed that filmed clouds
Might spread beneath, as o'er the stars of heaven.
So old the place was, I remembered none
The like upon the earth: what I had seen
Of grey cathedrals, buttressed walls, rent towers,
The superannuations of sunk realms,

Or Nature's rocks toiled hard in waves and winds,
Seemed but the faulture of decrepit things
To that eternal domèd monument.
Upon the marble at my feet there lay
Store of strange vessels and large draperies,
Which needs had been of dyed asbestos wove,
Or in that place the moth could not corrupt,
So white the linen; so, in some, distinct
Ran imageries from a sombre loom.
All in a mingled heap confused there lay
Robes, golden tongs, censer and chafing-dish,
Girdles, and chains, and holy jewelleries—

Turning from these with awe, once more I raised
My eyes to fathom the space every way—
The embossèd roof, the silent massy range
Of columns north and south, ending in mist
Of nothing, then to eastward, where black gates
Were shut against the sunrise evermore.
Then to the west I looked, and saw far off
An Image, huge of feature as a cloud,
At level of whose feet an altar slept,
To be approached on either side by steps,
And marble balustrade, and patient travail
To count with toil the innumerable degrees.
Towards the altar sober-paced I went,
Repressing haste, as too unholy there;
And, coming nearer, saw beside the shrine
One ministering; and there arose a flame.
When in mid-May the sickening East wind
Shifts sudden to the south, the small warm rain
Melts out the frozen incense from all flowers,
And fills the air with so much pleasant health
That even the dying man forgets his shroud—
Even so that lofty sacrificial fire,
Sending forth Maian incense, spread around
Forgetfulness of everything but bliss,
And clouded all the altar with soft smoke,
From whose white fragrant curtains thus I heard
Language pronounced: 'If thou canst not ascend
These steps, die on that marble where thou art.
Thy flesh, near cousin to the common dust,
Will parch for lack of nutriment—thy bones
Will wither in few years, and vanish so
That not the quickest eye could find a grain

Of what thou now art on that pavement cold.
The sands of thy short life are spent this hour,
And no hand in the universe can turn
Thy hourglass, if these gummèd leaves be burnt
Ere thou canst mount up these immortal steps.'
I heard, I looked: two senses both at once,
So fine, so subtle, felt the tyranny
Of that fierce threat, and the hard task proposed.
Prodigious seemed the toil; the leaves were yet
Burning—when suddenly a palsied chill
Struck from the pavèd level up my limbs,
And was ascending quick to put cold grasp
Upon those streams that pulse beside the throat.
I shrieked; and the sharp anguish of my shriek
Stung my own ears—I strove hard to escape
The numbness, strove to gain the lowest step.
Slow, heavy, deadly was my pace: the cold
Grew stifling, suffocating, at the heart;
And when I clasped my hands I felt them not.
One minute before death, my iced foot touched
The lowest stair; and as it touched, life seemed
To pour in at the toes: I mounted up,
As once fair Angels on a ladder flew
From the green turf to Heaven. 'Holy Power,'
Cried I, approaching near the hornèd shrine,
'What am I that should so be saved from death?
What am I that another death come not
To choke my utterance sacrilegious, here?'
Then said the veilèd shadow: 'Thou hast felt
What 'tis to die and live again before
Thy fated hour. That thou hadst power to do so
Is thy own safety; thou hast dated on
Thy doom.' 'High Prophetess,' said I, 'purge off,
Benign, if so it please thee, my mind's film.'
'None can usurp this height,' returned that shade,
'But those to whom the miseries of the world
Are misery, and will not let them rest.
All else who find a haven in the world,
Where they may thoughtless sleep away their days,
If by a chance into this fane they come,
Rot on the pavement where thou rotted'st half.'
'Are there not thousands in the world,' said I,
Encouraged by the sooth voice of the shade,
'Who love their fellows even to the death;
Who feel the giant agony of the world;

And more, like slaves to poor humanity,
Labour for mortal good? I sure should see
Other men here: but I am here alone.'
'They whom thou spak'st of are no visionaries,'
Rejoined that voice—'They are no dreamers weak,
They seek no wonder but the human face;
No music but a happy-noted voice—
They come not here, they have no thought to come—
And thou art here, for thou art less than they—
What benefit canst thou do, or all thy tribe,
To the great world? Thou art a dreaming thing,
A fever of thyself. Think of the Earth;
What bliss even in hope is there for thee?
What haven? Every creature hath its home;
Every sole man hath days of joy and pain,
Whether his labours be sublime or low—
The pain alone; the joy alone; distinct:
Only the dreamer venoms all his days,
Bearing more woe than all his sins deserve.
Therefore, that happiness be somewhat shared,
Such things as thou art are admitted oft
Into like gardens thou didst pass erewhile,
And suffered in these temples; for that cause
Thou standest safe beneath this statue's knees.'
'That I am favoured for unworthiness,
By such propitious parley medicined
In sickness not ignoble, I rejoice—
Ay, and could weep for love of such award.'
So answered I, continuing, 'If it please,
Majestic shadow, tell me: sure not all
Those melodies sung into the world's ear
Are useless: sure a poet is a sage,
A humanist, physician to all men.
That I am none I feel, as vultures feel
They are no birds when eagles are abroad.
What am I then? Thou spakest of my tribe:
What tribe?'—The tall shade veiled in drooping white
Then spake, so much more earnest, that the breath
Moved the thin linen folds that drooping hung
About a golden censer from the hand
Pendent.—'Art thou not of the dreamer tribe?
The poet and the dreamer are distinct,
Diverse, sheer opposite, antipodes.
The one pours out a balm upon the world,
The other vexes it.' Then shouted I,

Spite of myself, and with a Pythia's spleen,
'Apollo! faded, far-flown Apollo!
Where is thy misty pestilence to creep
Into the dwellings, through the door crannies,
Of all mock lyrists, large self-worshippers
And careless hectorers in proud bad verse.
Though I breathe death with them it will be life
To see them sprawl before me into graves.
Majestic shadow, tell me where I am,
Whose altar this; for whom this incense curls;
What image this, whose face I cannot see,
For the broad marble knees; and who thou art,
Of accent feminine so courteous?'

Then the tall shade, in drooping linens veiled,
Spake out, so much more earnest, that her breath
Stirred the thin folds of gauze that drooping hung
About a golden censer from her hand
Pendent; and by her voice I knew she shed
Long-treasured tears. 'This temple, sad and lone,
Is all spared from the thunder of a war
Foughten long since by giant hierarchy
Against rebellion; this old image here,
Whose carvèd features wrinkled as he fell,
Is Saturn's; I Moneta, left supreme
Sole priestess of his desolation.'
I had no words to answer, for my tongue,
Useless, could find about its roofed home
No syllable of a fit majesty
To make rejoinder to Moneta's mourn.
There was a silence, while the altar's blaze
Was fainting for sweet food: I looked thereon,
And on the pavèd floor, where nigh were piled
Faggots of cinnamon, and many heaps
Of other crispèd spice-wood—then again
I looked upon the altar, and its horns
Whitened with ashes, and its languorous flame,
And then upon the offerings again;
And so by turns—till sad Moneta cried:
'The sacrifice is done, but not the less
Will I be kind to thee for thy goodwill.
My power, which to me is still a curse,
Shall be to thee a wonder; for the scenes
Still swooning vivid through my globèd brain,
With an electral changing misery,

Thou shalt with those dull mortal eyes behold,
Free from all pain, if wonder pain thee not.'
As near as an immortal's spherèd words
Could to a mother's soften, were these last:
But yet I had a terror of her robes,
And chiefly of the veils, that from her brow
Hung pale, and curtained her in mysteries
That made my heart too small to hold its blood.
This saw that Goddess, and with sacred hand
Parted the veils. Then saw I a wan face,
Not pined by human sorrows, but bright-blanched
By an immortal sickness which kills not;
It works a constant change, which happy death
Can put no end to; deathwards progressing
To no death was that visage; it had passed
The lily and the snow; and beyond these
I must not think now, though I saw that face—
But for her eyes I should have fled away.
They held me back, with a benignant light,
Soft-mitigated by divinest lids
Half-closed, and visionless entire they seemed
Of all external things—they saw me not,
But in blank splendour beamed like the mild moon,
Who comforts those she sees not, who knows not
What eyes are upward cast. As I had found
A grain of gold upon a mountain's side,
And twinged with avarice strained out my eyes
To search its sullen entrails rich with ore,
So at the view of sad Moneta's brow
I ached to see what things the hollow brain
Behind enwombèd; what high tragedy
In the dark secret chambers of her skull
Was acting, that could give so dread a stress
To her cold lips, and fill with such a light
Her planetary eyes; and touch her voice
With such a sorrow—'Shade of Memory!'
Cried I, with act adorant at her feet,
'By all the gloom hung round thy fallen house,
By this last temple, by the golden age,
By great Apollo, thy dear foster child,
And by thyself, forlorn divinity,
The pale Omega of a withered race,
Let me behold, according as thou said'st,
What in thy brain so ferments to and fro.'
No sooner had this conjuration passed

My devout lips, than side by side we stood
(Like a stunt bramble by a solemn pine)
Deep in the shady sadness of a vale,
Far sunken from the healthy breath of morn,
Far from the fiery noon and eve's one star.
Onward I looked beneath the gloomy boughs,
And saw, what first I thought an image huge,
Like to the image pedestailed so high
In Saturn's temple. Then Moneta's voice
Came brief upon mine ear: 'So Saturn sat
When he had lost his realms.' Whereon there grew
A power within me of enormous ken
To see as a God sees, and take the depth
Of things as nimbly as the outward eye
Can size and shape pervade. The lofty theme
At those few words hung vast before my mind,
With half-unravelled web. I set myself
Upon an eagle's watch, that I might see,
And seeing ne'er forget. No stir of life
Was in this shrouded vale, not so much air
As in zoning of a summer's day
Robs not one light seed from the feathered grass,
But where the dead leaf fell there did it rest.
A stream went voiceless by, still deadened more
By reason of the fallen divinity
Spreading more shade; the Naiad 'mid her reeds
Pressed her cold finger closer to her lips.
Along the margin-sand large footmarks went
No farther than to where old Saturn's feet
Had rested, and there slept—how long a sleep!
Degraded, cold, upon the sodden ground
His old right hand lay nerveless, listless, dead,
Unsceptred; and his realmless eyes were closed,
While his bowed head seemed listening to the Earth,
His ancient mother, for some comfort yet.

It seemed no force could wake him from his place;
But there came one who, with a kindred hand
Touched his wide shoulders, after bending low
With reverence, though to one who knew it not.
Then came the grieved voice of Mnemosyne,
And grieved I hearkened. 'That divinity
Whom thou saw'st step from yon forlornest wood,
And with slow pace approach our fallen King,
Is Thea, softest-natured of our brood.'

I marked the goddess in fair statuary
Surpassing wan Moneta by the head,
And in her sorrow nearer woman's tears.
There was a listening fear in her regard,
As if calamity had but begun;
As if the vanward clouds of evil days
Had spent their malice, and the sullen rear
Was with its stored thunder labouring up.
One hand she pressed upon that aching spot
Where beats the human heart, as if just there,
Though an immortal, she felt cruel pain;
The other upon Saturn's bended neck
She laid, and to the level of his hollow ear
Leaning with parted lips, some words she spake
In solemn tenor and deep organ tune,
Some mourning words, which in our feeble tongue
Would come in this-like accenting—how frail
To that large utterance of the early Gods!—
'Saturn! look up—and for what, poor lost King?
I have no comfort for thee, no—not one;
I cannot cry, *Wherefore thus sleepest thou*?
For Heaven is parted from thee, and the Earth
Knows thee not, so afflicted, for a God;
And Ocean too, with all its solemn noise,
Has from thy sceptre passed, and all the air
Is emptied of thine hoary Majesty.
Thy thunder, captious at the new command,
Rumbles reluctant o'er our fallen house;
And thy sharp lightning, in unpractised hands,
Scorches and burns our once serene domain.
With such remorseless speed still come new woes
That unbelief has not a space to breathe.
Saturn! sleep on. Me thoughtless, why should I
Thus violate thy slumbrous solitude?
Why should I ope thy melancholy eyes?
Saturn, sleep on, while at thy feet I weep.'

As when, upon a trancèd summer-night,
Forests, branch-charmèd by the earnest stars,
Dream, and so dream all night without a noise,
Save from one gradual solitary gust,
Swelling upon the silence; dying off;
As if the ebbing air had but one wave—
So came these words, and went; the while in tears
She pressed her fair large forehead to the earth,

Just where her fallen hair might spread in curls,
A soft and silken mat for Saturn's feet.
Long, long those two were postured motionless,
Like sculpture builded-up upon the grave
Of their own power. A long awful time
I looked upon them: still they were the same;
The frozen God still bending to the earth,
And the sad Goddess weeping at his feet;
Moneta silent. Without stay or prop,
But my own weak mortality, I bore
The load of this eternal quietude,
The unchanging gloom, and the three fixèd shapes
Ponderous upon my senses a whole moon.
For by my burning brain I measured sure
Her silver seasons shedded on the night,
And every day by day methought I grew
More gaunt and ghostly. Oftentimes I prayed
Intense, that death would take me from the vale
And all its burthens. Gasping with despair
Of change, hour after hour I cursed myself—
Until old Saturn raised his faded eyes,
And looked around and saw his kingdom gone,
And all the gloom and sorrow of the place,
And that fair kneeling Goddess at his feet.
As the moist scent of flowers, and grass, and leaves,
Fills forest dells with a pervading air
Known to the woodland nostril, so the words
Of Saturn filled the mossy glooms around,
Even to the hollows of time-eaten oaks,
And to the windings in the foxes' hole,
With sad low tones, while thus he spake, and sent
Strange musings to the solitary Pan:

'Moan, brethren, moan; for we are swallowed up
And buried from all godlike exercise
Of influence benign on planets pale,
And peaceful sway above man's harvesting,
And all those acts which deity supreme
Doth ease its heart of love in. Moan and wail.
Moan, brethren, moan; for lo! the rebel spheres
Spin round, the stars their ancient courses keep,
Clouds still with shadowy moisture haunt the earth,
Still suck their fill of light from sun and moon,
Still buds the tree, and still the sea-shores murmur.
There is no death in all the universe,

No smell of death—there shall be death—moan, moan,
Moan, Cybele, moan; for thy pernicious babes
Have changed a God into a shaking palsy.
Moan, brethren, moan, for I have no strength left,
Weak as the reed—weak—feeble as my voice—
O, O, the pain, the pain of feebleness.
Moan, moan, for still I thaw—or give me help:
Throw down those imps, and give me victory.
Let me hear other groans, and trumpets blown
Of triumph calm, and hymns of festival,
From the gold peaks of heaven's high-pilèd clouds—
Voices of soft proclaim, and silver stir
Of strings in hollow shells; and let there be
Beautiful things made new for the surprise
Of the sky-children—' So he feebly ceased,
With such a poor and sickly sounding pause,
Methought I heard some old man of the earth
Bewailing earthly loss; nor could my eyes
And ears act with that pleasant unison of sense
Which marries sweet sound with the grace of form
And dolorous accent from a tragic harp
With large-limbed visions. More I scrutinized:
Still fixed he sat beneath the sable trees,
Whose arms spread straggling in wild serpent forms,
With leaves all hushed; his awful presence there
(Now all was silent) gave a deadly lie
To what I erewhile heard—only his lips
Trembled amid the white curls of his beard.
They told the truth, though, round, the snowy locks
Hung nobly, as upon the face of heaven
A midday fleece of clouds. Thea arose,
And stretched her white arm through the hollow dark,
Pointing some whither; whereat he too rose
Like a vast giant, seen by men at sea
To grow pale from the waves at dull midnight.
They melted from my sight into the woods;
Ere I could turn, Moneta cried: 'These twain
Are speeding to the families of grief,
Where roofed in by black rocks they waste, in pain
And darkness, for no hope.'—And she spake on,
As ye may read who can unwearied pass
Onward from the antechamber of this dream,
Where even at the open doors awhile
I must delay, and glean my memory
Of her high phrase—perhaps no further dare.

CANTO II

‘Mortal, that thou mayst understand aright,
I humanize my sayings to thine ear,
Making comparisons of earthly things;
Or thou mightst better listen to the wind,
Whose language is to thee a barren noise,
Though it blows legend-laden through the trees—
In melancholy realms big tears are shed,
More sorrow like to this, and such-like woe,
Too huge for mortal tongue, or pen of scribe.
The Titans fierce, self-hid or prison-bound,
Groan for the old allegiance once more,
Listening in their doom for Saturn’s voice.
But one of our whole eagle-brood still keeps
His sovereignty, and rule, and majesty;
Blazing Hyperion on his orbed fire
Still sits, still snuffs the incense teeming up
From man to the sun’s God—yet unsecure.
For as upon the earth dire prodigies
Fright and perplex, so also shudders he:
Nor at dog’s howl or gloom-bird’s even screech,
Or the familiar visitings of one
Upon the first toll of his passing-bell:
But horrors, portioned to a giant nerve,
Make great Hyperion ache. His palace bright,
Bastioned with pyramids of glowing gold,
And touched with shade of bronzèd obelisks,
Glares a blood-red through all the thousand courts,
Arches, and domes, and fiery galleries;
And all its curtains of Aurorian clouds
Flush angerly: when he would taste the wreaths
Of incense breathed aloft from sacred hills,
Instead of sweets, his ample palate takes
Savour of poisonous brass and metals sick.
Wherefore, when harboured in the sleepy West,
After the full completion of fair day,
For rest divine upon exalted couch
And slumber in the arms of melody,
He paces through the pleasant hours of ease
With strides colossal, on from hall to hall;
While far within each aisle and deep recess
His wingèd minions in close clusters stand
Amazed, and full of fear; like anxious men,

Who on a wide plain gather in sad troops,
When earthquakes jar their battlements and towers.
Even now, while Saturn, roused from icy trance,
Goes, step for step, with Thea from yon woods,
Hyperion, leaving twilight in the rear,
Is sloping to the threshold of the West—
Thither we tend.'—Now in clear light I stood,
Relieved from the dusk vale. Mnemosyne
Was sitting on a square-edged polished stone,
That in its lucid depth reflected pure
Her priestess-garments. My quick eyes ran on
From stately nave to nave, from vault to vault,
Through bowers of fragrant and enwreathèd light
And diamond-pavèd lustrous long arcades.
Anon rushed by the bright Hyperion;
His flaming robes streamed out beyond his heels,
And gave a roar, as if of earthly fire,
That scared away the meek ethereal Hours,
And made their dove-wings tremble. On he flared ...

'*The day is gone, and all its sweets are gone*!'

The day is gone, and all its sweets are gone!
   Sweet voice, sweet lips, soft hand, and softer breast,
Warm breath, light whisper, tender semi-tone,
   Bright eyes, accomplished shape, and languorous waist!
Faded the flower and all its budded charms,
   Faded the sight of beauty from my eyes,
Faded the shape of beauty from my arms,
   Faded the voice, warmth, whiteness, paradise—
Vanished unseasonably at shut of eve,
   When the dusk holiday—or holinight—
Of fragrant-curtained love begins to weave
   The woof of darkness thick, for hid delight;
But, as I've read love's missal through today,
He'll let me sleep, seeing I fast and pray.

What can I do to drive away

What can I do to drive away
Remembrance from my eyes? for they have seen,
Ay, an hour ago, my brilliant Queen!
Touch has a memory. O say, love, say,
What can I do to kill it and be free
In my old liberty?

When every fair one that I saw was fair,
Enough to catch me in but half a snare,
Not keep me there;
When, howe'er poor or parti-coloured things,
My muse had wings,
And ever ready was to take her course
Whither I bent her force,
Unintellectual, yet divine to me—
Divine, I say! What sea-bird o'er the sea
Is a philosopher the while he goes
Winging along where the great water throes?

How shall I do
To get anew
Those moulted feathers, and so mount once more
Above, above
The reach of fluttering Love,
And make him cower lowly while I soar?
Shall I gulp wine? No, that is vulgarism,
A heresy and schism,
Foisted into the canon law of love;
No—wine is only sweet to happy men;
More dismal cares
Seize on me unawares—
Where shall I learn to get my peace again?
To banish thoughts of that most hateful land,
Dungeoner of my friends, that wicked strand
Where they were wrecked and live a wrecked life;
That monstrous region, whose dull rivers pour,
Ever from their sordid urns into the shore,
Unowned of any weedy-haired gods;
Whose winds, all zephyrless, hold scourging rods,
Iced in the great lakes, to afflict mankind;
Whose rank-grown forests, frosted, black, and blind,
Would fright a Dryad; whose harsh-herbaged meads
Make lean and lank the starved ox while he feeds;
There flowers have no scent, birds no sweet song,
And great unerring Nature once seems wrong.

O, for some sunny spell
To dissipate the shadows of this hell!
Say they are gone—with the new dawning light
Steps forth my lady bright!
O, let me once more rest
My soul upon that dazzling breast!

Let once again these aching arms be placed,
The tender gaolers of thy waist!
And let me feel that warm breath here and there
To spread a rapture in my very hair—
O, the sweetness of the pain!
Give me those lips again!
Enough! Enough! It is enough for me
To dream of thee!

'I cry your mercy, pity, love—ay, love!'

I cry your mercy, pity, love—ay, love!
   Merciful love that tantalizes not,
One-thoughted, never-wandering, guileless love,
   Unmasked, and being seen—without a blot!
O! let me have thee whole,—all, all, be mine!
   That shape, that fairness, that sweet minor zest
Of love, your kiss—those hands, those eyes divine,
   That warm, white, lucent, million-pleasured breast—
Yourself—your soul—in pity give me all,
   Withhold no atom's atom or I die;
Or living on perhaps, your wretched thrall,
   Forget, in the mist of idle misery,
Life's purposes—the palate of my mind
Losing its gust, and my ambition blind!

'Bright star! *would I were steadfast as thou art'*

Bright star! would I were steadfast as thou art—
   Not in lone splendour hung aloft the night
And watching, with eternal lids apart,
   Like nature's patient, sleepless Eremite,
The moving waters at their priestlike task
   Of pure ablution round earth's human shores,
Or gazing on the new soft-fallen mask
   Of snow upon the mountains and the moors—
No—yet still steadfast, still unchangeable,
   Pillowed upon my fair love's ripening breast,
To feel for ever its soft swell and fall,
   Awake for ever in a sweet unrest,
Still, still to hear her tender-taken breath,
And so live ever—or else swoon to death.

King Stephen. A Fragment of a Tragedy

ACT I

SCENE I. *Field of Battle.*

[*Alarm. Enter* KING STEPHEN, *Knights, and Soldiers.*]

STEPHEN. If shame can on a soldier's vein-swollen front
Spread deeper crimson than the battle's toil,
Blush in your casing helmets! for see, see!
Yonder my chivalry, my pride of war,
Wrenched with an iron hand from firm array,
Are routed loose about the plashy meads,
Of honour forfeit. O, that my known voice
Could reach your dastard ears, and fright you more!
Fly, cowards, fly! Gloucester is at your backs!
Throw your slack bridles o'er the flurried manes,
Ply well the rowel with faint trembling heels,
Scampering to death at last!
FIRST KNIGHT. The enemy
Bears his flaunt standard close upon their rear.
SECOND KNIGHT. Sure of a bloody prey, seeing the fens
Will swamp them girth-deep.
STEPHEN. Over head and ears,
No matter! 'Tis a gallant enemy;
How like a comet he goes streaming on.
But we must plague him in the flank—hey, friends.
We are well breathèd—follow!

[*Enter* EARL BALDWIN *and Soldiers, as defeated.*]

STEPHEN. De Redvers!
What is the monstrous bugbear that can fright Baldwin?
BALDWIN. No scarecrow, but the fortunate star
Of boisterous Chester, whose fell truncheon now
Points level to the goal of victory.
This way he comes, and if you would maintain
Your person unaffronted by vile odds,
Take horse, my Lord.
STEPHEN. And which way spur for life?
Now I thank Heaven I am in the toils,
That soldiers may bear witness how my arm
Can burst the meshes. Not the eagle more

Loves to beat up against a tyrannous blast,
Than I to meet the torrent of my foes.
This is a brag—be't so—but if I fall,
Carve it upon my 'scutcheon'd sepulchre.
On, fellow soldiers! Earl of Redvers, back!
Not twenty Earls of Chester shall browbeat
The diadem. [*Exeunt. Alarum.*]

SCENE 2. *Another Part of the Field.*

[*Trumpets sounding a victory. Enter* GLOUCESTER, *Knights, and Forces.*]

GLOUCESTER. Now may we lift our bruised vizors up,
And take the flattering freshness of the air,
While the wide din of battle dies away
Into times past, yet to be echoed sure
In the silent pages of our chroniclers.
FIRST KNIGHT. Will Stephen's death be marked there,
I my good Lord,
Or that we gave him lodging in yon towers?
GLOUCESTER Fain would I know the great usurper's fate.

[*Enter two Captains severally.*]

FIRST CAPTAIN. My Lord!
SECOND CAPTAIN. Most noble Earl!
FIRST CAPTAIN. The King—
SECOND CAPTAIN. The Empress greets—
GLOUCESTER. What of the King?
FIRST CAPTAIN. He sole and lone maintains
A hopeless bustle mid our swarming arms,
And with a nimble savageness attacks,
Escapes, makes fiercer onset, then anew
Eludes death, giving death to most that dare
Trespass within the circuit of his sword!
He must by this have fallen. Baldwin is taken;
And for the Duke of Bretagne, like a stag
He flies, for the Welsh beagles to hunt down.
God save the Empress!
GLOUCESTER. Now our dreaded Queen:
What message from her Highness?
SECOND CAPTAIN. Royal Maud
From the thronged towers of Lincoln hath looked down,
Like Pallas from the walls of Ilion,

And seen her enemies havocked at her feet.
She greets most noble Gloucester from her heart,
Entreating him, his captains, and brave knights,
To grace a banquet. The high city gates
Are envious which shall see your triumph pass;
The streets are full of music.

[*Enter* SECOND KNIGHT.]

GLOUCESTER. Whence come you?
SECOND KNIGHT. From Stephen, my good Prince—
Stephen! Stephen!
GLOUCESTER. Why do you make such echoing of his name?
SECOND KNIGHT. Because I think, my lord, he is no man,
But a fierce demon, 'nointed safe from wounds,
And misbaptizèd with a Christian name.
GLOUCESTER. A mighty soldier!—Does he still hold out?
SECOND KNIGHT. He shames our victory. His valour still
Keeps elbow-room amid our eager swords,
And holds our bladed falchions all aloof—
His gleaming battle-axe being slaughter-sick,
Smote on the morion of a Flemish knight,
Broke short in his hand; upon the which he flung
The heft away with such a vengeful force,
It paunched the Earl of Chester's horse, who then
Spleen-hearted came in full career at him.
GLOUCESTER. Did no one take him at a vantage then?
SECOND KNIGHT. Three then with tiger leap upon him flew,
Whom, with his sword swift-drawn and nimbly held,
He stung away again, and stood to breathe,
Smiling. Anon upon him rushed once more
A throng of foes, and in this renewed strife,
My sword met his and snapped off at the hilts.
GLOUCESTER. Come, lead me to this Mars—and let us move
In silence, not insulting his sad doom
With clamorous trumpets. To the Empress bear
My salutation as befits the time.

[*Exeunt* Gloucester *and Forces.*]

SCENE 3. [*The Field of Battle. Enter* Stephen *unarmed.*]

STEPHEN. Another sword! And what if I could seize
One from Bellona's gleaming armoury,
Or choose the fairest of her sheaved spears!
Where are my enemies? Here, close at hand,
Here comes the testy brood. O, for a sword!
I'm faint—a biting sword! A noble sword!
A hedge-stake—or a ponderous stone to hurl
With brawny vengeance, like the labourer Cain.
Come on! Farewell my kingdom, and all hail
Thou superb, plumed, and helmeted renown,
All hail! I would not truck this brilliant day
To rule in Pylos with a Nestor's beard—
Come on!

[*Enter* DE KAIMS *and Knights, etc.*]

DE KAIMS. Is't madness, or a hunger after death,
That makes thee thus unarmed throw taunts at us?
Yield, Stephen, or my sword's point dips in
The gloomy current of a traitor's heart.
STEPHEN. Do it, De Kaims, I will not budge an inch.
DE KAIMS. Yes, of thy madness thou shalt take the meed.
STEPHEN. Darest thou?
DE KAIMS. How dare, against a man disarmed
STEPHEN. What weapon has the lion but himself?
Come not near me, De Kaims, for by the price
Of all the glory I have won this day,
Being a king, I will not yield alive
To any but the second man of the realm,
Robert of Gloucester.
DE KAIMS. Thou shalt vail to me.
STEPHEN. Shall I, when I have sworn against it, sir?
Thou think'st it brave to take a breathing king,
That, on a court-day bowed to haughty Maud,
The awèd presence-chamber may be bold
To whisper, there's the man who took alive
Stephen—me—prisoner. Certes, De Kaims,
The ambition is a noble one.
DE KAIMS. 'Tis true,
And, Stephen, I must compass it.
STEPHEN. No, no,
Do not tempt me to throttle you on the gorge,

Or with my gauntlet crush your hollow breast,
Just when your knighthood is grown ripe and full
For lordship.
A soldier Is an honest yeoman's spear
Of no use at a need? Take that.
STEPHEN. Ah, dastard!
DE KAIMS. What, you are vulnerable! my prisoner!
STEPHEN. No, not yet. I disclaim it, and demand
Death as a sovereign right unto a king
Who 'sdains to yield to any but his peer,
If not in title, yet in noble deeds,
THE EARL OF GLOUCESTER. Stab to the hilts, De Kaims,
For I will never by mean hands be led
From this so famous field. Do ye hear! Be quick!

[*Trumpets. Enter the* EARL OF CHESTER *and Knights.*]

SCENE 4. *A Presence Chamber.*

[QUEEN MAUD *in a Chair of State, the* earls of GLOUCESTER *and* CHESTER, *Lords, Attendants.*]

MAUD. Gloucester, no more: I will behold that Boulogne:
Set him before me. Not for the poor sake
Of regal pomp and a vainglorious hour,
As thou with wary speech, yet near enough,
Hast hinted.
GLOUCESTER. Faithful counsel have I given;
If wary, for your Highness' benefit.
MAUD. The Heavens forbid that I should not think so,
For by thy valour have I won this realm,
Which by thy wisdom I will ever keep.
To sage advisers let me ever bend
A meek attentive ear, so that they treat
Of the wide kingdom's rule and government,
Not trenching on our actions personal.
Advised, not schooled, I would be; and henceforth
Spoken to in clear, plain, and open terms,
Not sideways sermoned at.
GLOUCESTER. Then, in plain terms,
Once more for the fallen king—
MAUD. Your pardon, brother,
I would no more of that; for, as I said,
'Tis not for worldly pomp I wish to see
The rebel, but as dooming judge to give

A sentence something worthy of his guilt.
GLOUCESTER. If't must be so, I'll bring him to your presence.
[*Exit* GLOUCESTER.]
MAUD. A meaner summoner might do as well—
My Lord of Chester, is't true what I hear
Of Stephen of Boulogne, our prisoner,
That he, as a fit penance for his crimes,
Eats wholesome, sweet, and palatable food
Off Gloucester's golden dishes—drinks pure wine,
Lodges soft?
CHESTER. More than that, my gracious Queen,
Has angered me. The noble Earl, methinks,
Full soldier as he is, and without peer
In counsel, dreams too much among his books.
It may read well, but sure 'tis out of date
To play the Alexander with Darius.
MAUD. Truth! I think so. By Heavens it shall not last!
CHESTER. It would amaze your Highness now to mark
How Gloucester overstrains his courtesy
To that crime-loving rebel, that Boulogne—
MAUD. That ingrate!
CHESTER. For whose vast ingratitude
To our late sovereign lord, your noble sire,
The generous Earl condoles in his mishaps,
And with a sort of lackeying friendliness,
Talks off the mighty frowning from his brow,
Woos him to hold a duet in a smile,
Or, if it please him, play an hour at chess—
MAUD. A perjured slave!
CHESTER. And for his perjury,
Gloucester has fit rewards—nay, I believe,
He sets his bustling household's wits at work
For flatteries to ease this Stephen's hours,
And make a heaven of his purgatory;
Adorning bondage with the pleasant gloss
Of feasts and music, and all idle shows
Of indoor pageantry; while siren whispers,
Predestined for his ear, 'scape as half-checked
From lips the courtliest and the rubiest
Of all the realm, admiring of his deeds.
MAUD. A frost upon his summer!
CHESTER. A queen's nod
Can make his June December. Here he comes. ...

'This living hand, now warm and capable'

This living hand, now warm and capable
Of earnest grasping, would, if it were cold
And in the icy silence of the tomb,
So haunt thy days and chill thy dreaming nights
That thou would wish thine own heart dry of blood
So in my veins red life might stream again,
And thou be conscience-calmed—see here it is—
I hold it towards you.

The Cap and Bells; *or*, *The Jealousies*

A FAERY TALE—UNFINISHED

I

In midmost Ind, beside Hydaspes cool,
There stood, or hovered, tremulous in the air,
A faery city, 'neath the potent rule
Of Emperor Elfinan—famed everywhere
For love of mortal women, maidens fair,
Whose lips were solid, whose soft hands were made
Of a fit mould and beauty, ripe and rare,
To pamper his slight wooing, warm yet staid:
He loved girls smooth as shades, but hated a mere shade.

II

This was a crime forbidden by the law;
And all the priesthood of his city wept,
For ruin and dismay they well foresaw,
If impious prince no bound or limit kept,
And faery Zendervester overstepped.
They wept, he sinned, and still he would sin on,
They dreamt of sin, and he sinned while they slept;
In vain the pulpit thundered at the throne,
Caricature was vain, and vain the tart lampoon.

III

Which seeing, his high court of parliament
Laid a remonstrance at his Highness' feet,
Praying his royal senses to content
Themselves with what in faery land was sweet,
Befitting best that shade with shade should meet:
Whereat, to calm their fears, he promised soon
From mortal tempters all to make retreat—
Ay, even on the first of the new moon,
An immaterial wife to espouse as heaven's boon.

IV

Meantime he sent a fluttering embassy
To Pigmio, of Imaus sovereign,
To half beg, and half demand, respectfully,
The hand of his fair daughter Bellanaine.
An audience had, and speeching done, they gain
Their point, and bring the weeping bride away;
Whom, with but one attendant, safely lain
Upon their wings, they bore in bright array,
While little harps were touched by many a lyric fay.

V

As in old pictures tender cherubim
A child's soul through the sapphired canvas bear,
So, through a real heaven, on they swim
With the sweet princess on her plumaged lair,
Speed giving to the winds her lustrous hair;
And so she journeyed, sleeping or awake,
Save when, for healthful exercise and air,
She chose to *promener à l'aile*, or take
A pigeon's somerset, for sport or change's sake.

VI

'Dear Princess, do not whisper me so loud,'
Quoth Corallina, nurse and confidant,
'Do not you see there, lurking in a cloud,
Close at your back, that sly old Crafticant?
He hears a whisper plainer than a rant.
Dry up your tears, and do not look so blue;

He's Elfinan's great state-spy militant,
His running, lying, flying footman too—
Dear mistress, let him have no handle against you!

VII

'Show him a mouse's tail, and he will guess,
With metaphysic swiftness, at the mouse;
Show him a garden, and with speed no less,
He'll surmise sagely of a dwelling house,
And plot, in the same minute, how to chouse
The owner out of it; show him a—' 'Peace!
Peace! nor contrive thy mistress' ire to rouse!'
Returned the Princess, 'my tongue shall not cease
Till from this hated match I get a free release.

VIII

'Ah, beauteous mortal!' 'Hush!' quoth Coralline,
'Really you must not talk of him, indeed.'
'*You* hush!' replied the mistress, with a shine
Of anger in her eyes, enough to breed
In stouter hearts than nurse's fear and dread:
'Twas not the glance itself made Nursey flinch,
But of its threat she took the utmost heed,
Not liking in her heart an hour-long pinch,
Or a sharp needle run into her back an inch.

IX

So she was silenced, and fair Bellanaine,
Writhing her little body with ennui,
Continued to lament and to complain,
That Fate, cross-purposing, should let her be
Ravished away far from her dear countree;
That all her feelings should be set at naught,
In trumping up this match so hastily,
With lowland blood; and lowland blood she thought
Poison, as every staunch true-born Imaian ought.

X

Sorely she grieved, and wetted three or four
White Provence rose-leaves with her faery tears,
But not for this cause—alas! she had more
Bad reasons for her sorrow, as appears
In the famed memoirs of a thousand years,
Written by Crafticant, and publishèd
By Parpaglion and Co. (those sly compeers
Who raked up every fact against the dead)
In Scarab Street, Panthea, at the Jubal's Head.

XI

Where, after a long hypercritic howl
Against the vicious manners of the age,
He goes on to expose, with heart and soul,
What vice in this or that year was the rage,
Backbiting all the world in every page;
With special strictures on the horrid crime
(Sectioned and subsectioned with learning sage),
Of faeries stooping on their wings sublime
To kiss a mortal's lips, when such were in their prime.

XII

Turn to the copious index, you will find
Somewhere in the column, headed letter B,
The name of Bellanaine, if you're not blind;
Then pray refer to the text, and you will see
An article made up of calumny
Against this highland princess, rating her
For giving way, so over-fashionably,
To this new-fangled vice, which seems a burr
Stuck in his moral throat, no coughing e'er could stir.

XIII

There he says plainly that she loved a man!
That she around him fluttered, flirted, toyed,
Before her marriage with great Elfinan;
That after marriage too, she never joyed
In husband's company, but still employed
Her wits to 'scape away to Angle-land;

Where lived the youth, who worried and annoyed
Her tender heart, and its warm ardours fanned
To such a dreadful blaze, her side would scorch her hand.

XIV

But let us leave this idle tittle-tattle
To waiting-maids, and bedroom coteries,
Nor till fit time against her fame wage battle.
Poor Elfinan is very ill at ease—
Let us resume his subject if you please:
For it may comfort and console him much
To rhyme and syllable his miseries;
Poor Elfinan! whose cruel fate was such,
He sat and cursed a bride he knew he could not touch.

XV

Soon as (according to his promises)
The bridal embassy had taken wing,
And vanished, bird-like, o'er the suburb trees,
The Emperor, empierced with the sharp sting
Of love, retirèd, vexed and murmuring
Like any drone shut from the fair bee-queen,
Into his cabinet, and there did fling
His limbs upon a sofa, full of spleen,
And damned his House of Commons, in complete chagrin.

XVI

'I'll trounce some of the members,' cried the Prince,
'I'll put a mark against some rebel names,
I'll make the Opposition benches wince,
I'll show them very soon, to all their shames,
What 'tis to smother up a Prince's flames;
That ministers should join in it, I own,
Surprises me!—they too at these high games!
Am I an Emperor? Do I wear a crown?
Imperial Elfinan, go hang thyself or drown!

XVII

'I'll trounce 'em!—there's the square-cut chancellor,
His son shall never touch that bishopric;
And for the nephew of old Palfior,
I'll show him that his speeches made me sick,
And give the colonelcy to Phalaric;
The tip-toe marquis, moral and gallant,
Shall lodge in shabby taverns upon tick;
And for the Speaker's second cousin's aunt,
She shan't be maid of honour—by heaven that she shan't!

XVIII

'I'll shirk the Duke of A.; I'll cut his brother;
I'll give no garter to his eldest son;
I won't speak to his sister or his mother!
The Viscount B. shall live at cut-and-run;
But how in the world can I contrive to stun
That fellow's voice, which plagues me worse than any,
That stubborn fool, that impudent state-dun,
Who sets down every sovereign as a zany—
That vulgar commoner, Esquire Biancopany?

XIX

'Monstrous affair! Pshaw! pah! what ugly minx
Will they fetch from Imaus for my bride?
Alas! my wearied heart within me sinks,
To think that I must be so near allied
To a cold dullard fay—ah, woe betide!
Ah, fairest of all human loveliness!
Sweet Bertha! what crime can it be to glide
About the fragrant pleatings of thy dress,
Or kiss thine eyes, or count thy locks, tress after tress?'

XX

So said, one minute's while his eyes remained
Half lidded, piteous, languid, innocent;
But, in a wink, their splendour they regained,
Sparkling revenge with amorous fury blent.
Love thwarted in bad temper oft has vent:
He rose, he stamped his foot, he rang the bell,

And ordered some death-warrants to be sent
For signature—somewhere the tempest fell,
As many a poor felon does not live to tell.

XXI

'At the same time Eban' (this was his page,
A fay of colour, slave from top to toe,
Sent as a present, while yet under age,
From the Viceroy of Zanguebar—wise, slow,
His speech, his only words were 'yes' and 'no',
But swift of look, and foot, and wing was he),
'At the same time, Eban, this instant go
To Hum the soothsayer, whose name I see
Among the fresh arrivals in our empery.

XXII

'Bring Hum to me! But stay—here, take my ring,
The pledge of favour, that he not suspect
Any foul play, or awkward murdering,
Though I have bowstrung many of his sect;
Throw in a hint, that if he should neglect
One hour, the next shall see him in my grasp,
And the next after that shall see him necked,
Or swallowed by my hunger-starvèd asp—
And mention ('tis as well) the torture of the wasp.'

XXIII

These orders given, the Prince, in half a pet,
Let o'er the silk his propping elbow slide,
Caught up his little legs, and, in a fret,
Fell on the sofa on his royal side.
The slave retreated backwards, humble-eyed,
And with a slave-like silence closed the door,
And to old Hum through street and alley hied;
He 'knew the city', as we say, of yore,
For shortest cuts and turns, was nobody knew more.

XXIV

It was the time when wholesale houses close
Their shutters with a moody sense of wealth,
But retail dealers, diligent, let loose
The gas (objected to on score of health),
Conveyed in little soldered pipes by stealth,
And make it flare in many a brilliant form,
That all the powers of darkness it repell'th,
Which to the oil-trade doth great scathe and harm,
And supersedeth quite the use of the glow-worm.

XXV

Eban, untempted by the pastry-cooks
(Of pastry he got store within the palace),
With hasty steps, wrapped cloak, and solemn looks,
Incognito upon his errand sallies,
His smelling-bottle ready for the alleys.
He passed the hurdy-gurdies with disdain,
Vowing he'd have them sent on board the galleys;
Just as he made his vow, it 'gan to rain,
Therefore he called a coach, and bade it drive amain.

XXVI

'I'll pull the string,' said he, and further said,
'Polluted Jarvey! Ah, thou filthy hack!
Whose springs of life are all dried up and dead,
Whose linsey-woolsey lining hangs all slack,
Whose rug is straw, whose wholeness is a crack;
And evermore thy steps go clatter-clitter;
Whose glass once up can never be got back,
Who prov'st, with jolting arguments and bitter,
That 'tis of modern use to travel in a litter.

XXVII

'Thou inconvenience! thou hungry crop
For all corn! thou snail-creeper to and fro,
Who while thou goest ever seem'st to stop,
And fiddle-faddle standest while you go;
I' the morning, freighted with a weight of woe,
Unto some lazar-house thou journeyest,

And in the evening tak'st a double row
Of dowdies, for some dance or party dressed,
Besides the goods meanwhile thou movest east and west.

XXVIII

'By thy ungallant bearing and sad mien,
An inch appears the utmost thou couldst budge;
Yet at the slightest nod, or hint, or sign,
Round to the curb-stone patient dost thou trudge,
Schooled in a beckon, learned in a nudge,
A dull-eyed Argus watching for a fare;
Quiet and plodding, thou dost bear no grudge
To whisking tilburies, or phaetons rare,
Curricles, or mail-coaches, swift beyond compare.'

XXIX

Philosophizing thus, he pulled the check,
And bade the Coachman wheel to such a street,
Who, turning much his body, more his neck,
Louted full low, and hoarsely did him greet:
'Certes, Monsieur were best take to his feet,
Seeing his servant can no further drive
For press of coaches, that tonight here meet
Many as bees about a straw-capped hive,
When first for April honey into faint flowers they dive.'

XXX

Eban then paid his fare, and tip-toe went
To Hum's hotel; and, as he on did pass
With head inclined, each dusky lineament
Showed in the pearl-paved street, as in a glass;
His purple vest, that ever peeping was
Rich from the fluttering crimson of his cloak,
His silvery trousers, and his silken sash
Tied in a burnished knot, their semblance took
Upon the mirrored walls, wherever he might look.

XXXI

He smiled at self, and, smiling, showed his teeth,
And seeing his white teeth, he smiled the more;
Lifted his eye-brows, spurned the path beneath,
Showed teeth again, and smiled as heretofore,
Until he knocked at the magician's door;
Where, till the porter answered, might be seen,
In the clear panel, more he could adore—
His turban wreathed of gold, and white, and green,
Mustachios, ear-ring, nose-ring, and his sabre keen.

XXXII

'Does not your master give a rout tonight?'
Quoth the dark page. 'Oh, no!' returned the Swiss,
'Next door but one to us, upon the right,
The *Magazin des Modes* now open is
Against the Emperor's wedding—and, sir, this
My master finds a monstrous horrid bore,
As he retired, an hour ago I wis,
With his best beard and brimstone, to explore
And cast a quiet figure in his second floor.

XXXIII

'Gad! he's obliged to stick to business!
For chalk, I hear, stands at a pretty price;
And as for aqua-vitae—there's a mess!
The *dentes sapientiae* of mice,
Our barber tells me too, are on the rise—
Tinder's a lighter article—nitre pure
Goes off like lightning—grains of Paradise
At an enormous figure! Stars not sure!—
Zodiac will not move without a sly douceur!

XXXIV

'Venus won't stir a peg without a fee,
And master is too partial, *entre nous*,
To—' 'Hush—hush!' cried Eban, 'sure that is he
Coming down stairs. By St Bartholomew!
As backwards as he can—is't something new?
Or is't his custom, in the name of fun?'

'He always comes down backward, with one shoe',
Returned the porter, 'off, and one shoe on,
Like, saving shoe for sock or stocking, my man John!'

XXXV

It was indeed the great Magician,
Feeling, with careful toe, for every stair,
And retrograding careful as he can,
Backwards and downwards from his own two pair:
'Salpietro!' exclaimed Hum, 'is the dog there?
He's always in my way upon the mat!'
'He's in the kitchen, or the Lord knows where,'
Replied the Swiss, 'the nasty, yelping brat!'
'Don't beat him!' returned Hum, and on the floor came pat.

XXXVI

Then facing right about, he saw the Page,
And said: 'Don't tell me what you want, Eban;
The Emperor is now in a huge rage—
'Tis nine to one he'll give you the rattan!
Let us away!' Away together ran
The plain-dressed sage and spangled blackamoor,
Nor rested till they stood to cool, and fan,
And breathe themselves at th'Emperor's chamber door,
When Eban thought he heard a soft imperial snore.

XXXVII

'I thought you guessed, foretold, or prophesied,
That's Majesty was in a raving fit?'
'He dreams,' said Hum, 'or I have ever lied,
That he is tearing you, sir, bit by bit.'
'He's not asleep, and you have little wit,'
Replied the page, 'that little buzzing noise,
Whate'er your palmistry may make of it,
Comes from a play-thing of the Emperor's choice,
From a Man-Tiger-Organ, prettiest of his toys.'

XXXVIII

Eban then ushered in the learned seer:
Elfinan's back was turned, but, ne'ertheless,
Both, prostrate on the carpet, ear by ear,
Crept silently, and waited in distress,
Knowing the Emperor's moody bitterness;
Eban especially, who on the floor 'gan
Tremble and quake to death—he feared less
A dose of senna-tea or nightmare Gorgon
Than the Emperor when he played on his Man-Tiger-Organ.

XXXIX

They kissed nine times the carpet's velvet face
Of glossy silk, soft, smooth, and meadow-green,
Where the close eye in deep rich fur might trace
A silver tissue, scantly to be seen,
As daisies lurked in June-grass, buds in treen.
Sudden the music ceased, sudden the hand
Of majesty, by dint of passion keen,
Doubled into a common fist, went grand,
And knocked down three cut glasses, and his best inkstand.

XL

Then turning round, he saw those trembling two.
'Eban,' said he, 'as slaves should taste the fruits
Of diligence, I shall remember you
Tomorrow, or the next day, as time suits,
In a finger conversation with my mutes—
Begone!—for you, Chaldean! here remain!
Fear not, quake not, and as good wine recruits
A conjurer's spirits, what cup will you drain?
Sherry in silver, hock in gold, or glassed champagne?'

XLI

'Commander of the Faithful!' answered Hum,
'In preference to these, I'll merely taste
A thimble-full of old Jamaica rum.'
'A simple boon!' said Elfinan, 'thou mayst
Have Nantz, with which my morning-coffee's laced.'
'I'll have a glass of Nantz, then,' said the Seer,

'Made racy (sure my boldness is misplaced!)
With the third part (yet that is drinking dear!)
Of the least drop of *crème de citron*, crystal clear.'

XLII

'I pledge you, Hum! and pledge my dearest love,
My Bertha!' 'Bertha! Bertha!' cried the sage,
'I know a many Berthas!' 'Mine's above
All Berthas!' sighed the Emperor. 'I engage,'
Said Hum, 'in duty, and in vassalage,
To mention all the Berthas in the Earth—
There's Bertha Watson, and Miss Bertha Page,
This famed for languid eyes, and that for mirth—
There's Bertha Blount of York—and Bertha Knox of Perth.'

XLIII

'You seem to know—' 'I do know,' answered Hum,
'Your Majesty's in love with some fine girl
Named Bertha, but her surname will not come,
Without a little conjuring.' ''Tis Pearl,
'Tis Bertha Pearl what makes my brains so whirl;
And she is softer, fairer than her name!'
'Where does she live?' asked Hum. 'Her fair locks curl
So brightly, they put all our fays to shame!—
Live?—O! at Canterbury, with her old grand-dame.'

XLIV

'Good! good!' cried Hum, 'I've known her from a child!
She is a changeling of my management.
She was bom at midnight in an Indian wild;
Her mother's screams with the striped tiger's blent,
While the torch-bearing slaves a halloo sent
Into the jungles; and her palanquin,
Rested amid the desert's dreariment,
Shook with her agony, till fair were seen
The little Bertha's eyes ope on the stars serene.'

XLV

'I can't say,' said the monarch, 'that may be
Just as it happened, true or else a bam!
Drink up your brandy, and sit down by me,
Feel, feel my pulse, how much in love I am;
And if your science is not all a sham,
Tell me some means to get the lady here.'
'Upon my honour!' said the son of Cham,
'She is my dainty changeling, near and dear,
Although her story sounds at first a little queer.'

XLVI

'Convey her to me, Hum, or by my crown,
My sceptre, and my cross-surmounted globe,
I'll knock you'—'Does your majesty mean—*down*?
No, no, you never could my feelings probe
To such a depth!' The Emperor took his robe,
And wept upon its purple palatine,
While Hum continued, shamming half a sob,
'In Canterbury doth your lady shine?
But let me cool your brandy with a little wine.'

XLVII

Whereat a narrow Flemish glass he took,
That since belonged to Admiral de Witt,
Admired it with a connoisseuring look,
And with the ripest claret crownèd it,
And, ere one lively bead could burst and flit,
He turned it quickly, nimbly upside down,
His mouth being held conveniently fit
To save 'the creature'. 'Best in all the town!'
He said, smacked his moist lips, and gave a pleasant frown.

XLVIII

'Ah! good my Prince, weep not!' And then again
He filled a bumper. 'Great Sire, do not weep!
Your pulse is shocking, but I'll ease your pain.'
'Fetch me that ottoman, and prithee keep
Your voice low,' said the Emperor, 'and steep
Some lady's-fingers nice in Candy wine;

And prithee, Hum, behind the screen do peep
For the rose-water vase, magician mine!
And sponge my forehead—so my love doth make me pine.

XLIX

'Ah, cursèd Bellanaine!' 'Don't think of her,'
Rejoined the Mago, 'but on Bertha muse;
For, by my choicest best barometer,
You shall not throttled be in marriage noose.
I've said it, Sire; you only have to choose
Bertha or Bellanaine.' So saying, he drew
From the left pocket of his threadbare hose,
A sampler hoarded slyly, good as new,
Holding it by his thumb and finger full in view.

L

'Sire, this is Bertha Pearl's neat handy-work,
Her *name*, see here, *Midsummer*, *ninety-one.*'
Elfinan snatched it with a sudden jerk,
And wept as if he never would have done,
Honouring with royal tears the poor homespun,
Whereon were broidered tigers with black eyes,
And long-tailed pheasants, and a rising sun,
Plenty of posies, great stags, butterflies
Bigger than stags, a moon—with other mysteries.

LI

The monarch handled o'er and o'er again
These day-school hieroglyphics with a sigh;
Somewhat in sadness, but pleased in the main,
Till this oracular couplet met his eye
Astounded: *Cupid I—do thee defy*!
It was too much. He shrunk back in his chair,
Grew pale as death, and fainted—very nigh!
'Pho! nonsense!' exclaimed Hum, 'now don't despair;
She does not mean it really. Cheer up, hearty—there!

LII

'And listen to my words. You say you won't,
On any terms, marry Miss Bellanaine;
It goes against your conscience—good! Well, don't.
You say you love a mortal. I would fain
Persuade your honour's Highness to refrain
From peccadilloes. But, Sire, as I say,
What good would that do? And, to be more plain,
You would do me a mischief some odd day,
Cut off my ears and hands, or head too, by my fay!

LIII

'Besides, manners forbid that I should pass any
Vile strictures on the conduct of a prince
Who should indulge his genius, if he has any,
Not, like a subject, foolish matters mince.
Now I think on't, perhaps I could convince
Your Majesty there is no crime at all
In loving pretty little Bertha, since
She's very delicate—not over tall—
A faery's hand, and in the waist, why—very small.'

LIV

'Ring the repeater, gentle Hum!' ''Tis five,'
Said gentle Hum, 'the nights draw in apace;
The little birds I hear are all alive;
I see the dawning touched upon your face;
Shall I put out the candles, please your Grace?'
'Do put them out, and, without more ado,
Tell me how I may that sweet girl embrace—
How you can bring her to me.' 'That's for you,
Great Emperor! to adventure, like a lover true.'

LV

'I fetch her!'—'Yes, an't like your Majesty;
And as she would be frightened wide awake
To travel such a distance through the sky,
Use of some soft manoeuvre you must make,
For your convenience, and her dear nerves' sake.
Nice way would be to bring her in a swoon,

Anon, I'll tell what course were best to take;
You must away this morning.' 'Hum! so soon?'
'Sire, you must be in Kent by twelve o'clock at noon.'

LVI

At this great Caesar started on his feet,
Lifted his wings, and stood attentive-wise.
'Those wings to Canterbury you must beat,
If you hold Bertha as a worthy prize.
Look in the Almanack—*Moore* never lies—
April the twenty-fourth, this coming day,
Now breathing its new bloom upon the skies,
Will end in St Mark's Eve—you must away,
For on that eve alone can you the maid convey.'

LVII

Then the magician solemnly 'gan frown,
So that his frost-white eyebrows, beetling low,
Shaded his deep-green eyes, and wrinkles brown
Plaited upon his furnace-scorchèd brow:
Forth from his hood that hung his neck below,
He lifted a bright casket of pure gold,
Touched a spring-lock, and there in wool, or snow
Charmed into ever-freezing, lay an old
And legend-leavèd book, mysterious to behold.

LVIII

'Take this same book,—it will not bite you, Sire—
There, put it underneath your royal arm;
Though it's a pretty weight it will not tire,
But rather on your journey keep you warm.
This is the magic, this the potent charm,
That shall drive Bertha to a fainting fit!
When the time comes, don't feel the least alarm,
Uplift her from the ground, and swiftly flit
Back to your palace, where I wait for guerdon fit.'

LIX

'What shall I do with that same book?' 'Why merely
Lay it on Bertha's table, close beside
Her work-box, and 'twill help your purpose dearly.
I say no more.' 'Or good or ill betide,
Through the wide air to Kent this mom I glide!'
Exclaimed the Emperor. 'When I return,
Ask what you will—I'll give you my new bride!
And take some more wine, Hum—O Heavens! I burn
To be upon the wing! Now, now, that minx I spurn!'

LX

'Leave her to me,' rejoined the magian,
'But how shall I account, illustrious fay!
For thine imperial absence? Pho! I can
Say you are very sick, and bar the way
To your so loving courtiers for one day;
If either of their two Archbishops' graces
Should talk of extreme unction, I shall say
You do not like cold pig with Latin phrases,
Which never should be used but in alarming cases.'

LXI

'Open the window, Hum; I'm ready now!'
'Zooks!' exclaimed Hum, as up the sash he drew,
'Behold, your Majesty, upon the brow
Of yonder hill, what crowds of people!' 'Whew!
The monster's always after something new,'
Returned his Highness, 'they are piping hot
To see my pigsney Bellanaine. Hum! do
Tighten my belt a little—so, so—not
Too tight. The book!—my wand!—so, nothing is forgot.'

LXII

'Wounds! how they shout!' said Hum, 'and there,—see, see!
The Ambassador's returned from Pigmio!
The morning's very fine—uncommonly!
See, past the skirts of yon white cloud they go,
Tinging it with soft crimsons! Now below

The sable-pointed heads of firs and pines
They dip, move on, and with them moves a glow
Along the forest side! Now amber lines
Reach the hill top, and now throughout the valley shines.'

LXIII

'Why, Hum, you're getting quite poetical!
Those *nows* you managed in a special style.'
'If ever you have leisure, Sire, you shall
See scraps of mine will make it worth your while,
Tit-bits for Phoebus!—yes, you well may smile.
Hark! Hark! the bells!' 'A little further yet,
Good Hum, and let me view this mighty coil.'
Then the great Emperor full graceful set
His elbow for a prop, and snuffed his mignonette.

LXIV

The morn is full of holiday: loud bells
With rival clamours ring from every spire;
Cunningly-stationed music dies and swells
In echoing places; when the winds respire,
Light flags stream out like gauzy tongues of fire;
A metropolitan murmur, lifeful, warm,
Comes from the northern suburbs; rich attire
Freckles with red and gold the moving swarm;
While here and there clear trumpets blow a keen alarm.

LXV

And now the faery escort was seen clear,
Like the old pageant of Aurora's train,
Above a pearl-built minster, hovering near:
First wily Crafticant, the chamberlain,
Balanced upon his grey-grown pinions twain,
His slender wand officially revealed;
Then black gnomes scattering sixpences like rain;
Then pages three and three; and next, slave-held,
The Imaian 'scutcheon bright—one mouse in argent field.

LXVI

Gentlemen pensioners next; and after them,
A troop of wingèd Janizaries flew;
Then slaves, as presents bearing many a gem;
Then twelve physicians fluttering two and two;
And next a chaplain in a cassock new;
Then Lords in waiting; then (what head not reels
For pleasure?) the fair Princess in full view,
Borne upon wings—and very pleased she feels
To have such splendour dance attendance at her heels.

LXVII

For there was more magnificence behind.
She waved her handkerchief. 'Ah, very grand!'
Cried Elfinan, and closed the window-blind.
'And, Hum, we must not shilly-shally stand—
Adieu! adieu! I'm off for Angle-land!
I say, old Hocus, have you such a thing
About you—feel your pockets, I command—
I want, this instant, an invisible ring—
Thank you, old mummy! Now securely I take wing.'

LXVIII

Then Elfinan swift vaulted from the floor,
And lighted graceful on the window-sill;
Under one arm the magic book he bore,
The other he could wave about at will;
Pale was his face, he still looked very ill.
He bowed at Bellanaine, and said, 'Poor Bell!
Farewell! farewell! and if for ever! Still
For ever fare thee well!'—and then he fell
A-laughing!—snapped his fingers!—shame it is to tell!

LXIX

'By'r Lady! he is gone!' cries Hum, 'and I
(I own it) have made too free with his wine;
Old Crafticant will smoke me by the bye!
This room is full of jewels as a mine—
Dear valuable creatures, how ye shine!
Sometime today I must contrive a minute,

If Mercury propitiously incline,
To examine his scrutoire, and see what's in it,
For of superfluous diamonds I as well may thin it.

LXX

'The Emperor's horrid bad—yes, that's my cue!'
Some histories say that this was Hum's last speech;
That, being fuddled, he went reeling through
The corridor, and scarce upright could reach
The stair-head; that being glutted as a leech,
And used, as we ourselves have just now said,
To manage stairs reversely, like a peach
Too ripe, he fell, being puzzled in his head
With liquor and the staircase: verdict—*found stone dead.*

LXXI

This as a falsehood Crafticanto treats;
And as his style is of strange elegance,
Gentle and tender, full of soft conceits
(Much like our Boswell's) we will take a glance
At his sweet prose, and, if we can, make dance
His woven periods into careless rhyme.
O, little faery Pegasus! rear—prance—
Trot round the quarto—ordinary time!
March, little Pegasus, with pawing hoof sublime!

LXXII

Well, let us see—*tenth book and chapter nine*—
Thus Crafticant pursues his diary:
''Twas twelve o'clock at night, the weather fine,
Latitude thirty-six; our scouts descry
A flight of starlings making rapidly
Toward Tibet. Mem.—birds fly in the night;
From twelve to half-past—wings not fit to fly
For a thick fog—the Princess sulky quite
Called for an extra shawl, and gave her nurse a bite.

LXXIII

'Five minutes before one—brought down a moth
With my new double-barrel—stewed the thighs
And made a very tolerable broth—
Princess turned dainty; to our great surprise,
Altered her mind, and thought it very nice.
Seeing her pleasant, tried her with a pun,
She frowned. A monstrous owl across us flies
About this time—a sad old figure of fun;
Bad omen—this new match can't be a happy one.

LXXIV

'From two to half-past, dusky way we made,
Above the plains of Gobi—desert, bleak;
Beheld afar off, in the hooded shade
Of darkness, a great mountain (strange to speak)
Spitting, from forth its sulphur-baken peak,
A fan-shaped burst of blood-red, arrowy fire,
Turbaned with smoke, which still away did reek,
Solid and black from that eternal pyre,
Upon the laden winds that scantly could respire.

LXXV

'Just upon three o'clock a falling star
Created an alarm among our troop,
Killed a man-cook, a page, and broke a jar,
A tureen, and three dishes, at one swoop,
Then passing by the Princess, singed her hoop.
Could not conceive what Coralline was at—
She clapped her hands three times and cried out "Whoop!"
Some strange Imaian custom. A large bat
Came sudden 'fore my face, and brushed against my hat.

LXXVI

'Five minutes thirteen seconds after three,
Far in the west a mighty fire broke out.
Conjectured, on the instant, it might be
The city of Balk—'twas Balk beyond all doubt.
A griffin, wheeling here and there about,
Kept reconnoitring us—doubled our guard—

Lighted our torches, and kept up a shout,
Till he sheered off—the Princess very scared—
And many on their marrowbones for death prepared.

LXXVII

'At half-past three arose the cheerful moon—
Bivouacked for four minutes on a cloud—
Where from the earth we heard a lively tune
Of tambourines and pipes, serene and loud,
While on a flowery lawn a brilliant crowd
Cinque-parted danced, some half-asleep reposed
Beneath the green-faned cedars, some did shroud
In silken tents, and 'mid light fragrance dozed,
Or on the open turf their soothed eyelids closed.

LXXVIII

'Dropped my gold watch, and killed a kettledrum—
It went for apoplexy—foolish folks!—
Left it to pay the piper—a good sum
(I've got a conscience, maugre people's jokes).
To scrape a little favour 'gan to coax
Her Highness' pug-dog—got a sharp rebuff.
She wished a game at whist—made three revokes—
Turned from myself, her partner, in a huff.
His Majesty will know her temper time enough.

LXXIX

'She cried for chess—I played a game with her.
Castled her king with such a vixen look,
It bodes ill to his Majesty (refer
To the second chapter of my fortieth book,
And see what hoity-toity airs she took).
At half-past four the morn essayed to beam—
Saluted, as we passed, an early rook—
The Princess fell asleep, and, in her dream,
Talked of one Master Hubert, deep in her esteem.

LXXX

'About this time, making delightful way,
Shed a quill-feather from my larboard wing—
Wished, trusted, hoped 'twas no sign of decay—
Thank heaven, I'm hearty yet!—'twas no such thing.
At five the golden light began to spring,
With fiery shudder through the bloomèd east.
At six we heard Panthea's churches ring—
The city all her unhived swarms had cast,
To watch our grand approach, and hail us as we passed.

LXXXI

'As flowers turn their faces to the sun,
So on our flight with hungry eyes they gaze,
And, as we shaped our course, this, that way run,
With mad-cap pleasure, or hand-clasped amaze.
Sweet in the air a mild-toned music plays,
And progresses through its own labyrinth.
Buds gathered from the green spring's middle-days,
They scattered—daisy, primrose, hyacinth—
Or round white columns wreathed from capital to plinth.

LXXXII

'Onward we floated o'er the panting streets,
That seemed throughout with upheld faces paved.
Look where we will, our bird's-eye vision meets
Legions of holiday; bright standards waved,
And fluttering ensigns emulously craved
Our minute's glance; a busy thunderous roar,
From square to square, among the buildings raved,
As when the sea, at flow, gluts up once more
The craggy hollowness of a wild reefed shore.

LXXXIII

'And "Bellanaine for ever!" shouted they,
While that fair Princess, from her winged chair,
Bowed low with high demeanour, and, to pay
Their new-blown loyalty with guerdon fair,
Still emptied, at meet distance, here and there,
A plenty horn of jewels. And here I

(Who wish to give the devil her due) declare
Against that ugly piece of calumny,
Which calls them Highland pebble-stones not worth a fly.

LXXXIV

'Still "Bellanaine!" they shouted, while we glide
'Slant to a light Ionic portico,
The city's delicacy, and the pride
Of our Imperial Basilic. A row
Of lords and ladies, on each hand, make show
Submissive of knee-bent obeisance,
All down the steps; and, as we entered, lo!
The strangest sight—the most unlooked-for chance—
All things turned topsy-turvy in a devil's dance.

LXXXV

''Stead of his anxious Majesty and court
At the open doors, with wide saluting eyes,
Congées and scapegraces of every sort,
And all the smooth routine of gallantries,
Was seen, to our immoderate surprise,
A motley crowd thick gathered in the hall,
Lords, scullions, deputy-scullions, with wild cries
Stunning the vestibule from wall to wall,
Where the Chief Justice on his knees and hands doth crawl.

LXXXVI

'Counts of the palace, and the state purveyor
Of moth's-down, to make soft the royal beds,
The Common Council and my fool Lord Mayor
Marching a-row, each other slipshod treads;
Powdered bag-wigs and ruffy-tuffy heads
Of cinder wenches meet and soil each other;
Toe crushed with heel ill-natured fighting breeds,
Frill-rumpling elbows brew up many a bother,
And fists in the short ribs keep up the yell and pother.

LXXXVII

'A Poet, mounted on the Court-Clown's back,
Rode to the Princess swift with spurring heels,
And close into her face, with rhyming clack,
Began a Prothalamion—she reels,
She falls, she faints! while laughter peals
Over her woman's weakness. "Where!" cried I,
"Where is his Majesty?" No person feels
Inclined to answer; wherefore instantly
I plunged into the crowd to find him or to die.

LXXXVIII

'Jostling my way I gained the stairs, and ran
To the first landing, where, incredible!
I met, far gone in liquor, that old man,
That vile impostor Hum—'
So far so well,
For we have proved the Mago never fell
Down stairs on Crafticanto's evidence;
And therefore duly shall proceed to tell,
Plain in our own original mood and tense,
The sequel of this day, though labour 'tis immense!

LXXXIX

Now Hum, new fledged with high authority,
Came forth to quell the hubbub in the hall....

To Fanny

I

Physician Nature! let my spirit blood!
O ease my heart of verse and let me rest;
Throw me upon thy tripod till the flood
Of stifling numbers ebbs from my full breast.
A theme! a theme! Great Nature! give a theme;
Let me begin my dream.
I come—I see thee, as thou standest there,
Beckon me out into the wintry air.

II

Ah! dearest love, sweet home of all my fears,
And hopes, and joys, and panting miseries,
Tonight, if I may guess, thy beauty wears
A smile of such delight,
As brilliant and as bright,
As when with ravished, aching, vassal eyes,
Lost in a soft amaze,
I gaze, I gaze!

III

Who now, with greedy looks, eats up my feast?
What stare outfaces now my silver moon!
Ah! keep that hand unravished at the least;
Let, let, the amorous burn—
But, prithee, do not turn
The current of your heart from me so soon.
O save, in charity,
The quickest pulse for me!

IV

Save it for me, sweet love! though music breathe
Voluptuous visions into the warm air,
Though swimming through the dance's dangerous wreath,
Be like an April day,
Smiling and cold and gay,
A temperate lily, temperate as fair;
Then, Heaven! there will be
A warmer June for me.

V

Why, this—you'll say, my Fanny!—is not true:
Put your soft hand upon your snowy side,
Where the heart beats; confess—'tis nothing new—
Must not a woman be
A feather on the sea,
Swayed to and fro by every wind and tide?
Of as uncertain speed
As blow-ball from the mead?

VI

I know it—and to know it is despair
   To one who loves you as I love, sweet Fanny!
Whose heart goes fluttering for you everywhere,
      Nor, when away you roam,
      Dare keep its wretched home.
   Love, Love alone, has pains severe and many:
      Then, loveliest! keep me free
      From torturing jealousy.

VII

Ah! if you prize my subdued soul above
   The poor, the fading, brief, pride of an hour,
Let none profane my Holy See of Love,
      Or with a rude hand break
      The sacramental cake;
   Let none else touch the just new-budded flower;
      If not—may my eyes close,
      Love! on their last repose.

'*In after-time, a sage of mickle lore*'

   In after-time, a sage of mickle lore
   Y-cleped Typographus, the Giant took,
   And did refit his limbs as heretofore,
   And made him read in many a learned book,
   And into many a lively legend look;
   Thereby in goodly themes so training him,
   That all his brutishness he quite forsook,
   When, meeting Artegall and Talus grim,
The one he struck stone-blind, the other's eyes wox dim.

Three Undated Fragments

I

I am as brisk
As a bottle of whisk—
Ey and as nimble
As a milliner's thimble.

II

O grant that like to Peter I
May like to Peter B,
And tell me, lovely Jesus, Y
This Peter went to C.
O grant that like to Peter I
May like to Peter B,
And tell me, lovely Jesus, Y
Old Jonah went to C.

III

They weren fully glad of their gude hap
And tasten all the pleasaunces of joy.

Doubtful Attributions

'See, the ship in the bay is riding'

See, the ship in the bay is riding,
Dearest Ellen, I go from thee—
Boldly go, in thy love confiding,
Over the deep and trackless sea:
When thy dear form no longer is near me,
This soothing thought shall at midnight cheer me:
'My love is breathing a prayer for me'.

When the thunder of war is roaring,
When the bullets around me fly,
When the rage of the tempest pouring,
Blends the billowy sea and sky,
Yet shall my heart, to fear a stranger,
Cherish its fondest hopes for thee—
This dear reflection disarming danger,
'My love is breathing a prayer for me'.

The Poet

At morn, at noon, at eve, and middle night,
   He passes forth into the charmèd air,
   With talisman to call up spirits rare
From plant, cave, rock, and fountain. To his sight
The husk of natural objects opens quite

To the core, and every secret essence there
Reveals the elements of good and fair,
Making him see, where Learning hath no light.
Sometimes above the gross and palpable things
Of this diurnal sphere, his spirit flies
On awful wing; and with its destined skies
Holds premature and mystic communings;
Till such unearthly intercourses shed
A visible halo round his mortal head.

Gripus

GRIPUS. And gold and silver are but filthy dross.
Then seek not gold and silver which are dross,
But rather lay thy treasure up in heaven!—
SLIM. Hem!
GRIPUS. And thou has meat and drink and lodging too
And clothing too, what more can man require?
And thou art single—
But I must lay up money for my children,
My children's children and my great-grandchildren;
For, Slim! thy master will be shortly married—
SLIM. Married!
GRIPUS. Yea! married. Wherefore dost thou stare,
As though my words had spoke of aught impossible?
SLIM. My lord, I stare not but my ears played false.
Methought you had said married.
GRIPUS. Married, fool!
Is't aught unlikely? I'm not very old,
And my intended has a noble fortune.
SLIM. My lord 'tis likely.
GRIPUS. Haste, then, to the butchers,
And ere thou go, tell Bridget she is wanted—
SLIM. I go—Gods! what a subject for an ode.
With Hymen, Cupids, Venus, Loves and Graces!

[*Exit.*]

GRIPUS. [*solus.*] This matrimony is no light affair;
'Tis downright venture and mere speculation.
Less risk there is in what the merchant trusts
To winds and waves and the uncertain elements—
For he can have assurance for his goods
And put himself beyond the reach of losses—
But who can e'er ensure to me a wife

Industrious and managing and frugal,
Who will not spend far more than she has brought,
But be almost a saving to her husband?—
But none can tell—the broker cannot tell
He is not cheated in the wares he buys,
And to judge well of women or the seas
Would oft surpass the wisest merchant's prudence;
For both are deep alike—capricious too—
And the worst things that money can be sunk in.
But Bridget comes—
BRIDGET. Your pleasure, Sir, with me?
GRIPUS. Bridget, I wish to have a little converse
Upon a matter that concerns us both
Of like importance both to thee and me.
BRIDGET. Of like importance and concerning both!
What can your Honour have to say to me?
[*aside.*] O lord! I would give all that I am worth
To know what 'tis—
GRIPUS. Then prithee rein thy tongue
That ever battles with thine own impatience.
But to the point. Thou knowst, for twenty years
Together we have lived as man and wife,
But never hath the sanction of the Church
Stamped its legality upon our union.
BRIDGET. Well, what of that?
GRIPUS. Why, when in wiser years
Men look upon the follies of their youth,
They oft repent, and wish to make amends,
And seek for happier in more virtuous days.
In such a case, and such is mine I own,
'Tis marriage offers us the readiest way
To make atonement for our former deeds.
And thus have I determined in my heart
To make amends—in other words to marry.
BRIDGET. O Lord! how overjoyed I am to hear it!
I vow that I have often thought myself,
What wickedness it was to live as we did!
But do you joke?
GRIPUS. Not so upon my oath.
I am resolved to marry and beget
A little heir to leave my little wealth to.
I am not old, my hair is hardly grey,
My health is good—what hast thou to object?
BRIDGET. O dear! how close your honour puts the question!
I've said as much already as was fit

And incompatible with female modesty—
But would your honour please to name a day?
GRIPUS To name a day! But hark! I hear a knock—
'Tis perhaps young Prodigal, I did expect him.
BRIDGET. But Sir—a day?
GRIPUS. Zounds! dost thou hear the bell?
Wilt thou not run? He was to bring me money!

[*Exit* BRIDGET *and returns.*]

BRIDGET. 'Tis he, I've shown him to the little study.
GRIPUS. Then stay thee here, and when I've settled him
I will return and hold more converse with thee.

[*Exit.*]

BRIDGET. [*sola.*] My head runs round! O, what a happy change!
Now I shall be another woman quite.
Dame Bridget, then, adieu! and don't forget
Your Lady Gripus now that is to be;
Great Lady Gripus—O Lord!—
The Lady of the old and rich Sir Gripus!
O how will people whisper, as I pass,
'There goes my Lady'—'What a handsome gownd,
All scarlet silk embroiderèd with gold!'
Or green and gold will perhaps become me better—
How vastly fine, how handsome I shall be
In green and gold! Besides, a lady too!
I'll have a footman too, to walk behind me.
Slim is too slender to set off a livery,
I must have one more lustier than him,
A proper man to walk behind his lady.
O how genteel! methinks I see myself
In green and gold and carrying my fan—
Or perhaps I'd have a redicule *about me*!
The lusty footman all so spruce behind me
Walking on tip-toes in a bran new livery;
And he shall have a favour in his hat
As sure as ever I am Lady Gripus!

[*Enter* SLIM.]

SLIM. Why how now, Bridget, you're turned actress sure!
BRIDGET. An actor, fellow, no! To something better,
To something grander and more ladylike,

Know I am turned!
SLIM. A lunatic,'tis plain.
But, lovee, leave this jesting for a while,
And hear thy servant, who thus pleads for favour.
BRIDGET. For favour Sirrah! But I must be kind,
I will forget your insolence this once,
And condescend to keep you in my service.
But no! I want a much more lustier man,
You are too slender to become my livery
I must excard you, you must suit yourself!
SLIM. Why, how now, Bridget—
BRIDGET. You forget me, sure!
SLIM. Forget thee, Bridget? Never from my heart
Shall thy dear image part.
Ah! no,
I love you so
No language can impart!
Alas! 'tis love that makes me thin,
I have a fiery flame within,
That burns and shrivels up my skin—
'Tis Cupid's little dart,
And by this kiss I swear—

[*Attempts to kiss her.*]

BRIDGET. Ruffin, begone, or I will tell my lord.
Do you not care for difference of rank,
Nor make distinction between dirt and dignity?
SLIM. Why, Bridget, once you did not treat me thus.
BRIDGET. No, times are altered, Fortune's wheel is turned,
You still are Slim, but, though I once was Bridget,
I'm Lady Gripus now that is to be.
Did not his Honour tell you he should marry?
SLIM. Yea, to a lady of an ample fortune.
BRIDGET. Why, that, you fool, he said in allegolly.
A virtuous woman, is she not a crown,
A crown of gold and glory to her husband?
SLIM. Heavens is it possible? I pray forgive me
That I could doubt a moment of that fortune
Which is but due to your assembled merits.
BRIDGET. Well, Slim, I do not wish to harbour malice,
But while you show a proper due respect
You may be certain of my condescension.
But hark! I hear his lordship on the stairs,
And we must have some privacy together. [*Exit* SLIM.]

O lord, how overjoyed I am your honour—
GRIPUS. Bridget, I thank thee for thy friendly zeal,
That seems to glory in thy master's bliss;
And much it grieves me that I can't requite it
Except by mere reciprocal good-wishes.
For as a change in my domestic government
Will make thy place in future but a sinecure,
It grieves me much that I must warn you thus
To seek and get a situation elsewhere.
BRIDGET. O dear! O lord! O what a shock! O lord!

[*Faints.*]

GRIPUS. Ho! Slim—the devil's in the fool, to faint.
Halloo!—What shall I do? Halloo! Halloo!
Ho! Slim, I say—run, Sirrah, for the brandy!
SLIM. The brandy, Sir? there is none in the house!
GRIPUS. No brandy! None! What, none at all, thou knave?
What, none at all? Then rascal thou hast drunk it.
Why Bridget, Bridget—what, no brandy, knave?
Zounds! what a fit! Where is my brandy, wretch!
Thou toping villain, say, or I will slay thee!

[*Lets* BRIDGET *fall and collars* SLIM.]

SLIM. O lord! Forgive me, Bridget had the wind,
And drank the brandy up to warm her stomach.
GRIPUS. A tipsy Bacchanal! Then let her lie!
I'll not be drunken out of house and home.
Zounds! brandy for the wind—a cure indeed!
A little water had done just as well.
This is the way, then, when I want a drop;
I always find my cellar is stark naked.
But both shall go, yes, I discard ye. Thieves!
Begone, ye thieves!

[BRIDGET *jumps up.*]

BRIDGET. No, not without my wages!
I'll have a month's full wages or my warning!
I'll not be left at nonplush for a place.
GRIPUS. A month's full warning! What, another month,
To sack, to ransack, and to strip the house,
And then depart in triumph with your booty!
Begone, I say!

BRIDGET. No, not without my wages!
And I'll have damages, you cruel man!
I will convict you of a breach of marriage!
GRIPUS. Begone, I say! Deceitful thing! begone—
Who ever dared to promise such a match
But thy own fancy, and thy lying tongue?
What, marry one as poor as a church mouse,
And equally devoid of rank and beauty!
Reason would sleep and prudence would be blind,
And Gripus then would be no longer Gripus,
But only fitting for more sober men
To lodge in Bedlam and to call a lunatic.

THE END